F. E. PEACOCK PUBLISHERS, INC. ITASCA, ILLINOIS 60143

national government and policy in the United States

edited by
randall b. ripley
and
grace a. franklin

the Ohio State University

table of contents

contents

introduction:

government and policy

This volume seeks to introduce students to important aspects of how national public policy gets made in the United States through the interaction of the organs of the national government with various major private institutions. Whether the formal focus of study is American governmental institutions, the national policy process, or the substance of American public policy, the selections that make up the lion's share of this book will provide the reader with insights and information. The material that we, as editors, have provided to introduce the volume as a whole and to introduce each of the eleven different sections of readings seeks to underscore the specific relevance of individual readings to broader questions about American government, policy process, and policy substance.

In this present introductory essay we will first offer a broad overview of the major features of American national government, particularly as it is involved in the production of public policy. Second, we will make a few comments on the making of national policy, both in terms of the location for its creation and in terms of its effect. Third, we will outline the remainder of this volume.

An overview of American national government

The central features of American national government late in the 20th century are of two general kinds. First, there are features one would expect in any modern government of an industrialized nation set in a political system that can accurately be characterized as "open" or "representative" or "democratic." Second, there are features that might be expected specifically in the United States because of aspects of its history and the development both of its institutions and its people.

national government of U.S. as an instance of modern representative government in an industrialized nation

Three important general features of American national government could also be expected in other modern industrialized nations with open political systems: (1) complexity, (2) some two-way channels of access between the governed and the government, and (3) the undoubted existence of coercive power in the hands of the government generally used selectively and with restraint.

The *complexity* of national government in the United States appears in two interrelated ways. First, the government has a very large and complicated agenda of subject matter with which it deals. Virtually no aspect of modern life in the nation is not at least touched by some form of governmental activity. This does not mean that the national government is in control of all of these aspects—there are still large spheres of activity that mainly relate to state and local government and there are still other spheres in which private activity is dominant. But it is very difficult to think of any major activity in which an American citizen might engage that is not in some way tied to activity undertaken by the national government.

Second, as a way of managing its complicated agenda the government has also proliferated over the years into a collection of a large number of different organizations with a large number of employees, most of which (both organizations and employees) specialize in only some small part of the total substantive activity and competence of the government.

The executive branch contains most of the employees of the national government. In 1976 the government estimated its full-time permanent civilian employment in the executive branch at almost 2.5 million people (almost 22 percent of whom were with the postal service). Military personnel on active duty were estimated at over 2.1 million. At the same time full-time permanent personnel for the legislative and judicial branches combined amounted to fewer than 50,000 people.

Within the executive branch virtually everyone is a specialist. Only the President and a few of his top advisors theoretically have a grasp of the "big picture" of all governmental policy activity.

Given 4.6 million military and civilian employees the executive branch is, of course, divided and subdivided into a large number of organizations spread not just throughout the United States but all over the world. The civilian employees (including almost 1 million working for the Defense Department) worked for 11 major Departments, each of which contained a great variety of subunits ("bureau" is a generic term often used for the subunits with the clearest programmatic focus), and for over 50 independent agencies not attached to one of the Departments.

Congress, by contrast, had 535 elected officials in its employ (100 Senators and 435 Representatives) and more than 31,000 additional individuals —including more than 2,000 on committee staffs, almost 9,000 on personal staffs, and over 20,000 scattered among such agencies as the Congressional Research Service, the General Accounting Office, and the Congressional Budget Office. In theory the elected members must be generalists because collectively they wield the congressional powers over the full governmental agenda. In practice, however, most are specialists in the subject matter coming before the specific subcommittees on which they serve. Their staff members are almost all specialists too—also organized along jurisdictional lines dictated by subcommittees in the case of staff members.

The judicial branch of the national government has about 10,000 employees. This figure includes nine Supreme Court justices, almost 100 courts of appeals judges, under 400 district judges, and a variety of judges in courts with special jurisdictions (tax matters, customs matters, military appeals). The other persons employed by the judicial branch include law clerks for individual judges and a variety of administrative officers to keep the court system functioning. The Supreme Court, courts of appeals, and district judges are, perforce, generalists because they must deal with a broad range of issues. Their law clerks also are generalists. Judges and clerks on special courts are, by definition, specialists and the administrative officers are functionaries with their own specialities. In some ways the judicial branch has the highest proportion of generalists but it also has the least consistent impact on the day-to-day changes in national public policy.

One final point about the complexity of government in the United States: state and local governments also have a vast array of organizations and a very large number of employees. In 1974, for example, there were about 11.5 million state and local government employees. And, since the post-World War II demobilization (that also reduced federal civilian employment) growth has been much faster on the part of state and local governments than on the part of the federal government. In 1947, for example, there were about 3.5 million state and local employees and almost 2.1 million federal employees. By 1974 these figures had become 11.5 million state and local employees (more than a three fold increase) and 2.8 million federal employees (an increase of about one-third) during a period in which the national population was increasing by over 46 percent.

There are several major *channels of access* between the citizens of the United States and their officials, both elected and unelected. It needs to be stressed that these channels afford the potential for influence in both directions. That is, the officials do not passively wait for public reaction to events or "instructions" about how to proceed. They also seek to influence the public in a variety of ways.

Another general point worth noting is that although there is a direct relationship between citizens and officials that flows both ways, there are also relationships in both directions that are "mediated" by other forces in society: specifically, specialized publics and interest groups, political parties, and the mass media. Figure 1 summarizes the general character of the access—both direct and mediated—afforded the mass public to national officials. Figure 2—in many ways a mirror image of Figure 1—summarizes the general character of the direct and mediated access afforded elected and unelected officials to the general public.

That *coercive power* resides in the hands of the national government can hardly be doubted. A number of less-than-willing participants in armed combat overseas throughout the years can testify to its existence, as can a number of less-than-willing taxpayers scattered throughout fed-

Figure 1: Channels of Access from the Public to Officials

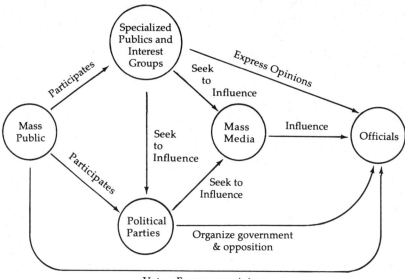

eral penitentiaries. However, the mark of a stable open society is that coercive power will not often need to be used and that, when used, its use will be limited and only enough to meet the specific situation with which it is intended to deal. There is, therefore, an inbuilt tension whenever the coercive power is openly called to play. How far should a government go in coercing individuals to fight in an unpopular war? What stance should the government take toward those who flee the country rather than submit to the draft? How real are the dangers of organized disruption that could threaten the existence of a relatively open system itself? What protective measures can the government legitimately take both to detect the possibility of organized disruption and to guard against it? All of these questions have been concretely posed in recent years in the United States by the issue of amnesty for Vietnam draft evaders and by the revelations of the use of the Federal Bureau of Investigation and the Central Intelligence Agency in connection with meeting alleged threats against the domestic tranquility and stability of the nation.

U.S. national government as an American phenomenon

Any government is the product in part of its unique historical and geographical setting and the government of the United States is no exception. At least six features of the history of the development of the American people, their opinions, and their institutions help explain features of the American governing apparatus today.

Figure 2: Channels of Access from Officials to the Public

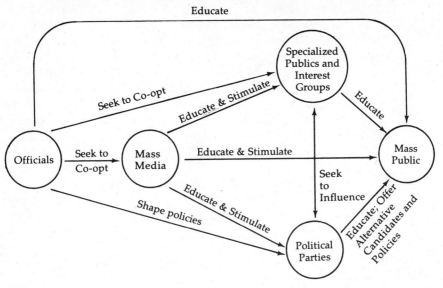

First, there has always been a profound strain of distrust of overly large and overly powerful government in the United States. This is hardly surprising given that a large number of the early settlers left Europe specifically to avoid some of the consequences of what they considered oppressive government (motives ranged from a concrete desire for religious freedom at the "noble" end of the spectrum to a desire for leaving a prison—a desire strong enough to outweigh the unknown terrors of the "new world"—at the "practical" end of the spectrum). Once here a large number of the inhabitants came to view the stance of the government in Westminster toward the American colonies as equally oppressive, particularly in economic matters. This heritage of the 17th and 18th centuries was very firmly in the minds of those who designed the national government in 1787. In subsequent years the suspicion of large, strong government has been kept alive both by the institutional innovations of the Founders and by a stream of rhetoric from almost every point on the political compass. In this case, although government and its functions have steadily grown, the core of the rhetoric is still believed in large part.

Second, the national government is only one of many governments in the United States. It has evolved to be the most powerful and, in some ways, the most important. But it is not necessarily the most consistently salient to the average citizen. The municipal government in Circleville, Ohio, or Shenandoah, Iowa, may not have the power to deliver a nuclear attack or raise billions of extra dollars by issuing bonds or jiggering income tax rates, but it can make decisions about who gets new sidewalks (and how much money they are assessed for them), who gets streetlights, where stoplights are placed, and whether a new member of the police force will be hired and who that person will be. And, to most citizens most of the time, the question of whether they will be assessed for a sidewalk that is only marginally desired or whether cousin Elmer will become a cop at $8,000 a year or continue pumping gas at $5,000 a year is more pressing than the question of U.S. policy toward Angola or detente with the Soviet Union or whether the rail system of the country requires a $10 billion subsidy or only a $2 billion subsidy.

The national government, then, undertakes only some of the governmental activities in the nation. And, particularly in recent years, there has been a strong urge on the part of the national government to pour both resources and decision-making authority back into state and local governments so that the national part of the federalistic edifice is not even as imposing as it looks on first glance.

Third, for a variety of reasons, Americans have long seemed to hold the judiciary in particularly high regard. Public opinion polls consistently show the Supreme Court to be more well thought of than either Congress or the Executive Branch. Judges are thought to be superior individuals. Although the public only realizes sporadically how important the judiciary can be in terms of impact on policy, the attitude of reverence toward courts and judges has helped sustain a judiciary that can become a vital and important part of the governing apparatus.

Fourth, given the design of the Constitution (and one needs only to read Articles I and II of that document to appreciate the point), the shared powers of Congress and the executive branch create a situation in which a relatively high degree of tension and conflict between the two branches is inevitable. But simultaneously, cooperation between Congress and the executive branch is essential if new public policy is to emerge and existing policy is to be changed. The Constitution created a strong President and a strong Congress (and a strong bureaucracy has emerged with the blessings of both). The shifting relationship between the legislative and executive branches—called "creative tension" by some and "hopeless stalemate" by others—has always been at the heart of the national government's formation of national public policy.

Fifth, when the 20th century public thinks of the national government they are very likely to think about the President in personal terms. He has become the focus of national activity. This does not accord with reality most of the time, but, nevertheless, it is a fact of life that sometimes influences what emerges from the government in the ways of policy.

Sixth, the particular history of the sequence in which varying demands of the domestic economy and society and, increasingly, the international economy and society came to the attention of and were acted on by the national government explains the details of why the government is doing what it is doing as we begin the last quarter of the 20th century.

Domestically the national government focused its attention almost exclusively on subsidizing a few specific private activities until after the Civil War. Most of the subsidies were aimed at developing the country by such measures as protecting industry from foreign competition and encouraging internal improvements such as canal building, railroad building, and homesteading. In the last few decades of the 19th century the national government also began to add a variety of regulatory concerns (for example, with interstate commerce of all forms) to its agenda as the fruits of the industrial revolution proved to be partially inedible or at least indigestible without some government help. Finally, after the Great Depression that began in 1929, the national government began to add a range of broad social concerns to its agenda that have continued to blossom (concerns such as the economic security of older persons, the health of older persons, the education of younger persons, and equal opportunities for persons of all races). At present the national government has a number of programs of all kinds—some that continue to subsidize a wide variety of private activities (growing or not growing specific crops, flying certain airline routes, making certain kinds of weapons), some that regulate a variety of activities (collective bargaining between labor and management, the stock exchanges and securities market, broadcasting), and some that are aimed at reducing the handicaps of the less fortunate (welfare, Medicare, busing to achieve racial balance in public school, public housing). Any of these policies may involve controversy although, predictably, the most controversial are those in the last category.

In terms of its activities on the world scene, the national government began to play a more aggressive role roughly beginning with the Spanish-American War in 1898. Slowly at first and then rapidly, the United States emerged as one of the few major powers in the world. This status has necessitated that the national government be increasingly concerned with its foreign relations and commitments and its military posture.

Even within shorter time periods than our entire national history the national government can be shown to be shifting priorities. For example, between 1960 and 1975 the national government's budget went up over threefold. But the increases were very different for different substantive areas. At one extreme, spending for health increased by more than 31 times. At the other extreme, spending for international affairs and finance increased by only 20 percent (which, in terms of "real

TABLE 1
RATIO OF FEDERAL BUDGET OUTLAYS IN 1975 COMPARED TO 1960, BY FUNCTION

Function	Ratio
National defense	1.9
Education and manpower	9.3
Health	31.5
Income security	4.8
Veterans' benefit and services	2.2
Agriculture and rural development	1.8
Natural resources and environment	5.6
Commerce and transportation	2.6
Community development and housing	5.4
International affairs and finance	1.2
Space research and technology	8.0
Total Budget Outlay	3.1

dollars" after an adjustment for inflation would have meant a decrease). Table 1 summarizes the budget changes in eleven different functional categories between 1960 and 1975 to give an idea of how priorities have been changing in recent years.

National policy

Two warnings need to be issued about the phrase "national policy" that has been used several times in the foregoing. One of the warnings involves the sources of national policy. The other involves the impact of national policy.

Where does national policy come from? An idealistic view is that a concerned and informed citizenry expresses its views to alert and responsive public officials who then proceed to develop the policy required to meet whatever problem is perceived. A cynical view is that an ill-informed public that cares little about government or policy, in effect, creates the conditions in which a small number of special interests can conspire with select public officials to produce parochial policy aimed primarily at the enrichment of the special interests and the security and tranquility of the public officials (and, often there are dark hints about their private enrichment).

Both views are extreme and usually inaccurate. There are, in fact, occasions on which a large number of citizens will mobilize themselves to express their opinions. On those occasions public officials will usually listen. On other occasions, even if no "voice of the people" can be heard, public officials will seek genuinely disinterested and effective national solutions to national problems. But there are also numerous instances in which what passes for national public policy is in fact the handiwork of a very small number of individuals—usually from Congress, the bureaucracy, and the private sector—who agree on what is best for some specific interest in society. Such clusters of individuals (called, appropriately, "subgovernments" in some writing on the subject) are not necessarily corrupt but they certainly can be said to take a limited view of the subject matter with which they are concerned. In some ways the widespread existence and importance of subgovernments can be expected in the fragmented situation produced by a large, complex governmental system interacting with a large, complex network of interest groups where subject matter specialization is encouraged and respected. The broadest impact of widespread subgovernment activity and dominance is that policy changes slowly in most areas most of the time and the existing policy is likely to have the dice loaded in its favor most of the time. Such a situation is not static nor inevitable and it does not always result in bad policy. But, in broad outline, it results in familiar policy that tends to be more responsive to particular interests than to general interests—which also means it tends to be more responsive to the more privileged than to the less privileged in society.

What impact does national policy have? Such a question is so broad as to be unanswerable in a few paragraphs. But what can be said is first that it is often difficult to prove that national policy has any particular effects. Second, it must also be noted that even if some of the intended consequences emerge from specific national policies and programs there are also likely to be some unintended consequences simultaneously. In short, two very different images—both of which have some basis in reality—can be drawn of the national government. One image is that of the large, powerful, well-run government addressing itself effectively to national problems and implementing solutions that at least begin to achieve the desired results. A second image is that of a large, confused collection of disparate organizations loosely united behind some rhetoric produced primarily in statutes and presidential speeches (and, occasionally, in decisions of the Supreme Court) fumbling fecklessly toward some noble ends but with little control over the situation in terms not only of external events, but also in terms of ability to predict the consequences of specific actions or evaluate the actual results of decisions made and actions taken.

The organization of this volume

All of the themes discussed thus far will emerge in a variety of settings in the specific readings that follow and in the short introductions we have prepared for each of the eleven clusters of readings. We want to explore—and, more important, we want each student to be able to explore—three major questions.

First, what linkages exist between society and government that help shape the nature of governmental institutions, the nature of governmental perceptions of problems, and the nature of attempted solutions to those problems in the shape of policies and programs?

Second, through what structures is policy produced and how?

Third, what policies and programs are, in fact, produced and with what effect?

Naturally, a single volume of readings cannot answer any of these questions fully. In fact, no volume of any sort and no course of any sort, could produce full, complete, and definitive answers. That fact is, after all, what makes the subject continually interesting. It is also what makes it particularly important for the student to be able to think for himself or herself when confronting questions about government and public policy.

The individual selections are organized in three parts suggested by the three questions above. However, any individual selection may well illustrate a number of points appropriate to all three questions. Any organization is, of course, arbitrary. And the more points that any selection illustrates, the better it is as far as we are concerned, because, what these readings and our introductory materials are portraying is a dynamic and interactive system, not a static system with neatly compartmentalized units and processes.

The readings are also chosen in part to raise a number of questions both about what exists and what ought to exist. In many areas both are open questions. "What exists?" is not itself an easy question to answer definitively. Interpretations by the observer almost always influence what gets reported as facts. "What ought to exist?" is an even more controversial question, as differing values of different individuals are explicitly called to the fore by merely posing the question. An educated person interested in matters of government and public policy needs to be able to comment on both what exists and what ought to exist. We certainly do not agree with all of the observations about facts in the following selections nor do we agree with all of the values suggested both indirectly and directly (in fact we could not hope to agree with all of them as we have sought some pieces that contain statements about both facts and values that differ markedly from similar statements in other pieces). We hope, however, that the selections will set the student using this volume off on a quest for the best possible approximation of a factual situation and the personally most satisfying pattern of values held in relation to government and policy in the United States.

II

the environment for government activity:

linkages between society and aovernment

public opinion

Public opinion is not easy to understand both because in the abstract it is a technically complex concept, and because in practice it is dynamic and constantly changing. Yet before being able to discuss intelligently the more interesting aspects about the place of public opinion in a representative government, one must have some grasp of the fundamentals of the nature of public opinion.

As a starting point, let's say that public opinion is the expressed set of views held by a large number of people on some issue of general importance. Even this seemingly simple definition raises questions. How many is a "large number" of people? Which people are expressing views? How are their views being expressed? What is an "issue of general importance"?

Some additional statements may help pin down the notion of public opinion. Opinion has certain measurable attributes—a subject (it is directed at something), directionality (one is either for, against, or neutral with respect to the topic), intensity (how strongly one feels about an issue), and stability (the length of time an opinion is held). Opinions are not necessarily formed as a result of a rational process of weighing competing views and information. More commonly, opinions are formed before information is available. Once an opinion is formed, conflicting information is usually discounted. Finally, the "public" in public opinion can be one of many publics—for example, mass public opinion is the opinion of the general population (which is usually measured on the basis of a sampling of adults). Smaller publics also express opinions—for example, elite or attentive publics that form around a temporary issue and then disband once the issue has become resolved, or special membership groups like hobby clubs, professional associations, business groups, and so on.

Many forces are important in shaping an individual's opinion on any particular issue. At the broadest level are forces of major historical and cultural significance such as wars, depressions, civic upheaval. One's direct or vicarious experience in such events can condition subsequent perception. The current state of affairs at both the national and local level also influence opinion formation. Included are factors such as the economic outlook (good times, bad times), the political context (party identification, election campaigns), social and civic conditions (riots, community needs). The individual's political socialization (his early molding into a politically-oriented creature—usually a result of family, school, church, and peer influences during youth) also has a long-term effect on how he perceives issues and reacts to them. The individual's awareness of a topic in objective informational terms (how much exposure to the topic has he had) is, of course, important and is a function of media coverage, his peer groups' attitudes, and his own "perceptual screen." (As mentioned above, opinions are often formed independent of unbiased information, but they definitely are formed as a result of media campaigns.) The individual's attitudes on other issues are important shapers of the issue in question. And finally there is a relationship between the individual's socio-economic characteristics and his opinions. In general, the upper strata of society (those with more income, education, and "better" occupations) tend to be more conservative in their opinions and outlook, while the more disadvantaged members of society (in terms of income, education, occupation) generally are of a more liberal persuasion. Similarly, increasing age and political conservatism are correlated.

What the above paragraph means in simple terms is that there are a number of factors that affect how an opinion is formed, that these factors may have different weights at different times and for different issues and for different kinds of persons, and that these influences are continuous (and often subtle) for every person.

The reason scholars spend so much time studying the myriad complexities of public opinion both in theory and in the real world is because of a long held and widely shared belief that in this country it is the people who are the source of power of the government. In Abraham Lincoln's words, government is "of the people, by the people, and for the people." Public opinion is thus a crucial component of our democracy, at least in theory, because it is an expression by the people who are governed. There are many explanations set forth by political scientists about how the public can, should, and does transmit its views to the government. For example, there is direct communication (the rational-activist model), communication through political parties and/or pressure groups, communication through shared values of the leaders and the led, and through socialization of leaders' roles. There are also theories about how the elected representatives of the public should respond to the public's views—the "instructed delegate" keeps his ear closely tuned to constituency wishes, the "trustee" acts on his own (presumably better informed) view of what is best for the public, and the "politico" does a little of both. There are elitist models and populist models. And many more.

The selection by Wahlke (reading 1) provides an interesting overview of the question of the role of the represented. In addressing the key question of what impact the public has in a democracy, Wahlke touches on a dilemma. Despite democratic theory, the public is not very informed about the government or attentive to its details, having only a vague knowledge about current policy proposals in government and about the stands of its representatives on those proposals. What happens to democratic theory, given an apparently unaware public? After surveying results of a number of research studies dealing with the behavior of the public, the behavior of elected representatives, and the influences on policy, Wahlke concludes that the key impact which the public may have is not a direct effect on specific policy proposals, but rather an intermediate impact by providing general support for the political system.

Following up on this suggestion, reading 2 (from a Senate Committee hearing) provides some evidence that although Americans may be disillusioned with their government, they have not lost confidence in the American system. Thus systematic support has not been withdrawn, although public confidence in leaders and institutions has declined. The hearing focuses on a national opinion poll conducted in the fall of 1973 explicitly for the Committee by a respected national polling organization. The poll sampled 1,596 people scientifically and asked them about their attitudes toward and relations with all levels of government. The main focus of the questions was on measuring public confidence in government. In the statement by the main witness and in the questions by committee members which followed, it is clear that while the public has "lost confidence, it has not lost faith." Disenchantment was with leaders, but not with the institutions or the system's ability to resolve problems. But the study confirmed that the public's level of knowledge about government was low, and legislators, while concerned with the general attitudes and confidence of the public, were not likely to view public opinion as a major determinant in shaping their own policy positions and proposals.

In summary, to the democratic idealist who is perhaps disillusioned by the state of affairs as depicted in this section, we would offer a word of encouragement. The world is never black or white. Public opinion is not rational, and government does not always function for the general good of the whole public, but the public does set the limits within which legitimate government activity can occur, and it does provide the important support function that is essential to continued stability of the nation-community. As Walter Lippmann has written, the people "can elect the government. They can remove it. They can approve or disapprove its performance. But they cannot administer the government . . . A mass cannot govern."

policy demands and system support: the role of the represented

reading 1

by John C. Wahlke

From John C. Wahlke, "Policy Demands and System Support: the Role
of the Represented," *British Journal of Political Science,* vol. 1 (July, 1971),
pp. 271–282, 284–288, 290.

DISCONTENT with the functioning of representative bodies is hardly
new. . . . This paper suggests how (and why) we might begin to reformu-
late representation theory and to identify the critical questions which
research must answer.

I

Much of the disillusionment and dissatisfaction with modern representative government grows out of a fascination with the policy decisions
of representative bodies which, in turn, reflects what may be called a
"policy-demand-input" conception of government in general and the representative processes in particular. Theorists and researchers alike have
long taken it for granted that the problem of representative government
centers on the linkage between citizens' policy preferences and the public-
policy decisions of representative bodies. . . .

THE SIMPLE DEMAND-INPUT MODEL

The basic elements in the general policy-demand-input conception
can be described, in necessarily oversimplified form, as follows. The principal force in a representative system is (as it ought to be) the conscious
desires and wishes of citizens, frequently examined in modern research on
representation under the heading of "interests." Interests are thought of
as constituting "policy demands" or "policy expectations," and the governmental process seems to "begin" with citizens exerting them on government. Government, in this view, is essentially a process for discovering
policies which will maximally meet the policy expectations of citizens. . . .

Analytically, the core of the representative process is the communication of these various forms of interest to governmental actors, which is thought to occur in either or both of two principal ways. It may take place through constituency influence, i.e., the communication of aggregated individual views by constituents to their "representatives." (The latter term theoretically includes administrative agency personnel, police officials, judges, and countless other governmental actors, but we shall deal here only with members of representative bodies.) Communication may also occur through group pressure or lobbying activities, conceived of as communication by group agents who are intermediaries between representatives and the aggregates of citizens for whom they (the group agents) speak.

The critical process for making representative government democratically responsible is, of course, election of the representatives. Elections are the indispensable mechanism for ensuring a continuing linkage between citizens' public-policy views (interests) and the public policy formulated by representatives (in cooperation, needless to say, with executives and administrators). The mechanism works in one or both of two ways. It may provide representatives with a mandate to enact into public policy at an early date the policy views expressed in the elections. It may also serve to legitimize, by stamping the *imprimatur* of citizen acceptance on, the policies most recently enacted by the representatives.

However logical and obvious such a conception of democratic representative governmental processes may seem, the observed behavior of citizens is in almost all critical respects inconsistent with it. Some of the more important established propositions about observed behavior which conflict with assumptions about the role of policy-demand inputs in politics may be listed here, even though there is no room to list in detail the evidence supporting them. They are, in most instances, propositions which are well known, although not normally brought to bear in discussions of representation:

1. Few citizens entertain interests that clearly represent "policy demands" or "policy expectations," or wishes and desires that are readily convertible into them.

2. Few people even have thought-out, consistent, and firmly held positions on most matters of public policy.

3. It is highly doubtful that policy demands are entertained even in the form of broad orientations, outlooks, or belief systems.

4. Large proportions of citizens lack the instrumental knowledge about political structures, processes, and actors that they would need to communicate policy demands or expectations if they had any.

5. Relatively few citizens communicate with their representatives.

6. Citizens are not especially interested or informed about the policy-making activities of their representatives as such.

7. Nor are citizens much interested in other day-to-day aspects of parliamentary functioning.

8. Relatively few citizens have any clear notion that they are making policy demands or policy choices when they vote.

None of this, of course, is new or surprising information. But it is sometimes forgotten when working from slightly less naïve models of the representational system than the one sketched out above. Each of the alternative models familiar to students of representative bodies, however, must sooner or later reckon with these facts.

A RESPONSIBLE-PARTY MODEL

Whatever else they are doing in the electoral process, voters in most political systems are certainly choosing between candidates advanced by political parties. It is therefore easy to assume that electoral choice between party-candidates is the vehicle for making policy-choices and to derive logically plausible mechanisms by which that choice might be made. For such mechanisms of demand-input to operate, several requirements would have to be met. In the first place, there must be a party program formulated and it must be known to the voters. Second, representatives' policy-making behavior must reflect that program. Third, voters must identify candidates with programs and legislative records, and base their choices on reaction to them. The arguments against the American party system and in favor of the British on grounds of systemic capacity for meeting these requirements are well known.

In most American contexts, the failure of party and legislative personnel to provide appropriate policy cues makes the applicability of the responsible-party model dubious to begin with, no matter what voters might be doing. But there are also signs of voter failure to respond appropriately to whatever such cues might be available. . . . With respect to public reaction to party at the national level, Miller and Stokes have demonstrated that party symbols are almost devoid of policy content, which is not surprising in view of what they call the legislative party "cacophony." And Converse, in one of the few relevant studies using panel data, found that party identification was far more stable among American voters sampled in 1958 and 1960 than their opinions on any "issues." We can only conclude, at least for the American case, that, with or without policy content, party symbols do not serve the American voter as the responsible party model would wish. . . .

But the most persuasive reason for questioning that model is what we know about the phenomenon of party identification itself. For the mere fact that one political party (or coalition) is replaced in government by another as a result of changing electoral fortunes, together with the fact that voters are making electoral choices between parties, does not in itself demonstrate anything at all about the relationship between election results and the public's views about party programs or policy stands. There is abundant evidence, on the contrary, that in many political systems voters identify with a political party much as they identify with a baseball or soccer team. Many voters in many lands are better described as "rooters," team supporters, than as policy advocates or program evaluators. The authors of *The American Voter* have acquainted us with the importance of that phenomenon in the United States. Of special interest here is their finding that, far from serving as a vehicle for the voter to express prior formed policy views, it is more likely that "party loyalty plays no small role in the formation of attitudes on specific policy matters". . . . [Editors' note: The authors of *The American Voter* are Angus Campbell, Philip E. Converse, Warren E. Miller, and Donald E. Stokes.]

It can hardly be said, then, that the responsible-party model solves any of the theoretical problems encountered in the elementary atomistic model of representative democracy. If anything, it raises further and more serious ones.

POLYARCHAL AND ELITIST MODELS

Historically, the awareness that few human beings are politically involved or active was at the core of many anti-democratic theories. More recently it has been the starting assumption for various elitist conceptions of power structure, particularly at the level of local communities. Still more recently the empirical accuracy of the assumption as well as the justifiability of "elitist" conclusions drawn from it have been questioned and subjected to empirical research.

Our concern here is not with the general theoretical problems raised by such approaches, however. It is rather with their implications for the demand-input conception of representative processes. The chief implication, of course, is that policy demands and policy expectations are manifested by a relative few and not by citizens in general. This implication is hardly to be questioned. . . .

The crucial question, then, concerns the extent to which and the mechanisms by which elites' policy-demanding activities are connected to the representational activities of the mass public. One possibility is that there is competition for different policy satisfactions among different elites, that this competition is settled initially in the governmental process, much as Latham has described the group process. . . .

What Latham leaves unsaid is how members of the voting public enter into this process "within the body of agreed principles that forms the consensus upon which the political community rests." Does it, by electoral decision, provide the ultimate ratification of policies formulated in the process of compromise among elites (groups)? At the very most, one might look for some "potential" power in the hands of the general public which it could use, if it wished, to ratify or reject policies and programs thus put before it. But all the considerations which made the simple atomistic and responsible-party conceptions implausible apply with equal force and in identical fashion against such an interpretation.

Thus, when we look for public participation through electoral choice among competing elites, we encounter the same difficulties we have encountered before. So-called polyarchal or elite-democracy models are no more helpful in connecting policy-making to policy demands from the public than were the atomistic and party models.

II

Demand-input emphases have tended also to color our views of what constitutes responsible behavior by elected representatives. Since the kind of findings just surveyed are well known, few modern studies consider Edmund Burke's "instructed delegate model" appropriate for modern legislators. Most report without surprise the lack of connection between any sort of policy-demand input from the citizenry and the policy-making behavior of representatives.

Nevertheless, most empirical studies of representative behavior accept the premise that conformity between legislators' actions and the public's policy views is the central problem of representative government, usually envisioning some kind of role-conception or normative mechanism through which the agreement comes about. . . .

[The findings of such studies,] while in some respects striking, are nonetheless ambiguous. From the standpoint of our understanding of representative government, the results of studies of the behavior of representatives are as unsatisfactory as the studies of citizen behavior seem disquieting. Many important questions are left unanswered, theoretically or empirically. Often the differences on which theoretically important distinctions are based are found to be small. Above all, in spite of the fact that legislative policy decisions are universally taken to be the most important type of legislative output, we know almost nothing about the character, let alone the conditions and causes, of how they vary in content. We now turn briefly to this problem.

III

"Policies" have been described as the most important variety of political output, and legislative policy decisions are commonly understood to be the most important type of legislative output. . . . So it is rather startling to discover that the term "policy" remains almost totally unconceptualized, i.e., that the literature provides "no theoretically meaningful categories which distinguish between types of policies."

There is, however, a recent series of methodologically sophisticated but theoretically unstructured inquiries into possible variations in public policy which tends still further to challenge the relevance of demand-input conceptions to understanding the representative process. . . .

It is the general import of these studies that, with only rare and minor exceptions, variations in public policy are *not* related to variations in political-structure variables, except insofar as socio-economic or environmental variables affect them and public policy variations together. Variations in policy output can be almost entirely "explained" (in the statistical sense) by environmental variables, without reference to the variables supposedly reflecting different systems and practices of representation. . . .

It is possible, of course, that these remarkable findings are unique to the American political system. That such is not the case, however, is strongly suggested by Cutright's discovery that variations in the national security programs of seventy-six nations appear to be explainable directly in terms of economic-development level and to be unrelated to differences in ideology or type of political system (including differences between communist and capitalist systems). . . .

In sum, then, the policy-environment correlation studies imply that stimuli which have been thought to be policy demands are really just automatically determined links in a chain of reactions from environment to policy output, a chain in which neither policy demands, policy expectations, or any other kind of policy orientation plays any significant role. There is no room, in other words, for any of the policy-related behaviors and attitudes of citizens which we examined in the preceding section of this paper to enter into the policy process.

IV

The foregoing arguments are not especially "anti-democratic" or "anti-representative." They are just as damaging to much anti-democratic theory and to elitist criticisms of representative democracy. It is not only policy-opinions of citizens in the mass public which are demoted in the rank order of policy determinants but policy opinions of elites and group leaderships as well. The principal implication is that "policy-process" studies whose aim is primarily to discover the political bases of policy decisions conceived of as choices between policy alternatives contended for by divergent political forces, or to explain why a particular decision went one way instead of another, comprehend too little of the political life of man, and that the part they do comprehend is probably not its most vital. The appropriate conclusion is not the grandiose notion that representative democracy is chimerical but the limited recognition that our conceptions of government, politics, and representation are somehow deficient, that "policy making" plays a different and evidently smaller role in the governance of society than we thought. . . .

A plausible working hypothesis which directs the study of representation toward "strong political behavior" is provided by Easton's discussion of "support." Viewed from this perspective, previous studies are seen to presume that political systems stand, fall, or change according to the "specific support" accorded them, the "consent" granted "as a consequence from some specific satisfaction obtained from the system with respect to a demand that the members make." But the arguments above show that specific support, the support attaching directly to citizens' reactions to policy decisions, does not adequately describe the relationship between citizen and government. We must also recognize and take into account what Easton calls "diffuse support," the support constituted by "generalized attachment to political objects, . . . not conditioned upon specific returns at any moment."

There is good warrant for the working hypothesis that,

> Except in the long run, diffuse support is independent of the effects of daily outputs. It consists of a reserve of support that enables a

system to weather the many storms when outputs cannot be balanced off against inputs of demands. It is a kind of support that a system does not have to buy with more or less direct benefits for the obligations and responsibilities the member incurs. If we wish, the outputs here may be considered psychic or symbolic, and in this sense, they may offer the individual immediate benefits strong enough to stimulate a supportive response. . . .

The shift of attention from "demands" to "support". . . calls for a corresponding shift of research emphasis from the behavior of representatives which has hitherto preoccupied most of us, to the perceptions, attitudes, and behaviors of the people whom representatives collectively represent, about which as yet we really know very little. The most immediate task is a primarily conceptual one—to identify the dimensions of support behavior, to map the incidence and variations of support in specific systems, and through comparative analysis of support mechanisms in different systems, to formulate hypotheses about its conditions and correlates.

v

David Easton's definition of support as affective orientation toward political objects, and his analytical distinction of political community, political regime, and political authorities as the three principal categories of such political objects is a useful starting point. We can probably assume, to begin with, that support for the political community is the most pervasive, general (diffuse), and stable element in the overall support mechanism of any political system. Basic group-identification, the sort of "pre-political" sentiment giving all segments of the community "a we-feeling . . . , not that they are just a group but that they are a political entity that works together and will likely share a common political fate and destiny," is surely a major dimension of this level of support. Everything we know about the historical evolution of nation-states, tribal societies, and all other political forms, as well as everything modern research tells us about the processes of political socialization, indicates that the loyalties, identifications, and cognitive-affective structures which make up this communal-loyalty dimension are acquired and shaped in early childhood and are affected little, if at all, by any political events, let alone such little salient events as the functioning of representative bodies. The indispensability of this kind of support for any political system was noted by V. O. Key: "A basic prerequisite is that the population be pervaded by a national loyalty. Or perhaps, more accurately, that the population not consist of segments each with its own sense of separateness." Almond and Verba, whose concept of "systems affect" approximates the concept of support for political community, likewise appear to take for granted (at least in the five countries they studied) the existence of a nationality sentiment or similar community sense defining a political community toward which members respond with varying effect.

But what if no sentiment of political community binds together a group of people who are, in fact, being governed (as is the case in many new African nations, to give an obvious example)? Or if segments seem increasingly to develop "each with its own sense of separateness" (as may well be the case in Canada or Belgium)? Can we be sure that "the sense of community must also be in part a product of public policy?" If not "policy," what aspect then of governmental activity, and especially of representative bodies' activity, affects it? At this stage we can only wonder —and begin to design research to find out.

A second major dimension of political community support is suggested by Almond and Verba's typology of political cultures, comprising what we may interpret as the political roles of "parochial," "subject," and "participant." The authors' original formulation differentiates these three types primarily in terms of their relative participation in demand-input activities. There is justification even in the original formulation, however, for viewing these roles as differentiated also by the extent of conscious support for the political community, or "the gradation from 'public' to 'private'.". . . Viewed this way, the second component of community support, which might be labelled "political commitment," appears as an autonomously defined political variable, a kind of participation through sensitivity and alertness to political events and objects as well as participation in civic and political roles—participation in politics per se, not necessarily in the sense of power seeking, however, and not participation in primarily instrumental activities. . . .

A number of familiar concepts bear on this second dimension of political-community support. Most of the phenomena usually treated under the heading of "political alienation," for example, represent an extreme negative value, ranking above only such anti-supportive positions as rebellion itself. "Political apathy," in a sense related to Almond and Verba's "parochialism," is more supportive than alienation but less so than "compliance." More supportive still is active "interest and involvement," although one must be careful to remember that support for the political community here is perfectly compatible (perhaps often associated?) with failure of support for regime or authorities. Beyond active spectator interest there is participation of varying degrees—ranging from nothing more than sporadic voting to regular and intensive political communication, to participation in authority or other "trans-civic" roles.

Such a conception of supportive political commitment seems perfectly consistent with what we do know about the relevant behavior of citizens. For example, once-depressing statistics about "low levels" of citizen interest take on quite different meaning in this light. The finding that "only" 27 per cent of the American public could be considered politically active, . . . or the countless similar readings of political interest and involvement in other political systems, must now, if there is no other different evidence on the point, be read not as sure signs of "apathy" or "negativism" but as probable indications of moderate support for the political community.

Still, on balance, we know much less than we should about the dynamics of support for the political community. Though we can recognize that communal loyalty and political commitment constitute important dimensions of it, we do not know how one dimension relates to the other, or how the day-to-day functioning of government, including the input-output functioning of representative institutions, relates to either.

The situation is not much different when we consider the problem of support for the "political regime." One major dimension here appears to be the level of conscious support for broad norms and values which apply to the political world generally, i.e., to "rules-of-the-game," or standards by which regimes are judged. . . .

The level of support for the institutional apparatus of government seems to be another major dimension of regime support, empirically distinguishable from generalized "agreement on fundamentals." Citizens are apparently able to dislike something or other about the actions of government and at the same time support its continuation institutionally unchanged, and their levels of support in this respect apparently fluctuate over time. . . . This perspective also leads us to view not as deviant, undemocratic views, but as probable indicators of probably normal regime support, the fact that more Americans think the majority of people usually *in*correct in their ideas on important questions (42 per cent) than think the majority correct (38 per cent), or that Congress is thought more correct than "the people" in its "views on broad national issues," (42 per cent as against 38 per cent). . . .

Our information about regime support phenomena, then, is no more adequate or satisfactory than our information about support for the political community. What there is of it, however, does seem to indicate that symbolic satisfaction with the process of government is probably more important than specific, instrumental satisfaction with the policy output of the process. . . .

Whereas political research has by and large neglected to study support for the political community and the political regime, it has paid considerable attention to support for "political authorities." Elections, of course, are considered an indispensable feature of representative government by anybody's definition, and election results in representative systems are almost universally interpreted as indices of support for incumbent authorities. The innumerable public opinion polls between elections which ask the level of voters' satisfaction or dissatisfaction with the ruling Government's performance in general, with the performance of various individual office holders or agencies, or with the handling of particular problems, are likewise taken as indicators of the rising and falling level of support for authorities.

No doubt such data are properly interpreted as measures of such support. But the question is, what should be read into them beyond that simple indication? . . .

VI

The conceptualization of support sketched out here is only that. It is not a theory, nor even a few hypotheses. Indeed, it is not even a very complete conceptualization, since many important questions are left open—how do we visualize support in a complex, multi-level, pluralistic government? What is the connection between support for local as against national (and, in federal systems, intermediate) authorities, regime, and political community? Between support for different segments of the regime at different levels? What is the relevance of the notion to supranational and intergovernmental politics?

What bearing has all this on representative government? Surely it does not suggest that to maintain representative democracy is more difficult, or that representative democracy is less desirable, just because it might seem to depend less on support deriving from mechanically satisfying demand-inputs than it does on the generation of support through quite different mechanisms. The question still is, how do representative bodies contribute to the generation and maintenance of support? In what respects and for what particular aspects of the task are they superior to non-representative institutions? These are questions to be answered by empirical research.

confidence and concern: citizens view American government

reading 2

From *Confidence and Concern: Citizens View American Government,* a hearing before the Subcommittee on Intergovernmental Relations, Committee on Government Operations, United States Senate, 93rd Cong., 1st sess. (December 3, 1973), pp. 1–2, 4–15, 17–18, 20–27.

[EDITORS' NOTE: The participants in the following discussion are Senator Edmund S. Muskie (D-Me.), Senator Bill Brock (R-Tenn.), Senator Lawton Chiles (D-Fla.), and Louis Harris, president of a well-known public opinion polling company.]

Senator MUSKIE. The committee will be in order.

I suppose this an unusual forum for discussing a public opinion survey but the survey is so comprehensive that it seemed to me the best way of presenting it and also of probing some of its more salient points. . . .

[The survey] shows us that people are very poorly informed, in general, about their Government at all levels and have only the most limited and basically self-centered contact with Government services.

Yet, contrary to the public apathy described by so many of the officials questioned, the study finds citizens anxious to take part in the affairs of their community, respectful of the organized groups which already do so, and eager to receive inspiration for their efforts in trustworthy, vigorous central leadership. It also shows a common desire on the part of the people and the State and local officials who were interviewed to see Federal responsibilities more widely shared with other levels of government.

Putting those conclusions together spells out a need for programs which bring citizens to participate in the decisions of their Government. And with this need came the call in the report for the allocation of more Federal funds and power to the cities, towns, counties, and States—those places where many Americans perceive their influence now has the most impact. When the Congress enacted general revenue sharing last year, for example, it hoped to develop a means for greater citizen participation, but so far very few positive results have come from that effort. . . .

Senator BROCK. . . . One of the things I would like you to address most particularly as we go along is the point that Senator Muskie touched on, the section relating to making shared responsibilities work. . . . It is backed up by polls throughout the document but, if I read it correctly, what the American people are asking for is a strong central government that exercises leadership, together with stronger State and local governments which initiate and undertake the action programs. I was fascinated, for example, with the statistics on health care. With all the discussion of a national health program, only 18 percent of the people wanted a Federal program, while 23 percent wanted a State program, 28 percent wanted a local program and 31 percent wanted something else.

It seems to me that the word is fairly clear here that people feel they are distanced too far from the source of power. There is a hunger expressed throughout the report for a greater voice in the process of Government, the allocation of resources and in the selection and implementation of programs. This is something that I feel very deeply about. It is surprising, too, that although we can take issues like health care or education where you have a great deal of difference between Senator Muskie's home area in the Northeast and mine in the South, this particular commonality of desire for greater and stronger local Government and a greater voice in Government is so strong. The breadth of it north, south, east, and west stands out boldly in the report, and I think it is fascinating to note. . . .

Mr. HARRIS. . . . For the first time in over a decade of opinion sampling, this survey shows that disaffection has now reached majority proportions. On a scale of powerlessness, cynicism, and alienation used by our firm since 1966, an average of 55 percent of the American people expressed disenchantment, compared with no more than 29 percent who felt that way only 7 years ago. The trend, however, has not been precipitous; it has been steadily and almost unabatingly upward from 29 percent in 1966 to 36 percent in 1968 to 42 percent in 1971 to 49 percent in 1972, all the way up to 55 percent this fall in 1973, a veritable flood-tide of disenchantment, seemingly gaining momentum with each passing year. . . .

Any objective analysis of such results can only conclude that a crisis of the most serious magnitude now exists in the responses and assessment of the people to their Government. While there are some traditional strains of feelings of economic injustice, the main thrust of the people's disaffection can be traced to a growing sense of powerlessness, to a deep feeling that those with power seek to abridge, deny, and even strip away the ultimate power of the governed. This felt tyranny of erosion of the people's power and freedom has not been viewed as a sudden development, is not limited to one act or one leader or one period in recent history. It has been taking place for several years, and its very duration escalates a serious and even dangerous condition into what I view as a full-blown crisis of confidence.

The study probed in considerable depth to determine just how much this crisis exists across the boards for the leadership of nearly all major institutions in America and how much it is centered on Government at various levels. Basically, by any standard, there has been a fall in respect and confidence in the people running almost every major U.S. institution compared with 1966, when we first measured it. . . .

Only one area of leadership shows any increase in public confidence since 1966: the media, a source of controversy in any era and probably never more than today. Television news and the press have risen in public esteem, although having said this the 41 percent high confidence in TV news and the 30 percent for the press are still accolades from only a minority of the people. Of perhaps greater significance is the wide gulf that exists in the estimate of the media by local and State officials surveyed and the public. While 41 percent of the public gave TV news high marks, only 17 percent of the leaders did the same. While 30 percent of the public expressed high regard for the press, no more than 19 percent of the leaders were willing to give a similar vote of confidence.

The inescapable conclusion is that the public has roughly twice as much confidence in the media as State and local public officials have today. . . .

Public confidence in government generally must be reported as being lower than a constituent democracy can afford. Since 1966, high confidence in the U.S. Supreme Court, our highest court in the land, has fallen away from a majority 51 percent to a minority 33 percent; in the U.S. Senate from 42 to 30 percent; in the House of Representatives from 42 to 28 percent; and in the executive branch of the Federal Government from 41 to 19 percent. All but the executive branch, however, did make some gains of between five and nine points just in the past year. The executive branch by contrast slipped another eight points lower.

Although the Federal Establishment ranks low by any standard, State and local government can take little comfort, for no more than 28 percent of the people expressed high confidence in leadership of local government and, even lower, 24 percent in State government, although a much higher 52 percent praised local trash collection, 44 percent their local police, and 39 percent their local public school leadership.

However, at the very bottom of the list came the leadership in the White House. . . .

While disenchantment among the public runs deep, it is important to point out that this disaffection is far more directed at the leadership of our institutions than at the institutions themselves. . . .

In the 26 years in which I have been engaged personally in analyzing public opinion as a professional, I have been singularly struck by the fact that most Americans have rather strong opinions on most important subjects, but that their views are marked by much more emotion than a thorough grounding in knowledge. In the surveys we take, people are giving us their feelings on a subject, much more than a final rendering of judgment when all the facts have been sifted and carefully weighed. This survey offers ample documentation of this basic observation.

By their own admission, a majority of people are not well informed about what is going on in government or politics at the Federal, State, or local levels. Although 89 percent correctly can identify their own State's Governor, no more than 59 percent can name one U.S. Senator from their State, only 39 percent can name the other U.S. Senator, only 36 percent can name both Senators and a minority of 46 percent really know who their Congressman is. Substantive knowledge about the details of legislation or foreign policy might be even lower than those levels.

Yet, for all of this lack of specific information, a striking finding of this study is that the American people are far from apathetic, uninterested in the public affairs of their country, nor uninvolved. It is only at their peril that public officials can assume an apathetic public, or one which will not respond.

Part of the problem exposed by the survey is that other than in paying their taxes and filing the necessary forms to receive licenses, social security, and other direct Government benefits, the American people have had remarkably little direct contact with their Government at any level. No more than 9 percent of the public have had "a highly satisfying experience" with local government, a low 5 percent at the State level, and a similar 5 percent at the Federal level. . . . Unfortunately, for most of the public, government at all levels means only slightly more than paying taxes, which, indeed, most feel are too high to begin with.

Both the public and the leadership tend to parallel each other's views about which level of government authority can best respond to a broad range of concerns ranging from world peace to garbage collection, from highway accidents to inflation. But two areas—political corruption and social welfare—are felt to deserve high priority attention from all levels of government. And the public and the leaders are also convinced that to make government function better—and this is Senator Brock's point— State and local government should be strengthened and the Federal Establishment should have power taken away from it, despite a clear mandate for the Federal Government to take the primary responsibility for such major issues as war and peace, the economy, and the quality of life. . . .

As a nation, over three out of every four adult citizens belong to some organization, and half of these are active in them. Only one in three people has some real organizational experience. But a much higher 58 percent, a majority, of the public expressed the view that they personally feel they could do something about an unjust or corrupt public official, and when asked what they would do "if they wanted to see a change take place in government," 94 percent said they would vote against a public official, 91 percent would talk to their friends and neighbors about the question, 84 percent would write their Congressman, 81 percent would write their U.S. Senator, 79 percent would work through a group they belong to, 76 percent would contact local law enforcement officials, 75 percent would contact someone in local politics, 72 percent would join a local citizens group, 66 percent would join a political party and work to make changes, 65 percent would write a letter to the newspaper, 62 percent would send money to support a local citizens group to demand action, 61 percent would talk to a newspaper reporter or editor, and 55 percent would vote against the public official's party at the next election.

Significantly, no more than 17 percent said they would "do nothing."

Clearly, there are literally masses of the American people poised out there with the notion of becoming more involved in the process rather than withdrawing from it. Indeed, half the public feels that "groups of citizens and organizations are having more effect in getting government to get things done." A much higher 68 percent of the State and local leaders share this view, and there is real hope there, Mr. Chairman. It is perfectly apparent that the public is looking in the future to vastly greater citizen participation in their governmental decision-making process than was ever the case before. . . .

Specifically, the American people desperately want a condition in the country in which government secrecy can no longer be excused as an operational necessity since it can exclude the participation of the people in their government, and, indeed, can be used as a screen for subverting their freedom. But just as important, the public is also demanding that any kind of successful future leadership must possess iron bound integrity. This matter of honesty and straight-dealing is one that the public is deeply alarmed about. It cannot be underestimated. The American people simply will not rest easy until they feel that integrity in government at all levels is secured.

Once these preconditions of openness and integrity have been fulfilled, then the time may well come when the people can be approached to make the sacrifices necessary to solve the common problems of the country. Indeed, as we have found out since the energy crisis descended upon us, the people are well out ahead of their leaders in willingness to sacrifice. But if the preconditions to open government are not met, then frustration, alienation, and polarization are likely to proceed apace. And the distrust of the governed for those who govern is a dangerous development indeed. . . .

Senator BROCK. Mr. Harris, just a few points. First of all, I think one of the more fascinating parts of this report is the difference of opinion between leaders and the people, and I would draw a parallel. Senator Chiles and others early this year sponsored a measure to open up the committee process—Senator Muskie was very active in this area—because I think we felt that an open government is absolutely essential. There was an awful lot of criticism that the committees would not work if our executive sessions were open to the public and, as a matter of fact, it has turned out that they work very well. But that was done, was it not, about March or April, Lawton?

Senator CHILES. Yes, I think it was March.

Senator BROCK. And yet your poll was run in September and there seems to be no indication of any perception of a more open government, so my question would be, I think Lawton addressed it in his opening remarks, how do we communicate this? Maybe it is just a first step, but I think it was a rather significant one. I think there are others that are going to be taken. I have never seen the Congress in the mood for reform as it has been this year in terms of the budgetary process and in terms of responsiveness. And yet the confidence level continues to decline. Perhaps it is due to our inability to communicate or articulate what we are doing. But I wonder if there is any approach you might suggest to us that would help.

Mr. HARRIS. Senator Brock, may I respond to that and say that there are two areas, I think, that are critical in terms of convincing the American people of the openness of government, on the one hand, and a willingness on the part of government leadership to share responsibility, on the other.

I think one feels that it has not been made clear, I think, to the people, to the American people, that the Federal Establishment is willing to share many of these substantive problems, at least the solutions to them, with the State and local governments. Now, I realize all of you gentlemen worked on this constantly, and yet the people themselves, when we surveyed them, felt basically that the Federal Government ought to have power taken away from it rather than added to it, which is a sign they feel that the Federal Government has too much power.

Now, I think the missing ingredient here is a necessary welcome on the part of leadership in Government to say to the people: "We want not only to have the Federal Establishment share responsibility with the State and local governments, but we would like the people to share in the decisionmaking along with us." People may not be terribly well informed about the workings of government, but they also feel quite well informed about what the problems are in the country, especially their own problems, and they are willing to go to great lengths through their citizen organizations, forming new ones or going through old ones, to participate, and I would think not just the act of open hearings but even making well known—if you can do this, and I do not see any reason why it cannot be done—that groups of citizens have an opportunity to participate at all levels in the planning, conception, and then indeed even in the monitoring of the execution of government programs.

In another study we did—not this one—we asked people about environmental controls: "Would you trust Government to monitor whether the controls were being really enforced?" And while people said, "Well, in the end, I suppose, Government has the facility to do it," believe it or not people would more trust a citizens' group to monitor whether controls were really being carried out than they would Government at any level.

Now, I do not propose a whole group of citizen bands roaming the country monitoring, but I must say there is a way to get at it. Senator Chiles, you went out to the people when you campaigned, and walked all around the State and saw them, and I think that's probably one of the major reasons you got elected. They felt you went out and cared.

I think basically it is about time that Government went out to the people and said, "We care"—and it is not, let me say, it is not the handout. People do not want government to say, "We are going to take care of you."

It is just the opposite today. People want to be told by their leaders, "We may not have all the answers, but we sure want you to share in formulating the answers."

That is what the people are saying fundamentally, Senator. . . .

Senator BROCK. Would you say one of the problems faced in the Senate or in the House is how to obtain input from the public when we are presented with a piece of legislation? The committee I have got to go to next is the Banking, Housing and Urban Affairs Committee. We are considering an omnibus housing bill and we are in the midst of a rather severe debate over the type of housing program we are going to have. The debate is not over whether we should have 235 or 236 but over who is going to run it. The question is whether or not we should have bloc grants, an allocation to local officials who would set up within the community, housing programs responsive to the community's needs.

Now, while I am for that, I can understand the position of others who are against it, because they read this poll the same way I do and they do not have any more confidence in local officials than the people do in us. So, this restoration of faith that we are seeking becomes a difficult question and is not something that is subject to a simple answer. It would be ill-advised for the Democratic Party and the Republican Party to open up to anything other than the individual. If it begins opening up to groups, lobbies, if you will, then there is a potential for shoving the party's philosophy out of line under the pressure of those very well-organized sub-groups. I think that will—

Mr. HARRIS. Senator, if I might say, I think one of the things that does come out of this study is that the people in terms of the lobbies and organized spokesmen whom you gentlemen see, I think, with regularity, are not in many cases always representative of the broad mass of the public out there in terms of for whom they try to speak. This is a serious problem, I think, in our kind of Republic, because those who are organized, those who have the money, if you will, to be represented, those who can be vocal, and those who have the time and the energy and the resources to be at those focal points of legislation—it seemed to me, and I tried to make that clear in my testimony—are also on the spot. The public's confidence in these special interest groups is also rather low, so I say it behooves them to take just as much warning for this as indeed the governmental levels, Federal, State, and local. I think you will find the various constituencies, whether it is within business, labor or education, or you name it, right down the line, who misspeak for special privilege as opposed to representing their constituency, will find themselves just as much on the spot and in trouble in the long pull, as I think elected public officials are.

In moving about in the private sector, one of the things I find most difficult to communicate to people who are not elected, who do not have to go back to face voters, if you will, is the fact that they are as much on trial, they are as much sensitized by public opinion these days, as anyone who has to face an election every 2 years or every 6. So that I would hope that one of the fall-outs or impacts of this study would be a going back to the people whom they claim to speak in behalf of—I do not want to single out farmers or workers or business or consumers or whatever, but all groups, I would say. The public may not know all the facts, but they have a pretty good instinct about knowing when the voices who speak are false voices and selfish voices and corrupt voices, and when they are voices of integrity. . . .

Senator MUSKIE. Let me . . . pull three points together. One, you made the point in your opening statement this morning that although television and the written press came off better than the rest of us, they still received a minority high confidence rating.

Mr. HARRIS. Yes.

Senator MUSKIE. Only a minority, 41 percent, gave them high confidence.

Second, you made the point, and the study makes the point, that the public considers itself poorly informed. And third, of course, is the point that a restoration of our own credibility rating is going to depend to a great deal upon communication which includes the press.

What can the press do to improve its performance, improve its credibility and, at the same time, contribute to whatever we might do to improve our own credibility? It seems to me the press is rather the key to an informed public and to a better perception of what we are actually doing, as well as to the improvement of its own performance.

Mr. HARRIS. Mr. Chairman, I think you put your finger on one key, if you will, a serious indictment of the media. When you get 60 percent of the public who say they do not feel well informed, I do not see how the media can escape some responsibility for that. It seems to me as one who indeed is part of the working press in a sense, in that I report publicly to over 200 newspapers twice a week, I would say woe betide the editor or the reporter who said, "Well, how can I help it if the people do not care or they do not take the trouble to listen or to view or to read. It is not my fault people do not hear or read me." The fact is you have a real responsibility to communicate if you are going to be in the communications business. . . .

I think people today are in a different mood. They are in a mood to want to participate. In fact, a new trend which has emerged is people are far less interested and desirous of the media endorsing candidates. They would much rather be assured that in elections both sides are heard and that all candidates have ample opportunity. This was supposed to be a great breakthrough, let us say, when television stations were allowed to endorse candidates. Yet now we are reaching a point where the public says, "We are less interested, Mr. Publisher or Mr. Television Station Owner, in what your views are. We want to be sure that our views are a pluralism of expression through the media here." It is having it wide open that people want. So in a sense the media, perhaps by being somewhat more responsive to this, have improved their credibility; and now it is Government's turn, business's turn, education's and the military's, and a whole lot of other institutions' turns.

I do not know whether that answers it but I think it is certainly one of the keys.

In the individual reporter's area, which I did touch on in my testimony—and I owe it to my colleagues to explain—I do not mean for a minute that reporters ought to let up and go easy on men in public life or on public officials, or on anybody anywhere. But often—or at least sometimes—I have observed that reporters are all too quick, without investigating carefully, to draw conclusions that might be the most negative about the motives or reasons someone in public life did something; and I think they have an obligation to say, "Look, what I have got to do is objectively examine this to see if it is indeed the fact or not the fact."

If they have come to the conclusion that it is the fact then they have an ironbound obligation to report it. I think these quick and easy shooting from the hip conclusions are a disease that not only affects a number of people in public life but also affects a lot of people in journalistic life. . . .

Senator CHILES. . . . I am very interested in the polls or the different sets of figures that would show where the people feel something can be done about corrupt officials and where they feel something should be done. Each one of those polls just tends to indicate to me so clearly that the people are ahead of their leaders, that they feel that we should be taking action in so many areas that we are failing to take action in. Do you not think this same feeling would come through with something like dealing with the energy crisis, that the people are ready for hard solutions if those are necessary, that we should not be trying to pablum feed them or trying to lead them into this thing.

I continue to hear people say all the time "Well, we have got to condition the people for this" or "we have got to condition them for that," what are your comments on that condition? . . .

Mr. HARRIS. I just reported this morning the fact that by any measure the public is quite far ahead of at least the articulated program that they have been asked to put up with in the way of sacrifice on the energy question. . . .

Senator CHILES. Your figures indicate the same thing is true of inflation, of trying the steps to control inflation.

Mr. HARRIS. Yes, sir. . . .

In fact, I just wrote a book on this subject called "The Anguish of Change," in which I showed, Senator, the leadership of this country, consistently over the past 10 years, has really misread the public and been out of touch in terms of what the public is willing to do. I do not believe that the public is right in a lot of cases, maybe not even in most cases, but I would have to conclude in this period of time that the public has been vastly ahead of its leaders. And one of the reasons for this crisis of confidence has to be the inability of leadership to credit the people with being interested in something more than just their own narrow selfish interests. . . .

Senator CHILES. The other area that I wanted to touch on was the question that Senator Brock raised that we continue to say that we really are afraid to give more power back to State or local governments even though we all want to do that and even though we all recognize that that is how it should work, "but State and local governments are not quite ready. They just do not have the leadership now or we are just afraid of this.". . .

Does your poll indicate, or does it not indicate, that if you gave this power and authority back to State and local government the people could work their will and they could be much closer in contact and then could hold these people accountable for their acts and could judge them and that you would have a different breed of State and local officials if they were not carrying out their mandate? . . .

Mr. HARRIS. Senator, there is no question about that. The only level of government in which we got a positive reading when we asked people, "How does local government, State government, Federal Government affect your lives," was local government. . . .

As important as anything, though, I think is the fact that people also thought it was at the local and State level as well as the Federal level that social programs should be worked on and corruption should be worked on. In other words, there is implicit in this, it seems to me, that people are saying, "We must have perhaps broad policies set at the Federal level, but the followthrough must be done at every State and every local level because it is in our own communities that it has got to be done, and if it is not done in the local communities then it will not be done anywhere, in effect."

So it would seem to me that again, through the sixties, we have been polarized to the point where you have a lot of adversarism between State and local government, on the one hand, and Federal Government on the other. Perhaps the time to take some of the chips off the shoulder in these areas is now—at least in terms of the public—to allow Federal and State and local people to feel they are all working for the same end here. . . .

As I think about it, perhaps it has been a mistake to lead with what has been called revenue-sharing. The reason I say that is because when you talk about revenue-sharing, people tend to think about tax money rather than to think in terms of the substance of what that money is to be used for; and once they hear revenue-sharing they may say, "Well, maybe I will get back some of the taxes I am paying," rather than the substance—if revenue-sharing were simply to reduce taxes.

Senator CHILES. If it was responsibility-sharing it would be better.

Mr. HARRIS. Right. It seems to me it would be better if Government people talked in terms of the substance of these programs and said, "Here is what we would like to see carried out on the local level and right straight through localities, through communities, throughout the country," and if you talked more in terms not of the benefits that individuals will get but rather the good that their communities will get and, as such, as their communities thrive and prosper and do well so they as individuals prosper. There is great identity today with communities if one will talk in the language that the people talk in.

Obviously, one can say, "Well, you must have the money to back it up and revenue-sharing is critical to backing it up." But I would say, if you start with the money you may end with the money, and the substance of what indeed it is all about may get lost in the shuffle.

Senator CHILES. The people are saying "That those services that could be done for me at the local level, be they social, fire protection, or police protection, should be done for me at the local level before we go to the next level or layer of government." . . .

Senator MUSKIE. We have talked a lot about the desire, as revealed in this report, that responsibilities and resources be turned back to State and local government. I think to leave the record standing at that would be a little misleading and so I would like you to comment on another finding you made . . . : "When offered the extreme case of Jefferson's classic formulation—'That government is best which governs least'—a majority of Americans and a near majority of their leaders disagreed. Nearly 9 Americans in 10 believe the Federal Government has 'a deep responsibility for seeing to it that the poor are taken care of, that no one goes hungry, and that every person achieves a minimum standard of living.' In fact, two-thirds of the public would agree that 'It's about time we had a strong Federal Government again to get this country moving again.' "

How does that finding square with others in the report that we ought to turn back responsibilities to State and local government and that we ought to take some power away from the Federal Government?

Mr. HARRIS. Well, I think the answer to that, Mr. Chairman, is that people feel what the Federal Government turns back to the States and localities has to be selective. It was not just an abdication of Federal responsibility. I think, for example, if the Federal Government announced suddenly one day that all responsibility for the economy was being given up by the Federal Government and each State was being allowed to set its own regulations and policies, I think the people would be horrified at this. Or if, and this is against the Constitution, the Federal Government said, "Each State can set its own foreign policy and negotiate with the Russians or the Chinese," I think the people would also be horrified.

So I think what people are saying here is that we want leadership to lead.

I hope nothing I have reported here this morning will indicate in any way that people want weaker leadership. They want stronger leadership, and the definition of strong leadership is open leadership, leadership which is willing to tear down the veils of secrecy and say, "We have nothing to hide, only full disclosure at every hand;" that kind of leadership which is willing to say "Here is the sum and substance of what we are thinking, your leadership is thinking, and we are willing to engage even your disagreement and your hostility in coming down to this kind of position on a particular issue." Whether it is an energy crisis or something else, the public would welcome that, more than welcome that. . . .

mass media

Our society has become more and more dependent on nonpersonal means of communication and information sharing as the size of the population and the amount of knowledge increase. We are deluged with books, newspapers, radio broadcasts, television shows, telephone calls, magazines, films, photographs, and computer printouts. The spread of nonpersonal communication is especially evident in politics, where candidates have to cover more ground than ever before in campaigning to get votes. The geographic size of the country hasn't changed since 1959, but the number of people to be reached has grown, as has the number of politically significant groups. A candidate who wants to win has to get to the people, but it is not physically possible to meet personally with a majority or even a plurality of the national electorate, and covering smaller areas is also demanding. Thus the officeholders and candidates of the 60's and 70's have come to realize the importance of the mass media in presenting themselves to the people, and hopefully in winning the votes of the people. Incumbents and candidates do things that they hope will receive attention from the news media, so they might win a film clip on the evening news, or a story in the paper, be it the local one or a national chain. News coverage is a great way of getting exposure, of conveying a name to the public, and it's free. Paid advertisements in the media are also used.

The mass media thus have an important function in American political life both between and during elections as they focus on candidates and what they say and do. In acting as a filter or conveyer of reality for the millions of people who must rely on the media to report the political events that have occurred during the day, the media are performing a subset of a larger function, which journalists have called "agenda-setting." Agenda-setting is what the term implies—helping to set the public's agenda for thought and talk. The media are influential in agenda-setting for a number of reasons. First, because of the complexity of society, people have to rely on an intermediary to report what has happened—no one can personally do his own investigating and reporting. This is one task of the media. Second, the media, particularly the television networks, are pervasive throughout most parts of society, so most people can hear the news if they want to. And third, although there are many regional and ideological interpretations of events, there is a fair degree of consensus among the media on what the major news stories are from day to day. So the same issues tend to get presented to the public, with various twists, by the media.

In performing this agenda-setting function, editors and broadcasters first are presenting information to the public in a relatively objective fashion about important topics. (The degree of objectivity and the definition of "important topics" are, of course, subject to discussion.) Which topics the press focuses on, how much attention over time those topics receive, the size of a story, the placement of a story on the page or in a broadcast are all cues to the public about the importance of what is being reported. Thus the media's most significant impact on public opinion is one of increasing public awareness about issues by presenting selected information on those issues. There is a direct correlation between the amount of media coverage of an issue and the salience of that issue to the public—for example, fully 96 percent of the public had heard about or read about the Watergate affair by May of 1973, according to a Gallup poll. McCombs and Shaw (in reading 3) explore the concept of agenda-setting in an election context in an easy-to-understand empirical test conducted during the 1968 presidential campaign in a single community.

The media have an impact on policy-makers and policy-making by providing information to governmental and nongovernmental elite who are involved in policy decisions, by serving as a forum for the exchange of ideas, and occasionally by creating issues. But more often, the media impact on policy is not a direct one, but rather indirect—by serving as a watchdog for the public over the operations of government, the media help to keep the government honest and open and on its toes. There is a natural tension between government officials and media representatives, because they have differing goals—the government person wants to have his product presented in the best light and would prefer to talk only about the success stories, while the reporter is interested in finding out if there is anything amiss in the agenda, and if so, why. Cater felt this tension significant enough to label the press the fourth branch of government since it served so well as a check and balance on the other three constitutional branches. In reading 4, Weaver addresses the issue of natural tension between reporters and reported, and describes the dilemma facing journalists as they exercise their craft—on the one hand they need access to and information from the government, but on the other hand, they also need to maintain their independence in interpreting and presenting that information to the public. Weaver describes two kinds of journalist practice, the liberal tradition (objective, factually oriented) and the adversary tradition (beginning in the 60's), and discusses the implications for the future of both styles.

the agenda-setting function of mass media

by Maxwell E. McCombs and Donald L. Shaw

From Maxwell E. McCombs and Donald L. Shaw, "The Agenda-Setting
Function of Mass Media," *Public Opinion Quarterly,* vol. 36 (Summer, 1972),
pp. 176–185.

IN OUR DAY, more than ever before, candidates go before the people through the mass media rather than in person. The information in the mass media becomes the only contact many have with politics. The pledges, promises, and rhetoric encapsulated in news stories, columns, and editorials constitute much of the information upon which a voting decision has to be made. Most of what people know comes to them "second" or "third" hand from the mass media or from other people.

Although the evidence that mass media deeply change attitudes in a campaign is far from conclusive, the evidence is much stronger that voters learn from the immense quantity of information available during each campaign. People, of course, vary greatly in their attention to mass media political information. Some, normally the better educated and most politically interested (and those least likely to change political beliefs), actively seek information; but most seem to acquire it, if at all, without much effort. It just comes in. As Berelson succinctly puts it: "On any single subject many 'hear' but few 'listen'." But Berelson also found that those with the greatest mass media exposure are most likely to know where the candidates stand on different issues. Trenaman and McQuail found the same thing in a study of the 1959 General Election in England. Voters do learn.

They apparently learn, furthermore, in direct proportion to the emphasis placed on the campaign issues by the mass media. Specifically focusing on the agenda-setting function of the media, Lang and Lang observe:

The mass media force attention to certain issues. They build up public images of political figures. They are constantly presenting objects suggesting what individuals in the mass should think about, know about, have feelings about.

Perhaps this hypothesized agenda-setting function of the mass media is most succinctly stated by Cohen, who noted that the press "may not be successful much of the time in telling people what to think, but it is stunningly successful in telling its readers what to think *about.*" While the mass media may have little influence on the direction or intensity of attitudes, it is hypothesized that *the mass media set the agenda for each political campaign, influencing the salience of attitudes toward the political issues.*

METHOD

To investigate the agenda-setting capacity of the mass media in the 1968 presidential campaign, this study attempted to match what Chapel Hill voters *said* were key issues of the campaign with the *actual content* of the mass media used by them during the campaign. Respondents were selected randomly from lists of registered voters in five Chapel Hill precincts economically, socially, and racially representative of the community. By restricting this study to one community, numerous other sources of variation—for example, regional differences or variations in media performance—were controlled.

Between September 18 and October 6, 100 interviews were completed. To select these 100 respondents a filter question was used to identify those who had not yet definitely decided how to vote—presumably those most open or susceptible to campaign information. Only those not yet fully committed to a particular candidate were interviewed. Borrowing from the Trenaman and McQuail strategy, this study asked each respondent to outline the key issues as he saw them, regardless of what the candidates might be saying at the moment. Interviewers recorded the answers as exactly as possible.

Concurrently with the voter interviews, the mass media serving these voters were collected and content analyzed. A pretest in spring 1968 found that for the Chapel Hill community almost all the mass media political information was provided by the following sources: Durham *Morning Herald,* Durham *Sun,* Raleigh *News and Observer,* Raleigh *Times,* New York *Times, Time, Newsweek,* and NBC and CBS evening news broadcasts.

The answers of respondents regarding major problems as they saw them and the news and editorial comment appearing between September 12 and October 6 in the sampled newspapers, magazines, and news broadcasts were coded into 15 categories representing the key issues and other kinds of campaign news. Media news content also was divided into "major" and "minor" levels to see whether there was any substantial difference in mass media emphasis across topics. For the print media, this major/minor division was in terms of space and position; for television, it was made in terms of position and time allowed. More specifically, *major* items were defined as follows:

1. Television: Any story 45 seconds or more in length and/or one of the three lead stories.

2. Newspapers: Any story which appeared as the lead on the front page or on any page under a three-column headline in which at least one-third of the story (a minimum of five paragraphs) was devoted to political news coverage.

3. News Magazines: Any story more than one column or any item which appeared in the lead at the beginning of the news section of the magazine.

4. Editorial Page Coverage of Newspapers and Magazines: Any item in the lead editorial position (the top left corner of the editorial page) plus all items in which one-third (at least five paragraphs) of an editorial or columnist comment was devoted to political campaign coverage.

Minor items are those stories which are political in nature and included in the study but which are smaller in terms of space, time, or display than major items.

FINDINGS

The over-all *major* item emphasis of the selected mass media on different topics and candidates during the campaign is displayed in Table 1. It indicates that a considerable amount of campaign news was *not* devoted to discussion of the major political issues but rather to *analysis of the campaign itself.* This may give pause to those who think of campaign news as being primarily about the *issues.* Thirty-five percent of the major news coverage of Wallace was composed of this analysis ("Has he a chance to win or not?"). For Humphrey and Nixon the figures were, respectively, 30 percent and 25 percent. At the same time, the table also shows the relative emphasis of candidates speaking about each other. For example, Agnew apparently spent more time attacking Humphrey (22 percent of the major news items about Agnew) than did Nixon (11 percent of the major news about Nixon). The over-all *minor* item emphasis of the mass media on these political issues and topics closely paralleled that of major item emphasis.

Table 2 focuses on the relative emphasis of each party on the issues, as reflected in the mass media. The table shows that Humphrey/Muskie emphasized foreign policy far more than did Nixon/Agnew or Wallace/Lemay. In the case of the "law and order" issue, however, over half the Wallace/Lemay news was about this, while less than one-fourth of the Humphrey/Muskie news concentrated upon this topic. With Nixon/Agnew it was almost a third—just behind the Republican emphasis on foreign policy. Humphrey of course spent considerable time justifying (or commenting upon) the Vietnam War; Nixon did not choose (or have) to do this.

The media appear to have exerted a considerable impact on voters' judgments of what they considered the major issues of the campaign (even though the questionnaire specifically asked them to make judgments with-

TABLE 1
MAJOR MASS MEDIA REPORTS ON CANDIDATES AND ISSUES, BY CANDIDATES

	Quoted Source					
	Nixon	Agnew	Humphrey	Muskie	Wallace	Lemay [a] Total

	Nixon	Agnew	Humphrey	Muskie	Wallace	Lemay [a]	Total
The issues							
Foreign policy	7%	9%	13%	15%	2%	—	10%
Law and order	5	13	4	—	12	—	6
Fiscal policy	3	4	2	—	—	—	2
Public welfare	3	4	(*) [b]	5	2	—	2
Civil rights	3	9	(*) [b]	0	4	—	2
Other	19	13	14	25	11	—	15
The campaign							
Polls	1	—	—	—	1	—	(*) [b]
Campaign events	18	9	21	10	25	—	19
Campaign analysis	25	17	30	30	35	—	28
Other candidates							
Humphrey	11	22	—	5	1	—	5
Muskie	—	—	—	—	—	—	—
Nixon	—	—	11	5	3	—	5
Agnew	—	—	(*) [b]	—	—	—	(*) [b]
Wallace	5	—	3	5	—	—	3
Lemay	1	—	1	—	4	—	1
Total percent	101% [a]	100%	99% [c]	100%	100%	—	98% [c]
Total number	188	23	221	20	95	11	558

[a] Coverage of Lemay amounted to only 11 major items during the September 12–October 6 period and are not individually included in the percentages; they are included in the total column.

[b] Less than .05 per cent.

[c] Does not sum to 100% because of rounding.

out regard to what politicians might be saying at the moment). The correlation between the major item emphasis on the main campaign issues carried by the media and voters' independent judgments of what were the important issues was +.967. Between minor item emphasis on the main campaign issues and voters' judgments, the correlation was +.979. In short, the data suggest a very strong relationship between the emphasis placed on different campaign issues by the media (reflecting to a considerable degree the emphasis by candidates) and the judgments of voters as to the salience and importance of various campaign topics.

But while the three presidential candidates placed widely different emphasis upon different issues, the judgments of the voters seem to reflect the *composite* of the mass media coverage. This suggests that voters pay some attention to all the political news *regardless* of whether it is from, or about, any particular favored candidate. Because the tables we have seen reflect the composite of *all* the respondents, it is possible that individual differences, reflected in party preferences and in a predisposition to look mainly

TABLE 2
MASS MEDIA REPORT ON ISSUES, BY PARTIES

	Republican			Democratic			American		
	Nixon/Agnew			Humphrey/Muskie			Wallace/Lemay		
Issues	Major	Minor	Total	Major	Minor	Total	Major	Minor	Total
Foreign policy	34%	40%	38%	65%	63%	64%	30%	21%	26%
Law and order	26	36	32	19	26	23	48	55	52
Fiscal policy	13	1	6	10	6	8	—	—	—
Public welfare	13	14	13	4	3	4	7	12	10
Civil rights	15	8	11	2	2	2	14	12	13
Total percent [a]	101%	99%	100%	100%	100%	101%	99%	100%	101%
Total number	47	72	119	48	62	110	28	33	61

[a] Some columns do not sum to 100% because of rounding.

at material favorable to one's own party, are lost by lumping all the voters together in the analysis. Therefore, answers of respondents who indicated a preference (but not commitment) for one of the candidates during the September-October period studied (45 of the respondents; the others were undecided) were analyzed separately. Table 3 shows the results of this analysis for four selected media.

The table shows the frequency of important issues cited by respondents who favored Humphrey, Nixon, or Wallace correlated *(a)* with the frequency of *all* the major and minor issues carried by the media and *(b)* with the frequency of the major and minor issues oriented to *each party* (stories with a particular party or candidate as a primary referent) carried by each of the four media. For example, the correlation is .89 between what Democrats see as the important issues and the New York *Times's* emphasis on the issues in *all* its major news items. The correlation is .79 between the Democrats' emphasis on the issues and the emphasis of the New York *Times* as reflected *only* in items about the Democratic candidates.

If one expected voters to pay more attention to the major and minor issues oriented to their own party—that is, to read or view *selectively*—the correlations between the voters and news/opinion about their own party should be strongest. This would be evidence of selective perception. If, on the other hand, the voters attend reasonably well to *all* the news, *regardless* of which candidate or party issue is stressed, the correlations between the voter and total media content would be strongest. This would be evidence of the agenda-setting function. The crucial question is which set of correlations is stronger.

In general, Table 3 shows that voters who were not firmly committed early in the campaign attended well to *all* the news. For major news items, correlations were more often higher between voter judgments of important

TABLE 3

INTERCORRELATIONS OF MAJOR AND MINOR ISSUE EMPHASIS BY SELECTED MEDIA WITH VOTER ISSUE EMPHASIS

Selected Media	Major Items		Minor Items	
	All News	News Own Party	All News	News Own Party
New York *Times*				
Voters (D)	.89	.79	.97	.85
Voters (R)	.80	.40	.88	.98
Voters (W)	.89	.25	.78	—.53
Durham *Morning Herald*				
Voters (D)	.84	.74	.95	.83
Voters (R)	.59	.88	.84	.69
Voters (W)	.82	.76	.79	.00
CBS				
Voters (D)	.83	.83	.81	.71
Voters (R)	.50	.00	.57	.40
Voters (W)	.78	.80	.86	.76
NBC				
Voters (D)	.57	.76	.64	.73
Voters (R)	.27	.13	.66	.63
Voters (W)	.84	.21	.48	—.33

issues and the issues reflected in all the news (including of course news about their favored candidate/party) than were voter judgments of issues reflected in news *only* about their candidate/party. For minor news items again voters more often correlated highest with the emphasis reflected in all the news than with the emphasis reflected in news about a favored candidate. Considering both major and minor item coverage, 18 of 24 possible comparisons show voters more in agreement with all the news rather than with news only about their own party/candidate preference. This finding is better explained by the agenda-setting function of the mass media than by selective perception.

Although the data reported in Table 3 generally show high agreement between voter and media evaluations of what the important issues were in 1968, the correlations are not uniform across the various media and all groups of voters. The variations across media are more clearly reflected in Table 4, which includes all survey respondents, not just those predisposed toward a candidate at the time of the survey. There also is a high degree of consensus among the news media about the significant issues of the campaign, but again there is not perfect agreement. Considering the news media as mediators between voters and the actual political arena, we might interpret the correlations in Table 5 as reliability coefficients, indicating the extent of agreement among the news media about what the important political events are. To the extent that the coefficients are less than perfect,

TABLE 4

CORRELATIONS OF VOTER EMPHASIS ON ISSUES WITH MEDIA COVERAGE

	Newsweek	Time	New York Times	Raleigh Times	Raleigh News and Observer
Major items	.30	.30	.96	.80	.91
Minor items	.53	.78	.97	.73	.93

	Durham Sun	Durham Morning Herald	NBC News	CBS News
Major items	.82	.94	.89	.63
Minor items	.96	.93	.91	.81

TABLE 5
INTERCORRELATION OF MASS MEDIA PRESIDENTIAL NEWS COVERAGE FOR MAJOR AND MINOR ITEMS

Major Items

	Newsweek	Time	New York Times	Raleigh Times	Raleigh News & Observer	Durham Sun	Durham Morning Herald	NBC	CBS
Newsweek		.99	.54	.92	.79	.81	.79	.68	.42
Time	.65		.51	.90	.77	.81	.76	.68	.43
New York Times	.46	.59		.70	.71	.66	.81	.66	.66
Raleigh Times	.73	.66	.64		.85	.89	.90	.72	.62
Raleigh News and Observer	.84	.49	.60	.74		.84	.93	.82	.60
Durham Sun	.77	.47	.47	.70	.80		.94	.91	.77
Durham Morning Herald	.89	.68	.68	.80	.93	.73		.89	.76
NBC News	.81	.65	.38	.87	.73	.84	.75		.82
CBS News	.66	.60	.83	.88	.79	.76	.78	.72	

Minor Items

the pseudo-environment reflected in the mass media is less than a perfect representation of the actual 1968 campaign.

Two sets of factors, at least, reduce consensus among the news media. First, the basic characteristics of newspapers, television, and newsmagazines differ. Newspapers appear daily and have lots of space. Television is daily but has a severe time constraint. Newsmagazines appear weekly;

news therefore cannot be as "timely." Table 5 shows that the highest correlations tend to be among like media; the lowest correlations, between different media.

Second, news media do have a point of view, sometimes extreme biases. However, the high correlations in Table 5 (especially among like media) suggest consensus on news values, especially on major news items. Although there is no explicit, commonly agreed-upon definition of news, there is a professional norm regarding major news stories from day to day. These major-story norms doubtless are greatly influenced today by widespread use of the major wire services—especially by newspapers and television—for much political information. But as we move from major events of the campaign, upon which nearly everyone agrees, there is more room for individual interpretation, reflected in the lower correlations for minor item agreement among media shown in Table 5. Since a newspaper, for example, uses only about 15 percent of the material available on any given day, there is considerable latitude for selection among minor items.

In short, the political world is reproduced imperfectly by individual news media. Yet the evidence in this study that voters tend to share the media's *composite* definition of what is important strongly suggests an agenda-setting function of the mass media.

DISCUSSION

The existence of an agenda-setting function of the mass media is not *proved* by the correlations reported here, of course, but the evidence is in line with the conditions that must exist if agenda-setting by the mass media does occur. This study has compared aggregate units—Chapel Hill voters as a group compared to the aggregate performance of several mass media. This is satisfactory as a first test of the agenda-setting hypothesis, but subsequent research must move from a broad societal level to the social psychological level, matching individual attitudes with individual use of the mass media. Yet even the present study refines the evidence in several respects. Efforts were made to match respondent attitudes only with media actually used by Chapel Hill voters. Further, the analysis includes a juxtaposition of the agenda-setting and selective perception hypotheses. Comparison of these correlations too supports the agenda-setting hypothesis.

Interpreting the evidence from this study as indicating mass media influence seems more plausible than alternative explanations. Any argument that the correlations between media and voter emphasis are spurious—that they are simply responding to the same events and not influencing each other one way or the other—assumes that voters have alternative means of observing the day-to-day changes in the political arena. This assumption is not plausible; since few directly participate in presidential election campaigns, and fewer still see presidential candidates in person, the information flowing in interpersonal communication channels is primarily relayed from, and based upon, mass media news coverage. The media are the major primary sources of national political information; for most, mass media provide the best—and only—easily available approximation of ever-changing political realities.

It might also be argued that the high correlations indicate that the media simply were successful in matching their messages to audience interests. Yet since numerous studies indicate a sharp divergence between the news values of professional journalists and their audiences, it would be remarkable to find a near perfect fit in this one case. It seems more likely that the media have prevailed in this area of major coverage. . . .

reading

4

the new journalism
and the old—
thoughts after
Watergate

by Paul H. Weaver

Reprinted with permission of Paul H. Weaver from *The Public Interest,* No.
35, Spring 1974. Copyright © 1974 by National Affairs, Inc.

. . . WATERGATE was more than a series of criminal and corrupt actions; it also has raised basic Constitutional questions concerning the inter-
relationship among all our political institutions, including of course the
press. One of these issues was the freedom of the press. Many of the
abuses symbolized by Watergate—the Plumbers, unjustified investigations and wiretaps, and so forth—were in fact directed at the press as part
of the Administration's campaign to make the news media less critical. If
these efforts had been successful, they would have reduced press freedom
and altered the balance between government and the press in favor of the
former. For the time being at least, that danger has been averted.

So the press emerges from Watergate as free, self-confident, and
enterprising as at any other time in its history. But it also emerges a bit
different from what it was before. For the press today is an institution in
limbo—an institution in that distinctive kind of trouble which derives
from not having a settled idea of its role and purpose. It is in limbo because
it now occupies an ambiguous middle ground between its longstanding
tradition of "objective" journalism and a new movement for an "adversary" journalism—no longer massively committed to the one but not yet
certain, let alone unanimous, about the other. To the extent that it is
committed to the new movement, it is committed to a journalistic idea that
is not easily compatible with American institutions in their current form,
nor easily reconciled with some of its most valuable traditions. And to the
extent that the press embraces this movement, its political role will remain
in flux until some new practical adaptation to adversary journalism is
worked out by government, public opinion, and the press itself. Watergate
did not create this problem—it has been growing for a decade now—but

it did intensify it. And this is the problem which confronts American journalism after Watergate.

TWO KINDS OF JOURNALISM

To put the matter briefly: Traditionally, American journalism has been very close to, dependent upon, and cooperative with, official sources. This has been one of its problems, but it has also been its greatest strength and virtue. For in various ways this arrangement has maximized both the openness and flexibility of American government and the amount of information available to the citizenry. Over the past ten years, however, a small but significant and still-growing segment of the journalistic community has begun to revise this relationship by assuming a posture of greater independence and less cooperativeness. They see this change as a modest reform which will render American journalism purer, better, and truer to its traditional aspirations. In fact, it represents a radical change. In the long run it could make the press "freer" but also less informative and possibly more partisan; and this in turn could make the political system more closed, less flexible, and less competent.

To appreciate the meaning of what has happened, we may begin with the simple fact that journalism is the enterprise of publishing a current account of current events.[1] As such, it cannot proceed until three prior questions have been settled. First, there is the question of how, where, and on what basis to find and validate information. Second, there is the question of the point of view from which events are to be surveyed and characterized. And third, there is the question of the audience to be addressed and the basis on which it is to be aggregated. Abstractly, one can imagine any number of possible resolutions of these issues, but in practice things work out more simply. For wherever one looks in the modern world, daily journalism seems to assume one of two general forms: the partisan and the liberal.

Partisan journalism, which prevails in many European countries, and which has traditionally been represented in the United States by the "journal of opinion" rather than the newspaper, begins with an explicitly political point of view. It is ideological journalism. It aims at assembling an audience that shares its point of view; its object is to interpret public affairs from within that point of view; and it gathers information for the purpose of illuminating and particularizing such interpretation. Such a journalism is less concerned with information as such than with the maintenance and elaboration of its point of view. To it, events are more interesting for the light they cast on its "position" than for what they are, or seem, on their face.

Liberal journalism, by contrast, which prevails in the English-speaking world, is characterized by a preoccupation with facts and events as such, and by an indifference to—indeed, a systematic effort to avoid—an explicitly ideological point of view. It aims instead at appealing to a universal audience on the basis of its non-political, "objective" point of view and its commitment to finding and reporting only "facts" as distinct from "opinion.". . .

Throughout the 20th century, American journalism has been solidly in the liberal camp, but [there are] tensions inherent in the very idea of a liberal journalism.

The first of these is the tension between access and autonomy, between the effort of the press to get as much unambiguously true information about as many events as possible—which requires a maximum of access to the actors in these events, which in turn entails a maximum of dependency on these actors—and its effort to preserve its capacity for independent judgment. The second tension arises out of the desire of liberal journalists to avoid taking a political point of view, which conflicts with the inevitability that, in the course of describing events, some sort of point of view will be assumed (observation and writing cannot proceed in the absence of one), and that no point of view will ever be totally devoid of political implications.

ACCESS AND INDEPENDENCE

To these complex problems, the established liberal tradition of American journalism provides a suitably complex resolution. As between access and autonomy, the tradition opts massively and with a clear conscience for access. This choice is reflected not only in the way newsmen go about their work, but in almost every other feature of American journalism as well, from the form of the news story to the role of the newspaper owner. By opting for access, the American press has given priority and reality to its ideals of acting as a *tabula rasa* and maximizing the amount of raw information it provides to the electorate. This same emphasis on access also goes a long way toward settling, if only unintentionally, the problem of point of view. A *tabula rasa* that is written on primarily by persons involved in events inevitably reflects their slant on the world.

In practice, then, this emphasis on access means the following:

First, virtually all the information published by the press is derived from (and is validated by) "high-level sources," i.e., persons, officials, and organizations actively involved in the events in question.

Second, what newsmen know about the events and issues they cover, and about the general context in which these occur, they acquire almost exclusively from the persons involved rather than from external professional, academic, or ideological sources and authorities.

Third, the point of view from which newsmen write is largely determined by the views, concerns, vocabularies, and situations of those actually involved in public affairs. The viewpoint of the American press is thus a practical rather than ideological or theoretical one.

And fourth, as a result of this emphasis on access, newsmen are routinely aware of—or can easily gather—a truly immense amount of information. They are authentic ringside observers of men and events. They can never publish more than a small fraction of what they know (or have reason to believe), and what they do publish is backed up by a large, if often unarticulated, familiarity with the persons, institutions, and issues involved.

Yet if the "objective" tradition defines American journalism as a primarily derivative and dependent enterprise, it also provides the newsman with a limited but still quite important sphere of independence. Partly this independence has existed by virtue of the sheer volume of events and information which are routinely available to the working newsman. He therefore is confronted with the daily and hourly necessity of choosing, and to choose is to exercise a measure of independent power. This power is enhanced by the fragmentation and indiscipline of American government. Not only do they increase the number of points of access for the newsmen seeking a given bit of information, but they also create for him the opportunity—often exploited in practice—to follow the maxim *divide et impera,* an approach whose utility is made much greater by the almost insatiable appetite of most officials for the two political resources which the newsman possesses automatically: publicity and information. The traditional journalist, then, is not utterly at the mercy of his sources. . . .

THE LIBERAL TRADITION

In the liberal tradition, then, the relationship between newsman and source, between press and government, is one of structured interdependence and bartering within an atmosphere of amiable suspiciousness. Each side knows its role. The job of government is to give access and information—*and to do so to a far greater extent than would or could be required by law.* This last point is worth emphasizing, since in this respect American government differs markedly from European (even British) governments. All European journalists are immediately struck by this difference. The American reporter not only has access to official announcements and press releases; he also has the opportunity of becoming the confidant of the official and of enjoying limited but regular access to his personal thoughts, official secrets, internal departmental gossip, and the like.

Of course, there is a price tag on such extraordinary access. The reporter is expected to be generally sympathetic to the public official and his government and to cooperate with them as far as his sense of professionalism permits. Beyond that, the press is expected to have no strong and comprehensive ideas about the general shape of public affairs; it is officialdom which is collectively entitled to define the topography and limits of public discussion and the news—and each individual official is to have the further opportunity of attempting to shape the content of news to suit his own preferences or purposes.

But the press also has its role and rights. Its main job is to exploit its access and, one way or another, to get as much information as it can into public circulation. It has the right to select freely among the often widely divergent ideas and information circulating within officialdom and to expose corruption and foulups. In exchange, it is expected to see to it that the impression being made on the public is not radically at odds with the reality of affairs as newsmen and officials, from their "inside" perspective, know it to be.

At the level of day-to-day individual interaction, of course, the relationship between press and government in the "objective" tradition is ill-defined and highly variable. There are a few rules of thumb that all parties are expected to observe. Officials are not supposed to lie—at least, hardly ever, and then only for some good public reason. They are also supposed to keep their efforts to deceive newsmen and the public to modest proportions. And they are not ever to use the powers of government to harass or coerce newsmen. Newsmen, for their part, are expected not to "editorialize" in their news stories and are supposed to give persons accused or disputed in a story an opportunity to tell their own side of the matter. And newsmen are also expected not to publish certain kinds of information without permission: official secrets, information about the seamy side of officials' private lives, and "inside dope" of no particular relevance to public policy. But within these limits, more or less anything goes. There is much uncertainty and much room for maneuver, manipulation, and enterprise on both sides—and for all their mutuality and cooperation, there is also endless conflict between government and press. But in this general scramble there are limits that both of the parties respect.

The great virtue of the liberal tradition of American journalism is that it enables the press to find and print a great deal of information—much more of it, and more quickly, than partisan newspapers can. For the newsman, it has the further advantage of affording him an opportunity to become truly learned and sophisticated about public affairs through an informal process of close personal observation. And for the citizen it has the virtue that it produces news which is generally intelligible. One can know that the content of news is a more or less faithful reflection of affairs as they are understood by the persons engaged in them, or at least as officialdom as a whole sees them. What is more, the general perspective on events is a practical one. News presented in this way is sensitive to the practitioner's questions of "What next?" and "How to?" and "Who are my friends and enemies?"—and this in turn increases the possibilities that public opinion, reacting to the news, will have significant impact on the day-to-day conduct of government.

Of course, the established tradition has its shortcomings as well, and some of them are quite severe. It is a kind of journalism that is very easily (and very often) manipulated, especially by government but also by newsmen themselves. In any particular instance, the reader can never be absolutely sure that the impression being conveyed to him is a reasonably accurate reflection of the reality of affairs. And beyond that, traditional liberal journalism is perhaps excessively controlled by the ethos and conventional wisdom prevailing among "insiders" and shared by newsmen. In short, the "objective" tradition has the vices and virtues inherent in the idea of acting as a *tabula rasa*. But the virtues are substantial ones too, and the vices, serious though they are, are to no small extent inherent in the very mission of journalism as defined by the liberal tradition: publishing a current account of current events for "the general reader," i.e., the ordinary citizen.

THE ORIGINS OF "ADVERSARY" JOURNALISM

What I have just described is the operational reality of the liberal tradition of American journalism. The image which that journalism has of itself is not exactly congruent with the reality. Some elements of this image, to be sure, are accurate enough. . . . But in other respects, and especially as it depicts the relationship between press and government, the image is a romantic fiction. To listen to traditional newsmen, one would think that the press is completely independent of government in its quest for news, that it routinely searches out vast amounts of hidden, jealously guarded information, that it is constantly defying persons in high office, and that it is the day-in, day-out adversary of "the Establishment" and the equally faithful defender of "the People.". . .

The movement for a new, genuinely adversary journalism which has gained such ground over the past decade arises out of this romantic myth; it is to the liberal tradition of our press what, in a religious context, heresy is to orthodoxy. It is the nature of a heresy to isolate a part of a tradition or doctrine and to treat the part as if it were the whole. The current "heretical" movement in American journalism is defined by the fact that it takes the mythical part of the "orthodox" tradition—the fiction of the autonomous, investigative, adversary press—for the whole of that tradition. It presents itself as an effort to make our press live up to what it always said it was: a journalism that is autonomous instead of interdependent, original instead of derivative, and in an adversary instead of cooperative relationship with government and officialdom. Like religious heresies, the movement *appears* to be a "reformation"—an effort to recover the core of a partially but not irrecoverably corrupted tradition. But such appearances are misleading. For, because heresies are simplificatory, what they profess to be "recovering" is actually something that never was and that was never intended to be. What they really advocate, therefore, is the creation of something quite new and different under a smokescreen of rhetoric about restoring what is old and familiar.

Although this movement for a newly purified journalism did not attain real strength until the late 1960's, its origins lay somewhat farther in the past. Within the journalistic community, three events were critical in fomenting dissatisfaction with the existing press-government relationship: McCarthyism, the U-2 incident, and the Bay of Pigs. Each cast discredit upon the Cold War itself or the spirit in which government conducted it, and together they caused newsmen to revise their opinion of American institutions and their own relationship to them.

THE EXPERIENCE OF THE 1960'S

These events marked the beginning of both the "credibility gap" theme in public affairs reporting and a growing truculence among newsmen. . . .

This issue might have been resolved satisfactorily had not four further developments supervened. One of these was the steep decline, during the 1960's, in the competitiveness of the "prestige" newsmarkets, especially New York, which quietly but effectively shifted the balance of power between newsmen and sources. When *The New York Times* had been actively in competition with the *Herald-Tribune,* their newsmen felt constrained to maintain friendly relationships with sources so that their opposite numbers would not get "exclusives"—and sources, as a consequence, could "whipsaw" newsmen to keep them in line. When the *Times,* the Washington *Post,* and other leading newspapers no longer had any true local competitors, their newsmen became less beholden, and sources became relatively weaker.

A second important development was the growth in the visibility, self-consciousness, and self-confidence of the journalistic profession, and especially of the Washington press corps. Traditionally, reporting had been a low-prestige occupation; some studies reported it to rank *between* the blue-collar and white-collar occupations. In the 1960's this began to change.

Third, there was the extraordinary political and cultural ferment of the 1960's, involving a dramatic expansion and intensification of political conflict and the emergence of countercultural, anti-establishment, and other oppositional movements. . . .

More important than this direct form of cultural influence, however, was the indirect influence of the spirit of the 1960's upon journalism. As we have noted, the traditional mode of American journalism was dependent and derivative; the press largely reflected the ideas and balance of power in official circles. . . . Thus, as ideological movements of opinion became stronger, traditional journalism found itself having to choose from among a variety of perspectives, all of which could claim some official standing. Merely by continuing to report public affairs in the traditional way, the press gave increasing exposure to the ideas and symbols of the oppositional movements.

THE WHITE HOUSE VS. THE PRESS

This led in turn to the fourth development which fostered the current movement for a "new journalism": the intensification of opposition to the movements of the 1960's, both in public opinion at large and within specific institutions and political circles. One of the ways in which such "backlash" sentiment expressed itself was by attacking the press for giving exposure to those movements, and one of the most prominent sources of such attacks was the White House, beginning with Lyndon Johnson. . . .

At first the belligerents fought their battles with the conventional weapons of legitimate political warfare. . . .

As feelings on both sides grew more embittered, their tactics became more unconventional and the struggle more total: It was an omen of the Watergate era to come. The Administration—which in this escalation was clearly the aggressor—launched FBI investigations of newsmen it felt to be hostile; deprived the press of traditional forms of access, such as the press conference, the casual telephone conversation, and the cocktail party; threatened television stations with loss of their licenses; in the first case of prior censorship in American history, brought suit to enjoin the publication of the Pentagon papers; and set up the Plumbers to stop unauthorized leaks. The press countered with heavy coverage of anti-Nixon political elements, publication of secret government documents (the Pentagon and Anderson papers) which they would not have dreamed of making public ten years earlier, and a growing pattern of refusing to accept the legality of subpoenas issued by courts in the course of due legal processes. There was also a certain tendency to begin ignoring traditional journalistic standards of fairness and truth. When the Supreme Court issued its "Caldwell" decision in 1972, which at most only upheld the existing rules defining the testimonial obligations of newsmen, the press interpreted this as a *change* in Constitutional law that reduced freedom of the press. A year before, in "The Selling of the Pentagon," CBS-TV editors falsified the continuity of a filmed interview with a Pentagon official. And when the actions of any newsman were challenged or criticized, increasingly the journalistic community as a whole drew together in defense of its own, right or wrong. Jack Anderson was given the Pulitzer prize for publishing a National Security Council minute concerning the American position in a current, explosive diplomatic situation, and "The Selling of the Pentagon," despite its dubious editing, was cited for excellence in the television documentary category.

THE NEW MOOD

The upshot of these developments was that the liberal press particularly—and to an increasing extent other parts of the journalistic community as well—found itself ever more committed to a stance of truculent independence from government and officialdom. Increasingly it felt that its proper role was not to cooperate with government but to be independent of it, or even opposed to it. Increasingly newsmen began to say that their job was to be an autonomous, investigative adversary of government and to constitute a countervailing force against the great authority of all established institutions. And increasingly they began to see as illegitimate the few traditional formal constraints upon the press: libel law, "fair trial" restrictions on news coverage, testimonial obligations upon all citizens to give their evidence under subpoena, and the laws defining and protecting government secrets. These sentiments, and the actions which in modest but growing number gave concrete expression to them, define the movement for a "new journalism" which exists today and which poses the central question which the press will have to cope with after Watergate.

It is impossible to state with any precision or sense of certainty just how widespread and securely entrenched this movement is. Its only clearly identifiable location seems to be generational: It is young reporters, in their twenties and early thirties, who seem most to share the attitudes that define the movement. In general, though, it is more a mood than a settled, behavioral pattern; a thing more of the spirit than of the flesh; a tendency or yearning more than an established and institutionalized accomplishment. And yet it is a fact. If it is not so widespread or influential as current conservative critics of the media insist, it is also more substantial than defenders of the movement admit. It exists; it really is unlike that which has prevailed in our journalism for decades; it could yet become dominant; and it makes a difference. . . .

ISSUES OF CONFIDENTIALITY

These developments have raised two large and disagreeable issues which our political and legal processes are now forced to grapple with.

One of these is the problem posed by the unauthorized publication of secret or confidential government documents, ranging from White House memoranda and secret depositions before grand juries to Jack Anderson's National Security Council minute or William Beecher's summary of the U.S. fallback position in the SALT-I negotiations. In large part, to be sure, the issue here should focus more on the persons responsible for leaking documents than on the press, which merely publishes them; surely the proper initial defendant, in a legal test of this process, is not *The New York Times* but Daniel Ellsberg, not Jack Anderson but his sources (apparently in the Pentagon). Yet it is also an issue that concerns the press itself because, until recently, the press, out of regard for national security or fear of the consequences, would not have published the Pentagon papers (though it might well have written *about* them, in a veiled and guarded way). Today, obviously, it will publish them, and the result is that we are confronted squarely with a new issue that we would be better off not having to deal with.

It is an impossible issue. However it is resolved, or even if it is not resolved, we will be worse off than we were before it was raised. It involves a conflict among three valuable traditions—press freedom, confidentiality in government, and the relatively open or amorphous quality of American government. Conflicts among these traditions have heretofore been resolved on an informal, *ad hoc* basis. To attempt to resolve them systematically and formally is to lose much and to gain little, if anything. One does need secrecy and confidentiality in government: to protect national security from enemy powers, to ensure that persons in government will feel free to write down on paper their best individual judgments on issues of fact and policy, and perhaps most of all to preserve the ability of officials (especially the President) to be flexible and to take initiatives. (Premature leaks are the tried-and-true device for forestalling Presidential initiatives in policy and administration, or for rendering them ineffective once taken.) On the other hand, one does not want Congress to make any law abridging the freedom of the press in order to preserve this confidentiality. Nor does one want to take the path of enacting an official secrets act that provides severe penalties for any civil servant who leaks information without formal approval from the highest authorities. This last measure would sharply reduce the amount and range of perfectly harmless and also useful information that would be made—is now made—available to the press, usually to the benefit of us all; it would also reduce the ability of Congress to oversee the Executive, since it would know less about what was going on. Thus, by retreating from its old cooperative notion of public responsibility, the press has created an issue which cannot be resolved without changing the American system as a whole in some fundamental—and unattractive—way.

More or less the same is true of the second issue raised by the current movement for a new journalism: the question of the testimonial obligations of newsmen. In the past several years, journalists have begun to insist with increasing frequency and vehemence that they should not be compelled by grand juries or courts to disclose information they have gathered from sources on a confidential basis. To do so, they say, will cause sources to give less information to the press, which in turn will reduce the amount of information citizens can glean from newspapers. Previously, newsmen had generally cooperated with the law enforcement establishment. . . .

Should we then enact shield legislation exempting newsmen from their testimonial obligations? Perhaps, but to do so is not without its costs. With certain minor and traditional exceptions, all citizens are now obligated to give their evidence before courts of law. It is hard to see why newsmen should be made a class apart in this respect; and it is likely that such an exemption would render our system of criminal justice less effective. The price of immunity for journalists would be less justice for everyone else. Here, too, we have a dilemma that is created by the newsman's increasing withdrawal of his consent from the traditional covenant of cooperative suspiciousness between the press and government. To resolve the issue is to change the American system in fundamental—and, again, unattractive—ways.

A RETREAT FROM THE LIBERAL IDEAL

The deeper problem with this movement for a new journalism, however, is that it represents an incipient retreat, not merely from an intelligible idea of the public interest and of the responsibility of the press to serve it, but also from the entire liberal tradition of American journalism and the system of liberal democracy which it has fostered and served. The problem of the press publishing a few government secrets or withholding the names of an occasional criminal may be serious in principle but it is usually negligible in practice. But there is a larger practical question raised by "adversary" journalism that is not at all negligible: the question of the persistence of the open, fragmented, liberal system of American democracy as we have known it and benefited from it for the past many decades.

Our instinct is to assume that this system is virtually indestructible, rooted as it is in the pragmatic temper of the American people, the Constitutional system of division of powers, and other such factors apparently beyond the influence of what we do or think. This is a reasonable assumption within limits, but it isn't entirely true. The system also depends on many institutions and attitudes which are indeed changeable, and one of the most important—if least acknowledged—of these is the kind of press we have. Its capacity to find and publish vast amounts of information about politics and government, and its success in reaching universal audiences without regard to ideology or political affiliations, have contributed in an important way to the openness and flexibility of American government and to the ability of public opinion to influence the conduct of public affairs and to attain consensus. As the press has become wealthier in recent decades, its ability to gather and print information has increased; as political party organizations have declined, the need and willingness of officials to give newsmen access have also grown; so even while the complexity of government and the amount of "classified" information have increased, the capacity of the press to help the American system realize its ideals has at least kept pace.

The new movement abroad in the journalistic community threatens all this. For the press can make its contribution to the system only by maintaining close access—a closer access, as I have said, than can ever be provided by law. The price of such access is some degree of cooperation and sympathy for government—*not* a slavish adulation, as is sometimes said, but a decent respect for authority, a willingness to see government and persons in government given the opportunity to do their job, and at least a slight sense of responsibility for and commitment to the goals inherent in those jobs. When these are not present, access diminishes. And when newsmen begin to assert they are positively the adversaries of government, access diminishes drastically. . . . In order to work, [liberal] journalism needs reporters to have access to government, and when they no longer have it the capacity of newspapers to maintain the other features of the existing form is weakened, as is the whole idea of and justification for those features. Journalism will change—and the logical direction of change is toward the partisan form of journalism, with its ideological basis, politically based relationship to the government in power, and fractionated audiences. It is possible, of course, that an adversary journalism could persist indefinitely, but this seems unlikely. A stance of "pure" opposition —opposition as an end in itself, rather than as an expression of some larger, positive political commitment—is self-contradictory in theory and likely to be short-lived in practice. The probability is that an adversary press would eventually ally itself with a political faction and so become partisan—an ideologically divisive factor rather than a politically unifying force. The consequences could be enormous.

TWO SCENARIOS FOR THE FUTURE

Now the partisan mode of journalism has its virtues. It does not evade the problem of "point of view" as liberal journalism does, and in this sense it has an appealing honesty. It also has the capacity to create and sustain coherent bodies of political opinion; at a time when political opinion in this country is so often contradictory and inchoate, that is a very important trait. This is why "journals of opinion," existing on the margins of American journalism, have been so important and desirable.

But if, over the long run, American journalism were ever to turn massively to the partisan mode, the consequences of this development would extend to nearly every aspect of our political system. Partisan journalism would not increase the openness of the system, it would sharply decrease it. It would not reduce the scope of political conflict, but enlarge it. It would not increase the capacity of American government to act effectively and flexibly in meeting emergent needs, but would tend to paralyze it. It would not empower public opinion as a whole, but would transform it into a congeries of rigid ideological factions eternally at war with one another and subject to the leadership of small coteries of ideologues and manipulators. Indeed, it would tend to transform the entire nature of American politics: From having been a popular government based on a flexible consensus, it would become Europeanized into a popular government based on an equilibrium of hostile parties and unchanging ideologies.

The alternative to such a "Europeanization" of journalism and politics, it should be emphasized, does not have to be a massive and uncritical reversion to the way things were during the 1950's and early 1960's. Even if this were possible—which it isn't—it would clearly be undesirable. Both officialdom and the press were then busily abusing the "objective" tradition, officialdom by treating the media as an institution to be deliberately "managed" for its own expediential purposes, and the press by encouraging and acquiescing in these efforts out of inertia and a generalized avidity to print "big news" as often and as easily as possible.

There are ways to curb these abuses while still preserving the benefits of the liberal tradition of our press which the "adversary" approach would squander. Government can increase the amount of information which is formally made available on the public record. It can scale down its "public relations" operations to the point where they cannot easily operate as instruments of press management and are content instead merely to disseminate information. As Josiah Lee Auspitz and Clifford W. Brown, Jr., have suggested, the "strategic" cast of mind giving rise to, among other things, the habit of "managing" the press for purposes of personal power can be discouraged by strengthening the political party, which embeds individual actors in an institutional context, channels and restrains their ambition, and promotes a "representative" as against a "strategic" ethos. And the press, for its own part, can help to recover the objective tradition by abandoning its flirtation with the "oppositional" posture and by ceasing to exploit public affairs for their sensation value (since the desire to exploit public affairs in this way is the main incentive leading the press to acquiesce in the manipulations of "strategically"-minded officials). The result, I believe, will be a journalism that provides more, and more useful, information to the citizenry, and a political system that, in consequence, comes a bit closer than in the past to realizing its historic ideals.

NOTES

1. I should point out that I am using the terms "journalism" and the "press" in these pages to refer to *daily* journalism only—that is, to daily newspapers and broadcast news programs. There are other forms of journalism, of course: weekly, monthly, quarterly, general purpose, special purpose, and so on. These other forms are important and interesting, and they perform crucial functions vis-à-vis government and the daily press itself. Unfortunately, space prevents me from considering them in this essay.

IIC

political parties and the electoral process

American political parties are, in some ways, wraithlike. In an organizational sense at times they appear barely to exist. Large sections of the public denounce them as irresponsible or crooked. Other sections of the public ignore them as irrelevant to the problems they see and feel in everyday life. They are excoriated by journalists and academics both for standing for too little in substantive terms and for trying to be too inclusive in what they promise. The commentators attack the two major parties for not presenting many real differences on policy; yet when one or both of the parties does in fact try to take a clearly distinctive position, it is often denounced by the same set of commentators as being too extremist and therefore out of tune with American politics in general.

Somehow, despite all of the criticisms by the political analysts and all of the expressed negative feelings throughout virtually all of our national history, the American party system has survived. A variety of changes has characterized that survival but a remarkable amount of stability has also characterized it. The Democratic party is, for example, the oldest continuously existing political party in the world. A partisan in the late 1970's would not feel uncomfortable were he or she suddenly transported back to the first decade of the 19th century and asked to live and function as a partisan then. Likewise, a contemporary of Thomas Jefferson or Andrew Jackson suddenly placed among us would have to make major adjustments to dealing with many of the appurtenances of modern American life, but the adjustments in reacting to and understanding the essential nature of the functioning of the party system would be only relatively minor. Then and now there are national parties in name that dominate the closing aspects of the campaigns for the presidency. In both periods all aspects of the contests for state and local office are in the hands of state and local parties, usually using the national names. Likewise, in both periods these same state and local parties play an important role in the presidential contest and also determine nominations to the national Congress. In both periods legislatures at all levels also usually organize themselves using the party labels under which members find themselves victorious.

In short, parties throughout our history have appeared partly in the flesh and partly in the spirit. Now you see them; now you don't.

We have chosen to focus on two features of political parties and the electoral process in the two readings we have chosen for this section. The first feature is the changing pattern of popular support for the two major parties—Democratic and Republican—since the modern period of Democratic dominance began in the late 1920's and early 1930's. The classic Democratic-Republican alignment in terms of what kinds of people supported which party that was forged in the

1930's has clearly changed even though, with only a few breaks, more Democrats have won more elections than Republicans for close to the last 50 years, regardless of whether those elections were for president, senator, U.S. representative, governor, state legislator, mayor, or more obscure offices.

One change involves growing evidence that more and more people are currently disenchanted with both of the major parties and, in some senses, with political parties altogether. Thus there has been a rise in self-identified "independents" among the electorate and relative decreases in the identification with either Democrats or Republicans (although, among those who do identify with one or the other, the Democrats continue to fare much better than the Republicans). Thus far the "independent" movement has not led to the creation of a genuine third party that has staying power beyond whatever votes a stray candidate here or there (even for president) might attract.

A second change is that of those persons eligible to vote, the percentage actually voting is going down. This also suggests disenchantment with the partisan political process as exemplified in elections.

A third change—and the one on which Ladd and Hadley focus in reading 5—is that the constituencies of the parties are shifting. Putting it most simply, more middle class whites are drifting away from Republican identification to Democratic identification and—at the same time— more blue collar whites are drifting toward Republican identification and away from the Democratic identification of their parents. If this trend continues the parties are likely to continue shifting their policy positions to accommodate their new constituencies and, at the same time, to try to find the magic formula for ensuring a good percentage of wins in head-to-head contests.

The second feature of the party-electoral system on which we have chosen to focus is the linkage between election results and the policy activities of the government. Some assert that parties afford the electorate a chance to choose among competing candidates and that that is enough to constitute the essence of representative government. Perhaps so, but we think there is also considerable evidence that elections do make a difference in the kind of policies that emerge from government. The difference is never as much or as clear as the most fervent partisans claim, but it is almost never as completely absent as the cynics claim. Pomper (in reading 6) focuses on the problem of the linkage between elections and policy guidance in the 1970's, but his conclusions seem applicable to at least the entire modern era of American politics.

transformations of the American party system

by Everett Carll Ladd, Jr.
with Charles D. Hadley

Reprinted from *Transformations of the American Party System* by Everett Carll Ladd, Jr., with Charles D. Hadley. By permission of W. W. Norton & Company, Inc. Copyright © 1975 by W. W. Norton & Company, Inc.

WHEN THE GREAT DEPRESSION broke, there were a variety of lags in the sociopolitical system which, apart from what contributions they may have made to the severity of the collapse, fueled a much more rapid and sweeping set of political transformations than would otherwise have occurred. In a space of a few short years, the American political agenda was rewritten. An unusually distinct policy cleavage appeared. And the parties dug into wholly new positions in a political battlefield so greatly altered. Neither before nor since the 1929–1936 period can one find partisan transformations of comparable magnitude occurring with such speed.

The New Deal party developments were also uniquely conclusive. In 1929 the Republicans were the national majority party. By 1936, they had been shoved firmly, decisively, into minority status. In 1929 they spoke for an ascendant public philosophy. By 1936 a new public philosophy was ascendant, with a new partisan home. Nothing so neat and definitive has prevailed in the contemporary transformations, nor did it occur earlier in the formation of the party system of the industrializing era.

Despite such ample evidence to the contrary, the notion that a single pattern underlies each of the American party transformations has crept into the literature on the subject, with unfortunate analytic consequences. In particular, we have been mesmerized by the New Deal experience, to the point of taking it to be a model. And since realignment was the most dramatic and visible component of the New Deal party transformation, realignment has become the prime focus in studies of partisan change. The New Deal model is so tantalizing, so compelling in its neatness and simplicity. The electorate was subjected to an overriding new issue. Under the impact of this new issue, the old structure of partisan alliances crumbled. A new majority party marched forth boldly, rallying a majority of the populace to the urgent business of the nation. Here was a realignment! When shall we see such another?

The search was on. Insightful observers detected a striking rhythm to the pattern of party realignment. Some came to believe that there was a natural interval of roughly a third of a century between realignments— the period of time required for a new generation of voters to come of age politically with perceptions sufficiently free from the searing experiences of the preceding realignment to be receptive to the call of a new. Count off thirty to thirty-six years from 1932 and what do you find? The United States is now overdue!

Alas, there is no realignment cycle, no striking rhythm, no necessity that the old majority party will be replaced by a new majority, no reason even to be particularly attentive to the prospects of the latter development. Over the course of American history, we hear only the ceaseless hum of societal change, detect only the intermittent accumulation of change sufficient to usher in a new sociopolitical period. And such a momentous shift in social setting requires basic transformations of the party system which may, or may not, feature prominently the type of transition which the classic New Deal realignment entailed.

We are now living through a transformation of the American party system. In its own way, it is quite as exciting and dramatic as that of the New Deal years. It is not as rapid, not as conclusive, not possessing of such elegant simplicity.

It surely has not, and will not, produce a new Republican majority. There has been a pronounced weakening of Democratic presidential support in a number of that party's old strongholds. If a solid Republican South is not in the offing, a solid Democratic South, so long a fixture in American politics, has now become an impossibility. But at no point in the last fifteen years has any set of indicators justified the conclusion that a coalition calling itself Republican would become majoritarian. The Republicans have shown no signs of becoming anything other than a reactive party. They have not approached articulation of a public philosophy comparable to the business nationalism of the old Republican majority or the governmental nationalism of the New Deal Democrats. And as a reactive party in a rapidly changing social setting, the Republicans have seen their support weaken steadily among ascendant political classes. Intellectuals, the college educated, the professional and managerial upper-middle classes, and privileged youth, have all moved decisively toward the Democrats.

Still, there is no indication of a new Democratic majority, comparable in policy coherence, scope, and regularity to that of the New Deal era. The Democrats have become an establishment party, in the sense of being home to major segments of the high socioeconomic and political classes of the contemporary United States. And in particular, their ascendant position within the intelligentsia permits them, much more than the Republicans, to be a generator of new responses rather than simply a reactor to past events and frustrations. Like the post-Civil War Republicans and the New Deal Democrats, they are a party of "new ideas." But the leadership of social and cultural change which the Democrats have assumed brings them into continuing tension with the white, middle-class majority of what remains—even in a time of inflation and recession, and the ongoing energy crisis—an affluent society. In the tentative, qualified manner which seems inevitable in so enormously diverse and multi-layered a party system as that of the United States, the Democrats will function as a top-bottom alliance, strongest among intellectuals and high status professionals, and among the deprived underclasses. Their vulnerability to neopopulist resistance and resentment, evident in 1972, will be recurring.

Another, very different reason why both new majority forecasts are in such grievous error involves an inherent blind spot in the realignment focus. Important facets of the contemporary partisan transformation simply do not comprise the movement of groups of voters from one party to another. The claims of any party, present or future, to majority status are blocked by the long-term weakening of popular partisan attachments. To a greater extent than ever before, the American electorate is candidate and issue oriented, rather than party oriented.

Political parties in the United States are now buffeted by an unusually powerful, and disparate, set of forces. However much advocates of disciplined, programmatic, responsible parties may lament this situation, increasing numbers of voters simply feel less dependent upon party-provided cues. An affluent, by all historical standards enormously leisured, highly educated populace, able to draw political information from an extraordinary national communications structure, will never bestow the kind of coherent and persisting attachments to parties which electorates of times past freely gave.

As the current thrusts of reform testify, what the ascendant professional classes want is not some strong party organizational structure able to barter, bargain, and dictate nominations, but open parties, porous electoral instruments which they can capture easily and use to advance favored candidates and the concerns which at a given moment seem to be of the most compelling importance. The reforms of the McGovern-Fraser, Mikulski, and Sanford Commissions, and of the 1974 Kansas City mini-convention, carry a clear message from the professional classes to the party regulars, organized labor, and other old claimants: "We want a permeable party, responsive to the kind of free-lance intervention in which we excel. Give us that and we will probably stay. Deny it, and we will leave." The party gave.

Current talk of a "Europeanization" of the parties is absurd. A European-type party isn't merely ideological. It is central-office directed, responsive to a party bureaucracy. Nothing done in the reforms of the 1970s is leading to such a development. Issue-oriented candidates and middle-class constituencies, not a muscular party apparatus, are the beneficiaries.

Even if the citizenry were not so inclined to independent electoral behavior, the weakening of political parties in the United States would be ordained by the extension of a national communications complex. Television news, not party handouts or doorbell ringing by precinct committees, is the primary source of information on candidates for much of the populace. The national media are candidate- and issue-emphasizing vehicles, not party emphasizing. Political parties have become ancillary structures in the whole process of communications between candidates and elected officials on the one side, and the electorate on the other.

In a perceptive essay, David Broder, the distinguished journalist of the *Washington Post,* has emphasized the extent to which the media have increasingly assumed, more through the unfolding of technology than by conscious design, various facets of the communications function which rested historically with political parties. Media personnel, Broder observes, serve as the principal source of information on what the candidate is saying and doing; act the part of talent scouts, screening candidates for national (and on another tier, state) office, conveying the judgment that some are promising, while dismissing others as of no talent; operate as the race-caller or handicapper, telling the public how the election contest is going, and why X is ahead of Y; function at times as self-perceived public defenders, bent on exposing what they consider the frailties, duplicities, and sundry inadequacies of a candidate; and in some instances serve as assistant campaign managers, informally advising a candidate, and publicly, if indirectly, promoting his cause. The press has long been linked in some way to such communications activities. But Broder is right in insisting that the preeminence of the media, vis-à-vis the parties, is something very recent and very important.

If substantial segments of the public feel much more confident than they did before in reaching electoral choices without the intervention of parties, and if the role of parties in the communications function has steadily diminished, is it surprising that citizenry loyalties or attachments to political parties have diminished? The lessened capacity of parties to organize and mobilize the electorate is a major feature of the contemporary partisan transformation. And, in the context of the American political system, it appears irreversible.

Some observers are wont to lament this decline of party. They see coherent party government as the only realistic answer to policy drift and governmental inertia. And they insist that political parties are the only available instrument through which the many who are individually weak can be organized and mobilized against the few who are powerful individually or organizationally. We do not share this view. Strong (organizationally, or in their hold on citizenry loyalties) parties are not the "last best hope" of democracy. The contemporary party system displays this dimension: nominee-oriented, issue-directed, media-utilizing, and media-assessed candidacies operating within the formal structure of political parties. We see no reason to lament this development. An electorate which engages with abandon in ticket splitting is much more volatile than one marked by party regularity, but it does not seem inherently less capable of effective democratic participation. It will indeed violate the political interests of some to see increasingly porous parties ever more susceptible to take-overs by successive waves of issue activists; but this involves the democratic power struggle, not a crisis of democracy.

If the new Republican and new Democratic prophesies are inaccurate and inadequate, they appear fortunate when compared to the prediction of long life and good health for the New Deal coalitions. In fact, the New Deal party system has vanished as certainly as that which featured the old Republican, post–Civil War majority. Could the indicators of this be clearer? Republicans and Democrats during the New Deal era grouped themselves rather nicely on opposite sides of the liberal-conservative polarity and were sharply distinguished thereby. The substantial inapplicability of this ideological division—focusing as it did on governmental nationalism vs. business nationalism, and the question of how expansive a role government should play—now has been widely noted. The class dimension of conflict was unusually salient (in terms of American experience) throughout the 1930s and 1940s, and as a consequence the class character of voting and party differentiation was unusually pronounced. There has been a long secular decline in class voting, however, since 1950, a decline which accelerated notably after 1964. The point was reached by the 1970s at which, within the white population, actual inversions of the New Deal class order began appearing frequently. In the New Deal context, the white working class provided regular, powerful sustenance for liberal programs. By the late 1960s and early 1970s, this social collectivity, its social and economic position so substantially altered, had come to occupy a position of persisting resistance to many of the claims for extensions of liberalism—involving new beneficiary groups in some instances, and altered policy objectives in others. (Support for busing on behalf of integration, and support for a minimum wage, both receive in the casual nomenclature of American politics the description "liberal"; but these policies obviously impact most directly on different population groups and evoke contrasting ideological dimensions.)

In the New Deal context, the Republicans qualified as the establishment party, representing the business elites. But in postindustrial America, the elite structure of the society has been substantially changed, and the composition of the upper classes has been massively altered by an expansion of college-educated, professional, and managerial cohorts. In 1975, the Democrats, as much as the Republicans, can lay claim to being an establishment party—in the sense of representing collections of prominent, established interests and a large, apparently growing proportion of persons of high socioeconomic status. During the New Deal era, labor unions became the pivotal organized interest within the Democratic party. Now in 1975, the capacity of labor to dominate Democratic national politics has been ended, with power gravitating decisively toward professional cohorts. The New Deal Democratic majority was built upon support of the solid South, but today the South is less supportive of the national Democratic party than any other region.

Both Republicans and Democrats in the New Deal era enjoyed a high measure of regular support from their respective "believers." But all indicators now reveal major increases in the levels of independent electoral behavior, a pronounced weakening of party loyalties, and a general decline in the capacity of parties to organize and mobilize the electorate. The growth in numbers and influence of issue activists, a stratum polarized ideologically, conservative activists gravitating to the Republican party while liberal activists are ascendant in Democratic affairs—with the profound implications this has for the shape of intra-party and inter-party competition—comprises a development with no counterpart in the New Deal party system.

Change in the fabric of conflict has been the principal precipitant of all transformations of the American party system. And with movement from industrial to postindustrial, exceptional alterations of conflict have occurred. This is nowhere more evident than in the fracturing of American liberalism. New Deal liberals were occupied primarily with the need for economic reform: Imposing controls on corporate business; organizing the industrial labor force; using government to bolster the economic position of the working class, to provide it with a larger measure of economic security, and to extend the range of social services. Such objectives are still pursued today, of course, and to some extent receive the endorsement of a large majority of the population. But as primary concerns, these remain the property of what must now be called *old liberalism.*

A *new liberalism* has now grown up. Nurtured by a climate of affluence in which such values have been significantly realized, it places less emphasis upon economic well-being and security, is less materialistic. It rather more emphasizes civil liberties and civil rights. It looks to a more participant, less hierarchical society. It stresses the importance of self-development of the individual, even at the cost of some further economic expansion if that is necessary. It is less attentive to the demand for economic growth, stressing environmental costs of such growth. Not rejecting governmental nationalism, it is nonetheless much less sympathetic to it than is the old liberalism, and reveals a suspicion of the state and of the workings of bureaucracy not found in the latter. The new liberalism shares the equalitarian commitments and flavor of the old (surely the only excuse for attaching "liberal" to both positions); but its equalitarianism is more sensitized to the needs of deprived (often ethnic) minorities. The new liberalism is attracted to the socially and culturally avant-garde, to experimentation and change in life styles, personal values, and ethical or normative codes. . . .

Liberalism was a united camp in the New Deal era, but it is now divided; and with its fracturing has come a rending of the Democrats as the great American liberal party. Important segments of organized labor, reflecting a core constituency for the old liberalism, find their position notably weakened as groups attached to the new liberalism achieve more prominent representation in the national Democratic party. The 1972 presidential election was the first to present a real quandary for the old liberal, trade union leadership and its mass clientele. These groups could not respond enthusiastically to a Republican party and presidential candidate never supportive of the economic egalitarianism of the the old liberalism; but they resented the growing influence of the new liberals who had nominated McGovern, and rejected the style, social and cultural concerns, and many of the social groups' sympathies embodied in the new liberalism. The presidential election of 1972 was the first to manifest this split. It will not be the last.

In view of such sweeping changes in the structure of conflict within which the parties live and function, insistence that the New Deal party system is somehow still substantially intact can be accounted for only by a highly formalistic analytic focus. That is, a political party calling itself Democratic enjoyed a substantial lead over another party calling itself Republican in many sectors of electoral behavior in 1975, as it did in 1935. In both years, Democratic identifiers outnumbered Republican adherents by a large margin. Control of Congress and of state capitols was securely Democratic in both periods. Looking to party registration data, we find that the Democratic position was actually much stronger in 1975 than forty years earlier. Such data are, of course, important. But what they demonstrate is the persisting weakness of the Republican party, not the persistence of the New Deal party system.

The key feature of a party transformation involves the search for electoral organization and expression of a new conflict configuration generated by a new social setting. That is what we have tried to attend to—more than to the subsidiary although not unimportant matter of which party is coming out on top. From the perspective applied here, we see reasonably steady and coherent progression of partisan change, even while immediate electoral results bounce wildly, this way and that, from one election to the next.

In the absence of analysis which locates parties amid the larger context of change in the social system, one is left with short-term forecasting which inevitably overemphasizes currents in the last election. We have had altogether too much of this. In the Eisenhower years, there was much talk of a new Republican majority. But just a few years later, following the 1964 Goldwater debacle, some observers questioned whether the GOP could survive as a serious electoral contender. Then, in the early Nixon years, forecasts shifted once more, and visions of a Republican revival were again seen throughout the land. And now, after Watergate, economic woes, and the massive setback administered to Republicans in the 1974 elections, we see a revival of assessments with a 1964 flavor. The United States, we are told, no longer has a two-party system, so crippled are the Republicans; it is more a "one-and-a-half-party system." To bend in this fashion before the prevailing breeze is sheer nonsense.

Of course the Republicans lost badly in 1974. Starting from a weak minority position, they were associated with the biggest political scandal in American history, one which saw the resignation of both a Republican president and vice-president. They were holding control of the executive branch, too, at the time of a major downturn in the economy. And given the saliency of these circumstances, the Democrats were able to avoid temporarily the range of social and cultural issues which over the past decade have cut, and in the future will continue to cut, so very deeply. The Democrats put together a truly impressive alignment, but it was not the old New Deal coalition. It included majorities of blacks, Jews, big city folk, trade unionists, Catholics, southerners, young people . . . and businessmen, midwesterners, small town dwellers, whites, the very prosperous, old people, Protestants—virtually every identifiable social collectivity in the country. Such is obviously the stuff of electoral defeat and victory, but not necessarily of a transformation of the party system.

The party coalitions in 1975 look very much like they have over the past decade. In terms of secure adherents, both are narrow based. Of the two, the Republican is clearly the weaker. The political agenda continues to reflect the influx of issues and concerns peculiar to the postindustrial era. Although they presided over the creation of the New Deal programs and display something of the preservatism most parents feel toward their offspring, the Democrats are still the party of change and experimentation —in large part, we think, because of their success in attracting the intelligentsia, the idea generating and consuming community. Both party structures are weak and porous; in an age of ideologically polarized activist cohorts, they are notably susceptible to take-overs by movements and candidates which eschew a politics of accommodation, as well as to walk-outs when they appear insufficiently responsive. And conditions are such that the volatility displayed in national electoral politics over the last decade or so will surely persist through the next.

"The more things change, the more they are different," violates the French aphorism, but better approximates political experience. By the 1970s, enough had changed to usher in a basic transformation of the American party system. Let us, then, bid fond farewell to the old New Deal coalitions. The system of which they were parts, along with the social era which nurtured it, having served us well, have slipped into history. And let us read well the new chapter that is opening, in the hope that by understanding it we can proceed intelligently in the quest for a full and secure democracy.

controls and influence in American elections (even 1968)

by Gerald M. Pomper

"Controls and Influence in American Elections (Even 1968)," by Gerald M. Pomper is reprinted from *American Behavioral Scientist,* vol. 13, no. 2 (Nov./Dec. 1969), pp. 215–230 by permission of the Publisher, Sage Publications, Inc.

THE ROLE OF ELECTIONS

There have been two broad and opposing positions on the effects of elections on policy outputs. One position sees elections as directly controlling public policy. In the fullest elaboration of this theory, elections are considered as mandates, or binding popular determination of future governmental programs. The opposing position sees elections as indirect influences on public policy, which are particularly important as protections of the vital rights and interests of the voters.

In the American institutional context, direct control of a mandate is difficult to imagine. The impact of any or many elections is limited by the diverse checks and balances of the national government, the "multiple cracks" of a federal system, the proliferation of nonelected public authorities, the powers of bureaucracies and courts, and the undisciplined party system. However, the very dispersal of power which makes control unlikely also makes influence more probable. In the conflicts and bargaining of branches, states, authorities, bureaucracies, courts, and parties, some agency is likely to support the vital interests of any significant number of voters.

Voting studies lead to similar conclusions. Voters do not make general policy choices in elections. Asked to describe the parties and their policies, only a small minority spontaneously evaluate them in terms of a political ideology. Depending on the looseness of the definitions employed, only 2.5 percent to 15 percent of the electorate can be considered ideologues who "clearly perceived a fundamental liberal-conservative continuum on which various of the political objects could be located." Moreover, there is no meaningful coherence in mass attitudes toward specific policy questions. Opinions on federal aid to education, for example, show no correlation to opinions on federal aid to housing. Among many individuals, indeed, opinions on the same questions show only random consistency over short periods of time.

By contrast, the voting studies do yield evidence consistent with the alternative theory of elections as means of protecting vital interests. For 45 percent of the electorate, Democrats and Republicans are liked or disliked because of the group benefits they provide. As a whole, the electorate lacks conceptual clarity in regard to public policies. On particular programs, however, there are concentrated "issue publics" which are knowledgeable and able to defend their specific interest. Concern for these special interests can even overcome the great influence of party identification. . . .

Furthermore, while the voters are not prepared to decide policy questions prospectively, they are ready to judge the parties retrospectively on the basis of their performance. For a fourth of the population, politics is viewed in terms of the nature of the times. A party in power during periods of peace and prosperity is praised; a party associated with depression or war is condemned. Voting provides a means by which groups can effectively provide feedback and gain attention to their demands. . . .

Given American institutions and voting behavior, ballots are unlikely to be means of direct control, but can be a method for indirect influence over policy. Elections are best considered as control mechanisms. In regard to policy, their principal function is to set boundaries—to provide legitimation for elite initiatives, to prevent actions which infringe on perceived vital interests, and to pass a retrospective judgment on these programs. Voting does not define the entire political system. It is one, but only one, vital input, an input most readily used by unorganized and unprivileged masses in attempts to gain attention to their needs and wants. This function can be fulfilled in various ways.

Often, elections are most important for the actions they deter elites from undertaking. Thus, de Tocqueville found democracies hobbled in conducting foreign policy. Changing public moods made it difficult to "regulate the details of an important undertaking, persevere in a fixed design, and work out its execution in spite of serious obstacles." Defenders of a long-term American involvement in Vietnam could easily agree. For better or worse, electoral pressure in 1968 made inevitable the withdrawal of United States troops.

Similarly, the threat of popular reprisal may limit the ability of elites to make basic, although desirable, changes in existing practices, such as British union rules, Indian caste practices, or American racial discrimination. More satisfying is the restraint electoral power places on arbitrary treatment of the enfranchised. Police protection of Negroes, for example, has been most evident where and when blacks voted, while police brutality and condoning of lynching has been most frequent where and when blacks were disfranchised. Positive actions have not always been stimulated by the ballot, but fairness and restraint have been encouraged.

In particular elections, the significant effect of the vote is the popular legitimation of party coalition. The electorate chooses a party as well as a candidate, and the composition and commitments of the winning coalition will greatly shape the course of future events. The voters thus indirectly affect governmental action by supporting or rejecting the men associated with these actions.

A majority party coalition does not exist for one election only in most instances. American history typically has seen the domination of one party over long periods of time, such as the period of Republican hegemony from 1896 to 1928, or the era of Democratic dominance since the New Deal. During these periods, whatever the outcome of particular contests, the basic party coalitions and their voting support by geographic areas and social groups remain relatively constant.

On some occasions, more extensive and long range changes take place. The basic voting support of each party shifts, resulting in a "critical election." The majority party is now supported by a new coalition of voters. It must recognize different demands from the past. Voters intervene decisively to change the political terms of reference. Victory in a critical election does not provide detailed policy instructions for the winning party, but it produces an opportunity to meet the new needs of the time and the desires of the new coalition.

Another effect of elections is the manner in which they condition the policy initiatives of party elites. Attempting to win votes, the parties offer proposals to the electorate in their party platforms. Indirect popular influence over policy can be facilitated in two ways through the platforms. First, the documents may provide a means by which the voters deliberately choose parties and their policies. Second, the platform may be significant even if not widely read. The campaign manifesto may reflect program initiatives made by parties in anticipation of voter needs and demands. The electorate's choice of a party would then become a choice of policies as well.

To be significant, platforms must be specific, policy-oriented, and relevant to the voters' concerns. Since voters tend to make their party choices on the basis of performance, they would facilitate a comparison of the two parties' positions and actions, with special attention to the merits and defects of the incumbents' record. They would also indicate the future positions of the party, specifically enough to be meaningful to the voter, particularly on issues of immediate concern.

The Presidential election of 1968 offers valuable data for analysis of the effects of elections. These data suggest that the period of 1964–1968 contains a pair of critical elections, changing the political shape of the nation. An analysis of the major party platforms of 1968 provides further evidence of this change, while also allowing some insight into the nature of platforms and elite-mass linkages.

A CRITICAL ELECTION IN 1968?

The concept of a critical election, first introduced by Key, is well-known. Such decisive contests "reveal a sharp alteration of pre-existing cleavages within the electorate. Moreover, and perhaps this is the truly differentiating characteristic of this sort of election, the realignment made manifest in the voting in such elections seems to persist for several succeeding elections."

A major difficulty with this definition is the restraint it places on any attempt to classify contemporary elections. The investigator may suspect that he is living in a critical period, but the established criterion requires him to wait many years before he can make a definite judgment. By the time enough elections have passed to demonstrate persistence of an electoral change, the conclusion that such realignment has indeed occurred is almost trivial. For example, it requires no great insight for present-day scholars to assert that critical change occurred at the time of the New Deal. It is more risky, but more useful, to be able to make assertions about the character of the elections of 1964 and 1968.

To attempt such analysis, five statistical indicators of critical elections were developed. All measure the continuity in the geographical state-by-state distribution of the Democratic party vote for President. A critical election would be indicated by:

1. a low linear correlation between the election results in the given year and the preceding election year;

2. a low correlation between the results in the given year and the average results in the four preceding elections;

3. low correlations between the results in the given year and those in a consecutive series of preceding or succeeding elections;

4. a high (absolute) mean difference between state results in the given year and state averages in the preceding four elections; and

5. a high standard deviation of these differences.

By these standards, the election of 1964 appeared in earlier analyses to be a critical election. . . .

Aside from these statistical indicators, there were other manifestations of critical change in the 1964 election. Detailed study of the South and the Northeast indicated great changes within the electorate of these areas. The intensely ideological character of the Goldwater campaign suggested a basic alteration of the practice of American politics, and the most thorough study of this campaign discovered some meaningful changes in party identification as well. The overwhelming victory of Lyndon Johnson and the legislative innovations of the 89th Congress duplicated the pattern of previous critical elections which led to policy innovations.

The election of 1968 now provides data to test the persistence of the upheavals of the Goldwater-Johnson contest. If the 1964 election were but a quirk in American politics, it should stand alone statistically. If it did change the shape of the system, it would be revealed by continuity between the 1964 and 1968 results. The data support the latter hypothesis.

When the Humphrey Democratic vote is compared to the Johnson returns, there is a high degree of continuity. . . . [T]he sources of Democratic and Republican strength remained relatively unchanged from 1964 to 1968. The overall results were quite different, of course, as the entire nation moved considerably away from the party of Johnson and Humphrey. The important point, however, is that the character of each party's geographical coalition did not change greatly, although the size of the coalitions changed.

The other indices also indicate increased stability in the political system. . . .

Statistical evidence thus provides some reason for inferring that a critical election occurred in 1964 and that the pattern established in that year has persisted to 1968. It is still not clear whether the Democrats or Republicans are now the majority party. Both have won one of these two elections, and either result theoretically could be a deviation from the new norm. It would appear most likely, however, that the Democrats remain the majority party, subject to any innovations of the Nixon administration. The distribution of party identification still heavily favors the Democrats, although there have been major changes within the voting coalition. New voters have been won in suburban areas, among professionals and among blacks, replacing the votes lost among manual workers and Southerners. It should also be underlined that the Democrats nearly won the 1968 election, although short-term influences—urban riots, Vietnam, the Chicago convention, a third party movement, and the Humphrey candidacy—were severely unfavorable. Only a dominant party could be expected to survive and nearly overcome such disadvantages.

THE PLATFORMS OF 1968

Change in the parties can also be seen in their platforms, which are studied by means of content analysis. Each sentence of the major party manifestos is placed in one of three major categories, which are further subdivided into eleven minor categories. The categories are: (1) rhetorical or factual statements; (2) evaluations of the parties' records and past achievements, divided into four subcategories: general approval, general criticism, policy approval, and policy criticism; and (3) statements of future policies, divided into six subcategories, in order of increasing commitment and specificity: rhetorical pledges, general promises, pledges of continuity, expressions of goals and concerns, pledges of action, and detailed promises. The pledges of future action are also grouped into nine substantive areas.

The platforms of 1968 show both similarities to and differences from the platforms of the previous twenty years. In the general distribution of platform statements . . . somewhat greater emphasis is placed on the pledges of future action, particularly in the Republican party. This pattern is due in part to the G.O.P.'s platform theme, "We must think anew and act anew." It is also a reflection of the changing demands placed on the parties by the unusual events and problems faced by the nation in 1968.

In their evaluations of the past, the parties followed an established pattern. As was true in almost all previous documents of the previous twenty years, the emphasis was on the record of the incumbent party. In

1968, as in the earlier period, the frequencies of platform statements assumed the following order: approvals by the in-party, criticisms by the out-party, approvals by the out-party, criticisms by the in-party. The debate is over the record of the executive party. It is not a contrast between two different sets of policies argued during the past four years. . . .

This pattern is in keeping with the voters' own characteristic emphasis on retrospective judgments. The voters pass on the actual policies which they have experienced. The platforms are an aid to this consideration, praising or damning those policies as is respectively appropriate for the in-party and the out-party. It should also be noted that, as in the past, policy evaluations predominate over general comments on parties and leaders. Voters are thereby helped to see if the parties have acted to provide the group benefits and protection which they seek.

Continuities and changes are also evidenced in the pledges of future action made in the 1968 platforms. The topical distribution of pledges . . . is distinctive in the . . . three categories of welfare, government, and civil rights. By 1968, issues concerning black voters were no longer the matters of legal equality and nondiscrimination included in the heading of civil rights. Instead, they consisted of welfare questions, such as anti-poverty programs and aid to the cities. By 1968, the new issue of "law and order" had arisen, and this change is also reflected in the increased concern for governmental questions. . . .

A key question about platform pledges of future policy is their degree of specificity. Those with meaning to the voters tend to be concentrated in the four subcategories from pledges of continuity to detailed promises. In past manifestos, pledges of this character have constituted 62 percent of the category, and this proportion was continued in both parties' programs for 1968 (61 percent of the Republican and 64 percent of the Democratic platforms). . . .

The Democratic platform for 1968 shows a familiar pattern. Pledges are most definite in the areas of immediate and tangible interest to the voters—welfare, labor, agriculture, and natural resources, with civil rights in a middling position. Areas involving intangible and more ideological questions, such as foreign policy, defense, government, including law and order, and broad economic policy are handled through more vague statements. In this case, the party has responded to the particularistic interests of voters by including specific pledges on these topics in its platforms. Such pledges are the documentary expression of its concern for popular needs, and its recognition of the importance of group benefits in motivating the voters. . . .

The Republicans present a different pattern in some respects. While there has been some change from the strongly ideological effort of 1964, echoes of that campaign are audible in the 1968 platform. In the areas of tangible benefits, there actually has been a decrease from the specific pledges of 1964, although these changes are generally in the direction of moderating and obscuring previously forthright conservative positions. In the more general areas, continued specificity is evident. The notable vagueness and neglect of the 1964 platform on civil rights is continued, with the only specific points relating not to Negroes, but to the immigration laws.

Further comparisons can be made between the parties by noting differences in the amount of attention they devote to different topics. . . . In 1968, Democrats devoted more attention than Republicans to the more tangible issues of labor, agriculture, and welfare. Again, Republicans showed a greater concern for the more ideological issues of foreign, defense, and general economic policy, as well as issues of government, particularly law and order. Although similar to past patterns, the 1968 platforms indicate that the Democrats are becoming increasingly a party composed of a coalition of discrete interests, and the Republicans more one of ideological unity.

A sharp break from the past is apparent in the pledges on civil rights, although the small number requires caution in interpretation. In the past, the parties have matched one another in the degree of specificity, and often the content, of their pledges in this area. In 1968, the Democrats presented pledges of some specificity, although they made few statements. The Republicans not only made few promises, but they were almost entirely rhetorical in character. The platforms may be another indication of the new character of the Republican party, particularly its reliance on a strong Southern element. Both the earlier analysis of the changing geographical distribution of the vote and this analysis of civil rights provisions lends support to the belief that the Republicans have turned to a new base below the Mason-Dixon line and that they will no longer openly seek black votes.

Two major conclusions can be drawn from the study of the 1968 major-party platforms. First, as in previous years, the platforms provide a possible linkage between elite and mass. They present to the voters differing evaluations of the record of the incumbents. They concentrate on policy questions rather than the mindless rhetoric commonly assumed. In their future promises, pledges tend toward a meaningful degree of specificity, particularly in regard to those tangible benefits of most concern to the voters.

The 1968 platforms in particular also reveal the responsiveness of the parties to innovations in American policies. The relative attention devoted to the various subjects has been modified, reflecting new interests and demands by voters. In a time of change, more stress is placed on promises of future action. The altered coalitions of the parties, previously suggested in analysis of the voting returns, is also reflected in the emphases and contents of their platforms. Democratic party stress on economic, welfare, and racial benefits, and increased Republican attention to foreign policy and governmental questions indicate the development of new party alignments.

CONCLUSIONS

This analysis of the 1968 election provides some evidence of the indirect influence of elections on policy outputs. Statistical measures indicate that the voters are dissolving the bands of political loyalty which have constrained them since the New Deal. New coalitions of voters began to form in the 1964 election, and the new coalitions have been continued into the 1968 elections. These changes on the part of the voters can provide the popular support for a new elite coalition to initiate policies to meet the evident public needs of the nation.

The parties have also begun to display some responsiveness to public demands. The 1968 platforms were not simply repetitions of old and unfulfilled promises. The parties showed some awareness of the real problems of American society and some awareness of the existence of new voter alignments. In these two ways at least, elections have been shown to be a linkage between the mass and the elite.

In a time of crisis for the political system, however, it would be foolish to close on a note of complacency. Those unhappy with the choices and results of the 1968 campaign surely had good cause for their discontents. If changes are evident, it is not yet clear that innovations will be sufficiently rapid and decisive to meet the problems. It is not yet clear if there is enough political will in either mass or elite to meet the problems of racial division, urban decay, and foreign wars. It is not yet clear whether the Nixon administration will be any more successful than the Johnson administration in redeeming its most critical promises to diminish poverty and to end the war in Vietnam.

Even if these questions are successfully resolved, elections will remain a limited, although vital, means of effecting social change. Ultimately subject to the control of popular majorities, elections are not a sufficient means of achieving the goals of a distinct and permanent minority, particularly black voters in America. In a capitalist economy, votes and governmental action alone cannot assure economic progress. In a society of inevitably unequal status, the egalitarianism of the vote is only one resource for progress. Elections do provide a link between governed and governors, but forging a grid of interdependent relationships remains the unfinished business of American democracy.

interest groups

An interest group is an organization of people who share some common interest, and who act to promote their interest with members of the government—in Congress, executive branch agencies, and the courts. There are a multitude of these groups at work at all levels of government, and they cover a wide range of interests, although the majority of them stem from some kind of shared economic interest. There are representatives for labor unions, for management, for church groups, for ethnic and other minorities, for professional associations, for business firms, for peak associations (which are, in effect, holding companies of other groups), for trade associations, for farm organizations, for foreign, state and local governments, for education, for special "causes" (like the environment or wild horses), and so on.

But despite a recitation of neutral information, the fact remains that the mere mention of interest groups or lobbyists suggests to many people an image of a corrupt process in which policy outcomes are determined by the preferences of groups that can spend the most money to influence government officials. Interest group activities are not inherently corrupt or bad. In fact, the practice of nongovernmental groups providing information to decision-makers is an ancient tradition. But because trying to persuade lends itself to misinterpretation, because of some outright abuses, and because of the tradition in this country of an open press eager to expose what appear to be improprieties in government, interest group activities have perhaps had a worse time of it in the public image than they really deserve. Certainly interest groups are not limited to overt bribery as the only means of influence, nor are they always the ones who initiate contacts with government officials.

In communicating with government officials, interest group representatives rely on both direct and indirect contacts, but they prefer the direct mode, which includes personal presentations of viewpoints and research findings and testimony at congressional hearings (for symbolic reasons more than anything else). Techniques available include personal phone calls, office visits, formal briefings, and informal gatherings (meals, parties). Indirect contacts include appeals made through intermediaries, letter and telegraph campaigns, public relations campaigns, and publicizing the voting records of members of Congress. In all contact with government officials, the interest group representative follows a number of guidelines to gain and maintain access to policy-makers. Pleasantness is important in all interactions, as is the need to convince the official of the importance of the particular issue to him (this is often achieved through reference to his constituency's interest). Being well prepared and well informed is important (information is the single most valuable commodity interest group representatives have to trade) as is making presentations well organized and concise (government officials don't have time to waste, or at least they prefer to maintain that image). And a willingness to negotiate and compromise is important to achieving success (half a loaf is better than none).

The article by Wright demonstrates the impact that an organized, well-financed interest group can have when it pursues a single policy purpose with vigor. The case involves the dairy lobby and its efforts to overturn an administrative decision affecting the level of price supports for milk. The intensity of the group's effort, the range of techniques utilized, and the targets of the lobbying effort are all amply described in the dairy group's successful lobbying campaign.

Political scientists have spent a lot of time and paper theorizing about the group nature of representational politics (also called pluralism) and the implications of such a group pressure system. One argument is that in the pluralist system anyone can go out and form a group to represent any interest, and that on any issue there will be a balance between countervailing groups' positions; thus under pluralism everything is just fine. However, since the widespread acceptance of the pluralist line of thinking, there have been second thoughts about the lack of representation for many interests in society who are not organized and/or who lack the resources to organize and operate as an effective group. As E. E. Schattschneider has said, "The flaw in the pluralist heaven is that the heavenly chorus sings with a strong upper-class accent." There is a bias built into the pluralist perspective, and it roughly boils down to economics: the more well-off can afford to organize and represent their interests, and the poorer classes lack the resources and the know-how to organize and gain access to leverage points in the policy-making process.

Wolman and Thomas address the pluralist political system in their empirical examination of blacks' impact on federal housing and education policy, and conclude the system has real shortcomings. They show that, despite the presence of organized groups for black interests, blacks did not have access to and effective participation in crucial stages of the policy process. As effective interest groups, the black organizations suffered from several problems—a lack of resources, a conscious decision to concentrate efforts at the local level rather than the national level, and an overriding goal of attaining legal equality rather than focusing on improved economic conditions for black citizens.

the dairy lobby buys the cream of Congress

by Frank Wright

AS AGRICULTURE CEASES to be a major occupation for the American
people, it also loses prominence as the preserver of the country's values
and traditions. We still recognize democracy's debt to the soil through
terms like "fleecing the public," "milking the company," and "porkbarrel,"
but the words have followed technology and money to the cities and
attached themselves to the more glamorous industries like oil, banking,
and aerospace. The pork porkbarrel can't possibly stand up anymore to
the cadmium porkbarrel or the cable television porkbarrel.

This doesn't mean that farming has completely lost the ability to
favor—and be favored—by Congress. While newer industries may
monopolize the more experienced legislators in matters of give and take,
men like Thomas Dodd or the late Robert Kerr, the dairy lobby has gotten
remarkable results this year by investing in Senators and Congressmen
publicly thought to be less inclined to serve the lobbyists—men like Edmund Muskie, William Proxmire, Harold Hughes, Hubert Humphrey, and
Wright Patman.

These men would never be found doing the same thing for oil that
they have done for milk, but perhaps milk money is thought to enjoy the
sanctity of the product from which it is made. In any case, the dairy lobby's
investment in these legislators, and others, has paid off handsomely—
while the dairymen bought into last year's election campaigns for about
$1 million, they stand to get back as much as 300 times that amount after
congressional pressure, applied in large degree by those who received the
money, forced the Nixon administration to reverse itself on the question
of milk price supports for 1971.

On March 12, Secretary of Agriculture Clifford Hardin announced that the support level would remain at the $4.66 per hundredweight in effect for 1970. The price applies to what is called "manufacturing milk," a basic grade used to make butter, cheese, and nonfat powdered milk. Whenever the market price falls below the support price, the government begins buying, thus assuring the farmer he will have a place to sell at a guaranteed price. The Agriculture Department expects that these subsidy payments for the marketing year now ending will approximate $380 million, not quite as much as the C-5A overrun, but a goodly amount of pocket money, nonetheless. The government-owned milk goes into the school lunch program, is distributed among the poor, and is dispersed overseas.

In his March 12 announcement, Hardin said that production was adequate to meet the nation's needs, no surplus was accumulating, and most milk was being sold by farmers to processors at prices higher than the support level, so there was no reason to raise the support. It was all very much in keeping with the Administration's general desire in farm affairs to rely as much as possible on the free market.

However, by March 25, just 13 days later, the Secretary had changed his mind. The support level would be raised after all, to $4.93, an increase of 27 cents. The price took effect April 1, the beginning of the new marketing year under the farm subsidy law.

The dairy industry, with a few noteworthy exceptions, like Land O'Lakes, was ecstatic, declaring the increase a great break for the milk-producing farmer. Some industry experts, though, saw trouble ahead. If farmers responded by sharply increasing production, there would be an oversupply, and free market prices would likely drop accordingly. Under those circumstances, they said, the Administration's action could cost the taxpayers up to $300 million in increased subsidies to buy the surplus.

In view of that financial risk and the fact that President Nixon's proposed budget for the coming year already envisions a deficit of several billion dollars, the success of the lobbying campaign that prompted Hardin's turnabout was even more impressive. The leaders were the country's biggest milk-producing cooperatives, particularly the Associated Milk Producers, Inc. (AMPI) of San Antonio, Texas. AMPI, an outgrowth of the constantly burgeoning merger movement among farm co-ops, is only two years old. But it represents approximately 32,000 member farms in 20 midwestern states ranging from the Canadian border to the Gulf of Mexico, and it markets about 10 per cent of the nation's milk.

The milk co-ops descended on Washington, in person and by mail. Their allies in Congress helped in two ways—by rushing to introduce legislation that would require the Administration to raise the support price and by lining up in private to urge the Administration to reconsider. Generally speaking, Democrats took the former course, and Mr. Nixon's fellow Republicans, not wishing to break publicly with him, took the latter. (The lobbyists favored Administration action because it was easier than buying a new law.)

Some of the congressional support for the subsidy increase may have grown from a real interest in the welfare of farmers, but much of it seems to have grown out of large campaign contributions.

During the past two years, according to records filed with Congress, Representative W. R. Poage (D-Texas), chairman of the House Agriculture Committee, received $5,000 in contributions from the dairy industry political financiers—even though he had no opposition for reelection in 1970. The record says that an additional $11,500 was spent on an appreciation dinner (or dinners—it is difficult to tell from the record) for Poage and Representative Wright Patman (D-Texas), chairman of the House Banking and Currency Committee, who had only nominal election opposition last year. Similarly, $2,000 was spent on an appreciation dinner for Representative Carl Albert (D-Okla.), Speaker of the House, another who was re-elected last year without opposition.

Representative Ed Jones (D-Tenn.), a ranking member of the House Dairy and Poultry subcommittee, received $7,500 in campaign contributions—even though he ran without opposition. Another member of the subcommittee, Representative Watkins Abbitt (D-Va.), received $8,000 to help him in a three-way election contest against nominal opposition.

Others on the full committee received contributions, too. Rep. Page Belcher (R-Okla.), the ranking minority member, got $5,000. Rep. Graham Purcell (D-Texas), a senior member, was given $6,530.

Senator Hubert Humphrey received $10,625 from the dairymen for his 1970 Senate comeback in Minnesota. He now is a member of the Senate Agriculture Committee. Senator William Proxmire (D-Wis.), third-ranking majority member of the Senate Agriculture Appropriations subcommittee, received $8,160 to help his runaway reelection victory. Senator Gale McGee (D-Wyo.), chairman of that subcommittee, also received $2,000.

Senator Edmund Muskie got $7,132, according to the records, and Senator Harold Hughes of Iowa, $5,000. The contribution to Hughes was listed in the records as an "honorarium." He was not up for reelection last year, but traveled extensively on behalf of other Democratic candidates.

The legislation, which these funds helped to foster, was introduced less than a week after Hardin's first announcement and just a few days before his second. All the recipients of the lobby money listed above, except Albert and Belcher, were co-sponsors of the legislation. Albert's aides said he supported the bill actively and would have been a sponsor except for his custom, as Speaker, not to attach his name to any bills. Belcher worked internally, trying to persuade the Administration to change its mind without congressional action.

The main sponsor in the Senate was Gaylord Nelson (D-Wis.). He had about two dozen co-sponsors, and at least eight of those received contributions from the milkers, including the three on the key committees—McGee, Proxmire, and Humphrey.

In the House, more than 70 members signed up to support the legislation, including over 30 who received money from the industry during 1969 and 1970.

The dairy money was funneled through four funds set up by the dairy people, who obviously included among their number somebody with an eye for imaginative acronyms as well as for political use of a dollar.

The biggest is the Trust for Agricultural Political Education (TAPE), an arm of AMPI in San Antonio. Since the spring of 1969, when it went into business, TAPE has reported receipts of $1,053,571 and expenditures of $447,291. . . .

The second-largest fund, the Trust for Special Political Agricultural Community Education (SPACE), has reported receipts of $181,472 and expenditures of $126,170. It is the agent of Dairymen, Inc., a large cooperative milk group in the southeastern United States, headquartered in Louisville, Kentucky.

The other two funds are much smaller. One is the Agricultural and Dairy Educational Political Trust (ADEPT) of Mid-America Dairymen, Inc., Springfield, Missouri. The other is the Agricultural Cooperative Trust (ACT) of the National Milk Producers Federation, located in Washington.

The dairy lobby got a kind of beyond-the-call-of-duty service from a few key Senators who could never afford to be so acquiescent to the better-known special interest groups. For example, in the case of Nelson, no money, according to the records, was required to enlist his rapid assistance. A person who was in close touch with the Senator's role said that AMPI lobbyists delivered the text of their proposed legislation to his Capitol Hill office, and he introduced it in the Senate the same day. In addition, AMPI provided at least some of the data for a statement which Nelson inserted in the Congressional Record in support of the bill. AMPI calculated for him the claim that Hardin's refusal to raise the support price would cost dairy farmers $500 million nationally and $90 million in Wisconsin. Nelson neglected in his statement to give AMPI credit for its fact-finding assistance.

Likewise, Hubert Humphrey failed to acknowledge the industry's help in providing him with a long statement making the case for an increased support price that he inserted into the Record. An aide said later that it, too, had been provided by AMPI.

Such political assistance was augmented by other dairy weapons.

Letters from AMPI members deluged numerous lawmakers. AMPI claimed that more than 50,000 pieces of mail were generated by dairy farmers in its part of the country within a week. Pressure also was applied directly to the Agriculture Department. George Mehren, as Assistant Secretary of Agriculture under Democrat Orville Freeman in the 1960s, joined the AMPI staff and began making the rounds of his old departmental haunts.

And, as an added bit of whipped cream, the dairymen won an audience with the President himself. On the morning of March 23, 11 days after the first Hardin announcement, a group of 16 dairy industry spokesmen were ushered into Mr. Nixon's office for a 30-minute session. Also present were Secretary Hardin and representatives of the Office of Management and Budget. Nine members of the delegation were from AMPI, including President Butterbrodt. Two others were from Pure Milk Products Cooperative, a Wisconsin outfit that is merging with AMPI. Mid-

America and Dairymen were there, too. Apparently their arguments impressed Mr. Nixon because he heard them out for 58 minutes.

Not everybody gets a chance to plead their case with the President for an hour. But if they have recently spent more than $1 million on politics, it obviously helps. It also apparently helps if you speak for people from a segment of society that once supported Mr. Nixon at the ballot box but lately has shown signs of disenchantment—as the farmers did in the 1970 congressional elections.

Following the White House meeting, AMPI shut down the temporary command post it had set up at the Madison Hotel. "There was nothing left to do but wait," said one staff member.

The wait was short. Two days later, after reviewing all the evidence to make sure everything was perfectly clear, the Administration caved in. Hardin announced the increase in supports, and added that a "constant analysis" of the situation had provided new evidence of rising production costs which necessitated the higher price supports. Everyone concerned nodded and smiled.

The quick switch represented a defeat for one of AMPI's competitors, Land O'Lakes, Inc., a Minnesota-based cooperative best known for its butter. Prior to Hardin's first decision, Land O'Lakes officials had circulated among Administration farm officials a position paper opposing a price support increase and suggesting that AMPI had been manipulating the market to strengthen its argument in favor of one. The paper said higher government guarantees would only encourage greedy farmers to produce more, raise prices to consumers, forcing them to look for milk substitutes even more than they are now, and lead to higher government costs. The producer would be hurt in the long run, the paper said.

On the subject of price manipulation, Land O'Lakes claimed AMPI had been engaging early this year in "apparent" maneuverings to drive the market price paid to producers up to unrealistically high levels, about $5.10 for manufacturing milk in the Minnesota-Wisconsin area. This, it was claimed, laid the groundwork for the AMPI contention that support prices could be raised to almost that level for 1971 without boosting government costs—because free market milk prices paid to farmers would always be higher than the support level. . . .

One AMPI spokesman, Jim Hill of the northern regional staff in New Ulm, Minnesota, acknowledged in an interview that his organization "May have overpaid producers a little bit to prove our point—to get the market price up around $5." But, he claimed, the price was not unrealistically high, as claimed by Land O'Lakes, because the "consumers were not complaining." AMPI says it would welcome a "full" and "official" investigation.

In any event, the dairy industry seems to have learned how to make money talk in Washington—and is proud of it.

The reasons that some of the Senators and Congressmen lent their voices to that money are less clear. Maybe it's because a political hand in the pocket of a deserving milk farmer smarts less than one in the pocket of a military contractor. Or because many of the dairymen who benefit from the subsidy are small or middle-sized farmers, not greedy conglomerates. Or because politicians from dairy states run no risks in helping farmers and great risks in refusing to do so. Or perhaps, since there is no organized opposition to the milk subsidy, and since agriculture is becoming a vague memory in the public mind, Congress is not challenged enough to even think about its coziness with the milkers.

But for men who actively oppose strong lobbies, congressional conflicts of interest, and the power of vested interests to buy legislation, the dairy deal remains an unexplained aberration. The big money may have moved long ago from the cow to the C-5A, and other places, but the difference is in degree rather than in kind, and it is worth asking whether those who criticize special favors to the latter and offer them to the former are morally ahead of their time, or just tactically behind.

black interests, black groups, and black influence in the federal policy process: the cases of housing and education

reading 8

by Harold L. Wolman and Norman C. Thomas

From Harold L. Wolman and Norman C. Thomas, "Black Interests, Black Groups, and Black Influence in the Federal Policy Process: The Cases of Housing and Education," *Journal of Politics,* vol. 32 (November, 1970), pp. 875–877, 879, 882–897.

FEW WOULD DISAGREE that American politics is characterized by bargaining, negotiation, compromise, and mutual accommodation. But some have argued that these characteristics, rather than indicating consent as Dahl has suggested, indicate instead that dissent is being suppressed and that the political system is stable *because* of that suppression. Thus, Jack Walker has remarked that

> one of the chief characteristics of our political system has been its success in suppressing and controlling internal conflict. But the avoidance of conflict, the suppression of strife, is not necessarily the creation of satisfaction or consensus. The citizens may remain quiescent, the political system might retain its stability, but significant differences of opinion remain, numerous conflicts are unresolved and many desires go unfulfilled.

Walker and others dispute the assumption that the absence of articulated demands signifies consent. Rather, they believe that the absence of articulated demands reflects the fact that not all interests are expressed through organized groups and that not all organized groups have effective access to centers of decision making.

All interests do not become translated into group demands, it is argued, because certain segments of the population lack the resources for effective group participation. Studies of participation have shown that lower-class people in particular, possessing little education and low political efficacy, are less likely to join groups than are their middle- and upper-class counterparts. As a result, according to critics like E. E. Schattschneider, the interests of the lower classes are much less likely to be articulated through groups. Schattschneider concludes, "The flaw in the pluralist heaven is that the heavenly chorus sings with a strong upper-class accent."

Moreover, the critics contend, decision makers are likely to be much less receptive to certain types of groups, particularly those that put stress on the social system by pushing for change. The decision makers do not dispassionately weigh the relative forces of the contending groups and then register a decision. In many cases the decision makers can determine who has effective access on the basis of their own values. The "mobilization of bias" by political decision-making institutions plays a major role in determining which groups are heard and which are not.

The "Negro revolt" of the past decade provides an important and appropriate setting for an investigation of the relevance of some of the criticisms that have been made of the pluralist description of American politics. To the extent that black Americans do share common interests, how successful have they been in achieving effective access to federal decision makers and in helping to shape national policy to conform with those interests? The "Poor People's Campaign" of 1968 provided a dramatic indication that black participation in federal policy processes has not been satisfactory in the view of many black groups and their leaders.

Studies that we conducted during 1967–68, independently but in close contact with each other, of the process of formulating national policies in the areas of housing and education, have provided us with evidence that black participation in national policy processes is not as effective or as extensive as the pluralist description suggests it should be. (We are assuming the existence of relatively greater unmet demands, i.e., felt needs, among black Americans than among the rest of the population.) Specifically, we examined the federal policy-making processes to discover which groups had access and where, and at what points in the policy process that access occurred. We found an absence of black access and effective black participation at crucial stages in the process. It is our purpose in this paper to present that evidence, to suggest explanations for it, and to assess its significance in relation to the pluralist description of American politics. . . .

BLACK GROUPS AND PARTICIPATION IN POLICY MAKING

How do groups representing black interests attempt to influence public policy at the national level? Do they take advantage of the multiplicity of access points available in the education and housing policy processes? To answer these questions, we first considered the major black groups on the assumption that each represented interests held by some portion of the black community.*. . .

In summary, black groups have directed most of their efforts to influence national policies on issues involving civil rights. These have been largely formal and visible activities, e.g., lobbying and litigation, that occur fairly late in the policy process, particularly at the stages of legislative consideration and implementation. At those stages certain actions can be prevented and marginal changes in policy outputs affected, but the major thrust of policies cannot substantially be altered, for they have been shaped in the earlier innovative and formulative stages when the basic agenda is set.

BLACK GROUPS AND ACCESS TO THE POLICY-MAKING ELITE

The pattern of black participation in the policy-making process is quite similar in housing and education. Very few blacks were found in the policy-making elites that we studied.† In housing there were only two black members of the elite, including, of course, Robert Weaver who as the first Secretary of Housing and Urban Development was also the first black member of the Cabinet. . . .

But did the organized groups representing black interests have effective access to members of the policy-making elite? The evidence indicated that they did not. We asked the members of the education policy system: "What are the two or three groups or forces outside the government that have the most impact on federal policy involving elementary and secondary education?" and "higher education?" Not one of the 71 respondents cited a civil-rights organization or any other element in the black community. . . . We also asked the education respondents, "Outside your immediate office, who are the ten people whom you see most frequently, formally or informally, with respect to matters that involve federal educational policy?" None of the 71 respondents cited a representative of a civil-rights organization or any other black leader as a person whom they consulted. This is fairly impressive negative evidence of the absence of black access to the national educational policy-making elite. Members of the policy-making elite had neither reference groups nor personal contacts in the black community.

We obtained at least some positive evidence of the same phenome-

* [Editors' note: These groups included the National Association for the Advancement of Colored People (NAACP); the Legal Defense and Education Fund (LEAF); the Leadership Conference of Civil Rights (the Conference); the National Urban League; the Congress of Racial Equality (CORE); the Student Non-Violent Co-ordinating Committee (SNCC); and the Southern Christian Leadership Conference (SCLC).]

† [Editors' note: The "elites" that were studied included members of Congress, staff members from Congress, bureaucrats, individuals in the Executive Office of the President, representatives of clientele groups, and public interest representatives. Sixty-eight individuals were identified as being in the housing elite and 77 were identified as being in the education elite.]

non by asking 59 of the respondents: "Do you feel that all relevant and concerned groups have adequate opportunity to express their views concerning federal educational policies?" Thirty-six of those who responded to the question believed that certain groups did not have adequate access to the policy process in education. These groups included four distinct categories: the Negro-urban poor; various educational interests, including vocational education, independent schools, and private liberal-arts colleges; teachers, students, and parents; and state and local education officials. . . .

It should be noted, however, that while the Negro-urban poor are cited more than any other group, there was by no means a widespread sentiment among the respondents that any identifiable group was seriously underrepresented. Yet a substantial uneasiness was apparent over the representativeness of the education policy process as a whole. . . .

In housing, the pattern of responses was substantially the same. Members of the housing policy system were asked how often over the course of a year they communicated with the 16 interest groups identified as participants. The more moderate black organizations, the NAACP and the Urban League, ranked seventh in frequency of the policy-makers' contacts while the more militant groups, SNCC and CORE, ranked sixteenth, with many decision makers almost never communicating with them.

In sum, the responses indicate that black access to the policy-making elites is limited in terms of the reference groups and personal contacts with the influential policy makers and that a sizeable, but not substantial, number of those who are influential believe that black people lack adequate access to the process.

VIRTUAL AND INDIRECT REPRESENTATION

Although our findings strongly indicate that black groups on the whole do not possess effective access to the major centers of decision making in the domestic policy-making process, it does not follow that black interests are ignored by the policy-making elite. Indeed, members of the elite themselves may share these interests. Thus, when housing decision makers were questioned about their agreement with the policy positions of the four major black organizations, 34 of the 42 who responded either generally agreed or agreed very strongly with the NAACP or Urban League, while 13 answered similarly for SNCC and CORE. Interestingly enough, 26 indicated that they did not know what SNCC's or CORE's policy positions were, tending to verify our previous observation that neither group makes much effort to achieve access. . . .

More specifically, certain units within the executive branch were institutionally structured and certain officials took it upon themselves to represent the interests of the black community—or at least some of the interests of some parts of the black community. In HUD, the Office of Community Development and the Office of Equal Opportunity, both headed by blacks, provided such representation, particularly in the implementation stage. Neither of these units, however, was a major center of policy making. Within HEW the Commissioner of Education and the Special Assistant to the Secretary for Civil Rights assumed a special responsibility for the interests of black people. At the time of this inquiry, the commissioner was a white man while the Civil-Rights Assistant was a black woman. The commissioner's record as a champion of civil rights had earned him the antipathy of most Southern congressmen. The Civil-Rights Assistant was concerned primarily with Title VI compliance and she did not participate in the overall development of educational policies except as they related to civil-rights matters. The U.S. Office of Education (USOE) also maintained an Office of Programs for the Disadvantaged which had the responsibility of receiving and processing suggestions and complaints from poor people about the operation of federal education programs.

Federal institutions outside the main policy system also represented some black interests. Demands from these institutions acted as inputs to the policy-making system from within the Administration. The Office of Economic Opportunity (OEO) in particular argued the case for black interests, although much more effectively in education than in housing. In education, the OEO administered two programs, Headstart (later transferred to USOE) and Upward Bound, oriented towards helping black children overcome cultural, economic, and educational obstacles. Through these programs, OEO was able to influence other programs that affect black children.

Probably the most important form of indirect representation of black interests came from demands on the policy-making elite made by certain non-governmental groups such as the Urban Coalition, the National Council of Churches, and the AFL-CIO. Of these groups, organized labor has clearly been the most important. Despite the fact that many rank-and-file unionists did not appear to support black-oriented policies, labor leadership consistently pushed for legislation favorable to moderate black interests. . . .

There are a number of other ways in which black "representation" is achieved in the policy process. Perhaps the most important in the minds of the policy-making elite, which tends to believe that there *should* be black representation, is the practice of consulting a few well-known black leaders or enlisting them in formal and highly visible advisory capacities. . . . The other aspect of this form of black representation is consultation with intellectuals and experts, e.g., educators, urbanologists, etc. who tend to be affiliated with universities, foundations, and research institutes. . . .

Although black interests are not excluded from any of the stages of the policy-making process, serious deficiencies do exist in efforts at interest articulation through indirect representation. The most obvious is that groups or institutions attempting to represent black interests are often restrained by their own constituencies from fully representing those interests. . . .

More important, however, is the question of which black interests get articulated through indirect representation. Obviously the black community is not monolithic; various segments within it do have interests that differ, and in some cases quite markedly. . . . It is quite apparent that the black interests articulated through indirect representation are those that are popularly termed moderate. . . . Thus, black interests that focus on integration and on relatively traditional governmental efforts to alleviate and ultimately to eliminate black poverty receive the bulk of indirect representation. . . .

Finally, at this point in history, the very existence of indirect representation—regardless of how adequate that representation may be—is unacceptable to many blacks. No matter how noble the intentions of liberal white groups, blacks frequently perceive white efforts to aid the black cause as paternalistic and patronizing. Blacks tend to regard such efforts as a continuation of the master-subordinate relation implicit in the history of race relations in America. . . .

ANALYSIS

Both pluralists and most of their critics have assumed that rational men who hold common interests will organize into groups in order to achieve their goals. Mancur Olson has recently argued, however, that exactly the opposite is true. The rational individual will not make the sacrifices—such as time, energy, money—necessary to join a large voluntary group. He reasons that his participation will not make any measurable difference in the group's accomplishments, yet he will benefit from the group's accomplishments whether he is a member or not. Successful groups are, by Olson's persuasive logic, necessarily small groups or groups that are "fortunate enough to have an independent source of selective incentives." Thus, in order to receive the AMA journal, which keeps them informed on recent advances in medicine, doctors must belong to the American Medical Association. Unfortunately for black groups no similar incentives provide an effective means of coercing black people to join and contribute to them.

The consequent lack of resources has meant that black groups have had to make hard choices about where to concentrate their energies. Because almost all of the black groups at the national level are no more than coalitions of local groups, there is a natural reluctance to expend already scarce resources at the national level. Instead, efforts have been concentrated on influencing policies at the local level where the problems and processes may be less complex, and where the payoffs will, in all probability, be more tangible and visible.

The emerging ideology of black power, shared to some extent by nearly all black groups, reinforces the tendency to focus on local politics. Local activity is consistent with an emphasis on direct citizen participation, which seems to form an integral part of the ideology. In addition, the more militant version of the ideology holds that it is pointless to work with or through a "racist white power structure" at the federal level. . . .

[T]he lack of special incentives and the concentration of effort at the local level means that black groups suffer from a severe lack of resources when they do attempt to influence policy at the national level. . . .

. . . the lack of technical expertise among black groups has been a major problem. On the whole, black organizations have not been able to develop coherent programs in either housing or education. . . .

In a sense, however, it is hardly surprising that blacks have not made a more extensive effort to develop national programs in housing and education. In education in particular white experts are divided and uncertain over how the federal government can most effectively improve the situation of black children. . . .

Probably a more serious lack has been the inability of black groups to develop more lobbyists of the quality of Clarence Mitchell. As a labor lobbyist remarked, "Negro groups make so little effort to learn Washington and to learn how to operate in Congress. The great lack in Negro organizations is for effective lobbyists, but it's hard to get people like Mitchell." The reason for this lack may be that the kind of temperament characteristic of a good lobbyist is not readily found in members of most black groups and particularly not in militant ones. "Lobbying emphasizes compromise, accommodation, patience," one lobbyist explained. Most black groups, however, have emphasized a highly moral and emotional approach better aimed at the mass public than at the policy-making elite. For whatever reasons, however, there is widespread agreement that most black groups do not have a good understanding of the operations of the policy process. One black observer commented, "The civil-rights groups have a total ignorance of how important appropriations and administrative guidelines are. They just don't understand the process."

In addition, black groups face a number of specific problems in securing access simply because they are black groups. The concentration of black people in the urban North and the rural South limits the willingness of many congressmen to pay them much heed since they are not major factors in their constituencies. Another problem is that relatively few black leaders have sufficient personal prestige or professional status to guarantee their inclusion, formally or informally, at the innovative and formulative stages. Aside from Whitney Young in housing and Kenneth Clark in education and a handful of others of similar stature, few blacks are actively consulted by the White House, the agencies, or the key congressional leaders. Nor do they have easy access to influential policy makers in those places. Finally, it may be that access is severely restricted by certain members of the elite who do not view some of the black groups—particularly the more militant ones—as legitimate participants in the political process.

SUMMARY AND IMPLICATIONS

The major reason for the ineffectiveness of black participation appears to be a severe lack of resources and a decision to concentrate most activity at the level of local communities. The result is that the few efforts made by black groups to influence national policy suffer from insufficient expertise, with respect to both the complexities of policy and the workings of the policy process. Black participation and representation occur primarily in the legislative-consideration and the implementation stages of the policy process. Black organizations and leaders have made little attempt to influence policy development at the innovative and formulative stage where meaningful choices between long-range alternatives are for the most part made.

The policy goals that black groups have pursued have been short-run, direct, and highly visible: principally to attack overt racial discrimination and to promote integration. Only recently have black groups begun to direct their efforts towards problems of black poverty rather than towards the lack of legal equality. Most black participation has been aimed at the courts and Congress through litigation and legislative lobbying.

Black interests are represented indirectly in the policy-making process through a variety of mechanisms. Probably the most important of these is that certain members of the decision-making elite may already share some attitudes of some black groups. Outside the elite, organized labor has often represented black interests to decision makers. But indirect representation is often incomplete and ineffective, and many blacks perceive it to be a demeaning survival of the paternal master-slave relation between blacks and whites.

It appears that the pluralist description of the American political system is not entirely adequate. Our research has shown that black interests and black groups do not, on the whole, possess effective access to the centers of decision making in federal education and housing policy. This lack of influence is not, however, due primarily to the causes that most critics of pluralism have suggested. Contrary to their analyses, channels of access do appear to be relatively open and most decision makers seem willing to listen to any groups who use them. The extremely limited use of the channels by groups with the most manifest set of unmet demands reveals a flaw in the pluralist analysis. As Mancur Olson has pointed out, the main assumption of the pluralists—that rational men sharing interests will form groups in order to accomplish their ends—is defective. This applies not only to the black community, but to other interests as well—for example, housewives, students, commuters or, more generally, consumers, as opposed to producers, of goods and services.

Furthermore, there are defects in the pluralist assumption that the response of the decision-making elite will normally be satisfactory. Without examining specific policy outcomes, it seems obvious that the response of federal policy makers to black demands, whether they are articulated by marginal black participation or indirect white representation, is inadequate. This inadequacy is reflected in continued social and economic discrimination against black Americans and in the rise of the black-power movement. Indeed, Dahl notes the "spirit of alienation and despair" that affects black ghetto dwellers and suggests that it is associated with the emergence of civil disorders. To us this constitutes recognition, *albeit en passant, that pluralism is not producing the social stability that ought to accompany the incremental change and mutual adjustment that, according to Dahl, are its byproducts.*

. . . We suggest that extensive efforts should be made to secure more effective and meaningful involvement of black interests and black leaders in all aspects of the federal policy process. It is appropriate to do so on the basis of democratic ideals alone; it also makes eminent sense as a possible means of strengthening the black community's support for the social and political systems. The civil-rights movement did not result in extensive involvement by black groups in the federal policy process in housing or education. It is apparent that the policy makers are aware of the need to represent the blacks and the poor, but that they are uncertain about what can and should be done. The dilemma of the decision makers extends not only to the process of representation of interests, but also to the substance of what should be done for the disadvantaged who are themselves unable to develop viable suggestions. Deliberately expanded black participation in the federal policy process will not solve these problems, but it should be an important step towards overcoming the lack of leadership, disorganization, and resultant frustration that now characterize black involvement in the pluralist system.

Finally, we must conclude with a disclaimer. This paper is not primarily an attack on pluralism nor is it a definitive examination of black involvement in the policy-making behavior of the national elite. It is a call for reassessment of some pluralist assumptions and an urgent plea for more research on the processes by which people with shared interests organize into groups and gain access to political decision makers.

III

the structure of government:

national institutions and policy

IIIA

the presidency

In many ways the American presidency is the center of American political life, or at least is so viewed by journalists, television commentators, political scientists, public officials, large segments of the public, and most presidents themselves. The president is often viewed personally not just as a chief executive of a vast governmental apparatus (the federal executive branch) but also as "leader of the Free World," national leader in a policy sense, national leader in a moral sense, and the chief political leader for his party.

Paradoxically, despite the attribution of semi-divine powers to the president, that individual often seems unhappily unable to do much to influence the course of life in the United States. A profoundly conservative man such as Gerald Ford can preside over a budget with a planned deficit of over $50 billion and an actual deficit of over $70 billion. A president dedicated to the eradication of poverty and peaceful improvement of the lot of the poor such as Lyndon Johnson can watch helplessly while the major cities of the country explode, thus accentuating class and race divisiveness for subsequent years. The president may make pronouncements about solutions to problems or may take preventive action on problems, but often such actions seem like feeble efforts when considered only a short time later in conjunction with news reports detailing the continued growth of some domestic or foreign problem seemingly beyond presidential ken or influence or both.

Presidents are constantly in the public eye—sometimes as heroes, sometimes as goats. Public approval of the presidential job vacillates considerably, frequently, and quickly, depending not just on the incumbent's skills or lack thereof but also depending on how the world seems to be going. No matter what stance or "style" a president may affect in approaching the public, he is likely to be severely criticized. The bland good will and equanimity of an Eisenhower, the frenetic vigor of a Kennedy producing a perpetual air of crisis and crisis management, the cattle-prod personal involvement and commitment of a Johnson, the aloofness and moral pretensions of a Nixon, and the earnest pragmatic conservatism of a Ford have all had their admirers, but all have also had their severe detractors. There is no winning formula that lasts for very long for very many. In recent years only Franklin Roosevelt and Dwight Eisenhower seemed to have a permanent hold on at least something like the support of a majority of politically interested citizens, and even they had large numbers of severe critics.

The one policy area in which presidents have a special role to play—less hampered by the range of forces and competing interests to which all presidents are subject most of the time in most areas—involves foreign policy. Both to give a sense of what a president can achieve when he devotes personal time and skill to foreign matters and in order to show President Nixon at his best (because, despite his deserved disgrace after Watergate and related crimes, he also had some genuine skills), we have included the picture drawn by Evans and Novak (reading 9) of his foreign policy initiatives early in his first term.

In domestic policy matters, the president must work with (and sometimes against) a large array of institutions and agencies that often have policy preferences different from his own. Over the course of the past several decades, the president has developed an array of his own "in house" resources to assist him in dealing with both the domestic and foreign policy. In reading 10 Shull summarizes briefly the development of this institutional presidency, assesses the major policy roles of the principal parts of the Executive Office of the president, and raises some questions about the overall impact of the institutional presidency on the capacity of the president to lead.

The largest and most consistently important parts of the institutional presidency are the White House Office and the Office of Management and Budget. The White House Office is the special personal preserve of any incumbent president. Its population is wholly determined by him or by his close advisors and its use is shaped to fit the needs and priorities of any given president. The Office of Management and Budget is peopled largely by career individuals (despite an increased political component added during the Nixon years). OMB has a more stable role in government although emphases may change with different presidents. But it has for almost the last four decades played important roles in coordinating the legislative program of the president, in preparing the budget that the president submits to Congress annually, in managing expenditures by operating agencies after the money has been appropriated or otherwise made available, in overseeing the management of the executive branch, and in generally monitoring the development and functioning of the executive branch from a central perspective (allegedly the president's). The triangular relationship between White House, OMB, and the operating agencies—with the occasional personal participation of the president—is at the heart of whatever constitutes executive management in the United States government at any given time. Gilmour's article (reading 11) on this relationship with reference to the "legislative clearance" function illustrates a number of broader themes.

Any president who has more than the most minimal aspirations in domestic policy must pay central attention to his relations with Congress. Some of this attention almost surely has to be personal, but a great deal of it also involves the corporate or institutional presidency. The Holtzman selection (reading 12) comes from the concluding section of a book that empirically investigated executive branch liaison efforts in the 1960's. The general points made in the selection are not, however, time-bound but relate to any modern president's personal and corporate efforts to deal with Congress in a routinized, productive way.

a very personal diplomacy

reading 9

by Rowland Evans, Jr.
and Robert D. Novak

IT WAS MELVIN ROBERT LAIRD, pragmatist and realist, who in the new
Nixon administration perceived the realities in Vietnam. Laird, as Secretary of Defense, approached the delicate, difficult problem of getting
American soldiers out of Vietnam like a ferocious bulldog gnawing on a
bone; he couldn't let it alone. It consumed his energies, stretched his
imagination and made him something of a terror to the nonpolitical advisers on foreign policy whom Nixon had surrounded himself with—principally Harvard history professor and long-time adviser to Presidents, Henry
M. Kissinger.

"Mel?" Kissinger mused long months later when asked about Laird.
"Mel is a rascal, but a good rascal."

Laird had carefully started to build his case for rapid U.S. pullout long
before he dreamed he would go to the Pentagon, long before the election,
long before even the Republican National Convention at Miami Beach.
As the powerful chairman of the House Republican Caucus, his politically
sensitive antenna was sending out quiet vibrations as early as February
1966, when Senator Robert F. Kennedy infuriated President Lyndon Johnson, Vice President Hubert Humphrey and the entire foreign and military
policy team then in power with his proposal for a coalition government
in Saigon. Laird took pains immediately to warn fellow Republicans not
to knock Kennedy, as Humphrey and other Johnson satellites were doing.
Instead, Laird counseled House Republican leaders to stay mute in the face
of Kennedy's challenge to Johnson. "We may be endorsing the same
proposal if we win the 1968 election," Mel Laird said. In short: Don't close
the negotiating door.

At the Miami Beach convention, it was Laird who spelled out his "de-Americanization" policy during the platform hearings. It was Laird who told the press, while riding with candidate Nixon from Bismark, N.D., to Boise, Ida., in October 1968, that up to ninety thousand American troops could be pulled out of Vietnam in the next twelve months (and was sharply rebuffed by Johnson's Secretary of Defense, Clark Clifford, who noted that the troop level was still going up in Vietnam).

As the brainiest politician in the Nixon circle of advisers during the campaign, Laird took it upon himself to educate Nixon on the absolute imperative of moving out of Vietnam immediately, not all at once, of course, but to set wheels in motion that would calm the antiwar passions beginning to spread beyond the peace bloc. He never lost a chance to try to proselytize Republican politicians, campaign advisers and candidate Richard Nixon himself.

Such missionary work was absolutely necessary. Nixon's entire public record had been that of a hard-line anti-Communist, eager to halt Red aggression all over the world—including Vietnam. After the Republican election debacle of 1964, Nixon assumed, incorrectly, that Johnson would be sparing in help for the beleaguered Saigon regime, and therefore proposed that the divided Republicans unify in 1965 around the issue of stopping Communist aggression in Southeast Asia, just as they had unified a century before on the issue of no more slave states. In the 1966 midterm election, he criticized the details of the Johnson intervention but defended fighting the war itself: "We believe this is a war that has to be fought to prevent World War III." Nixon was then an unequivocal hawk in Vietnam, favoring a military victory. By 1968, however, he was being advised that military victory was impossible. That, and the unpopularity of the war, watered down the militancy in his speeches. By the time the campaign for President opened in New Hampshire in February, Nixon was pledging to "end the war," implying he had a tidy plan to be unveiled in due time. It was not dovish and not hawkish but very Delphic, susceptible to favorable interpretation by dove and hawk alike.

Laird cautioned Nixon not to say "end the war." The phrase was not accurate, Laird explained, because the war might go on long after Nixon had completed his first term. The proper pledge was "end American participation in the war"—get American troops out and transfer the burden of combat to the South Vietnamese.

Nixon did not follow the advice and decided to keep things murky throughout the 1968 campaign. He never did spell out a detailed policy to fulfill his pledge to end the war. Indeed, Nixon's election found him uncertain on detailed planning of any kind for foreign policy, including the war in Southeast Asia. He possessed a strong, well-defined global strategy but few of the tactics to pursue it. Certain that he would win the election from the day the Democrats ended their bloody convention on the Chicago battlefield, Nixon saw no political need to get specific in a bid for votes. Although he was beginning to intellectualize a U.S. strategy that became the Nixon Doctrine, his specific plans for getting Americans out of Vietnam—throughout the campaign and right up to the inauguration—

scarcely advanced beyond this broad-brush campaign pledge (stated by Nixon behind closed doors to Southern delegates at the Miami convention): "We need a massive training program so that the South Vietnamese can be trained to take over the fighting, that they can be phased in while we phase out."

But what about a negotiated settlement? What were the chances for cease-fire? Would Hanoi settle for a fair distribution of power in South Vietnam, based on a genuinely free election? Or did "coalition government" doom South Vietnam to eventual Communist domination? These questions had not been considered by Richard Nixon, either as candidate or as President-elect.

The President-elect's first order to Henry Kissinger was succinct: Tell me where the United States stands today in Europe, Southeast Asia, the Middle East and lesser geographic regions, how to organize the National Security Council setup in the White House, what my immediate crises will be, how I should proceed with the Strategic Arms Limitation Talks, and on and on. The order to Kissinger was designed to produce a complete inventory of the entire range of U.S. foreign policy, upon which the new President would then construct the details of his own policy—details he had conspicuously avoided setting forth during the campaign.

Kissinger's first step was to call in half a dozen experts in national security affairs; several were to become bitter critics of Nixon foreign policy—such as Morton Halperin, who stayed with Kissinger in the White House until the Cambodian intervention in 1970, and Dan Ellsberg, a brilliant RAND Corporation analyst and a strong Vietnam dove.

Consulting frequently with Laird, Kissinger and his staff holed up at the Pierre Hotel and prepared five options for Nixon on how to deal with the war that had driven his predecessor out of the Presidency. The options, one or a combination of which would establish the Nixon war policy, were these: Option I—Immediate escalation, with full-scale bombing in the North including the supply port of Haiphong and industrial areas around Hanoi, aimed at quick military victory (or, if the North Vietnamese chose, a negotiated settlement in Paris); Option II—Vigorous military prosecution of the war, with steadily increasing U.S. pressure on the ground, but no escalation, also aimed at outright military victory. Options III, IV, and V all embraced the troop-withdrawal concept, with No. V calling for an immediate end to the U.S. combat role and total reliance on the Paris peace negotiations.

Kissinger was operating at the Pierre under a Nixon timetable that set Vietnam as the principal topic for discussion at the first National Security Council meeting, which the President-elect had scheduled for January 25, five days after the inauguration. Nixon wanted the options presented then.

Next, Kissinger turned to the mechanism that would soon be playing the vital role in the development and carrying out of U.S. policy: the National Security Council. Both he and Nixon wanted that mechanism to be more supple than the old NSC structure (with its Planning Board and Operations Coordination Board) under Eisenhower, but more precise in its procedures than the informal, conversational method which Lyndon Johnson employed to make high national policy at his famous Tuesday luncheons. Kissinger's assignment was to strike a balance, and as it turned out, he chose a form closer to John F. Kennedy's than either Eisenhower's or Johnson's.

On December 30 he took his completed memorandum on the new NSC system to Florida ("I apologize for the length," read a notation), and Nixon approved it on the spot. Kissinger's memorandum discussed the Johnson system briefly, pointedly criticizing the Tuesday policy-making luncheon for "the frequent uncertainty about precisely what was decided." As for the Eisenhower system, Kissinger told Nixon that "its very formality tended to demand too much of the participants' time and insufficient priority to issues of primary presidential concern."

Nixon's approval of the memorandum established the NSC as the only forum for top-level review and policy-making, and gave power over the agenda to a Review Group headed by Kissinger, with the State and Defense departments and the Central Intelligence Agency having one seat each—a division of power strongly advocated by Laird. It also proposed for the first time that the President, using the NSC staff, make an annual State of the World report to Congress to "permit a more extended discussion of the President's view of the international situation than is possible in the State of the Union message." [1] Thus, the great advantages that Kissinger brought into the White House in becoming Nixon's preeminent foreign policy adviser—his expertise against Secretary of State William Rogers' utter unfamiliarity with foreign affairs—were reinforced institutionally from the beginning.

Richard Nixon and Henry Kissinger, it quickly became happily clear to both, thought much alike on U.S. global strategy. At heart, Nixon perceives the world in classical balance-of-power terms and is totally unwilling to cede U.S. influence in any part of the world where it exists. But the United States, given the vast drain of the ten-year war in Vietnam and having lost the nuclear superiority that so well served Eisenhower (in Korea) and Kennedy (in Cuba), now had to define a strategy that would explain military withdrawal from Vietnam in terms other than the virtual surrender demanded by more and more war-weary Americans.

At that first NSC meeting called by Nixon to discuss Vietnam, a tentative decision was made to adopt a mix of options III, IV and V in Kissinger's five-choice scenario—a withdrawal keyed to the ability of South Vietnamese forces to take over the U.S. combat role. The strongest voice at the table for this option was Laird's, in keeping with his long-held views. He wanted the fastest withdrawal possible *within* the outer limits of what the President's military advisers, the Joint Chiefs of Staff, would accept (and Laird well knew that to get the Pentagon brass to accept *anything* in the way of meaningful withdrawals was going to demand all the President's and his own powers of persuasion).

Rogers spoke quietly for an even faster withdrawal. Unencumbered by military advisers, and by profession an expert negotiator and mediator (like all good lawyers), Rogers was convinced that the faster the pace of

structure of government

withdrawals, the more chance there was for a breakthrough at the Paris peace talks.

Kissinger, in those early NSC meetings that determined the course of the United States in Vietnam, was most skeptical about the South Vietnamese ever becoming the kind of fighting force that could assume a primary combat role against the legions from Hanoi, or even their Vietcong guerrilla allies in the South. To Kissinger, a far harder military posture—forcing North Vietnam to choose between devastation or genuine negotiation—seemed the best of a series of hideously bad alternatives. In those days, the generals and the admirals would rather have had Kissinger at the Pentagon than Laird.

But while Laird pressed for withdrawals as quickly as possible, Kissinger was scrupulously neutral, tossing in questions and making comments in a way calculated to conceal any preference of his own, and to define the choices available to Nixon in the clearest possible terms. ("I will never give advice unless you order me to," he told the President privately when he agreed to take the job. "But I will do my best to see that all options are fully exposed.")

On January 25, then, Nixon made the first and most difficult of his foreign policy decisions. He would withdraw, gradually but unilaterally. But like his Secretary of State, he had set far too high a probability on a breakthrough at the Paris peace talks. He had erred—and the months ahead would prove it—as Lyndon Johnson had erred, time and time again, by judging the actions of the tough and hardened Communists in Hanoi by Western standards of rationality.

In his very first press conference, on January 27, Nixon gave a revealing clue to his inner hopes for a negotiated settlement: "I believe that as we look at what is happening in the negotiations in Paris, as far as the American side is concerned, we are off to a good start . . . we have laid down those things which we believe the other side should agree to and can agree to"—mutual withdrawal of forces, exchange of prisoners and, although not yet spelled out, free elections. In Paris, Nixon's newly appointed chief Vietnam negotiator, Henry Cabot Lodge, was also optimistic. The optimism did not last long.

With or without success at Paris, Nixon's plan for withdrawal from Vietnam served as the centerpiece of the Nixon Doctrine, the President's still-developing scheme for a global American strategy in the era of nuclear parity. In essence, the doctrine was half a cover for getting U.S. troops out of Vietnam and half a challenge to U.S. allies elsewhere to do more in the common cause of resisting Communist aggressions. If Paris failed as a source for bringing the war to a negotiated end, Nixon had to have an explanation for Asian countries on the rim of Communist China as the troop-withdrawal process went on. He had to convince them, or at least make a valiant effort to convince them, that the United States was not turning its back and retiring across the Pacific. The Nixon Doctrine and its ramifications were to be a recurring theme in his Presidency.

First, however, there was an essential follow-up to the January 25 NSC decision. On March 6, Nixon sent Laird to Saigon to get the approval of General Creighton Abrams, the U.S. Field Commander in Vietnam, for the withdrawal concept. No figures were mentioned and the timing was left vague. Under those conditions Abrams acquiesced, but he did not attempt to conceal what he regarded as an overwhelming risk in the concept itself. Laird returned to Washington on March 10, reported to Nixon, and working through a Pentagon task force headed by Admiral William Lemos, began charting a withdrawal schedule under the imposing title "Conceptual Overview."

Kept in a locked cabinet in his own office, the Conceptual Overview of Laird and his Vietnam task force became the master chart that would determine the pace and size of U.S. troop withdrawals: which units would come out first, what balance should be kept between combat and logistical backup troops, and which geographic areas of combat should be gradually turned over to the South Vietnamese. It became the road map of Nixon's withdrawal journey.

Only one major decision now remained: the date and circumstances for announcing the withdrawal of the first contingent. Nixon wanted maximum publicity for this occasion. He decided to meet President Nguyen Van Thieu of South Vietnam on June 8 at Midway Island, the halfway point between the United States and Saigon. But a note of high drama awaited the President when, en route to his meeting with Thieu, he put down at Hickam Field in Honolulu on June 7 for a face-to-face consultation with General Abrams. The source of that drama was Abrams himself.

Ever since Nixon had chosen the troop-withdrawal option, the military high command had been seething, fighting the idea of spending scarce defense dollars to build up Saigon's military power. The principle of troop withdrawal—pulling out of a war in which forty thousand Americans had already given their lives—went squarely against their military training and strong convictions not to yield to Communist aggression. They also bitterly resented the President's decision to withdraw *combat* troops first and not backup support troops. They had offered their own troop-withdrawal schedule, based on quick pullback of up to seventy-five thousand supply troops. But to disengage the cream of Army and Marine Corps combat forces on some, to them, vague hope that Saigon's own army could take up the slack seemed the height of stupidity. During the four and one-half months preceding Nixon's trip to Honolulu and Midway, General Earle G. Wheeler, Chairman of the Joint Chiefs of Staff, and General William Westmoreland, Army Chief of Staff, had led an internal struggle to reverse or at least modify the President's plan.

But Nixon's tactic of withdrawing combat, not support, troops was grounded in concrete because it had become fundamental to his larger strategy to make the Paris peace talks come alive. What Nixon counted on was the impact that withdrawing combat troops would have on Hanoi. Once Ho Chi Minh, the North Vietnamese leader, perceived that the new President was in fact reducing U.S. war-making capability in South Vietnam, surely he would become less intransigent at the Paris peace talks. On the other hand, withdrawal of strictly noncombat troops would never be taken as evidence in Hanoi that Nixon was really moving toward winding down the war. To the contrary, Hanoi would sneer at it as sham, a maneuver to make negotiating points. All this was carefully spelled out to the American generals, but they resisted every step of the way.

The full force of this resistance did not strike Nixon until his meeting with Abrams in Honolulu. Abrams, as judged by one participant there, "oozed with distaste" when Nixon revealed the formal orders he was about to give that twenty-five thousand combat troops would be withdrawn as the first contingent. In tight-lipped politeness, Abrams raised hard questions: Was the U.S. risking the substance of four years of war? Would the withdrawal plan be interpreted as a sellout by the South Vietnamese, no matter what Thieu said publicly? Was not the U.S. taking a fantastic gamble? The opposition was so remorseless that the high civilian officials there "knew we had done something hard to do when we got through with the brass and made that first announcement."

And so President Nixon, in the hardest and most significant decision of his new Presidency, set an immutable course in Vietnam that reversed the long build-up of the previous decade, a build-up that had taken U.S. military strength from a handful of advisers to 543,400 troops. He desperately hoped that this evidence of good faith would persuade Ho Chi Minh to begin serious negotiating in Paris, but in this he would be disappointed (as Laird always suspected he would be). He desperately prayed that his policy reversal would cool domestic passions, but the political effect at home was neither dramatic nor permanent. He desperately trusted in the growing ability of Thieu's own army to fill the gaps left by the departing Americans—a trust yet to be entirely fulfilled. But the meeting with Thieu on Midway Island was set in circumstances inherited by Nixon at their most desperate stage. Given his commitment to withdraw from Vietnam with "honor," not surrender, the formula he devised was probably the best if not the only one available.

On March 21, Melvin Laird testified before the Disarmament Subcommittee of the Senate Foreign Relations Committee and, for the first time, faced the full force of antiwar passion from the committee's chairman, Senator J. W. Fulbright of Arkansas. "You've got to do something radical to change this war," Fulbright lectured Laird, "or we're going down the drain. Soon it will be Nixon's war, and then there will be little chance to bring it to an end. It is time to de-escalate and settle it."

Thus, with Richard Nixon barely two months in office, antiwar politicians were breaking their silence, feeling that Nixon was moving down the same path that sucked in Lyndon B. Johnson. One reason the political lid was lifting was the post-Tet offensive by Communist troops and a counteroffensive by the Americans and South Vietnamese. The other, more important reason was statements of administration officials. On March 14 at his televised news conference in the White House, Nixon was asked by Charles W. Bailey II of the *Minneapolis Tribune* whether he saw "any prospect for withdrawing American troops in any numbers soon." The President's reply set the official line that would have serious implications far into the future:

Mr. Bailey, in view of the current offensive on the part of the North Vietnamese and the Vietcong, *there is no prospect for a reduction of American forces* in the foreseeable future. [Emphasis added.]

When we are able to reduce forces as a result of a combination of circumstances—the ability of the South Vietnamese to defend themselves in areas where we now are defending them, the progress of the talks in Paris, or the level of enemy activity—when that occurs, I will make an announcement. But at this time there is no foreseeable prospect in that field.

Nixon administration spokesmen took up the line. On March 19, Laird told the Senate Armed Services Committee that the United States was planning no troop pullout "at the present time." When published reports appeared that indeed such a pullout was inevitable, administration spokesmen denied it. Confusion proliferated. John Gardner, the liberal Republican who had quit as President Johnson's Secretary of Health, Education and Welfare mainly over the war, talked privately with Nixon that spring of 1969 and was delighted to learn of the pullout, passing the good news on to his friends. Gardner and his friends were subsequently mystified and distraught by the official disclaimers of any withdrawal.

The logic behind this goes to the heart of the political strategy being practiced in 1969 by Richard Nixon and John Mitchell, and enunciated by Mitchell, in connection with civil rights. "Watch what we do instead of what we say," said Mitchell. The Nixon–Mitchell strategy was predicated on the fear of alienating the dominant conservative majority that voted for Nixon and Wallace in 1968. To prevent that alienation, progressive policies must be masked in conservative rhetoric. In the case of Vietnam, that meant *denying* reports of the decisions for a troop withdrawal that had already been made and were being relentlessly pursued against opposition from the uniformed military.

The self-inflicted damage stemming from this was incalculable. Had the withdrawal policy been clearly enunciated when first decided upon, the period of grace from Fulbright and the Senate doves would have been significantly lengthened. But, as it was, Fulbright and his allies were pulled prematurely into a posture of opposition from which it was difficult to withdraw. More important, Nixon's harsh rhetoric and soft policy built doubts within the intellectual and student peace bloc that he was really serious about taking troops out. Living in the world of rhetoric, students and intellectuals *believed* Nixon's rhetoric (which was misleading) and *doubted* his actions (which were genuine). Far into the future, doubt that Nixon really was pulling out of Vietnam would haunt the campuses.

Even after his June announcement of the first troop withdrawal, Nixon continued to talk a hard line. With one giant antiwar demonstration having taken place nationwide on October 15 and a massive march on Washington planned by more extreme leftist groups for November 15, Nixon had a golden opportunity in his speech to the nation of November 3 to soften dissent by simply emphasizing the extent of troop withdrawals, now and into the future. In this he failed to consult Laird and, instead, took an opposite course. In contrast to the preparation of his speech in May stating the U.S. negotiating position, before the first troop withdrawal was announced, foreign policy experts had no hand in preliminary drafts for this speech. It was written by one hand alone: Richard Nixon's. In a conscious imitation of Winston Churchill speaking without notes during the dark days of the Battle of Britain, the President memorized the speech for television.

Thus, the November 3 speech, embodying the political tactics of John Mitchell and the unmistakable political prose of Richard Nixon, appealed to those Americans who would *not* be demonstrating in the streets of Washington on November 15: the Silent Majority, so designated for the first time. Asking "you, the great Silent Majority of my fellow Americans" for support, the President declared, "I would be untrue to my oath of office if I allowed the policy of this nation to be dictated by the minority who . . . try to impose [their view] on the nation by mounting demonstrations in the streets." Instead of emphasizing the irreversibility of his withdrawal policy, the President stressed his willingness to re-escalate if need be: "If I conclude that increased enemy action jeopardizes our remaining forces in Vietnam, I shall not hesitate to take strong and effective measures to deal with that situation."

The explicit threat in those words was, of course, partly aimed at Hanoi in the hope that the prospect of escalation would loosen the adamant negotiating posture of the Communist mission in Paris. The impact there, however, was zero. At home, it was immediate and politically dangerous.

Liberals of both parties, infatuated with rhetoric, were dismayed by the November 3 speech. But all polls and other political barometers indicated it was a smash hit with that Silent Majority for which it was intended. Nixon and his aides were well satisfied, not realizing they had lost another opportunity to defuse antiwar sentiment by matching words to deeds. . . .

NOTES

1. The timing of that proposal, and its immediate acceptance by Nixon, clearly demonstrate how wrong certain critics were when, one year later, Kissinger was accused of deliberately undercutting Rogers and the State Department by persuading Nixon to shelve Rogers' own State of the World Report in favor of the Nixon-Kissinger report. In fact, the Nixon-Kissinger report had been in the planning stage for slightly more than one year.

the institutional presidency and policy-making

reading 10

by Steven A. Shull

This article was written expressly for the present volume. Professor Shull is a member of the Political Science Department at the University of New Orleans.

THE PRESIDENCY increasingly has become the locus for ideas and coordination of public policy in the American system of government. Partly due to greater public expectations and government complexity, the presidency today performs many functions (both symbolic and actual) that were scarcely envisioned by our forefathers. Such additional factors as increasing technology, the emergence of the United States as a world power, and the overflowing of public concerns across state boundaries have all enlarged the responsibility of the presidency.

In light of these governmental and societal changes, several tools for presidential leadership and policy coordination have been developed. As presidents have sought to exercise control over policy to meet these responsibilities, the notions of central clearance and agenda-setting appeared. These notions originally referred to financial supervision of agencies, but beginning with the administration of Franklin Roosevelt they have been broadened to include substantive program development and coordination as well. Presidents have exerted policy leadership through a variety of techniques in order to centralize and coordinate their relations with Congress and the bureaucracy.

A large number of presidential institutions have been created in the last four decades, principally within the structure of the Executive Office of the President. By Fiscal Year 1976 the EOP had grown to over 1,600 employees arranged in 42 different agencies or offices. The purpose of the various parts of the EOP, which was created in 1939, is to provide *information* to the President and to centralize his control over the rest of the executive branch. Collectively all such offices often are referred to as the "institutionalized presidency" with its many thousands of supporting personnel, in contrast to the president, as one man. While institutionalization was once touted by reformers as providing a president with leadership over a nonresponsive Congress and bureaucracy, it is now sometimes seen by these same observers as a mixed blessing. Institutions designed to lead the bureaucracy may have succeeded only in creating yet another layer of bureaucracy between the president and the bureaucracy he sought to direct. This may have occurred in spite of language in the act creating the EOP stating that "In no event shall the Administrative Assistance (to the President) be interposed between the President and the head of any department or agency."

The president's personal impact is, of course, limited to only a few major areas or stages of policy. He cannot possibly be involved directly in all decisions, and he is in need of loyalty and detachment in order to coordinate overall administration policy. The EOP and its component elements was created in order to help accomplish these goals.

Presidential staffing has provided many advantages to presidents. Since the selection process does not require Senate confirmation, the president can be concerned more with loyalty and character rather than political and/or interest group considerations. In addition to a loyalty that is never approached by bureaucrats, staff provides the president with information, privacy, and ego support.

Presidents have come to recognize that unquestioned support places the presidential advisory system in a cocoon and has costs associated with it. For it is clear that the presidential perspective may also be a limited one, if in a different way from that of the bureaucracy. Former White House Chief of Staff Donald Rumsfeld has said that "White House aides should be constantly aware that they are an extension of the presidency and are obliged to submerge their convictions, other than when acting in an adversary role." And yet, it must be a careful balancing act, because the aura of the White House may lead advisors (however unconsciously) to tailor their advice to please the president. Aides may come to confuse their own or even the president's wishes with the "public interest." This may result partially from their limited contact with interest groups, public opinion, and actual government operations. It is clearly possible for aides to lose their perspective with advice that can mislead, misinform, and even cripple the president.

Even before the creation of the Executive Office of the President, all presidents have relied on advisors, formal or informal, who are not part of the permanent bureaucracy or even the Cabinet. The procedure was merely extended and legitimized through the EOP framework.

The size of the institutional presidency varies considerably and the exact number of employees at any given time is somewhat unclear. This is because the president supplements the budgetary allotments to these organizations by utilizing temporary employees from other departments. Additionally, he can hire outside consultants. Ironically, it was the fiscally conservative Republican Nixon who had greater numbers of aides than any other president. The figures in Table 1 illustrate the substantial growth

TABLE 1
NUMBER OF EMPLOYEES IN MAJOR PRESIDENTIAL INSTITUTIONS, 1943–1976

	1943 Roose- velt	1950 Truman	1957 Eisen- hower	1962 Kennedy	1967 Johnson	1972 Nixon	1976 Ford
White House Office	40	238	267	273	250	540	500
National Security Council	—	25	28	50	48	75	70
Council of Economic Advisers	—	36	35	44	48	57	46
BOB/OMB	352	531	419	465	525	680	640
Domestic Council	—	—	—	—	—	70	30
Totals	492	830	749	832	871	1422	1286

that has occurred in the major presidential agencies. It is evident that the greatest increase took place during the Truman and Nixon Administrations. It also appears that President Ford is beginning to make good on his promise to reduce the presidential advisory system to a more manageable size.

Not only has the size of the institutionalized presidency differed across presidents, but so has its style and organizational complexion. Since presidents have wide latitude to revise these organizations by executive order, a considerable variety of configurations has developed.

Roosevelt set the tempo for presidential staffing arrangements by keeping a masterful hand in all executive branch activities. He developed a very loosely structured advisory system. It is biographer Arthur Schlesinger's view that while Roosevelt shared other presidents' distrust of bureaucracy, no president has surpassed his knowledge of the intricacies of departments and agencies. Roosevelt liked rivalry within his advisory system, which caused waste, but guaranteed retention of power in his hands.

Truman's organizational framework was more formal than his predecessor's and seems to have reflected a greater trust and utilization of the cabinet and bureaucracy. Like Eisenhower, his staff was less influential in presidential decision making than appears to have been the case with most other recent presidents.

The *Eisenhower* advisory system was very complex and hierarchical, with more clearly partitioned staff responsibilities than most other presidents have preferred. He had a passion for organization and utilized a large number of staff assistants to provide him with specific recommendations rather than a number of alternatives among which he could choose.

Kennedy utilized a relatively small, unstructured, and pragmatic personal staff as an instrument to control the bureaucracy as did Roosevelt, but he attempted to do so with less chaos. His staff was used more for initiating policy than has been the case with most other presidents. As President Ford has attempted to do, Kennedy had frequent communication with all senior aides.

structure of government

Like Eisenhower, *Johnson* relied more on the bureaucracy and Cabinet than did Kennedy and Roosevelt. And yet, he followed the Democratic penchant for more informal staffing arrangements. Johnson was more personally involved in policy formation than most presidents have chosen to be.

Nixon had the largest and most hierarchical personal staff of any president in history, with only a few senior aides having access to him. This arrangement provided him with the privacy and solitude he seemed to crave. The structure also reflected his preference for limited contact with others in government, and for written rather than oral communication.

The *Ford* style reflects the criticism of isolation and "palace guard government" directed at his predecessor. Ford's senior staff members all have access to him, and they appear to encompass a greater variety of viewpoints than was the case with the Nixon staff.

Presidents have found that there is probably no perfect staffing system and that each approach has its costs and benefits. In general, Democratic presidents have favored a relatively flexible White House bureaucracy; while Republicans, perhaps more concerned with order and efficiency, seem to have felt that a structured presidential establishment was necessary to coordinate the diverse executive branch.

Public policy is the end toward which many presidential and advisory activities are directed. Although advisors generally are not interested and involved in substantive policy or program concerns, there are three overall policy functions that do concern the presidential advisory system: policy initiation, policy advocacy, and policy implementation. While the line separating these activities is often blurred, the distinction is a useful way to understand executive responsibilities. Such functional compartmentalization includes both foreign and domestic policy considerations, and the continuing development of staffing arrangements has attempted especially to supplement the more limited presidential control in the latter realm.

Policy initiation refers to a relatively new presidential responsibility to formulate national programs and policies—a function that Congress seems increasingly unwilling or unable to perform. The president has a moderate amount of control over executive branch initiatives, and seeks to coordinate policies through organizations such as the Domestic Council, the National Security Council, the Council of Economic Advisors, and the Office of Management and Budget.

Policy advocacy is the process of promoting and communicating the president's wishes to others, both within and outside government. This responsibility was the first role performed by presidential staff, which seems increasingly to be moving into the other two policy areas as well. Such salesmanship is more commonly performed by personal rather than institutional advisors, and it appears to be the policy area over which the president has the greatest personal control. Policy advocacy is performed primarily by the White House office, including such activities as legislative and executive branch liaison, and press and public relations.

Policy implementation is the coordination and execution of specific presidential programs. While implementation of policy is the traditional function of the executive, it has also been the area that presidents and their advisors are least interested in, perhaps because it also appears to be least under their influence. In spite of the perception that implementation lacks glamor, presidents increasingly are adding advisors for specific policy areas, or using the Executive Office of the President to protect favored activities from "improper" bureaucratic implementation. There has also been a tendency for presidential agencies like OMB and the Domestic Council to be concerned increasingly with management as well as formulation functions. Perhaps this reflects a greater recognition that the presidential advisory system can exert influence in the entire gamut of the policy process, from policy formulation to policy execution. A brief profile of the major presidential institutions follows in terms of their policy roles.

The Domestic Council was established in 1970 to define national problems and propose a range of solutions in the domestic policy sphere. Patterned after the National Security Council, it attempts to clarify options for the president by setting national priorities formerly made by the Office of Management and Budget and the Cabinet. It performs the necessary and complex function of sorting out complex proposals from a myriad of agencies. The Domestic Council has undergone major changes in its organization and procedures during its short history. President Nixon developed the largest domestic staff ever in the somewhat ironic effort to reduce both expectations and realities in domestic policy. The association of its first director, John Ehrlichman, with the Watergate scandal corresponded with the diminution of its influence. President Ford has sought to reduce domestic programs even more, but he has broadened the mandate of the Council to what may have been envisioned originally by President Nixon. While the much smaller Domestic Council will likely be less a political force than it once was, it may expand its role in policy implementation through agency oversight.

Like the Domestic Council, the National Security Council (NSC) has a broad mandate to coordinate Cabinet-level policies (domestic, foreign, and military) as they relate to national security questions. Created in 1947, the NSC is more professional and less political than the Domestic Council. When Henry Kissinger was National Security Advisor under Presidents Nixon and Ford, the agency assumed for the first time in its history some responsibility for the implementation as well as the initiation of policy. It appears that the responsibility for the former function has waned since Kissinger relinquished directorship of the Council to continue as Secretary of State. Presidents have utilized the NSC in very different ways.

The Council of Economic Advisors (CEA) has the dual responsibility of reporting on the state of the economy to both Congress and the president. Like the Director of the OMB, its three members must be confirmed by the Senate. It is primarily a presidential institution, however, which provides the Chief Executive with position papers, and it began to take an active role in economic policy formulation during the Kennedy and Johnson administrations. The CEA has played a lesser role under Republican presidents, perhaps underscoring their dislike for government interference in the economy. The Council rarely met under Nixon and Ford, and both presidents relied much more heavily on other economic advisers.

Created in 1921, the Office of Management and Budget (OMB —formerly Bureau of the Budget) is the oldest institution in the presidential advisory system. Like the CEA, the OMB is also relied upon by Congress, and it has the closest relationship to Congress (especially committees) of any presidential institution. The OMB has long played a key role in policy formulation through central clearance and program development. Increasingly, however, the OMB has also been involved in policy management and it is probably the only presidential institution that recently has played a role in all three policy areas (initiation, advocacy, implementation). The reorganization to OMB in 1970 reflected President Nixon's desire to increase the management role of the agency in an effort to supervise the bureaucracy, in addition to its traditional responsibility of program and budgetary coordination. The impoundment policy and the agency's increasing politicization under the Nixon Administration brought the OMB considerable criticism. Opponents have charged that the agency has attempted too much and that its new management function should be deemphasized in favor of coordination. President Ford thus far has seemed to concur.

While the White House Office also shares some responsibility in policy formulation and initiation, its role is largely that of salesmanship. Although members of the White House Office are closer in physical proximity to the president than any other advisors, they often have been uninterested and uninvolved in substantive policy questions. Centralization of executive power with the president has also placed a good deal of influence in the hands of the White House Office, which is the president's private staff, and is often referred to by detractors as "gatekeepers" or "palace guards." Much of their time is spent on "image-building," ranging from extremely important issues to interpreting the First Lady's opinion on premarital sex and keeping the president up with Billy Graham on the list of most admired men.

The chief image-making organizations in the Ford White House are the Office of Communications headed by Press Secretary Ron Nessen and the White House Editorial Office directed by Robert Hartmann, the president's chief political officer. The Office of Communications under President Nixon was a large organization that attempted to coordinate information from throughout the executive branch as well as to respond to Watergate allegations. Ford's organization, with less than half as many employees, seems geared more toward informing than propagandizing. While the Office of Communications primarily informs the media and the public, the Editorial Office is responsible more for informing the president (via speeches and a daily news summary).

Beginning with Eisenhower and Kennedy, legislative liaison was recognized as a legitimate presidential function. Gradually congressmen have come to rely on such White House aides for information and the presidential perspective, while at the same time recognizing that such arrangements strengthen presidential leadership in agenda-setting. Although President Nixon and his aides seemed to distrust Congress, Presi-

TABLE 2
POLICY INFLUENCE OF PRESIDENTIAL ACTORS

Actor	Policy Area		
	Initiation	Advocacy	Implementation
President	+	++	
Vice President		+	
White House Office	+	++	
Domestic Council	++		
NSC	++		+(under Kissinger)
CEA	+		
OMB	++		+(since 1970)
Cabinet		+	+
Bureaus	+		++
Temporary Institutions	+		

Key: ++ = major role; + = moderate role; blank = minor role.

dent Ford has initiated more personal and direct contact with members of the House and Senate.

There are numerous other peripheral actors in presidential policy-making, including the vice president, the Cabinet, and temporary organizations such as task forces, commissions, and White House conferences. As with other advisors, their importance is determined by presidential personality, style, and preferences.

Although the role of vice president has varied widely, no vice president has emerged as a major advisor in presidential policy-making.

Cabinet officers serve as a bridge between the president and the permanent bureaucracy. In general, it has proven to be a difficult role as members try to reflect both perspectives. The Cabinet as a collective entity has not proven very useful to presidents as an advisory body, although individual members frequently have been important.

The temporary groups referred to above tend to be purely advisory and to focus on particular policy issues. Presidents have utilized these bodies for a variety of purposes, and while they normally are an extension of his influence, presidents have found that they are not always easy to influence, control, or ignore.

An impressionistic summary of the discussion of the influence of actors in the presidential policy process is presented in Table 2.

QUESTIONS ABOUT THE IMPACT OF THE INSTITUTIONALIZED PRESIDENCY

The growth of presidential staffing has accompanied a reduced White House dependence on departments. This may have its costs in discouraging qualified people in the bureaucracy from remaining in positions where they feel abused. White House aides have acquired power without corresponding accountability or responsibility, and overreliance on their perspectives may limit the ability of the president to choose among alternatives (as may have occurred under Presidents Eisenhower and Nixon). The president cannot rely too heavily on staff and still lead, as only he can provide both leadership and direction. Perhaps the most important consequence of institutionalization may have been a further widening of the gap between initiation and implementation, thereby reducing presidential control and prerogatives.

Institutionalization has been charged by some observers as having the unhealthy impact of leading to presidential insulation and isolation. The advisory system may be acquiring a bureaucratization that presidents find difficult to oversee. Staffing gives the president greater freedom of action but less control, as he may be unaware of the adviser's activities (at least Nixon so claimed). An atmosphere of infallibility may surround the White House, and according to former Nixon White House Chief of Staff, H. R. Haldeman, there is "an intoxication in the power laden White House atmosphere which affects the egos, judgments and perspectives of many of the people who work there." While presidents claim they desire independent-minded advisers, the role of "devil's advocate" may eventually come to be discouraged.

What factors might help the president avoid the dangers of isolation and assist him in maintaining contact with reality? He clearly needs outside information and to be aware of the danger of allowing one set of advisers to dominate his thinking. Kennedy attempted this through avid reading and through diverse contacts with a variety of people both in and out of government. The president needs advice from his Cabinet and bureaucracy, and perhaps a recognition of their natural adversary relationship with the White House staff will make him less likely to be suspect of their motives. He may not get complete loyalty from bureaucrats, but he should welcome their advocacy. Both the president and his staff should seek to maintain their perspective by keeping in touch with public and press opinion, by being sensitive to political realities, and by resisting (as put by former Johnson aide, George Reedy) the "temptation toward idolatry." Presidents should also recognize that a bigger staff is not necessarily a better one, and that their ability to accomplish major social change is likely to be limited.

central legislative clearance

by Robert S. Gilmour

From Robert S. Gilmour, "Central Legislative Clearance: A Revised Perspective," *Public Administration Review,* vol. 31 (March/April, 1971), pp. 150–158.

CENTRAL LEGISLATIVE CLEARANCE in the Executive Branch is widely regarded as one of the most powerful tools of the President. Under the aegis of the Office of Management and Budget (OMB, formerly the U.S. Bureau of the Budget) the hundreds of legislative proposals generated by federal departments, bureaus, and independent agencies are coordinated and reviewed to assess their acceptability as component parts of the presidential program. Here, many observers would argue, the substance of the congressional agenda is determined. Richard E. Neustadt's constantly cited history of central clearance describes legislative clearance as "by far the oldest, best intrenched, most thoroughly institutionalized of the President's coordinative instruments—always excepting the budget, itself. . . ." Others have reaffirmed the view that the President's program is arrived at primarily by Budget Bureau, now OMB, review of proposals "welling up" from the agencies.

While accepting the importance of centralized legislative advice within the Executive Branch, close students of presidential policy making have not always been enthusiastic about the results of this process. For example, Arthur Maass recorded his concern more than 15 years ago about Executive Office decision making through a process of "piecemeal review, rejection, and modification of individual proposals flowing up from the administrative units. . . ." More recently Norman Thomas and Harold Wolman have reported that even "Some participants in the policy process within the Executive Office of the President have contended . . . that this pattern has resulted in the adulteration of new ideas by internal bureaucratic considerations and clientele pressures exerted through the agencies."

During the 1960's, observers focused special attention on the academic community, presidential commissions, task forces, and the White House staff as the ascending stars of legislative initiation. One usually unstated but implicit conclusion is that these newer presidential agents significantly augmented or supplanted traditional Budget Bureau powers over central clearance and presidential program development. Indeed, there is considerable evidence that important aspects of legislative clearance have been recentralized in the White House staff during the Kennedy and Johnson presidencies.

These evaluations aside, there has been surprisingly little examination of the legislative clearance process—systematic or otherwise—on which to base a firm judgment.

Our purpose here will be to consider how legislation initiated by the Executive reaches the level of *central* clearance. What specific processes are involved and which actors figure most prominently at various stages in policy development? An attempt will be made, then, to reexamine the traditional conception of legislative proposals "welling up" from the bureaucracy for central clearance by the President's staff in the Executive Office.

Findings are based in part on interviews with career and political executives in eight of the 11 cabinet-rank departments and with officials in the Office of Management and Budget. Anonymity was offered all respondents, though some had no objection to being quoted or referred to as a source.

GROWTH OF LEGISLATIVE CLEARANCE

Development of presidential oversight of the legislative ideas and views of administrative agencies is usually associated with the Budget and Accounting Act of 1921, although no provision for central legislative clearance was contained in the Act, and there is certainly no record that Congress intended to invest the Executive with so powerful a tool in the legislative process. Ironically, it was the suggestion of a congressional committee chairman that, according to Richard Neustadt's sleuthing, "precipitated the first presidential effort to assert central control over agency views on proposed and pending legislation. . . ." A second irony was that the initial proclamation establishing the Bureau of the Budget as a legislative clearinghouse was issued and vigorously implemented by the generally "Whiggish" administration of Calvin Coolidge. As an economy move, Coolidge insisted on Budget Bureau approval of all legislation proposed by Executive agencies which committed the government to future expenditures. Budget Circular 49 required reports on pending fiscal legislation to be routed through the Bureau for the addition of BOB advice before they were submitted to Congress.

For reasons quite apart from those of Coolidge, President Franklin D. Roosevelt enlarged the scope of legislative clearance substantially. Acting on Roosevelt's instructions in 1935, Budget Director Daniel Bell required all agency proposals for legislation and advice on legislation pending to clear the Budget Bureau "for consideration by the President," before submission to Congress. Agency proposals subsequently sent to Congress were to include a statement that the "proposed legislation was or was not in accord with the President's program."

There is little question that the Budget Bureau took its expanded clearance role with utmost seriousness. Yet Budget apparently remained little more than a clearinghouse for sporadic, though numerous, agency proposals and reports on pending bills throughout the Roosevelt Administration. Neustadt credits "The custom of compiling formal agency programs as a preliminary stage in presidential program-making" to "White House requirements imposed . . . in the four years after World War II."

When the Republicans returned to power in 1953, the annual Budget call for departmental and agency programs initiated during the Truman Administration was continued without interruption. During mid-summer of 1953, President Eisenhower joined the Budget Bureau's call for legislative proposals in a personal letter "bearing signs of his own dictation" addressed to each cabinet officer. Neustadt notes that the cumulative response was "astonishing" to those members of the White House staff who either assumed or believed that Congress was the rightful place for legislative initiation. "For here were departmental declarations of intent to sponsor literally hundreds of measures great and small, *most of which the President was being asked to make his own by personal endorsement in a message.*"

In the present study, respondents whose experience extended to the Eisenhower period agreed that the Budget Bureau exercised extremely close supervision over Executive channels for legislative proposals. One suggested that it took the combination of CEA Chairman Arthur Burns and Secretary of the Treasury George Humphrey to end-play the Bureau in getting legislative proposals to the President. Similarly, others indicated it was easier to risk an end-run to Congress, skirting BOB authority.

During the 1960's, the Budget Bureau's veritable monopoly over Executive Branch legislation built up in the Eisenhower Administration appears to have eroded seriously. Nearly all "career" respondents having the perspective of relatively long tenure offered much the same view as one 30-year veteran: "Since the Kennedy Administration, the role of the White House in legislative clearance has been multiplied many times. White House staff members can operate at the highest level, hammering out programs directly with the Secretary. Sometimes during the Johnson Administration there was even direct communication between the White House and agency heads to develop legislative proposals."

Despite apparent changes in the relative importance of central clearance by the OMB, institutional procedures for agency submission of proposals and reports continue to operate much as they did in the Bureau of the Budget for more than 20 years. An examination of those procedures and processes should thus precede an evaluation of recent trends.

BUREAUCRATIC INITIATION

In the public mind, line bureaucrats appear to have been eclipsed as legislative innovators by presidential task forces and other outsiders to the traditional process. Nonetheless, in the business of elevating ideas as serious proposals and issues, bureaus remain well situated and prolific. To cite but one illustration, the Department of Housing and Urban Development alone proposes approximately 300 separate bills in the space of a single legislative year, most of which are initiated by the HUD bureaucracy. Although the great bulk of these proposals are "minor amendments" or bills of "middling importance," taken collectively they can hardly be ignored as the definers of larger policy.

Legislative drafting is a continuing activity in the agencies, but most bills are generated in a hurry-up response to the annual call for legislation. Budget Circular A-19 prompts agency action with the note that "annually proposed legislative programs for the forthcoming session of Congress . . . are to be used . . . in assisting the President in the preparation of his legislative program, annual and special messages, and the annual budget."

Not surprisingly, agency-initiated bills must run the gamut of clearance channels—in the sponsoring bureau and in the departmental hierarchy above—before the process is in any way centralized by the Office of Management and Budget. Each agency has its own routing procedure for legislative proposals, yet these will normally include critical reviews by finance officers, the agency planning units, and by line divisions of the agency which have a direct interest, depending upon the substance of each proposal. Typically, centralized responsibility for the coordination of agency bills is vested in a small staff such as the U.S. Forest Service Division of Legislative Liaison and Reporting. At a later stage, and with a fair assurance of departmental support, such bills are likely to be rendered as formal drafts by the agency's legislative counsel.

ASCENDING THE HIERARCHY

Assistant secretaries and their deputies in charge of designated line bureaus normally encourage their agencies—even the field offices—to send up ideas for legislative improvement. Successful efforts of this sort have the effect of maximizing supervisory control over agency submissions, making it possible for political executives to winnow out those proposals that they believe merit departmental support. The assistant secretaries also perform an important role as mediators in ironing out the inevitable differences among bureaus' plans for legislative enactment. And once they have formally approved an agency bill—offered by a bureau immediately subordinate—they may find themselves cast as negotiators with their departmental counterparts.

The legislative counsel (assistant or associate general counsel) of a department has strong potential influence over final clearance outcomes. He is characteristically not only a routing agent, but is also expected to offer advice on the language and general desirability of each proposal. Actual influence of this position varies greatly among departments canvassed. In departments such as Commerce and Treasury, which do not generate large numbers of bills, small legislative divisions occupy most of their time with the preparation of reports on bills pending in Congress, and principally serve an "editorial function" during the clearance process. In the action departments of the 1960's, legislative attorneys have played a much more vital role. Drafting of HEW bills, for example, has been centralized in the Division of Legislation. Clearance powers of the legislative counsel are even greater in Housing and Urban Development. Preparation of HUD's "omnibus package" of legislation involves both the collection of agency proposals and the sifting of ideas recommended by HUD's architectural, construction, housing, and mortgaging clientele groups. Associate General Counsel Hilbert Fefferman recalled, "We drafted major bills on model cities, rent supplements, FHA Title 10's 'new communities,' the College Housing Act, the Housing for the Elderly Act, and a good many others."

The general counsel in most departments is not only immediately superior to his legislative attorneys and, as one respondent described him, "the final arbiter for legal language," but he is also responsible for coordinating and compiling proposals and bills originating in the agencies. Some departments additionally rely on a program review committee for this purpose, but in any case the general counsel has substantial influence over the final shape of the department's legislative package. As an appointed official, however, and quite possibly a departmental newcomer, the general counsel can hardly help but place heavy reliance on the legislative counsel and other "career" subordinates.

In addition to the general counsel's office, other staff divisions of a department, especially the finance and planning divisions, may be consulted as a part of normal clearance procedure. Indeed, the OMB formally requires that an agency ". . . shall include in its letter transmitting proposed legislation or in its report on pending legislation its best estimate of the appropriations . . . which will be needed to carry out its responsibilities under the legislation." Budget officers are necessarily consulted when proposed legislation authorizes new departmental expenditures. Drafts may also be routed to departmental program planning officers, but this consultation appears often to be the exception rather than the rule.

Most departments have at least a pro forma routing of otherwise approved proposals across the desks of the secretary and his most immediate subordinates. It is understood that the secretary may intervene at any point during the process as an initiator, advocate, or veto agent, but the typical bill will not receive the secretary's or even the under secretary's personal attention. In effect, clearance of most departmentally generated legislative ideas takes place in the staff offices manned by career bureaucrats. "Political" oversight is largely exercised by the assistant secretaries and the general counsels. Of course the secretary and other high officials are likely to become deeply involved in clearance when this process takes the form of policy planning to develop major departmental or presidential program thrusts.

Most respondents indicated that the secretary also performs the roles of mediator and arbiter. One strategically placed observer in HEW remarked that the "settlement of disputes between assistant secretaries, career officials, or both is about the only way he can gain any real measure of control in this circus." Another, in HUD, recalled, "When Robert Weaver was Secretary during the Johnson Administration, he and Under Secretary Robert Wood held relatively frequent meetings to settle conflicts between assistant secretaries." If those differences were not "bargained out," then it was said that the Secretary or the Under Secretary "made the decision."

INTERDEPARTMENTAL CLEARANCE

Before reaching the Office of Management and Budget, there is often an interdepartmental phase in the clearance process that some consider to be as important as final OMB review. One respondent in Transportation explained, "Where there's a substantial outside interest in legislation that we're drafting, we generally clear it with other agencies before going to Management and Budget." Another in Justice held, "Usually you get things worked out without the necessity of OMB negotiations."

Apparently, the points of contact between departments vary with legislative complexity and with the relative importance attached to bills by their initiators, but most are made at the operating level—one agency to another. Liaison between departments on the few major, controversial bills is likely to take place at a higher level. As a legislative attorney in Transportation put it, "Of course, if the problem were significant enough, it would go to the secretarial level."

Consultation and coordination of agency and departmental positions are not in the least secretive or inappropriate. OMB guidelines actually encourage each agency:

> . . . to consult with other agencies concerned in order that all relevant interests and points of view may be considered and accommodated, where appropriate, in the formulation of the agency's position. Such consultation is particularly important in cases of overlapping interests, and intensive efforts should be made to reach inter-agency agreement before proposed legislation or reports are transmitted. . . .

The Office goes further to suggest that "Interagency committees and other arrangements for joint consultation may often be useful in reaching a common understanding."

In view of Management and Budget's limited staff—12 professionals—in its Division of Legislative Reference and the considerable technical complexity of many federal programs, OMB's formal encouragement of interdepartmental efforts to accommodate overlapping interests may be understood as a matter of practical necessity. Nonetheless, it's surprising that interdepartmental liaison in legislative policy making has drawn so little attention.

OMB CLEARANCE

Legislative proposals cleared in the departments and sent forward to Management and Budget in response to the annual call may be seized upon for translation to presidential prose and rushed to the drafting boards, or they may be shuffled to the files of good ideas in repose. In either case, formal clearance awaits the preparation of a draft bill submitted by the sponsoring department. These are typically sent separately, following the initial proposals by weeks or months.

When each draft arrives, OMB's Division of Legislative Reference assesses its general compatibility with the President's announced program and with current budgetary projections. In making these judgments, heavy reliance is placed on presidential messages, consultation with White House staff members, and perhaps direct communication between the Director and the President. "On the less important matters," as one assistant director admitted, "we rely primarily on the compromises that can be negotiated out among the departments and their respective agencies, these negotiations being within the general context of the President's objectives as he has stated them. In effect, a good portion of the President's program consists of the compromises that are struck here." Drafts deemed generally to be "in the right ballpark" are sent to the relevant line agencies for comments and deferred internally to the appropriate OMB program division where interagency negotiations over particular provisions will be held.

In dealing with each legislative proposal, Management and Budget has several alternatives. First, the Office may approve, stating with authority that the bill is "in accord with the program of the President," or appraising the bill "consistent with the objectives of the Administration," or noting feebly that there is "no objection from the standpoint of the Administration's program." Taking this option, OMB obviously offers varying degrees of support from strong backing to lukewarm tolerance. All the same, it here assumes a passive role which usually hinges on prior interdepartmental agreements, and it may be just those agreements that assure clearance at the lowest level of acceptance.

Secondly, Management and Budget may negotiate changes in a bill with the agencies immediately concerned to adjust differences. This course of action is much more commonly adopted, both as a means of resolving interdepartmental conflict and sometimes as a delaying tactic until a definite presidential position can be developed and enunciated. To reach agreement on points disputed in each bill, Legislative Reference may elect to act as a mediator or referee during formal meetings involving participants from departments and their agencies ranging from the assistant secretarial level downward. "The main task" of OMB, as one assistant director described it, "is that of persuading agencies to get together on proposed legislation, unless we hold strong independent views of our own. We suggest compromises and try to operate on a persuasive basis, but we stick to our guns in bargaining for the President's program."

On some occasions the OMB's efforts to "persuade" have been more direct, and the Office, as the Budget Bureau before it, takes the part of overt supervisor for legislative activities and pronouncements of line agencies. When negotiations were held over the Land and Water Conservation Fund in the early 1960's, for example, the Army Corps of Engineers and the Bureau of Reclamation (Interior Department) made known repeatedly their desire to be excluded from the Fund's provisions. One member of the OMB's staff recalled, "It was necessary for us to persuade the Corps and the Bureau of Reclamation to refrain from taking an official position against their inclusion under the new conservation law." A close observer in another agency remarked, "From where we sat, that 'persuasion' looked a good deal more like a firm command." However, respondents more often criticized Management and Budget's indecisiveness and apparent inability to "take a stand."

Performance of the Office's supervisory role may also take the form of its final alternative in the clearance process, an outright block of legislation under review causing permanent rejection or at least temporary delay. It is not at all uncommon for OMB to return an agency-sponsored bill indicating that it would not be in accord with the President's program. In the past this advice has occasionally been moderated with a notation that the offending bill would not be in accord "at this time" or "at least at this time."

Despite a firm prohibition against agency submission to Congress of bills which are held to be in conflict with the presidential program, it is well known that agencies frequently "get around" the confines of clearance procedures. This is accomplished through informal and nonofficial channels, most notably in the legislative drafting and information services agencies provide congressional committees and individual congressmen. Additionally, as one Budget officer expressed it:

> If an agency is dissatisfied with the outcome of our negotiations, it can quite easily arrange—and they often do—to have a congressman question them at the hearings in order to bring out that our office has made them water down the bill it wanted. Certainly the people I deal with play that game, but there are disadvantages as well as advantages involved.

By implication the prime disadvantage of this latter tactic, and apparently one that is well understood by the agencies, is the notion that OMB has a "long memory" for bureaus that repeatedly employ it. An agency must therefore weigh short-term tactical gains of a successful "end run" against longer-range objectives which may be jeopardized by opposition from Management and Budget in the future.

Continuing contact between OMB and line bureaus for general management, fiscal, and legislative matters is primarily maintained by the budget examiner assigned to each agency. The examiners have also become Budget and Management's chief mediators for interdepartmental disputes centering on their agencies' programs. Stalemate of interagency negotiations will, of course, receive the attention of an OMB division chief, an assistant director, or perhaps even the Director himself.

Traditionally, decisions of the Director "on behalf of the President" were understood to be final, or nearly so. After a contested ruling by the Director, an agency or department head was, in a formal sense, "always free to appeal to the President." But the success of this gambit was unlikely, and the logic of presidential denial in such cases seemed quite convincing. Former Budget Director Kermit Gordon has argued:

> If the President reverses his Budget Director fairly frequently, the latter's usefulness to the President will be gravely impaired if not destroyed, for it will have become evident that he has failed in his

effort to tune in on the President's wave length, and his desk will become only a temporary resting place for problems on the way to the President.

Nonetheless, there is mounting evidence that the pattern has changed. From the standpoint of increased influence, the White House staff appears to have been the prime beneficiary.

WHITE HOUSE INTERVENTION

Perhaps the best illustration is that of a young OMB examiner who explained to the writer, "I'll come to work and learn that 'There was a meeting at the White House last night, and it's all settled.' The bill I've been negotiating for weeks has been pulled up from the Office by the White House staff." It is quickly learned that this is not an isolated instance. High-level Management and Budget officers have had a role in these White House sessions, but OMB no longer has the monopoly claim on clearance decisions held by the Bureau of the Budget in the 1950's. Most of us were keenly aware of the strong legislative initiatives taken by the President and White House staff during the '60's, yet few students of administration noticed that the White House staff has directly intervened in central legislative clearance.

This change has been perceived by departmental and agency administrators throughout the Executive Branch. The opinion is widespread that the White House has taken over from Management and Budget on legislative matters of "any real importance." Said one respondent, "During the past ten years, especially, meetings have been called by the White House staff to hash out legislative agreements where the Department of Agriculture has been involved." The same point was made by others. In Transportation: "It is my experience that White House meetings to discuss our legislation have been called only after clearance by the Secretary. These meetings usually mean, then, that there is disagreement between our department and another." In HEW: "During the last five years there have been a great many meetings called by the White House to discuss our legislative items. The Nixon Administration hasn't changed that trend." A budget officer in Legislative Reference argues that the Nixon staff "has, if anything, been even more active in clearance than Johnson's or Kennedy's. The fact of the matter is that there are now many more men in the White House for this kind of work. They are better organized, and they have definite legislative and program assignments."

With this change there has apparently been a greater willingness on the parts of departmental officials to challenge the Budget Director. As one respondent put it, "There has got to be a way to go over the OMB on a regular basis without going directly to the President. There is. That's the White House staff. Ted Sorensen and Joe Califano, in the Kennedy and Johnson Administrations respectively, were constantly available to mediate and arbitrate between the secretary of a department and the Director of the Budget." In the Department of Transportation a respondent allowed "that the Office of Management and Budget still calls negotiations to iron out agreements on legislation, but once conflict over a bill escalates to the point that the Director becomes involved, the OMB is no longer in a position to act as a mediator. This is when the disagreement between parties is likely to be carried over to the White House." A Justice Department attorney in the early Nixon Administration stated flatly, "[Budget Director] Mayo doesn't overrule [Attorney General] Mitchell unless Mayo represents the President." Observations of this sort were volunteered in every department interviewed, and they were intended to apply to all three administrations of the '60's.

For Presidents Kennedy and Johnson, who wished to achieve a high level of legislative accomplishment, reliance on traditional initiatory and clearance procedures was understood to be inadequate. Neither President found that the bureaucracy could supply the ideas and advice needed for a major legislative program. William Carey reports, for example, that President Johnson "spent the better part of a year badgering the Budget Director to assign 'five of the best men you have' to drag advance information out of the agencies about impending decisions and actions so that he could preempt them and issue personal directives to carry them out, but the Budget Bureau never came anywhere near satisfying him because its own radar system was not tuned finely enough."

The answer to intelligence difficulties supplied by the Kennedy and Johnson Administrations was, in part, the establishment of congressional liaison offices operating closely with the secretary of each cabinet-rank department. It was reasoned that this machinery would highlight major policy questions and assist the President and the secretaries in dealing effectively with Congress. According to Russell Pipe's description:

> The Johnson Administration's legislative program has included many proposals affecting more than one Department. Liaison officers collaborate on such legislation to see that maximum effort is expended to promote the legislation. Omnibus bills require joint liaison ventures. In addition, personal friendships, political debts, and a kind of collegial relationship growing out of shared legislative skills bring liaison officers together to work on measures requiring all-out drives for passage. Thus, a network of liaison interaction has been created.

At the White House Joseph Califano's office became "a command post for directing the Great Society campaign, an operational center within the White House itself, the locus for marathon coffee-consuming sessions dedicated to knocking heads together and untangling jurisdictional and philosophical squabbles." Respondents in the departments indicated repeatedly that Califano was the presidential assistant who constantly "initiated negotiations," "called us in" for conferences, and "ironed out conflicts" among the agencies.

The Nixon Administration counterpart to Califano is Presidential Assistant John Ehrlichman, who has also become Executive Director of the newly established Domestic Council staff. The "Ehrlichman Operation" is considerably larger than any of its predecessors and, according to some informants, even more vigorous. The Domestic Council—functionally the cabinet without Defense and State Department components—was set in motion by President Nixon's Reorganization Plan No. 2 of 1970, and is intended to provide an "institutionally staffed group charged with advising the President on the total range of domestic policy." As yet Ehrlichman's staff shows no signs of becoming a career unit like the supporting staff of the National Security Council, but that is apparently what originators of the concept in the President's Advisory Council on Executive Organization have in mind for the future. With or without a careerist orientation, the Domestic Council staff under Ehrlichman has institutionalized the process of White House clearance for controversial or high-priority legislation beyond Management and Budget's Division of Legislative Reference.

The White House deadline is an additional structural device that has made an impact over the past decade and has had the effect of short-circuiting interdepartmental negotiations. A career attorney in Commerce commented, "It's not at all uncommon for legislative clearance to be greatly abbreviated because of short-fuse deadlines set by the White House, Management and Budget, or both." His counterpart in another department viewed this development as "unfortunate because it means that legislative outputs are uncoordinated and often drafted in a slipshod fashion."

Still others interpreted these deadlines as a means for agencies to avoid the rigors of interdepartmental bargaining. In HEW an experienced observer noted that deadlines have "more than once facilitated a shortcut in the clearance process." He went on to suggest:

> As a department strategy for approval of its bills, specific departments have dragged their feet until the eleventh hour. Thus when the draft went in from the line departments to the OMB there was virtually no time for Budget clearance, much less for a thoughtful and coherent response from other concerned departments. In the face of a firm White House deadline, the initiating department's proposal would earn the official blessing of the President as a reward for tardiness.

A respondent in Agriculture said, "Sometimes I think agencies wait until the deadline is upon them on purpose—so they won't have to consult and coordinate with other departments." Others added that deadlines imposed by the White House have been just as firm during the first year and a half of the Nixon Administration as they were under Johnson.

CONCLUSION

Of the approximately 16,000 bills annually processed by the Office of Management and Budget, probably 80 to 90 per cent do come "welling up" from the agencies to be cleared in the ascending hierarchy of career bureaucrats and political overseers in the line departments and finally to be negotiated by OMB and given a grade in the President's program. Treatment of the remaining bills, those singled out for special attention by the White House, provides the most striking change in central clearance during the past decade. All three Presidents of the '60's have short-circuited normal clearance channels to put a personal stamp on high-priority legislation. On crucial new programs, the White House has imposed strict deadlines for policy development, rushing Management and Budget coordination and allowing more discretion to individual departments. When OMB clearance negotiations have dragged or stalemated, the White House has not hesitated to intervene, dealing directly with departmental program managers. Indeed, this new process appears to have been institutionalized in the Domestic Council staff. At the same time, with the encouragement of the Budget Bureau and its successor, the Office of Management and Budget, line bureaucrats may have become their own best negotiators and mediators for clearance. The result, it appears, is a substantial challenge to OMB authority for central clearance from above and below.

legislative liaison: executive leadership in Congress

by Abraham Holtzman

reading 12

STRENGTHENING EXECUTIVE LEADERSHIP IN THE CONGRESS

IT IS CLEAR that the organization and upgrading of special legislative
liaison units represents a significant strengthening of the political executive in its relations with the Congress. In contrast to the deficiencies of
this political leadership as late as the 1940s and early 1950s, the necessary staff and the ability to mount concerted, well-organized campaigns
for legislation now exist in all the departments as well as the White
House.

In the departments, legislative liaison has won increasing recognition
as a key element in executive leadership. Its importance to the departmental secretaries is attested to by the fact that legislative liaison has been
differentiated from other dimensions of leadership, that special groups of
actors have been entrusted with this singular responsibility, and that they
hold positions of influence at the highest echelons of the departments. And
in the White House, recent Presidents have consistently relied upon legislative liaison agents so that they comprise today a vital unit in the President's personal staff.

Executive leadership is not merely a function of the policies, actions,
and personality of the departmental secretary or the President. Those
endowed with authority and responsible for leadership must have instruments for carrying out their policies. Leadership in large systems must be
institutionalized at various levels if it is to prove effective. Neustadt has
called attention to the fact that, while the President represents a tremendous source of power and influence, his leadership is dissipated and ne-

gated unless his decisions are carried through. The same holds true for departmental secretaries.

Legislative liaison agents provide these political leaders with specialized staff, actors who are concerned almost entirely with implementing their policies; who are experienced in relationships involving bargaining, compromise, and the aggregation of votes; and who are acutely sensitive to the problems and nature of the congressional actors. By filling such roles as adviser, spokesman, coordinator, intelligence agent, lobbyist, administration team player, and service expediter, liaison officers strengthen and carry out the leadership functions of the President and the departmental heads vis-à-vis the Congress. Since, moreover, the chief leaders of the executive are freed from the burdens of day-to-day relations with the Congress and afforded a superior, reliable source of advice and information, they gain by being able to concentrate upon the policy, strategy, and difficult problems concerning congressional relations. It must be assumed that they are also freed to devote themselves to their multifaceted administrative responsibilities.

Although executive lobbyists are not principally experts on substance and are not expected to serve as policy advisers, they do contribute to the development of realistic policy proposals. Substance and process are intimately related, especially in the Congress, where power is extremely fragmented. There, executive proposals are dependent upon a number of groups of actors and must proceed through a series of steps over a period of time. By speaking up within the inner circles of the departments and the White House on the substance of legislation as it is affected by the problems of the legislative process, the peculiarities of individual congressmen, and timing, liaison officers contribute to the policy proposals of their superiors. Bills may be altered and compromises advanced or rejected as a result of their advice and activity. Because they must pay attention to internal administrative decisions that have an impact upon the constituencies of congressmen and consequently upon the attitudes and behavior of legislative actors, the liaison agents affect another type of executive policymaking.

One danger is always present, of course, in allowing agents who process or sell policy to influence its nature. They may distort it by pressing too single-mindedly toward their own immediate goals of winning acceptance for the policy and keeping congressional relations from being exacerbated. Such a danger is inherent, however, in the design of all legislation, in packaging the proper mix of the desirable and the attainable. Moreover, any tendency on the part of liaison officers to overstress the practical side of winning can be resisted by other staff and senior members surrounding the executive leaders as well as by these leaders themselves.

The weakness of the Cabinet as a centripetal force in the executive system has long been recognized. Individual departments have traditionally made their own way in the Congress with little if any cooperation from the other departments or backup from the White House. To the extent that Presidents seek to shape a united administration behind policy and strategy determined at the highest political level, the liaison apparatus of the White House and of the departments are a great help. These actors have much in common so that cooperation is easy, White House and departmental resources supplement each other, and the departmental officers accept the superiority of White House priorities. The liaison apparatus contributes to the integration of the executive system in advancing its proposals to the Congress.

Effective executive leadership in shaping legislative policy is an absolute imperative for the proper functioning of the American national government. The President today has more effective means than ever before for mobilizing the leadership and resources of the executive system behind his program. How much further Presidents will proceed in this direction remains to be seen, but the structure has now been institutionalized and the practice established by which this can be accomplished.

STRENGTHENING EXECUTIVE LEADERSHIP IN RELATION TO THE BUREAUCRACY

The institutionalization of legislative liaison at the top levels of the departments and the White House signifies also a greater domination by executive leaders over the bureaucracy. Ensuring that the bureaucracy acts under the leadership of elected and politically responsible executive actors is a major problem in the modern democratic state. Liaison officers work to ensure that career administrators do not operate independently in the Congress, pursuing interests of their own in disregard of or contrary to the goals or strategies of the political leaders. The resources that bureaucrats command are also marshaled by liaison agents for the purposes of the political leadership. And the performance of bureaucratic actors is monitored to reduce the possibilities of antagonism between members of the legislative and executive systems.

Legislative liaison agents make a clear distinction between political leaders with whom they identify and career executive actors, a distinction that supports the thesis of those who suggest that the two represent different types. The interviews conducted with career administrators reinforce this conclusion. Patterns of cooperation and conflict appeared between both sets of actors in the Eisenhower and Kennedy Administrations. It is hypothesized that such patterns will continue in future administrations. Conflict should be minimal under a President and secretaries who sponsor ambitious legislative programs, since these are likely to coincide with the ambitions of the bureaucracy. Greater conflict may be expected when the executive leadership proposes extremely limited goals that it insists the bureaucracy support, and when the President and the majority of congressmen represent different parties.

The reaction of the Congress is always an uncertain and potentially dangerous restraint upon liaison officers' attempts to control bureaucrats in the interests of the departmental secretaries and the President. With regard to the Department of Defense, for example, congressmen have, through legislation as well as informal behavior, demanded that the services (bureaucrats) be free to pursue their own goals in relations with the Congress. Legislative actors insist, moreover, upon protecting their own pipelines into the bureaucracy. The instantaneous congressional reaction when State's Assistant Secretary for Congressional Relations sought to tap informal contacts between legislative and bureaucratic actors testifies to the congressional antagonisms that departmental political leaders face in attempting to maintain the boundaries of their own systems.

The close relationship that members of the House Appropriations Committee and the staffs of both Appropriations Committees maintain with special career officers in each department imposes another constraint upon the ability of the liaison officers to control the bureaucracy in its dealings with Congress. The extreme hostility of these legislative actors toward the departments' liaison officers reflects their reluctance to permit any interference in their special relations with the bureaucracy.

It is questionable, in view of the ambitions of bureaucratic actors and their support among congressmen and clientele groups, whether the political executive leadership could successfully displace bureaucrats in their special relations with the Congress, assuming it wished to do so. What is to be expected is that the liaison agents will constantly maneuver to place their superiors in the dominant position vis-à-vis the Congress and to enable them to take full advantage of ongoing bureau-congressional relations. The congressional response to these efforts needs to be studied further, as does the relationship between liaison and career actors and the means by which they solve their problems.

STRENGTHENING THE EXECUTIVE LEADERSHIP: OUTSIDE SUPPORT

The establishment of full-scale legislative liaison staffs has also strengthened the department heads by reorienting to their level the interests and activities of organized groups outside the national government. One of the principal defects in the department heads' relations with the Congress, according to Dr. John D. Millett of the 1949 Hoover Commission Task Force on Departmental Management, was the absence of any interest-group support in the Congress for the departmental position. As congressional relations within the departments have come increasingly under the control of the political head of the department, it is noteworthy that interest groups now find it to their advantage to work with and through this level of leadership. While the bureaucracy retains close ties with professional and clientele groups, political decisions of consequence that are made on programs and strategy are determined more and more at the level of the departmental secretary. To the extent that interest groups want to have a voice in departmental programs and relations with the Congress, they must address themselves to the levels where the decisions are ultimately made.

In a number of the departments the legislative liaison agent has become a focal point for rallying interest-group support for the departmental position and for marshaling the lobbying effort in which these groups can engage. And in the eyes of such groups, the liaison agent, who is one of the principal assistants to the secretary, becomes a very important channel to the secretary as well as to the rest of the department. The close relations between departmental and White House liaison units means, moreover, that the two sets of liaison agents afford interest groups extremely valuable access points for ascertaining executive decisions, for sharing in political intelligence, and for becoming involved in action patterns in the Congress. Interest groups now find it profitable to orient themselves to the departmental position in order to advance their own goals and operations in the legislative as well as the executive systems.

LOBBYISTS INSIDE AND OUTSIDE THE NATIONAL EXECUTIVE

Liaison agents for the departments and the White House may be compared to lobbyists for interest groups, public and private, that attempt to influence the policy outputs of the Congress. In many respects the two groups are similar: both represent political superiors and larger systems; both are employed to shape a favorable climate in which their leaders may interact with legislative actors; both are concerned with the legislative process and with policy output; both utilize somewhat similar stratagems and tactics.

Legislative actors consider both sets of lobbyists as representatives of groups whose interests have a legitimate right to be articulated in the legislative process. Congressmen and their staffs also perceive these lobbyists as functionally useful to themselves: service and collaboration are vital to legislative actors. Both lobbyists and legislative actors benefit, therefore, from an exchange of resources. At the same time, members of the legislature demand that lobbyists treat them with honesty and respect, and that they recognize the significance of the political situation in the legislators' constituencies and committees. Legislative actors can impose similar sanctions upon both sets of lobbyists: a withdrawal of trust and confidence and a denial of access. The legislators may also vote against their proposals and subject them to public attack. Both sets of lobbyists are keenly aware of the possibility of such sanctions, and shape their behavior accordingly.

The differences between the two sets of lobbyists and the differences in their relations with Congress are sufficient to suggest that executive lobbyists must be considered a distinct group. The two come from dissimilar backgrounds, liaison agents being much more partisan and more experienced in the Congress. In this respect the executive lobbyists are similar to the legislative actors, and the other lobbyists tend to be more like executive career administrators. Although both sets of lobbyists must also interact with executive actors, the liaison agents approach them as aides to the official leaders of the executive system, not as representatives of private groups. And, of course, as members of the official decision-making part of the executive system, the liaison agents are privy to matters not shared with lobbyists from groups outside the national government.

The relations that the two sets of lobbyists have with other actors within their own systems appear to differ markedly. Hence many of the opportunities, restraints, and problems that confront these lobbyists are dissimilar. However, these conclusions are advanced only provisionally. They need to be tested against data on liaison officers in future administrations. And before they can stand as valid, they must be supported by much more research than has yet been done on lobbyists for the private as well as public groups that seek to influence the decisions of the national government.

Liaison agents must cope with two sets of actors from within their own system—their political superiors and the bureaucrats whose attitudes and behavior have an important effect upon congressional relations. Congressmen are interested in and seek contacts with both sets of executive actors. Although this complicates tremendously the task of the executive lobbyists, it also affords them distinct advantages in dealing with the legislative system.

While the available research is meager and deals primarily with business groups and their lobbyists, it indicates that businessmen are more concerned with their businesses than with the politics of influencing government. They are involved only sporadically (and sometimes not at all) in trying to influence the Congress, and on the whole they find such politics distasteful. There is evidence, again scanty, that these leaders are somewhat contemptuous of the agents who lobby for them, and that the latter reciprocate this attitude. In other words, the close and cooperative relations that exist between most of the liaison officers and their superiors, their common recognition of the importance of dealing politically with the Congress (again with some exceptions), and the high degree of involvement of senior political executive actors in the Congress do not characterize the relations between the leaders of business and their lobbyists.

Secondly, the bureaucracy in the executive system at times constitutes a handicap for the legislative liaison officers with which other lobbyists, in all probability, do not have to contend. But this, too, calls for additional research. There has been virtually nothing published in this area. From what is known about institutional relations between subunits and their larger associations in agriculture, labor, and business, it is clear that the two differ often in their goals and politics. However, these associations are composed of more or less independent entities that may legitimately express their own self-interests politically, even if they diverge completely from those of their associations. The larger associations may be said to exist for their welfare and tend to be dependent upon the subunits for membership, funds, and support. These subunits are not bureaus, nor can they accurately be compared with them. Although bureaus and agencies—and even the service departments within Defense— have interests of their own, they are *supposed to subordinate themselves* to the broader general interest as defined by politically responsible leaders of the executive system. And of course they are not free to withdraw organically from the departments.

With regard to relations with Congress, the two sets of lobbyists differ on at least three major points. Congress specifically prohibits executive lobbying; it imposes only perfunctory regulations on lobbying by groups outside the boundaries of the national executive and legislative systems. True, the antilobbying law is honored only in the breach, and no prosecution of liaison officers has occurred or even appears likely as long as the leaders in one executive department, Justice, are responsible for prosecuting the leaders of other executive departments. Nevertheless, the liaison agents do feel somewhat inhibited in approaching Congress. Their counterparts in the outside interest groups may inundate Congress with their assistants, their allies, and their constituents; they may wine and dine the legislators. Executive lobbyists cannot directly employ such tactics. They recognize that Congress is jealous of its prerogatives as an independent and equal partner of the executive in the national government. Executive lobbyists are aware that the appearance in Congress of too many actors from their system is a source of irritation and resentment among legislators. The threshold of tolerance for executive intervention in the legislative process is much lower in this respect than for lobbyists representing outside groups. Nor do congressmen look favorably upon a massive lobbying effort by bureaucrats, whether they come from the capital or from the constituencies. On the other hand, constituents mobilized by outside interest groups are considered to be citizens and voters whom the legislators represent; the legitimacy of their appearance is unquestioned.

On another level, legislative liaison agents possess a tremendous advantage over the lobbyists for outside groups. As official members of the executive and representatives of its leaders, executive lobbyists, or their superiors or bureaucrats, are often permitted entrée into the executive sessions of the committees that work on legislation. Affording such access to private lobbyists is considered unethical and rarely occurs. Hence the liaison officers are in better position vis-à-vis the most important decision-making centers of the Congress to observe, obtain information, work out accommodations, and speak for their principals while a bill is still in the process of being shaped by the legislators.

Executive lobbyists and those from outside the national government differ also in their emphasis on and identification with partisanship. Since political party is treated separately, all that needs to be noted here is that outside lobbyists avoid partisan positions and identification. They want to work with all members regardless of party, and they represent groups that with one or two exceptions avoid an official identification with the campaigns or candidates of any of the political parties. These groups have members from both major parties. State and Defense are the departments that most closely approximate the nonpartisan approach of the other interest groups and lobbyists. Both of these departments seek bipartisan support and avoid playing partisan politics in committee. Nevertheless, some of the senior political leaders of Defense in the Kennedy Administration were utilized on partisan issues, and the tremendous resources of Defense were marshaled by White House lobbyists in support of their partisan politics.

POLITICAL PARTY AND THE
SEPARATION OF POWERS

Leon P. Epstein has pointed to the separation of powers in the American national government as "the crucial circumstance" in explaining non-cohesive congressional parties. The separation of executive and legislative actors into distinct systems also divides each of our major national political parties into two congressional parties, and it fragments one national party further by establishing in it an executive party. Assuming the Congress and the presidency are controlled by members from the same national party, the latter is composed of three different organizations with separate sets of leaders and intelligence apparatuses. Moreover, the separation of powers imposes a great strain upon cooperation between leaders and members of the legislative parties and the executive leaders of the same national party.

The President, as the official national leader of his party, is able to call upon his partisan legislative leaders for collaboration, a relationship functionally useful for both. He can also depend, to a large extent, upon ties of common party identification and a sense of obligation on the part of congressional leaders from his party to support him as the head of their party. To a lesser extent the rank and file among his fellow partisans in the Congress also feel the tug of common party ties.

It is necessary to perceive the legislative liaison agents for the President and for the secretaries of his departments as additional links between executive and legislative partisans. Hence, at another level of executive-legislative relations, linkages between partisans are strengthened and institutionalized. In effect, therefore, the new executive lobbyists help ameliorate the divisive impact of the separation of powers upon a political party, and their partisan identification with congressional leaders and their followers facilitates executive involvement in the legislative system.

Congressmen from both national parties consider lobbying by the President and his representatives legitimate. Legislators recognize that executive intervention and leadership are necessary for themselves as well as for the chief executive and his associates. Nevertheless, partisanship on the part of executive lobbyists can be either dysfunctional or functional, depending upon whether both systems are controlled by actors from the same national party or whether one party dominates the executive but not the Congress. In the latter case, liaison agents are handicapped, since they are identified by the leaders of the congressional majority party as representatives of the head of the opposite party and his colleagues. This does not mean that cooperation is impossible, but it does mean that the degree of entrée is restricted, a trust-confidence relationship is not fully developed, and collaborative endeavors are reduced to a minimum. While liaison agents in the White House and the departments (always with a few exceptions) feel closer to the members and leaders of their parties in the Congress, when the latter are in the minority they do not control the scheduling of legislation and they do not occupy the official leadership positions in the committees. Moreover, there is some evidence from the Eisenhower Administration, whose actors faced such a situation for six years, that with different parties in control of the Congress and the executive, the liaison agents felt more restrained in lobbying the Congress.

Criticism of executive lobbying emanates almost entirely from legislators whose party does not control the White House. When such members make up a majority in the Congress and control the Speaker, the majority leaders, and the committees, the dangers inherent in such criticism loom very large for the executive lobbyists. They need cooperation from the leaders of the majority party and a congenial atmosphere in which to deflect investigations and attacks. If it is the minority members who publicly complain about lobbying by executive actors whose administration their party does not control, the liaison agents may be temporarily embarrassed, but little else. The force of such accusations tends to be blurred by the fact that they come from members of the opposite party; legislators identified with the executive party tend to discount such charges as part of the normal course of partisan politics.

On the whole, legislative liaison agents in the White House and the departments have a strong background of political party activity and identification, as do legislative actors. The heads of the departments, unlike the official heads of private interest groups, either are experienced party leaders in their own right or are identified with the partisan administration of the President, who is the chief leader of his party in the nation. When their executive lobbyists approach the Speaker, the majority leaders, the whips, and the committee chairmen from the same party, they are contacting fellow partisans who share their attitudes and expectations. The legislative party leaders have already participated with the President in his weekly leadership meetings, at which program, strategy, and tactics are discussed.

The legislative liaison actors cooperate with these legislative leaders on strategy and tactics. The offices of the legislative leaders from their party are made available to executive lobbyists for more immediate lobbying with members before votes are taken, and the two intelligence networks mesh into each other freely, for both represent common leaders and both are actors in the same national party. In the case of the liaison unit in the Kennedy White House, efforts were also made to utilize state and local party leaders in lining up support for the President's legislation among fellow partisans in the Congress.

ADDITIONAL ASPECTS OF THE FUNCTIONAL UTILITY OF LIAISON AGENTS FOR THE DEMOCRATIC SYSTEM

In an essay on the future of legislative systems, David B. Truman raises the question whether, in the shift of legislation as a function away from national legislative bodies to bureaucracies, something essential to a system based upon universal suffrage may not be jeopardized. He suggests that administrators may be engaged in a different kind of political activity than are elected politicians, that the roles, skills, attitudes, and perceptions of the two may be dissimilar. The contribution of the elected politician to policy-making, assessing the proposals of substantive experts and reconciling them "with the feasibility that exists or can be created in the electorate," may be lost to the system. "It is the primacy of aggregate politics and its functionality for the system that may be at stake."

The better the staff that the political leadership of the executive system has at its disposal to direct bureaucratic actors on behalf of its goals and priorities, the smaller the likelihood that the skills, attitudes, and perceptions of elected politicians will be separated from the legislative function. The President himself is an elected politician, whose elevation to and continuance in office is premised upon his success in aggregate politics within the national electorate. His immediate staff and his associate leaders, who preside over the bureaucracies in each of the departments, are in many cases former elected politicians themselves or have been actively engaged in the winning of nominations and elections for others. The legislative liaison officers in the White House and the departments during the Kennedy Administration and many in the Eisenhower Administration represented this type of political actor. They helped sensitize their leaders to the needs of the elected politician in the legislature and they shared in mobilizing legislative majorities behind executive bills. They recognized, moreover, the problems of aggregate politics facing the President, both in marshaling public opinion behind his program and in assessing possibilities for the next election campaign.

While the legislative function may be shifting to the executive, it has not moved entirely to bureaucratic actors. The bureaucracy continues to be a source for many executive proposals to the Congress, but the goals and strategies are primarily those of the chief executive, his advisers, and his subleaders. Members of the White House staff think in the terms of the elected politician, and so do many Cabinet members and their assistants. As one group of assistants to the President and the secretaries of the departments, the liaison agents strengthen the number and influence of actors who are more similar to elected politicians in background and attitudes than to bureaucrats.

Political science must be concerned with the important question "Does it make any difference who governs?" Different ends are pursued and different groups represented when disparate groups of leaders contribute to the making of policy. By strengthening the senior political leadership of the executive system vis-à-vis both the Congress and the bureaucracy, the executive lobbyists contribute to a more unified central party. Thus they afford those groups—latent and organized—who associate their interests with the policy ends of the President and his leadership advantageous positions regarding policy. In other words, different groups are advantaged in the decision-making process of the national government and in its allocation of resources as a result of the strengthening of the President and his political associates.

Not only do the liaison officers deal directly in many cases with lobbyists from outside groups, but outside lobbyists seek them out as a point of access to the chiefs of the executive system and for collaborative endeavors in the Congress. The legislative liaison agents help also in reconciling the more parochial interests of the legislators and the narrow professionalism or clientele interests of the bureaucratic actors with the broader, more general set of interests represented by the elected leader of the executive system and his chief associates.

III B
the bureaucracy

Bureaucracies, both governmental and nongovernmental, impinge on many facets of our daily lives. Whether we are mailing a letter, filing an insurance claim, protesting a parking ticket, buying food, or requesting a Social Security pension, we must make our desires and actions conform to the routines and requirements of the particular bureaucracy involved—the Post Office, the insurance company, the Police Department, the grocery store, the Social Security Administration. Bureaucracies are a useful means of organizing human behavior, and they are apparently with us to stay; governmental bureaucracy especially is inevitable when a society has decided to provide services to its public.

Perhaps because we Americans have become more conscious of the pervasiveness of bureaucracies in our lives, and because we are suspicious of largeness *per se,* and because we sometimes feel like we are losing control of our lives to impersonal bureaucratic routines, the popular image of bureaucracies has not been a kind one. Mention "bureaucrat" or "bureacracy" and the connotation is of a faceless civil servant, a nonperson who is unambitious, conservative and content with the status quo, who specializes in red tape, confusion, and delay, and whose agency seems incapable of making a timely decision. However, a recent survey of public services and attitudes towards those services conducted by individuals at the University of Michigan suggests that, on the basis of their own personal concrete experiences, most people have a very good impression of bureaucracy and bureaucrats, but in the abstract they still think of them in negative terms. Thus bureaucracies may be doing a better job than they get credit for, but the old negative images may be a long time in dying.

Certain characteristics of governmental bureaucracy contribute to the poor image. Government is large—the national government alone had nearly 2.5 million civilian employees in 1976 and another 2.1 million in the military services—and it is complex—there are departments, bureaus, agencies, commissions and committees, each with its own hierarchical organization, formal and informal layers of authority, channels of communication, and patterns of decision making. These organizations are spread throughout Washington and state and local sites, and they implement (and make) policy in a vast range of issue areas. The president is only the nominal head of this enterprise—in no sense does he "control" it. Naturally, as the number of persons whose actions must be coordinated and supervised increases, so does the opportunity for duplication, confusion, and noncoordination. It is no surprise to learn of different government agencies doing the same thing, or living on after their original missions have been served, or sometimes working at cross purposes to each other.

The fragmented, special-purpose orientation of bureaucratic administration reflects the special interest nature of Congress, which in turn is a result of the particularistic nature of representative democracy. Another characteristic of governmental bureaucracies is that most civilian employees of the government are protected from the winds of political change in the presidency and Congress by the civil service system which replaced political patronage in the late 1800's as the chief means of gaining entry into government service. Although this protection has helped prevent massive, politically motivated shifts in personnel at periodic intervals, and although it has helped to build professionalism and expertise within the civil service, it also has the drawback of engendering a certain lassitude or complacence about job security that is detrimental to fresh thinking and innovative problem solution.

There are many policy consequences of government by bureaucracy (some of them are hinted at in the above paragraph), but we will address only four broad ones here and in the readings: administrative decision making and politicization of the bureaucracy; autonomy versus control of the bureaucracy; the importance of budgeting; and the predictability of bureaucratic behavior.

Formally, the bureaucracy evolved in order to administer policies that Congress had legislated. In practice, there is considerable policy-making by the agencies themselves through administrative decision making. This takes several forms. First, Congress lacks sufficient technical knowledge and time to write intricately detailed legislation spelling out just how a program should work, so it writes a general law and delegates authority to the administrative agency to operate the program within general guidelines. Thus most domestic agencies publish program regulations periodically in the *Federal Register* for public circulation and comment, and these rules and regulations comprise the written operating code for the program. But even this code is not detailed enough to anticipate all occurrences that might arise, and it often contains vague definitions. Thus, in day-to-day program operations bureaucrats have latitude to make personal judgments and interpretations of an informal (unwritten) nature that may constitute policy decisions. In addition to these written and unwritten decisions, most regulatory agencies are intimately involved in independently making rules and regulations that affect the public and in settling disputes between competing private interests or between private and public interests.

The stuff of administrative decisions and politics is inextricably linked. Who gets a television station license? Should a field office be closed? Where should a dam be built? These kinds of decisions all involve a winners or losers situation, where there is competition for a (presumably limited) resource. And given this competition, bureaus face many pressures to make their decisions favorable to some affected interest. Thus the process and outcome of administrative decisions (including how agencies dispense their tangible resources) is one way agencies become politicized. Another way concerns the resources that an agency can bring to bear on other actors to increase its own power, for example, by stimulating pressure from the general public, pressure from special interest groups, or pressure from other parts of the government. Elizabeth Drew in reading 13 depicts the power of the Army Corps of Engineers, a highly powerful agency with strong political allies and a rich pot of benefits to distribute, both of which contribute to its success and its politicization.

Despite the Hatch Act (which prohibits many partisan political activities by civil servants), despite the civil service, despite the textbook image of an apolitical administrator, bureaucrats are not neutral. The decisions they make daily are political in nature. Thus it becomes important to ask about the personal attitudes of these semi-permanent, non-elected bureaucrats who administer and make policy. What do they believe in? How do they view the world? What are their attitudes about democracy? What factors influence their thinking and outlook? This is exactly the inquiry pursued by Wynia in his article (reading 14), in which he finds that overall, bureaucrats are fairly tolerant, but their outlook depends on agency affiliation, years of formal education, and length of service in the bureaucracy.

Who controls the bureaucracy? Bureaucrats themselves operate under a variety of influences—their personal background and training, the formal and informal norms within the agency, the political context of the agency and the issue—as the preceding paragraphs make clear. Institutionally, there are several possible points of control and influence. We said earlier the president doesn't control the bureaucracy in a cause and effect sense. This is because he is confronted with a built-in system of semi-permanent employees—he himself makes fewer than 2,500 (political) appointments. Naturally bureaucrats owe allegiance to the president, but they also have allegiances to their agency, to their programs, to themselves.

The public doesn't really control the bureaucracy, at least not directly, since bureaucrats are not an elected group. There is indirect control in the sense that bureaucrats are recruited from the public and thus may reflect important cultural norms. There is control of a sort (or at least shared interests) from special publics who are allied with government agencies (the agencies' clients).

Congress doesn't really control the bureaucracy, although it is ultimately responsible for the care and feeding of the bureaucracy through the appropriations process. There is a close working relationship between agencies and "their" congressional committees that promotes cooperation and only gradual policy change, and discourages vigorous scrutiny of program operations. Although Congress is involved with agencies in many ways (appropriations, authorizations, confirmations, hearing, oversight), there is no way for it to get a handle on the whole bureaucracy because the congressional involvement is itself fragmented and decentralized.

In sum, the bureaucracy is not fully subordinate to any branch of government. It is a semi-autonomous phenomenon. The article by Drew illustrates how and why one agency, the Corps of Engineers, is autonomous—and successful.

Budgeting is an essential component of governmental bureaucracy, perhaps the most important routine a bureaucracy engages in. For without a budget an agency cannot plan, it cannot hire, it cannot build facilities, it cannot distribute, regulate, or redistribute things of value —in short, it cannot exist. The annual federal budget is a huge document that identifies the various program priorities of the government for the forthcoming fiscal year. The allocations recommended in the budget may be altered by Congress, but basically they set the boundaries within which agency officials must operate their programs. Le-Loup, in reading 15, discusses various aspects of the federal budget, including incremental budgeting and uncontrollability of the budget.

The final reading (16) in this section, by Bernstein, describes phases in the life of regulatory agencies, but the generalizations are applicable to many bureaucracies. The article suggests not only that agency behavior is often predictable at different times and under different conditions, but also that the close working relationship between many agencies and their clientele is often detrimental to agency policy-making when viewed from a public interest perspective.

dam outrage:
the story
of the
Army Engineers

reading

13

by
Elizabeth B. Drew

From Elizabeth B. Drew, "Dam Outrage: The Story of the Army Engineers," *Atlantic* (April, 1970), pp. 51–56, 61–62.

. . . FEW POLITICIANS publicly criticize the Corps, because almost all of them
want something from it at some point—a dam, a harbor, a flood-control
project. A combination of Corps diplomacy and congressional mutuality
keeps most of the politicians content, and quiet. The overwhelming
majority of Corps projects are attractive federal bonuses, given free of
charge to communities—some local contributions may be involved in small
flood-control or municipal-water-supply projects—and therefore they are
highly prized. "They take care of all of the states," said one Senate aide.
"If there's water in a faucet in one of them, they'll go in there and build
a dam."

There is no question that the civil works program of the Army Corps
of Engineers, viewed over its long history, has benefited the country. It
has made waterways navigable and provided hydroelectric power and
flood control. Communities to which it has brought help have been genuinely grateful. Now, however, it is a prime example of a bureaucracy that
is outliving its rationale, and that is what is getting it into trouble. As the
Corps, impelled by bureaucratic momentum and political accommodation,
has gone about its damming and dredging and "straightening" of rivers
and streams, it has brought down upon itself the wrath of more and more
people disturbed about the effects on the environment. A secret poll taken
by the White House last year showed environmental concerns to be second
only to Vietnam in the public mind. This rather sudden general awareness
of the science of ecology—the interrelationships between organisms and
their environment—has brought projects which disturb the environment
and the ecology, as Corps projects do, under unprecedented attack. The
Corps' philosophy, on the other hand, was recently expressed in a speech

by its chief, Lieutenant General F. J. Clarke. "With our country growing the way it is," he said, "we cannot simply sit back and let nature take its course.". . .

The major activities of the Corps are the damming, widening, straightening, and deepening of rivers for barge navigation, building harbors for shipping, and construction of dams and levees and reservoirs for flood control. It also works on disaster relief and tries to prevent beach erosion. A project can serve several purposes: building waterways, providing flood control, hydroelectric power, or water supply. As the Corps completed the most clearly needed projects in these categories, it found new purposes, or rationales, for its dams. The newer justifications are recreation and pollution treatment. . . .

[T]he military men in the civil works section of the Army Corps of Engineers represent only a thin superstructure over a large civilian bureaucracy. . . . The civil works section of the Corps . . . comprises about 200 military men, and under their direction, 32,000 civilians.

Generally, the career military engineers come from the top of their class at West Point, or from engineering schools. . . .

The civilian bureaucracy is something else. The Corps, like other government agencies, does not attract the brightest civilian engineering graduates, for it does not offer either the most lucrative or the most interesting engineering careers. . . .

The military patina gives the Corps its professional aura, its local popularity, its political success, and its independence. The military engineers are, as a group, polite, calm, and efficient, and their uniforms impress the politicians and the local citizens. The engineer who heads one of the Corps' forty district offices, usually a colonel, is a big man in his area; the newspapers herald his coming, and he is a star speaker at the Chamber of Commerce and Rotary lunches. But the military man gets transferred, so smart money also befriends the civilian officials in the district office. These men stay in the area, and want to see it progress. The Tulsa office of the Corps, for example, has about 1500 employees, of whom only three are military. The local offices are highly autonomous, for the Corps operates by the military principles that you never give a man an order he can't carry out, and that you trust your field commanders. If a district engineer believes strongly in a project, it is likely to get Corps endorsement. The Corps has mastered the art of convincing people that its projects are desirable, and so the projects are not examined very closely. Corps engineers are impressive in their command of details that non-engineers cannot understand, assiduous in publishing books that show what the Corps has done for each state, and punctilious about seeing that all the right politicians are invited to each dedication of a dam.

And so the Army Corps of Engineers has become one of the most independent bureaucracies in the federal government. The Corps' civil works section is neither of great interest to the Pentagon nor answerable to more relevant civilian bureaucracies. It makes its own living arrangements with the Congress, and deals not with the Armed Services Committees of the House and Senate, but with the Public Works Committees.

Theoretically, the Corps reports to the appointed civilian chiefs of the Department of the Army, but these men are usually preoccupied with more urgent matters than Corps projects, and after a spell of trying to figure out what the Corps is doing, or even to control it, the civilians usually give up. . . .

The power of the Corps stems from its relationships with Congress. It is the pet of the men from the areas it has helped the most, who also usually happen to be among the most senior and powerful members, and the ones on the committees which give the Corps its authority and its money. . . .

The legislation that authorizes and appropriates the money for Corps projects encourages manipulation and swapping because of the unusual way in which it parcels out the money on a project-by-project basis. It is as if a housing bill had designated X dollars for a development here and Y dollars for a development there.

A very formal document—known around Capitol Hill as "eighteen steps to glory"—explains the procedures by which a project is initiated. In actuality, what happens is that local interests who stand to gain from a Corps project—barge companies, industrialists, contractors, real estate speculators—get together, often through the Chamber of Commerce, with the district engineer and ask for a project. The Corps literature is quite explicit about this: "When local interests feel that a need exists for any type of flood control, navigation, or other improvement, it will be most profitable for them to consult at the outset with the District Engineer. He will provide full information as to what might be done to solve their particular problem, the authorities under which it might be accomplished, and the procedures necessary to initiate the action desired." Then the local groups ask their congressman, who is responsive to this particular segment of his constituency, to secure legislation authorizing the Corps to make a study of the project. Usually the Corps man is already aboard, but if not, he is not very far behind. "Sometimes," said a congressman who, like most of his colleagues, declined to be named when talking about the Corps, "the Chamber of Commerce will call me, and I'll say get in touch with Colonel So-and-so in the district office and he's over there like a shot; or the Corps will make an area survey and go to the community and drop hints that they might have a dam if they work on it." Frequently the project's promoters will form a group—the Mississippi Valley Association, the Tennessee-Tombigbee Association, the Arkansas Basin Development Association, and so on. The Florida Waterways Association, for example, boosters of the controversial Cross-Florida Barge Canal, has among its directors a realtor, representatives of a consulting engineering company, a dredging company, chambers of commerce, port authorities, newspapers, and a construction company. The associations meet and entertain and lobby. The Lower Mississippi Valley Association is noted for its days-long barge parties. Some twenty- to thirty-odd people from an association descend on Washington from time to time, to testify and to see the right people in Congress and the Executive Branch.

The power to authorize the study of a project, then to initiate it, and to appropriate the money for it is held by the Senate and House Public Works Committees, and by the Public Works Subcommittees of the Appropriations Committees of the two bodies. This is a total of seventy-one men; as is usual with congressional committees, a very few of the most senior men wield the key influence. It all comes down to a chess game played by the same players over the years—the committees, their staffs, and the Corps. There are always demands for more projects than can be studied, authorized, or financed, and so the Corps and the politicians are always in a position to do each other favors. One study can be moved ahead of another by the Corps if a man votes correctly. One project can get priority in the authorizing or appropriating stages. "Everyone is in everyone else's thrall," said a man who has been involved in the process, "unless he never wants a project."

The Corps has managed to arbitrate the demands for more projects than its budget can include through its highly developed sense of the relative political strengths within the Congress, and by making sure that each region of the country gets a little something each time. . . . The Secretary of the Army rarely changes the Corps' proposals. The Budget Bureau does examine the Corps' proposals on a project-by-project basis, but it runs a poor third to the Corps and Capitol Hill in deciding what the Corps program should be. The President, who is but a passerby, cannot establish control over the public works process unless he decides to make the kind of major political fight that Presidents usually do not think is worth it. On occasion, the White House will oppose a particularly outrageous project—or, out of political exigency, support one. Outsiders are unable to penetrate the continuing feedback between the Corps and the congressional committees, and are insufficiently informed to examine the rationale, the nature, and the alternatives of each project.

There may have been a Corps of Engineers project that was rejected on the floor of Congress, but no one can recall it. Every two years—in election years—a rivers and harbors and flood-control authorization bill is passed by Congress, and every year, money is appropriated. It has been calculated that, on the average, the authorization bills have provided something for 113 congressional districts (or more than one fourth of the House of Representatives) at a time, and the appropriations bills for 91 districts. "We used to say," said a man involved in the process, "that we could put our mortgage in that bill and no one would notice, and then the appropriations committees would cut it by 15 percent." The most recent appropriation carried something for 48 states. On occasion, a senator, Paul Douglas of Illinois for one, or William Proxmire of Wisconsin for another, has spoken out against a particular Corps project, or the "pork-barrel" technique of legislating Corps projects, but they have not been taken seriously. . . .

Douglas fought rivers and harbors projects for years and then, in 1956, made a speech saying that he was giving up. "I think it is almost hopeless," he said, "for any senator to try to do what I tried to do when I first came to this body, namely, to consider these projects one by one. The bill is built up out of a whole system of mutual accommodations, in which the favors are widely distributed, with the implicit promise that no one will kick over the applecart; that if senators do not object to the bill as a whole, they will 'get theirs.' It is a process, if I may use an inelegant expression, of mutual back scratching and mutual logrolling. Any member who tries to buck the system is confronted with an impossible amount of work in trying to ascertain the relative merits of a given project."

The difficulty in understanding what a given Corps project will do, and what its merits are, comes not from a lack of material supplied by the Corps, but from an overabundance of it. A Corps report on a proposed project—the result of a survey that may take three to five years—is a shelf-long collection of volumes of technical material. Opponents of the project are on the defensive and unequipped to respond in kind.

Most of the projects that Congress asks the Corps to survey are, of course, turned down, because a congressman will pass along a request for a survey of almost anything. By the time a project moves through the Corps' bureaucracy to the Board of Engineers for Rivers and Harbors in Washington—what the Corps calls an "independent review group"—it has a promising future. The Board is made up of the Corps' various division engineers, who present their own projects and have learned to trust each other's judgment.

The supposedly objective standard for deciding whether a project is worthy of approval is the "benefit-to-cost" ratio. The potential benefits of a project are measured against the estimated costs, and the resulting ratio must be at least one-to-one—that is, one dollar of benefit for each dollar spent (the Corps prefers the term "invested")—to qualify. There is, however, considerable flexibility in the process, and at times the benefit-cost ratios of controversial projects are recomputed until they come out right. This was true of the Trinity River project to make Fort Worth a seaport, the Cross-Florida Barge Canal, and projects along the Potomac River. "There is enough room in the benefit-cost ratio," said a man who has worked with the Corps on Capitol Hill, "for the Corps to be responsive to strong members of Congress who really want a project." It has been remarked that the measurements are pliant enough to prove the feasibility of growing bananas on Pikes Peak.

There is much argument over the Corps' method of arriving at prospective benefits. For example, business that might be drawn by a project is considered among the benefits, even though there is no real way of knowing what business the project will attract and what the effects will be. The lower prices to a shipper of sending his goods by barge rather than by rail is also considered a national benefit; such a benefit may involve the fact that a wheat farmer is growing and shipping more wheat because of the lower prices, even though we do not need the wheat. The windfalls to real estate investors who have been lucky or clever enough to have bought inexpensive land—some of it underwater—in the path of a future project can turn up as a boon to us all in the form of "enhanced land values." The land, which can then be sold and developed for industrial, housing, or resort development, undergoes extraordinary value increases. . . .

Since more projects are authorized than are given money to be begun, hundreds of them lie around for years, forgotten by all but the sponsors, or the sponsors' sons, and the Corps. If a project becomes too controversial, its backers can simply outwait the opponents. When old projects, sometimes thirty years old, are dusted off, they may be started without reconsideration of either the original purposes or the benefits and costs.

Once a project is begun, its costs almost invariably outrun the estimates. Project proponents, on the other hand, argue that the benefits are consistently underestimated. The Corps is very sensitive about cost "overruns." They say that one must keep inflation in mind, and that such projects get changed and enlarged as they go along. Such changes, undermining the original benefit-cost rationale, do not seem to trouble the Congress. The Trinity River project, estimated at $790 million when it was authorized in 1962, is now expected to cost a little over $1 billion, and construction has not yet begun. The increases are not limited to the controversial projects. A look at project costs in a 1967 Corps report, the most recent one available, shows "overruns" of over 300 percent. . . .

The Corps of Engineers public works program has been, among other things, an income-transfer program, and this is a good time to look more closely at who has been transferring what to whom. The federal government has been paying for the Corps program—or rather, all of the taxpayers have. And the Corps program consists in the main of subsidies for irrigation, navigation, and flood control. Some projects have been for the benefit of only one particular industry. . . .

Robert Haveman, an economist and author of *Water Resource Investment and the Public Interest,* has shown that the preponderance of Corps projects has gone to three regions: the South and Southwest, the Far West, and North and South Dakota, but mainly to the South, in particular the lower Mississippi River area. Within an area, the rewards are not evenly spread. The major beneficiaries of the flood-control projects which also provide water for irrigation have been the large landholders—in particular, in the Mississippi Delta and San Joaquin Valley. These are the same landowners who are paid the largest federal farm subsidies for not growing the crops which the federal water projects make it possible for them to grow. The Corps is still preparing to produce more farmland, in the name of flood control, in the Mississippi Delta region. . . .

The Corps established an environmental division a few years ago, to advise on the environmental effects of its projects. This summer it is sponsoring a seminar on how it can better "communicate" with the public. Corps officials have been urging greater environmental concerns on the Corps members, and on their clientele, appealing, among other things, to their self-interest. In a recent speech, Major General F. P. Koisch, director of the Corps' Civil Works Division, told the Gulf Intracoastal Canal Association to listen to "the voice of the so-called 'New Conservation.' ". . .

Clearly, no rational settlement of the conflict between "progress" and the environment is going to come from dam-by-dam fights between the Corps and the conservationists. The conservationists have been out there all alone all these years, and they have worked hard, but they have lacked a national strategy. In some instances, they have tried to have it all ways: opposing not only hydroelectric projects but also alternatives such as generating power through burning fuels (air pollution) or building a nuclear plant (thermal pollution and radiation hazards). Some conservationists have been interested in "preserving" the wildlife so that they could shoot it. Where engineers have been pitted against engineers, as in the case of the Oakley and Potomac dams, the opponents have been more successful. "The only way to resist," say Representative John Saylor of Pennsylvania, a critic of the Corps for years, "is to know a little more about the Corps than the Chambers of Commerce do." The new approach of trying to build a body of law on the basis of the "rights of the people" against a public works project could be of profound importance. . . .

[O]ne solution to the problems the Corps program creates would be simply to stop it. The Corps and the Public Works Committees and the river associations could give themselves a grand testimonial dinner, congratulate themselves on their good works, and go out of business. There are more effective ways of transferring money—for instance, directly—if that is what we want to do; there are others who need the money more. But such suggestions are not, of course, "practical."

For as long as anyone can remember, there have been proposals for removing the public works program from the military, and transferring the Corps' civil functions, or at least the planning functions, to the Interior Department or a new department dealing with natural resources. President Nixon considered similar ideas, but rejected them in preparing his message on the environment. The Corps likes being where it is, and the powerful Forest Service and Soil Conservation Service, which are secure in the Agriculture Department, and the congressional committees whose power derives from the present arrangements, have habitually and successfully resisted up to now. "The two most powerful intragovernmental lobbies in Washington are the Forest Service and the Army Engineers," wrote FDR's Interior Secretary Harold Ickes in his diary in 1937, in the midst of a vain effort to reorganize them and Interior into a new Department of Conservation. Whatever the chances for reform, it has never been clear who would be swallowing whom as a result of such a change. The closed-circuit system by which public works decisions are made should be opened to other interested parties. Certainly a federal program that is more than a century old should be overhauled. The Corps is now at work on some internal improvements, but bureaucracies are not notably rigorous about self-change, and the water interests do not want change.

If there are to be a Corps and a Corps public works program, then proposals to expand the Corps' functions make sense. Making the Corps responsible for sewage treatment, for example, would give it a task that needs to be done, local governments a benefit which they really need and which would be widely shared, and politicians a new form of largesse to hand around. Antipollution could be spared the pork barrel through a combination of requirements for local action and federal incentives, and through adequate financing. Yet making antipollution part of the pork barrel may be just what it needs. Programs which appeal to greed are notably more politically successful than those that do not. The Corps' engineering expertise, in any event, could be put to use for something other than building dams and straightening rivers. It is the judgment of just about every economist who has studied the public works program that there should be cost-sharing and user charges. There have been proposals for making the beneficiaries of flood-control and navigation projects and harbors pay for them, or at least part of them.

In a period of great needs and limited resources, a high proportion of the public works program amounts to inefficient expenditures and long-range commitments of money on behalf of those who make the most noise and pull the most strings. Despite all the talk about "reordering priorities," the Nixon Administration's budget for the next year increases the money for the Corps. Even if the nation should want to double its standard of living (leaving aside for the moment the question of whose standard of living) and even if the public works programs really could help bring that about, it would be good to know more about the nature and price of such a commitment. At a time when a number of our domestic arrangements are coming under re-examination, this one is a prime candidate for reform. Meanwhile, the changes it is making in the nation are irreversible.

federal bureaucrats' attitudes toward a democratic ideology

reading 14

by Bob L. Wynia

From Bob L. Wynia, "Federal Bureaucrats' Attitudes Toward a Democratic Ideology," *Public Administration Review,* vol. 34 (March/April, 1974),
pp. 156–162.

IN 1964 a prominent political scientist, Dr. Herbert McClosky, published a study on consensus and ideology in American politics.[1] His study,
which focused on popular and elite consensus surrounding American
democratic ideology, demonstrated that considerable variation exists
around the values held by two large segments of the American populace,
the "general electorate" and the "political influentials." This intriguing
analysis raised a number of legitimate questions which called for further
research. This article reports on research that serves as an expansion of the
McClosky study in some respects, but is original in other respects. We
chose to apply certain of the McClosky postulates and apply them to a
very unresearched segment of a "democratic" society, the career bureaucracy. Of principal concern was the attitude bureaucrats or national planners hold toward certain democratic ideals or principles. Also, what effect,
if any, do the agency affiliations, education levels, and years in the public
service have on their attitudes?

OVERVIEW OF THE FEDERAL BUREAUCRACY

Although often recognized as a "fourth branch" of government, the
federal career bureaucracy and the career bureaucrat in particular is undoubtedly one of the least studied phenomena of present-day American
government. The federal bureaucracy is a huge, complex mechanism comprising thousands of government agencies with over three million employees. Many of the most serious decisions which need to be made each
day are directly related to policy interpretations arrived at by the career
bureaucrat,[2] protected by the Civil Service system and not elected by the

public. What ideological views do these federal executives hold? Is there a common ideology among them? What democratic principles do they espouse? What level of faith do they have in the democratic process? How committed are they to democratic values?

One noted author (Frederick Mosher) makes the following premises about public service executives:

1. Governmental decisions and behavior have tremendous influence upon the nature and development of our society, our economy, and our policy;

2. The great bulk of decisions and actions taken by governments are determined or heavily influenced by administrative officials, most of whom are appointed, not elected;

3. The kinds of decisions and actions these officials take depend upon their capabilities, their orientations, and their values; and

4. These attributes depend heavily upon their backgrounds, their training and education, and their current associations . . .

The premise stated by Mosher and the further elaboration that little attention is paid to people who administer and plan government programs seem clear enough. A basic and accepted principle of democratic rule is that *elected* officials set policy which guides the nation, state, city, or school district. Often overlooked is that fact that much of the policy power of a democracy lies not in the hands of those elected officials, but rather is two steps removed from them (some of this power being drained off by political executives) in the personnel who are neither elected nor politically appointed and are protected from removal on political grounds—the career civil service. Mosher says:

They influence—or make—decisions of great significance for the people, though within an environment of constraints, controls, and pressures which itself varies widely from one jurisdiction to another, from one field or subject to another, and from one time to another.

A most critical need is to recognize to what extent policy decisions are made at the level of the career civil servant, what is policy and what is program (if indeed they are separable), and (the subject of this article) what the attitudes of the individual public executive are. If career executives are important in decision making, then certainly their attitudes are of importance to us. While long advocated (and made law by the Hatch Act) that career people should have no close political relationships, this policy has not recognized the fact that all people hold certain philosophical principles or attitudes which affect their actions. It is to these "principles" or "attitudes" we are addressing ourselves. Like Mosher we found little definitive research and only slightly more subjective reporting aimed at attitudes of public service officials.

No studies we are aware of have dealt with such important areas as attitudes or behavioral characteristics of top-level federal civil servants. Warner describes in detail the social, economic, and educational backgrounds of federal executives and their families. Stanley appraises various features of a personnel system for the higher civil service and considers the attractiveness of federal careers through the eyes of present and former federal employees. Kilpatrick was concerned with the image of federal service as held by employees themselves, the business community, college and high school groups, and the public generally.

Thus we may be able to accurately describe a "typical" executive's physical and historical characteristics almost down to hair and eye color, yet we are unable to compile comprehensive data (let alone cite exploratory research) on such gross characteristics as political party or organization affiliations. . . .

For this research, 42 of the attitude scale items were selected from McClosky's research on the basis of those most likely to fit a Guttmann scale. These 42 items fit into six subscales:

1. "Rules of the game," with emphasis on fair play, respect for legal procedures, and consideration for the rights of others;

2. "Support for general statements of free speech and opinion";

3. "Support for specific applications of free speech and procedural rights";

4. "Belief in equality"—broken down into political, social and ethnic, and economic equality;

5. "Political cynicism"—defined as a feeling that the system will not govern justly and for the common good;

6. "Sense of political futility"—defined as a feeling that one cannot reach an influenced system.

Agree-disagree statements covering the six subscales were administered to 405 federal executives representing 52 different federal agencies and all geographic areas of the country. From observation and past research studies we hypothesized that: (1) The career bureaucrat would demonstrate little consensus on democratic principles; (2) The bureaucrat who had worked primarily in a "social agency" would demonstrate a higher degree of agreement on statements relating to a positive attitude toward specific democratic privileges than executives from the other types of agencies ("defense related" and "others"); and (3) Variables, years in the federal service, employing agency, and years of education would affect attitudes on all of the value scales, with significant changes over time. . . .

ANALYSIS AND DISCUSSION

We have focused our analysis on those scales and items where the largest percentages of difference occur. Most of the percentages range from 20–30 per cent agreement. This seems exceedingly significant when one projects these figures over three million federal bureaucrats. While the overall data lend support to the fact that there is extensive agreement with the democratic philosophy within the bureaucracy, there are many areas of grave and undisputed disagreement on specific applications of democratic principles. These are highlighted [in Tables 1, 2, and 3].

The items in Table 1, when viewed as pertaining to specific applications of the democratic ideology, illustrate the percentage of bureaucrats who agree with democracy in the abstract. The table also points out at the same time that a significant number of bureaucrats (over one-third) do not hold to certain constitutional guarantees. . . .

For example 24.6 per cent of all bureaucrats agreed that "when the country is in great danger we may have to force people to testify against themselves even if it violated their rights."

A most noticeable and consistent attitude appears in items which advocate or at least accept the use of force, for whatever purpose. There is considerable acceptance of people "taking the law into their own hands," innocent people having to suffer, congressional committees breaking rules to explore "dangerous subversives," the use of "cruelty and even ruthlessness" in order to bring about changes for the "benefit of mankind," and using force to save the "American way of life."

Free speech in the abstract is an area where considerable agreement is apparent when analyzing gross percentages for the total subscale. As a basic freedom, bureaucrats want free speech protected; however, Table 3 illustrates how in specific situations some will agree to suspend this basic constitutional right and guarantee.

TABLE 1

Item	Percentage of Bureaucrats Who Agree with Item	[Percentage of General Populace Who Agree with Item *]
There are times when it almost seems better for the people to take the law into their own hands rather than wait for the machinery of government to act.	31.9	26.9
We might as well make up our minds that in order to make the world free a lot of innocent people will have to suffer.	31.0	41.6
We have to teach children that all men are created equal but almost everyone knows that some are better than others.	37.5	58.3

* Editors' note: The figures for the general populace came from McClosky (1964). See note 1 for citation.

TABLE 2

Item	Percentage of Bureaucrats Who Agree with Item	[Percentage of General Populace Who Agree with Item *]
There are times when it almost seems better for the people to take the law into their own hands rather than wait for the machinery of government to act.	31.9	26.9
We might as well make up our minds that in order to make the world free a lot of innocent people will have to suffer.	31.0	41.6
If congressional committees stuck strictly to the rules and gave every witness his rights, they would never succeed in exposing the many dangerous subversives they have turned up.	28.0	47.6
To bring about great changes for the benefit of mankind often requires cruelty and even ruthlessness.	27.0	31.3
The true American way of life is disappearing so fast that we may have to use force to save it.	18.6	34.6

* Editors' note: The figures for the general populace came from McClosky (1964). See note 1.

Once the variables, agency, education, and years in the public service become part of the analysis, a different picture of bureaucrat attitudes emerges. Data collection relating to these variables utilized the following definitions:

1. Social agencies, including the Departments of Health, Education, and Welfare; Labor; Housing and Urban Development; and the Office of Economic Opportunity

2. Defense-related agencies including all Department of Defense agencies and bureaus; and

3. "Other," including all other departments and independent agencies of the federal government.

TABLE 3

Item	Percentage of Bureaucrats Who Agree with Item	[Percentage of General Populace Who Agree with Item *]
A person who hides behind the laws when he is questioned about his actions doesn't deserve much consideration.	24.8	75.7
When the country is in great danger, we may have to force people to testify against themselves even if it violates their rights.	24.6	36.3

* Editors' note: The figures for the general populace are from McClosky (1964). See note 1.

Years of education was broken down into three specific groups: high school diploma or below, bachelor's degree, and above the bachelor's degree level.

Years in the public service was divided into four levels: 5 years or less, 6 through 15 years, 16 through 25 years, and people with over 26 years in the public service.

On all items defense agency executives agreed more often than the other two groups. Within each of the tables there are some notable differences in the levels of agreement. It is quite obvious that either defense agencies tend to draw more "anti-democratic" types of individuals to work there, or that attitudes are altered over time. Indeed, there is good evidence in our data to substantiate this change over time theory (see Table 4). . . .

Table 5 demonstrates the rather divergent view of the "rules of the game" aspect of democratic ideology. These items refer to consideration for the rights of others, respect for legal processes, and general fair play.

On specific items we note that defense agency executives are more inclined toward the use of force, approving the use of any methods to "get the right things done"; are willing to justify unfairness or brutality in order to carry out some "great purpose"; and even accept "cruelty and ruthlessness" in order to bring about great changes for the benefit of mankind. [See Table 6.]

Perhaps the most definitive attitudinal responses are apparent when analyzing a specific item within the scale. One gets a much clearer picture of attitudes both within the bureaucracy as a whole as well as across the boundaries of the variables. Thus, in an item dealing with exposing dangerous subversives, the contrast between social agency executives and defense agency executives takes on added significance when considering the more than two-to-one ratio of difference. [See Table 7.]

As was pointed out earlier, when we turn to the influence years of

TABLE 4

Item	Average	Agency			Years of Education			Years in Service			
		Social	Dept. of Defense	Other	0-12	13-15	16+	1-5	6-15	16-25	26+
When the country is in great danger, we may have to force people to testify against themselves even if it violates their rights.	24.6	25.3	30.9	20.4	25.6	26.3	22.5	15.2	23.3	24.6	28.8
Any person who hides behind the laws when he is questioned about his activities doesn't deserve much consideration.	24.8	19.0	29.3	24.4	41.0	26.6	19.1	12.1	16.5	24.6	37.5

Percentage of Agrees

TABLE 5

Rules of the Game Scale

Agency	Average Percentage Agree
Social	21.7
Defense	36.6
Other	24.6

TABLE 6

Percentage of Agreement

Item	Social Agencies	Defense Agencies	[General Populace*]
Almost any unfairness or brutality may have to be justified when some great purpose is being carried out.	19.3	22.0	32.8
To bring great changes for the benefit of mankind often requires cruelty and even ruthlessness.	25.0	33.3	31.3
The true American way of life is disappearing so fast that we may have to use force to save it.	9.5	29.3	34.6

* Editors' note: The figures for the general populace are from McClosky (1964). See note 1.

TABLE 7

	Percentage of Agreement	
Item	Social Agencies	Defense Agencies
If congressional committees stuck strictly to the rules and gave every witness his rights, they would never succeed in exposing the many dangerous subversives they have turned up.	17.9	38.5

schooling tends to play in developing or altering bureaucratic attitudes, we note that the less education the more "anti-democratic" the attitude. The effect of these negative attitudes toward basic human rights, minority peoples, and the American political system on the decision-making process seems obvious. From data in our research it is clear that these attitudes are considerably different depending on how many years he attended school. Table 8 illustrates this phenomenon.

The effect of years of education is equally apparent on the final item in Table 8 which calls for a reverse in the agree-disagree pattern to demonstrate democratic values.

Bureaucratic attitudes toward equality of people indicate a rather divergent spread. Defense agency executives, for whatever reasons, consistently demonstrate attitudes of an anti-democratic nature, whenever the

TABLE 8

	Percentage of Agreement		
	Years of Education		
Item	0–12	13–15	16+
We might as well make up our minds that in order to make the world better a lot of innocent people will have to suffer.	38.5	33.9	26.2
If congressional committees stuck strictly to the rules and gave every witness his rights, they would never succeed in exposing the many dangerous subversives they have turned up.	48.7	31.9	19.1
I don't mind a politician's methods if he manages to get the right things done.	20.5	15.7	11.0
Almost any unfairness or brutality may have to be justified when some great purpose is being carried out.	20.5	22.4	11.6
The true American way of life is disappearing so fast that we may have to use force to save it.	28.2	20.4	14.5
Any person who hides behind the laws when he is questioned about his activities doesn't deserve much credit or consideration.	41.0	26.6	19.1
Every person should have a good house, even if the government has to build it for him.	10.3	28.8	32.4

TABLE 9

Item	Percentage of Agreement		
	Agency		
	Social	Dept. of Defense	Other
We have to teach children that all men are created equal, but almost everyone knows that some are better than others.	34.6	43.9	34.7
Just as is true of fine race horses, some breeds of people are just naturally better than others.	19.5	28.5	17.3
Regardless of what some people say, there are certain races in the world that just won't mix with Americans.	13.3	26.0	13.8
The trouble with letting certain minority groups into a nice neighborhood is that they gradually give it their own atmosphere.	20.2	27.9	20.3

issue of racial or social equality is raised. Table 9 supports our contention that a large percentage of defense agency executives fail to support basic protections and social guarantees of a democratic system.

DISCUSSION

Several observations can be offered by way of summarizing and commenting upon the data. Earlier we discussed the critical role played by career executives in the policy-setting—decision-making process in our constitutional form of government. If we accept the earlier premise that career bureaucrats are vital components of this decision-making process, then clearly additional and extensive research is called for in order to attempt a clarification of some of our data. Do nonegalitarian attitudes affect the decision-making process, and how? Would higher-grade (GS 16, 17, 18) executives follow this same pattern? Are the variables interdependent, and if so to what degree?

Perhaps the most perplexing aspect of this inquiry is the social agency-defense agency differences. Both groups seem to indicate a molding of attitudes to fit the particular agency affiliation. The democratic principles and beliefs seem to be learned over time. Within the bureaucracy, it seems safe to suggest that, depending on the agency, these principles will be reinforced, thwarted, supported, or squelched. Our findings certainly support the long-espoused need to have a system for moving federal executives regularly across agency lines, providing for a variety of experiences and environments—thus allowing for the development of a more balanced set of attitudes.

Finally, to what degree is consensus on democratic principles really necessary? Can a "democratic system" stay democratic when a high percentage of its bureaucrats disagree with many of its fundamentals? Obviously consensus on fundamental principles among this most influential group is unnecessary if we are willing to accept the manner in which our present system operates. If on the other hand, as our evidence suggests, changes in attitude are desirable in order to provide a *more* "democratic" system, then we anticipate broad acceptance of these findings. Evidence suggests that the active, involved, and articulate classes rather than the public at large are the ones who serve as the major carriers of the democratic ideology; thus responsibility for keeping the system going depends heavily on them. We would certainly include federal career executives in this class. Yet it is apparent that a large number of them hold attitudes alien to democratic ideals. One senses that, like most Americans today, federal bureaucrats show little interest in political ideas because they are more concerned with personal affairs. Yet doesn't this lack of interest, lack of knowledge of fundamental rights, lack of understanding of basic constitutional guarantees stand out as evidence that many bureaucrats covertly feel our form of "democracy" by bureaucracy is failing? The effect of these attitudes, alien to the democratic ideology, is untested but worthy of much speculation and study.

NOTES

1. Herbert McClosky, "Consensus and Ideology in American Politics," *The American Political Science Review,* Vol. 58, No. 2 (June 1964), p. 361.

2. The terms career bureaucrat, federal executive, and public service official are used interchangeably throughout this article. All refer to executives of the federal government above the GS 12 level who are protected by Civil Service laws and regulations. This study focuses primarily on the GS 13, 14, and 15.

the federal budget and national policy

reading

15

by Lance T. LeLoup

This article was written expressly for the present volume. Professor LeLoup is a member of the Political Science Department at the University of Missouri—St. Louis.

EVERY YEAR since 1921 the President of the United States has begun the new year by sending Congress his annual budget; a series of requests to fund the thousands of federal programs. This annual phenomenon has been called the "world series of government" but in reality bears more resemblance to a long season of seemingly endless encounters. At a given time officials in Washington are working on three fiscal year budgets simultaneously: executive branch officials are preparing estimates for the next year, Congress is considering this year's requests, the Office of Management and Budget (OMB) is disbursing the current year's monies and the General Accounting Office (GAO) is auditing the past year's accounts.

The federal budgetary process is a microcosm of American politics and represents the most regularized pattern of interaction between institutions and interests. The budget documents, rivaling the New York City phone book in size, are not only a detailed map of what the government does but also a partisan statement of presidential priorities. While the constitution grants to Congress the power of the purse, it has been the president who has traditionally set the budget agenda, and congressional control of spending and budgetary influence has waned in recent years. A series of reforms passed in 1974 culminated an effort by Congress to get its own house in order and reassert itself in making budgetary decisions.

Budgetary decisions are the outcome of a complex set of interactions between social, economic, and political trends, national institutions, and interest groups. To understand the budget and its role in the formation of national policy, it is helpful to examine the nature of budgetary decisions, recent changes in the budget, questions of budget planning and control, budget reform, and current policy conflicts.

THE NATURE OF BUDGETARY DECISIONS

The federal budget is a compendium of policy recommendations and choices; priorities are plentiful and often in conflict with each other. For example, the goal of reducing unemployment conflicts with the goal of reducing the size of the deficit; decreasing military spending is in conflict with the goal of a well paid volunteer army. Besides the inherent tension between budgetary objectives, many decisions are carried over from previous years—what is referred to as "uncontrollable" spending. One result of these characteristics of budgetary decisions is that policy objectives are often not explicitly stated. To reduce conflict, budget officials use compromise budget figures rather than an elaborate statement of competing goals and choices.

Three kinds of budgetary decisions are particularly important; they include:

(1) Economic decisions: How large should the total budget be?
(2) Spending decisions: How is the money spent and who benefits from federal programs?
(3) Revenue decisions: How is money raised and who pays for government programs?

Economic Decisions: Budget Size

The Employment Act of 1946 gave the president the responsibility to maintain full employment and stable prices. This has proved a difficult task given his limited power and the fragile nature of the desired economic balance. Monetary policy, the regulation of the supply and cost of money (interest rates), is in the hands of the Federal Reserve Board and to a large extent insulated from presidential control. The main tool available to the president and shared with Congress is fiscal policy, the level of taxing and spending. Conventional Keynesian economic theory dictates that the government stimulate a sluggish economy out of a depression or recession by deficit spending (lowering taxes and increasing spending). The opposite situation of an overheated, inflationary economy calls for a surplus budget (raising taxes and decreasing spending) although these actions have proven distasteful to politicians in the past.

The absolute size of the budget (current dollars) has grown throughout our history. Expenditures as recently as 1935 were only $6.5 billion. By 1955 that figure had reached $68.5 billion and by 1977 it is close to $400 billion. In most years in the last several decades the government spent more than it took in, running a deficit in sixteen of the past twenty years. Growth in the past two years has been remarkably large by past standards; almost $100 billion or a 34 percent increase between 1974 and 1976. These figures give impetus for those who complain bitterly about the unchecked growth of federal spending. However, answers to questions on budget size and its economic impact are dependent on more than current dollar figures. This recent expansion is a function of high inflation and a series of automatic increases built into the federal budget to counteract a sagging economy.

How big is the federal budget? One way to gauge it is to look at total dollars. A better way to gauge the *relative size* of the budget over time is as a percentage of the Gross National Product (GNP), the total of all goods and services produced in the United States. Federal spending in 1976 will account for a little over one fifth of the GNP (21.5 percent). While this has risen since 1960 from the figure of 18.3 percent, the relative growth of the budget appears much smaller in the context of the growth of the economy.

Criticisms concerning the size of the budget go hand in hand with those observers who view the national debt of over $400 billion as a national disgrace and economic fiasco. But the analogy of governmental finance with a household budget is a poor comparison. Who holds the national debt? American citizens and financial institutions hold a majority of the debt ("Buy savings bonds in school or where you work"); governmental agencies hold most of the remainder (creating the situation where the government owes itself money). Interest on the national debt goes to banks, insurance companies and private citizens, i.e., back into the U.S. economy. Most of the national debt was accumulated during wartime to finance defense efforts. Further, fiscal policy depends on the manipulation of revenue and expenditures; given the growth of uncontrollable spending, a requirement of a balanced budget would render the government impotent to affect the economy and point us back towards the nineteenth century.

Relative to economic growth as measured by the GNP, the national debt has actually been *decreasing* since 1950. The decline has been from over 80 percent in 1950 to a current proportion of approximately 30 percent. A national debt *per se* is not unhealthy, but legitimate concerns arise when annual deficits become very large or continue over a long period of time.

While the size of the budget has increased rapidly in recent years, it by no means has taken over the private economy. Economic decisions concerning the size of the budget are extremely difficult in the face of economic uncertainty, different priorities concerning inflation and unemployment, and the conflict over these choices between the legislative and executive branches. They are made more difficult by simultaneous conflict over the scope of government.

Spending Decisions: Who Benefits?

While attempting to affect the performance of the U.S. economy through decisions on budget and deficit size, government officials also must make decisions on where the money will go. Will more money go to cancer research or welfare; to long range bombers or agricultural subsidies? From year to year, there is a basic consistency in governmental policies and spending. Yet in spite of this relative stability, significant shifts in the composition of the federal budget have occurred in the last 30 years and particularly in the last decade. Table 1 in the general introduction to this volume details some of those shifts between 1960 and 1975.

Income security, government payments to individuals in the form of Social Security, Aid to Dependent Children, and other cash transfer programs, have risen from less than 5 percent of all spending in 1946 to over 34 percent in 1976. At the same time, the share of the budget going to national defense has fallen from 75 percent in 1946 (World War II high) to 27 percent in 1976. While the defense budget in dollars has not declined, in recent years it has not grown as fast as other programs. Education, manpower, social services, and health programs have increased their share of the budget dramatically.

While annual shifts may be modest, significant changes in the composition of the budget have occurred in a relatively short period of time. Almost half of the 1976 federal expenditures ($160 billion) represent payments to individuals. This money does not purchase goods or services, but rather is given directly to recipients of veterans, social security, welfare and other benefits. The Brookings Institution has characterized this shift as "the transformation of the federal government into largely a check-writing organization." Spending decisions of these types have important policy implications for income distribution in the United States and long term consequences since they are not necessarily made every year.

In any given year, then, officials have only a certain proportion of the budget to allocate differentially to new and existing programs because of uncontrollable or multiyear decisions, and concurrent decisions on budget size.

Revenue Decisions: Who Pays?

In addition to size and spending decisions, budgetary decisions concerning revenues are made. The amount of revenue received by the federal government is determined by the tax structure and the economy. Tax laws in the U.S. are a tremendously complex set of codes and rules, that unlike appropriations, do not change every year. Taxes, combined with expenditures, affect the distribution of income and determine who pays for federal programs. While the progressive federal income tax (which taxes higher income groups more heavily than lower income groups) remains the main source of revenue, the proportion of revenue generated by the progressive income tax has declined since 1950. Several other changes have occurred in revenue patterns. One is the decline in the proportion of corporate taxes; the other is the increase in payroll taxes like Social Security. The effect of these changes has been to cause the tax structure in the U.S. to become more regressive (taxing lower income groups more heavily than higher income groups).

Of all sources of revenues, the progressive federal income tax is most important for redistributive policy. Yet in the past twenty years, the total tax structure in the United States has become less effective in income redistribution. Pechman and Okner concluded that for 95 percent of the population, the total effect of *all* state, local and federal taxes is equivalent to a flat rate tax of around 25 percent. This includes annual incomes from $5000 up to $100,000. The redistributive impact of all taxes (the difference in the distribution of income before and after taxes) is less than *one* percent.

Revenue questions represent a crucial aspect of budgetary decisions. Taxes not only affect who pays and how much but can be used to provide public incentives and disincentives. One of President Ford's major energy proposals was the tax on imported crude oil; the President and his advisors intended to use the tax to make the oil more expensive so people would use less. The Democratic Congress objected to the underlying assumptions of this approach and its impact on lower income groups, favoring other policy actions to lower oil consumption.

The total amount of revenues raised in a given year depends not only on the tax structure, but also on the state of the economy. A given set of tax laws will generate billions more revenue at 4 percent unemployment than at 8 percent unemployment. One dramatic example of this was the tax cut in the early sixties. Cutting taxes successfully stimulated the economy to a degree that the revenue generated by the lower tax rates was greater than the revenue originally anticipated under the higher rates.

Tax laws and revenue decisions are related to other budgetary actions. They constrain, but they do not determine expenditure levels. Taxes have not changed radically from year to year, if at all, but remain a potent budgetary and fiscal tool.

BUDGET CONTROLLABILITY

One of the newest controversies in budgeting is over controllability. The term "uncontrollable" is an unfortunate choice because it connotes something unanalyzable or outside the normal range of decision-making. In addition, it implies a clear difference between controllable and uncontrollable in a given year that actually does not exist. The implication is clear, however, that the decision-makers who shape the U.S. budget have discretion over only part of it in a given year. This presents a critical set of constraints on Congress and the President.

Uncontrollable budget items represent spending decisions made in prior years that carry into the current year, i.e. multiyear decisions. Yet all these decisions were made consciously at an identifiable time and all are ultimately controllable in the long run. In addition, there is a great deal of variation in controllability of budget items, not the popularly pictured dichotomy between controllable and uncontrollable items. While both interest on the national debt and payments to individuals through Social Security, Medicaid, etc. are classified as uncontrollable, the former is "less uncontrollable" than the latter. Congress, for example, clamped a ceiling and an individual state maximum on the social services grants programs, in asserting control. Congress also has made certain entitlements like the 1972 Education Amendments subject to the normal appropriations process and the availability of money. President Ford has attempted to reduce federal commitments to social welfare programs like food stamps. In contrast, the only way to avoid paying interest on the national debt would be to default or pay it off—neither is a likely outcome.

At the same time, some of the items classified as controllable actually leave little room for discretion. Over 60 percent of the controllable items are in the forms of wages and salaries which are difficult to manipulate from year to year. One observer, Robert Haveman, concluded that of the $67.5 billion for defense and $34.9 billion for domestic programs classified as controllable, only $5 and $3 billion respectively could actually be cut immediately.

The domination of uncontrollable budget items is not necessarily an evil. It represents a combination of fixed costs, long term commitments, and *collective choices that certain beneficiaries should receive payments regardless of other conditions.* At the same time it mandates who benefits, however, these multi-year decisions restrict policymakers' ability to use fiscal policy to effectively alter the economy. As a series on concurrent policy choices, one set of budgetary decisions can impinge on and restrict another set of decisions. Budget controllability will be a continuing issue throughout the seventies not only over the question of budget manipulability, but because uncontrollable spending has grown primarily in the area of social welfare programs. Under Nixon and Ford, the White House has held different priorities concerning social welfare policy than the Congress.

BUDGETARY DECISION-MAKING

Allocating over 20 percent of goods and services produced in the U.S., the process of deciding on budget figures is obviously a crucial one. The budgetary process involves agencies and departments, the OMB and the president, key committees in Congress, as well as numerous groups and interests. The interaction of these participants provides annual and multi-year decisions that direct the course of governmental policy. Yet, we have contradictory images of the budgetary process. On one hand the budget represents a plan of action; explicit decisions on goals and objectives and how money will be spent to achieve these goals. This is sometimes referred to as the *"rational"* model of budgeting. In contrast to this view of budgeting is the *"incremental"* model; a view that budgets and policies change very slowly and only in small increments. Incrementalism pictures budgeting as a series of limited considerations of small changes; decision makers do not start from base zero every year but rather make minor changes in last year's figures. While the rational model depends on goals and objectives, incrementalism argues it is impossible to agree on goals.

Which view is correct? Actually both are partially correct. The incremental model points out serious flaws in the rational model of budgeting: goals are not often precise, all possible alternatives are not considered, and many spending totals change less than 10 percent per year. However, incrementalism as a view of budgeting has its own limitations. Excessive concentration on budget stability shields from view a number of significant policy changes at the agency level and ignores a number of non-incremental spending changes.

Budget stability from year to year is a function of several of the factors mentioned above; primarily because most decisions commit money for more than one year. In addition, the political process arrives at some consensus on the scope of federal policy and the funding changes for these programs usually proceed slowly until new controversies arise. Budget change occurs simultaneously with policy change when new functions for government are agreed upon. This occurred with the space program in the late fifties, federal aid to education and health programs in the mid-sixties, income maintenance programs in the late sixties, revenue sharing in the seventies. New programs in federal energy development that will undoubtedly grow to significant proportions are being formulated at the present time.

In this manner, budgeting as a reflection of political change and policy choices is a function of many factors. Changes are often a response to economic and social trends. Change can also be initiated through actions by agencies, the President, and the Congress or their combined efforts. Agencies generally seek to maintain their current programs and often seek to develop new ones. They solicit support from the public and with the President and Congress to foster their goals. Many budget changes in the sixties were a result of presidential initiative, particularly the Great Society programs. Certain changes, like the space program, were largely a function of congressional moves.

Agencies, the executive, and Congress have been found to develop a set of fairly consistent budget roles in their mutual relationships. Agencies have been characterized as *advocates* of greater spending. The OMB and the President have tried to channel these demands to fit the President's priorities. Congress has been characterized as a *guardian;* protector of the public purse consistently cutting budget requests. Under Nixon and Ford, a variation on these roles has emerged. While agencies remain advocates, the executive has emerged as the treasury guardian and main restraining force. Both Nixon and Ford attempted to cut back the role of the federal government in domestic programs. Both have been partially rebuffed by the Democratic Congress which finds itself playing alternate roles of advocate and guardian, attempting to protect and expand existing programs and to have a greater impact on the economic health of the nation.

Both images of the budget as a rational planning device and a stable, incremental statement of government activity have some validity. However, understanding the role of budgeting in national policy demands a fuller explanation of stability and change than either can provide.

BUDGET REFORM

Reformers have attempted to improve the budgetary process throughout the 20th century and undoubtedly will continue to do so. Recent attempts at reform have focused at both the agency level and Congress. Planning Programming Budgeting (PPB), prevalent in the 1960's and instituted for the entire federal government in 1965, was an effort to make budgeting conform to the rational model. PPB was a formal system that attempted to make agencies justify all expenditures every year. Budget officials were required to specify objectives, propose alternative means for achieving those objectives and select the alternative that provided the greatest benefits at the least cost. While PPB looked good in theory and actually performed well in some agencies, it proved unworkable and was dropped in 1971. It proved difficult to agree on objectives, and it was impossible to choose quantitatively between competing qualitative objectives. No budgeting system could provide easy answers to value questions such as whether to spend money on foreign aid or veterans' benefits. While the PPB system failed, much of its philosophy succeeded in changing the decision-making process. The legacy of PPB in the executive branch is a greater concern with efficiency, program evaluation, and cost benefit analysis, but in a more limited, decentralized manner.

One of the most important changes in national policy making to occur in years was Congressional Budget Reform. Seeing their influence and ability to deal with the budget slip away, the early 1970's saw a growing movement to improve the way Congress dealt with the budget.

A major problem before budget reform was the fragmentation of the process. After Congress received the President's budget it was broken down into a dozen separate appropriation bills and was never considered as a whole again. Each subcommittee of the Appropriations Committee had considerable autonomy in determining the agency budgets it reviewed. The end results were a set of little budgets; total spending and deficit totals were arrived at by default.

The Budget Control and Impoundment Act not only restricted the President's ability to impound funds (not to spend what Congress had appropriated), but most importantly it changed budget procedures in Congress. New Budget Committees were established to consider the budget as a whole and, in effect, produce a congressional budget. Spending guidelines are established by the first budget resolution in May which directs the Appropriations Committees in their subsequent actions. The second resolution, to be completed in September after the appropriations bills have been passed, sets binding totals. In addition the Congressional Budgeting Office (CBO) was established to provide the House and Senate with "independent" sources of monitoring and information. Many members of Congress felt that reliance on the President and the OMB had left them at a disadvantage in attempting to decide on budget figures. The budget resolutions provide an opportunity for Congress to review the budget in its entirety for the first time as a legislative body.

1975 saw a partial and cautious attempt to implement the reform procedures and 1976 was the first year of full implementation. Senator Muskie (D-Maine) and Representative Adams (D-Washington) have received high marks for their performance as chairmen of the new Budget Committees although the success or failure of the process will not be known for several years. President Ford's attempts to rescind prior appropriations (a new procedure in lieu of impoundment) were uniformly unsuccessful with the exception of appropriations for the White House Staff and Executive Office of the President. Congress was happy to cut back on the President's funds.

A major obstacle to the new budget procedures is the makeup of congressional coalition supporting budget reform—a mixture of fiscal conservatives who see it as an opportunity to control growth, and liberals, who see it as an opportunity to debate and reshape national priorities. The fragile nature of this coalition in the House of Representatives and the difficult task of reconciling the wide range of views were evidenced in 1975 and 1976 by the close margins of the vote on the budget resolutions. These reforms offer the Congress an opportunity to use its power of the purse more effectively but the final verdict on their impact is not yet in.

BUDGET ISSUES IN THE SEVENTIES

The federal budget remains mysterious and inaccessible to the casual observer; shrouded in bureaucratic jargon and confusing figures, the budget has never been subject to widespread public understanding and debate. With the budget becoming more complex rather than simpler, increasing public awareness and attention on a large scale is unlikely. There are, however, a number of budget issues that can be anticipated in the coming years, that are suitable to public debate and scrutiny.

The size of the annual deficit and the growing national debt seems to rise and fall as a salient issue. As the U.S. economy recovers from the 1973-75 recession, this will probably subside from prominence before it rises again. The question of budget controllability, on the other hand, will in all likelihood remain an important issue in coming years. As short run discretion is reduced, decision makers are justifiably concerned with their potential impact. However, budget makers can retain adequate fiscal control through the use of expenditures and revenues if the proportion of uncontrollable expenditures does not rise any further and if budget reform succeeds.

Taxes seem to be a perennial issue but the tax structure carries on with only minor adjustments along the way. The House Ways and Means Committee has consistently failed to produce major reform because of the necessity to satisfy a vast array of interests satisfied with the status quo. As more wage earners move into the middle income ranges without a concomitant shift upward in tax rates, the overall tax burden shifts gradually down to the lower income scale. This has occurred over the past two decades and the high percentiles of taxpayers contribute relatively less than they did in the 1950's. Other tax issues will arise around the method of funding Social Security and the growth of other largely regressive payroll taxes.

The direction and nature of budgetary issues are greatly affected by the person occupying the White House. In coming years, a Republican will probably continue to oppose congressional domestic spending initiatives. A Democrat with a healthy economy might begin to initiate a new federal role (and increased program spending) in health, income maintenance, transportation, or other areas. Substantial tax reform may also be on the agenda. This situation may turn the tables in presidential-congressional budgeting relationships with the Congress proceeding slowly and cautiously on executive initiatives.

Budgetary decisions are the essence of political choice; understanding their stability and change is to understand our complex system of making national policy. A single year is but a small moment in our history and radical changes in any given year will be the exception rather than the rule. Over time, however, the shifting of attitudes, structure and environment leads us in directions often far removed from our past priorities and choices.

reading 16

the life cycle of regulatory commissions

by Marver H. Bernstein

Selection from Chapter 3, "The Life Cycle of Regulatory Commissions,"
in Marver H. Bernstein, *Regulating Business by Independent Commission* (copyright 1955 by Princeton University Press), pp. 74–95. Reprinted by permission of Princeton University Press. Footnotes have been deleted.

ADDITIONAL LIGHT can be shed on the process of regulation by the
historical pattern followed by commissions from birth to decay. While the
experience of each commission has unique elements, the history of commissions reveals a general pattern of evolution more or less characteristic
of all. Despite variations in time sequence and the particular circumstances
surrounding the creation of each one, the national independent commissions have experienced roughly similar periods of growth, maturity, and
decline. These common experiences can be generalized into a rhythm of
regulation whose repetition suggests there is a natural life cycle for an
independent commission.

The life cycle of an independent commission can be divided into four
periods: gestation, youth, maturity, and old age. The length of each phase
varies from one commission to another, and sometimes a whole period
seems to be skipped. Some commissions maintain their youthfulness for
a fairly long time, while others seem to age rapidly and apparently never
pass through a period of optimistic adolescence. Some are adventurous,
while others are bound more closely to the pattern established by the
oldest commission, the ICC. Such differences add an element of interest
and reality to the evolution of commission regulation, but they do not
invalidate generalizations about the administrative history of regulation.

GESTATION: PHASE 1

Frequently twenty years or more may be required to produce a
regulatory statute. First, there is a period of slowly mounting distress over
a problem. When the strain or oppression is felt by organized groups or

is dramatized by public scandal or economic depression, it may gather momentum quickly. Recognition of acute distress promotes discussion of complaints and abuses and may lead to the organization of groups to fight for governmental regulation to eliminate the source of complaint. Organized groups will seek to widen their membership and strengthen their resources for the legislative battle ahead. Demands will be made on the legislature for corrective action to protect the interests of the groups affected. Throughout this period the organized groups favoring regulation intensify the search for a proposed public policy around which they can rally. . . .

After a period of earnest agitation for enabling legislation, the statute is finally enacted. It represents the culmination of study of what has come to be recognized as an acute public problem. Usually the legislature can be galvanized into action only after the problem has become extremely serious. At first the objectives of the legislation are limited and generalized in somewhat vague language. The approach of the statute tends to be restrictive and to concentrate attention on eradicating abuses. The prevailing view is that the elimination of abuses will bring public and private interests into harmony again.

The statutory mandate lacks clarity. Although it climaxes a prolonged struggle for reform, the policy which it establishes rarely provides clear directions to the new agency. Despite the effort to produce a consensus in favor of *regulation,* the legislation reflects unsettled national economic policy. The agency of regulation is created at the peak of organized fervor for reform. But agitation for regulation rarely produces a first statute that goes beyond a compromise between the majority favoring and the powerful minorities opposing regulation. . . .

The desire for regulation in this early period takes precedence over attempts to refine regulatory goals and basic policies. It is the battle for legislation that captures public attention, not the hammering out of a carefully articulated set of regulatory goals. What is wanted is immediate relief from an intolerable situation, not the development of a philosophy for ordering economic relations. It is the short-run, rather than the long-term, implications of regulatory policy which preoccupy the advocates of regulation. . . .

YOUTH: PHASE 2

When a regulatory commission is established, its real and potential capacities contrast sharply with those of the regulated groups. It lacks administrative experience, its policy and objectives are vague or unformed, its legal powers are unclear and untested, and its relations with Congress are uncertain. On the other hand, the regulated groups are well organized, with vital interests to protect against the onslaught of the regulators. The regulatory agency usually begins to formulate its program and to block out its major policies at a time when the regulated enterprises are highly developed and their technologies far advanced.

At this stage the atmosphere surrounding the regulatory process is far from placid or neutral. The animosities generated during the period of

structure of government

agitation and legislative enactment do not subside quickly, and the new administrators are reminded of the strength of the regulated groups at every possible opportunity. . . .

On the other hand, the agency ordinarily begins its administrative career in an aggressive, crusading spirit. It may resolve to meet the opposition of the regulated with firmness in order to promote the public interest. It tends to take a broad view of its responsibilities; and some members of the commission, at least, will develop a fair measure of daring and inventiveness in dealing with their regulatory problems. . . .

In view of the high hopes for administrative regulation and the great faith placed in the commission as an agent of reform, commissioners are urged to define their role in expansive rather than restrictive terms. In the period of Progressive reform politics early in the twentieth century, one commentator observed: "Public service commissions are administrative bodies. They are charged with duties of constant supervision. They are empowered to initiate all proceedings necessary to accomplish the purposes of the laws. Merely passive enforcement of commission laws will not long command public respect and confidence and serve as a remedy for abuses, alike on the part of the public and the corporations, which it is the purpose of the commissions to prevent. Aggressiveness should be found in public service commissions."

If the agency is to act in the public interest, it must do so while it still commands public support and can count on sympathetic political leadership both in the Presidency and in Congress. If powerful political support and leadership are available to the commission, it may have "the opportunity—perhaps the only one it will ever have—to make a material contribution to the shape of things." But the opportunity does not last very long. It is remarkable how quickly political interest disappears. If an agency is to take advantage of the favorable political situation, "it must establish its beachheads quickly, and extend and fortify its lines without delay. Standards for conduct of private enterprise, guiding standards for the administrative agency, and the position of the agency may be established before the political force behind the agency's directive is spent and the dissident groups have found ways of moderating or checkmating the new program."

The regulatory commission soon discovers that it can accomplish little until the Supreme Court has passed on the validity and constitutionality of its powers and authority. Immediately the scene of battle changes to the courtroom. Litigation forms the framework for the regulatory process until the courts have issued an authoritative decision or series of decisions outlining the legal scope of regulatory powers. The trial by legal combat gives most of the advantage to the private parties. An untried and untested regulatory statute comes under attack by extremely skillful lawyers traditionally opposed to governmental efforts to control economic affairs. The arena in which the legitimacy of regulation is attacked and defended is highly specialized, technical, and frequently obscure. Few nonlawyers are able to follow the legal proceedings, which appear incredulous or mysterious to the uninitiated.

While the enactment of a statute is clear proof that the about-to-be-regulated groups have lost the first round in the struggle against regulation, it is equally clear that they do not give up when the law is passed. Instead, as Graham has suggested, the regulated group ". . . attempts immediately and persistently to get 'sound' men appointed to the independent commission. The distinguished members of the bar who represent it can be most gracious, not to say ingratiating, to members of the commission who seem to deserve the industry's confidence. Some commissioners so win the confidence of industry that industry weans them away from the public service into its own employ. Commissioners who prove 'difficult' are subject to constant attack in the public press, in trade publications, before committees of Congress and on the floor of Congress itself; and their reappointment is bitterly opposed."

It is not difficult to account for the loss of public support and the decline of political leadership on behalf of effective regulation. First, the public support that has been built up laboriously during the period of gestation reaches a climactic peak at the moment that the enabling legislation is passed. Public support can be maintained at this peak for only a short time. Attention has been directed for so long to the issue of whether or not to regulate that the public heaves a sigh of relief when an affirmative decision is made. The organized groups that propagandized in behalf of regulation are tired after their long struggle and believe that they have earned a rest from political turmoil.

Second, after concentration on the enactment of legislation, there is a tendency to regard administration as automatically following legislation. If statutory authority is available, the expectation is that it will be exercised. At least, it is felt, someone else will see that the administrative wheels are set in motion and directed along the prescribed legislative lines. Lack of concern with administration, growing out of its undramatic nature, helps to account for the rapid decline of public interest.

Third, the necessity to defend its powers and methods in the courts forces a commission to operate during its period of youth in a technical environment that defies general comprehension by the public.

Fourth, the resourcefulness of regulated groups helps to account for changes in public attitudes and the outlook of the commissioners. Various social opportunities may be open to commissioners who are or may become sympathetic to the position of the regulated groups. The chance to secure an executive post with a firm subject to regulation may urge a certain kind of restraint upon the commissioners. This is not to suggest that there is a conspiracy between the regulated and the regulator but rather a more subtle relationship in which the mores, attitudes, and thinking of those regulated come to prevail in the approach and thinking of many commissioners.

Fifth, Congress can ill afford to perpetuate the acrid animosities and scars of political battle. Senators and representatives hesitate to remain identified as champions of public control of business except in periods when support for such control is overwhelming in their constituencies. Divisons within each major party are aggravated by regulatory controversies, and each party is anxious to heal the wounds to party unity. And finally, the cohesiveness of industrial groups cannot be matched by the inchoate, relatively unorganized (and frequently disorganized) public. Consequently, the new commission may be left in splendid isolation until some new crisis attracts public attention and regulation again becomes a vital public issue. . . .

MATURITY: THE PROCESS OF DEVITALIZATION: PHASE 3

Gradually the spirit of controversy fades out of the regulatory setting, and the commission adjusts to conflict among the parties in interest. It relies more and more on settled procedures and adapts itself to the need to fight its own political battles unassisted by informed public opinion and effective national political leadership. . . .

In the period of maturity, regulation usually becomes more positive in its approach. Its functions are less those of a policeman and more like that of a manager of an industry. The approach and point of view of the regulatory process begin to partake of those of business management. The commission becomes accepted as an essential part of the industrial system. As the program of regulation becomes broader in scope and impinges more directly on the functions of management, the stakes become greater. Hence the struggle to control the formulation of regulatory policies and to influence the conditions surrounding the regulatory process becomes more carefully calculated. The commission becomes more concerned with the general health of the industry and tries to prevent changes which adversely affect it. Cut off from the mainstream of political life, the commission's standards of regulation are determined in the light of the desires of the industry affected. It is unlikely that the commission, in this period, will be able to extend regulation beyond the limits acceptable to the regulated groups.

In method as well as policy, the commission loses vitality. Davis describes the pattern in these words: "The early experimentation yields forms, patterns, routines. Problems tend to be solved not by original thought but by digging up precedents. A member of the staff who is abruptly confronted with the question why he follows a particular method, inevitably responds: 'Why, we've always done it that way.' " Precedent, rather than prospect, guides the commission. Its goals become routine and accepted.

Perhaps the most marked development in a mature commission is the growth of a passivity that borders on apathy. There is a desire to avoid conflicts and to enjoy good relations with the regulated groups. Without the spur of Congressional demand for regulatory progress and without prodding and leadership from the White House, a commission is apt to take a rather narrow view of its responsibilities. . . .

The tendency of commissions to be passive toward the public interest is a problem of ethics and morality as well as administrative method. Graham compares the "passive immorality" of mature commissions to the willingness of many municipal police systems to come to terms with the forces of organized crime. Acceptance by government officials of an alliance with regulated groups is an abdication of responsibility and must be considered a blow to democratic government and responsible political institutions.

A mature agency cannot count on Congressional support for firm regulation. Congress, in this stage, is reluctant to increase the commission's authority and finds it difficult to overcome its traditional particularism and localism and devote constructive attention to national economic policies. Scarcely a note of concern can be heard from the public. Popular apathy indicates that more energetic action is not desired. Those few concerned with effective regulation are satisfied with the progress made to date and see only disaster ahead if the regulatory program is expanded. Complacency and lethargy become firmly rooted.

The approach of a mature commission is heavily judicialized. It routinely devotes most of its time to the adjudication of individual cases. Any latent ability to reconsider regulatory objectives and formulate programs of action is buried under a burden of cases awaiting decision. In an effort to meet charges of arbitrary action and unfairness toward individuals in the adjudication of disputes, the commission makes available to the private parties almost unlimited opportunities to challenge its position and to persuade it that its contemplated action is incorrect or unfair.

Important developments concerning staff, work load, and appropriations should be noted. A spirit of professionalism gradually becomes entrenched in the staffs of most mature commissions. Lawyers, engineers, and economists vie with each other for dominance in the policy-making channels of the agency. Each professional group likes to have veto power over the policy proposals of the other. Professional interests tend to narrow the point of view adopted with respect to regulatory matters, and the dependence on precedent becomes almost iron-bound. The major result is a myopic view of the public interest which rationalizes the regulatory *status quo*. In terms of work load, the commission tends to get further and further behind in managing its activities. Backlogs keep attention focused on yesterday's problems. Little or no attention is given to the need for progressive revision of regulatory methods and statutory standards. Both Congress and the Bureau of the Budget tend to be unsympathetic to the commission's plea for larger appropriations for the purpose of hiring more staff to dispose of backlogs. Lack of confidence in the commissions as well-managed agencies results in reduced appropriations and budgetary decline.

The close of the period of maturity is marked by the commission's surrender to the regulated. Politically isolated, lacking a firm basis of public support, lethargic in attitude and approach, bowed down by precedent and backlogs, unsupported in its demands for more staff and money, the commission finally becomes a captive of the regulated groups.

The gradual loss of youthful energy and the transition to the infirmities of old age are not uniquely applicable to regulatory commissions. Because of the economic and political stakes of regulation, however, commissions seem to be more subject than other types of government agencies to passivity and inability to interpret the public interest. Commissions need to be forewarned, more than other agencies, about their prospects. If there are ways of guarding against easy acceptance of the traditional and hesitancy to question its adequacy or propriety, commissions have not yet discovered or applied them. . . .

OLD AGE: DEBILITY AND DECLINE: PHASE 4

All social institutions are subject to inertia and loss of vitality. Procedural patterns tend to become sanctified as unalterable guides for bureaucratic conduct and accepted and defended as the traditional and correct way of behavior. The power to resist debilitating pressures and to maintain administrative vigor varies markedly from one association to another. In governmental activity some agencies develop a sense of mission and attract competent personnel and adequate political leadership that enable them to retain their creative powers for a long period. Other agencies fall victim more quickly to traditional modes of thinking and behavior and become passive instruments of public policy rather early in their administrative career.

The development of the characteristics of old age is not confined exclusively to the independent regulatory commission. But commissions seem more susceptible to debility and eventual collapse than other types of agencies. As multiheaded agencies normally cut off from continuing political support from the chief executive, they tend to lack dynamic administrative leadership. As government agencies operating in a web of controversial and hostile economic relationships, they tend to relate their goals and objectives to the demands of dominant interest groups in the economy. Ignored or abandoned by an unorganized public, commissions tend to play for safety in policy decisions. Passivity deepens into debility. . . .

During old age the working agreement that a commission reaches with the regulated interests becomes so fixed that the agency has no creative force left to mobilize against the regulated groups. Its primary mission is the maintenance of the *status quo* in the regulated industry and its own position as recognized protector of the industry. The institutionalization of favoritism toward dominant groups in the regulated industries is fostered by the narrow jurisdiction of the commission. Dealing with only one industry or a group of related industries, its vision of the public interest lacks the breadth and scope that a wider jurisdiction would tend to force upon it.

The final debilitation of the commission does not go unnoticed in the executive and legislative branches. Congressional appropriations committees and budget examiners of the Bureau of the Budget grow increasingly reluctant to approve funds needed to permit the agency to dispose of its growing backlogs. There is the fear that further additions to budget and staff will not make the agency more efficient and only commit it irrevocably to outworn procedures and policies. If a commission is overtaken by a serious governmental crisis or emergency brought on by war, defense mobilization, or economic depression, it will recede into the background and lose additional budgetary support.

Budgetary decline will in turn have debilitating effects on the personnel of the commission who elect to stay. Employees tend to become less able and imaginative in meeting their responsibilities. The commission will become more dependent than before upon the regulated industries to supply staff. Thus the staff continually reinforces its commitment to the maintenace of the *status quo* in the industry. . . .

Symptoms of debility and old age also include poor management and doubt about regulatory objectives. The managerial qualities of an independent commission decline as the commission passes the first blush of youth. Splintered responsibility at the top level, the growth of passivity, acceptance of the judicial model as sacred, and inability to take the initiative required for planning its operations reduce the commission to managerial ineptitude. The need for commissioners to work as a team makes for certain understandings among them which act as powerful deterrents to efforts to improve their managerial quality. Occasionally a particularly disaffected member may refuse to accept the going relations among commissioners. But his opposition may only unite other commissioners more strongly in their defense of the accepted pattern of operation.

A significant indication of senescence is the failure of regulatory objectives to keep pace with changes in technology, economic organization, and popular views about the proper scope of governmental activity. In the phase of old age the regulatory objectives of a commission are no longer meaningful and appropriate. Not only are there growing doubts about the original objectives laid down vaguely in the enabling statute, but there is even greater doubt about what the objectives ought to be. In their declining days commissions can be described as retrogressive, lethargic, sluggish, and insensitive to their wider political and social setting. They are incapable of securing progressive revision of regulatory policies and fall further and further behind in their work. . . .

The period of old age is unlikely to terminate until some scandal or emergency calls attention dramatically to the failure of regulation and the need to redefine regulatory objectives and public policies. In this fashion, the historical pattern of regulation might come full circle, although no important regulatory function of a commission has actually been eliminated. If a new agency is established to achieve the promise of modifying economic relations in the public interest, it will probably embark on its career full of hope, inspiration, and zeal, alert to its responsibilities, and driven by ambition, ingenuity, and public spirit.

congress

The United States Congress is the most important national legislature in the world. It is also often misunderstood and both attacked and praised for the wrong things as well as for some of the right things. Critical commentators often try to portray Congress as an easily described and understood body whose principal faults are slowness and alleged unresponsiveness to national needs that can easily be cured by a few institutional reshufflings such as a mandatory retirement age, a new and vigorous party leader, an end to the Senate filibuster, or a rejection of the seniority system for selecting committee chairmen. Supportive commentators also often come out with a simple pronouncement that basically boils down to the assertion that Congress is so complex that it cannot really be understood except as a mystical organic whole, and, when looked at in that light, it does a splendid job of reflecting the shifting and contesting streams of opinion and interest in the country through its slow-moving incremental approach to change in public policy.

Congress is, indeed, complex. But it can be understood in other than mystical terms, and faults can be uncovered that can be, and in fact sometimes are, remedied by rather sophisticated actions by the Congress itself (actions well beyond some simple-minded tinkering with mechanics). Both the critics and supporters of the institution often write and talk as if Congress is an unchanging phenomenon. To be sure, what might be called the "modern Congress" has existed in broad outline for roughly a century but during that century there have been many important changes, both planned and unplanned.

A single sentence definition of Congress (albeit a lengthy sentence) can identify some of the major questions about the nature and functioning of that body in the last part of the 20th century. Congress, a body of 535 representatives, virtually all of whom call themselves Democrats or Republicans and who are all elected from specific states and districts, is organized into two houses (a House and a Senate) and many committees and subcommittees within those two houses, and is required, among other things, to legislate in all substantive areas on the governmental agenda (most of which have a wide range of competing interests including, sometimes, something amorphous called the national interest) in an institutional setting in which power is shared with the president and a vast executive branch.

From that single sentence a number of observations of central importance in understanding Congress follow.

The fact of *election* of the members means that, since they are eligible and since the job is viewed as desirable, they will be concerned with re-election and with keeping favor with at least enough of their constituents so that their chances of re-election are maximized.

The fact of coming from *specific states and districts* means that members are given a geographical focus for their re-election concerns. It also gives them a natural focus for at least some policy concerns.

The fact that members virtually all call themselves *Democrats or Republicans* means that inside the House and Senate members organize into a nominal majority party and a nominal minority party and select leaders for those two contending groups. At minimum the leaders then provide the organizational and procedural framework that allows the House and the Senate to process a great deal of work on the floor. The parties and their leaders may also provide differing substantive positions around which large numbers of partisans rally. The fact of party is pervasive but not necessarily dominant in many of the workings of Congress.

That fact that Congress is organized into *two houses* means that agreement between those two houses on details is necessary before laws can be passed. The bodies are also natural competitors, both jealous of their prerogatives as co-equals. Each is quite different in size (the House with 435 and the Senate with 100) and this leads to additional differences in how they approach their legislative tasks. Each also has some unique powers—the Senate being particularly important with regard to foreign affairs and to presidential nominations and the House being particularly important with regard to taxing and spending.

The fact that Congress is organized in numerous *committees and subcommittees* is in part a response to a large agenda and in part a response to a large bureaucracy also struggling with the same agenda but with many more people and resources. In order to cope both with the agenda and the bureaucrats, most substantive impact of Congress emerges through subcommittee and committee decisions.

The fact of being required to legislate on a *vast array of topics* in a setting of *competing interests and powers shared extensively with the executive branch* has at least the following major results: (1) representation in practice means many different things—that is, many different entities (individuals, districts, organized groups, classes, races, the national good) receive representation; (2) Congress will almost always appear to be behind in its work; (3) Congress can have impact only on some topics and in limited ways despite its imposing formal powers; (4) Congress will seek to aid itself by providing professional staff; (5) it will automatically look to the president and executive branch for much legislative initiative; (6) it will necessarily delegate much authority to the president and executive branch; and (7) it will only be able to monitor part of the executive branch's performance in carrying out congressional intent in the myriad of federal programs authorized and funded by Congress.

Given the competing substantive and institutional demands on the individual senator and representative, it is hardly surprising that the policy output of the institution is the result of a series of compromises reached both within Congress and between individuals and groups within Congress and individuals and groups outside Congress.

In the readings that follow the dialogue between Gerald Ford (then House minority leader) Charles Wiggins, and John Culver (reading 17) illustrates a number of points about the interactions of committees, outside interests, and parts of the executive branch in producing policy. The Ripley article (reading 18) focuses on the interaction between party leaders and committee leaders. The final two readings address two different aspects of the substantive impact of Congress: Moe and Teel (reading 19) deal mainly with the legislative impact, whereas Ogul (reading 20) assesses the importance of Congress in oversight of executive branch activities.

structure of government

committee organization in the House

by Gerald R. Ford,
Charles E. Wiggins,
and John C. Culver

reading
17

From *Committee Organization in the House*, hearings before the Select Committee on Committees, House of Representatives, 93rd Congress, 1st sess. (1973), vol. 1, part 1, pp. 38, 41–45. The participants in this colloquy were all members of the House at that time.

Mr. WIGGINS. . . . Congressman Ford, you made the point quite properly that the Members are spread thinly because of the multiple committee assignments and, to some extent, their work product suffers, and Congress suffers as a result of that. The reason we have so many committees is because the work of the Congress has increased. The role of the Federal Government has increased and that trend is probably irreversible.

The problem, therefore, it seems to me, is to group these functions into a manageable number of committees and presumptively the groupings should have some relationship to each other. I want to talk about some specific committees with respect to this goal of grouping and to solicit your ideas. It has generally been regarded, Congressman Ford, that the members of the committees should almost be partisans for the legislation that goes through the committee and for the special interest groups that are affected by it. Given that present reality, would it be possible to group a labor function with a management function in some sort of a commercial committee?

Mr. FORD. I may be unrealistic, but I have more faith in my colleagues than to assume that just because they come from an area which is more oriented, say, to management than to labor or vice versa, that those Members cannot have a broader viewpoint than just a parochial interest.

I know from practical experience—if I might change the committee—that most people who want to go on the Committee on Agriculture come from agricultural districts. The net result is there has been some criticism, valid or not, that the Committee on Agriculture is too prone to support just the interest of agriculture without a broader point of view.

As long as the House can work its will, I think that is the crux of the matter. Any overemphasis of one committee toward a particular subject or a particular problem, I think, can be overcome.

I know, if I could again change the subject to another committee, many people say that too many members of the Committee on Armed Services represent areas where there is an emphasis on armed services installations. Therefore, it is said, they are parochial and, therefore, they cannot be objective. Again, as long as the House can adequately work its will and as long as you have a broad viewpoint that Members are not that parochial, I don't think it is a matter of too serious concern.

Mr. WIGGINS. I am pleased with your comments but I am not as confident that the House can effectively work its will against a committee that is loaded on one side because the committee has the upper hand. There is a tendency on the part of many Members who are not on a given committee to go along with the committee. They have the notion that committees should have a healthy degree of friendly antagonism within them.

It seems to me that is also healthy and we should not tend to load up committees with partisans of one or two vested interests. . . .

Mr. CULVER. . . . One of the more fundamental questions, I believe, Mr. Ford, that this committee is going to have to eventually grapple with and reach a conclusion about is what is the role of the Congress within our political system? Are we a coequal, independent branch of the Government with an independent legislative policy creating responsibility or are we some other adjunct to the executive branch with a responsibility to essentially accept and perhaps modify but in most cases simply ratify like an echo chamber what is being recommended from the other end of Pennsylvania Avenue?

Now, I would be interested in what your thoughts are more fundamentally.

Mr. FORD. I am a partisan in the strongest sense for the role and the responsibility of the legislative branch. I am even more emphatic in that regard as far as the House of Representatives is concerned. Any downgrading of that responsibility or that role I would vigorously oppose.

Mr. CULVER. In that connection, it seems to me that if we are agreed that the Congress in this instance specifically the House of Representatives should be possessed with the capability to perform that constitutional responsibility as an independent legislative policy creating body, it does get to the question then as to the structural design of our committees to perform that responsibility.

As you know, at the time of the floor debate when this committee was established, there was some colloquy between Chairman Bolling and the other Members of the House, concerning whether or not our committee would be addressing itself to a structural reorganization to mirror and reflect the executive branch reorganization proposals that have been recently recommended in connection with the executive. There was some exchange on that point.

It seems to me this is a very important question, the extent to which our committee is preoccupied attempting to devise an appropriate structure and design for the House to the extent to which we should be sensitive at all to what is deemed by the executive to constitute the appropriate realinement [sic] functionally for the performance of the executive branch mission and the discharge of the executive branch responsibility. Whether we should be influenced by that particular categorization or function and realinement [sic] or whether we should be viewing this entire question totally independent of that and looking upon our responsibility to recognize as unique and independent the responsibility of the Congress and the House and to proceed along that way.

What I am getting at is the extent to which you feel there is any requirement to dovetail the executive and congressional design or whether, in fact, you think that would be contrary to the development of an independent capability that doesn't go to the merits of the executive branch recommendations that would seem fitting and appropriate for reorganization of the Capitol or other executive departments.

Mr. FORD. Mr. Culver, although I generally agree with the executive reorganization proposals that were made last year or the year before by the administration, I have never felt that we had to follow suit item for item if those executive reorganizations had taken place.

I think we ought to make up our own minds. We might or we might not take certain departments or certain agencies and put them in under the jurisdiction of the specific committee that might follow the executive reorganization proposed by the administration. Their problems might not be the same as our problems. I don't think overlapping jurisdiction of a committee with a department is necessarily bad, although in general those things that fall under the jurisdiction of the Department of Agriculture probably ought to be considered by the Committee on Agriculture. That is simply one committee.

Some of the others might not be quite as precise or simple. However, we shouldn't be just hog-tied to whatever the executive branch proposes in the realinement [sic] of departments or agencies in fixing our committee responsibilities.

Mr. CULVER. Mr. Wiggins was pursuing a line of inquiry that many critics of the Congress and those concerned with congressional reform have expressed concern about. That is the problem of special interest domination of a particular committee or its membership because of the nature of the political system and processes.

As you are very much aware, the argument is advanced particularly at the time of increasing complication with sophistication, that the expertise that is derived by the individual Members as the result of extensive service on a particular committee is both necessary and desirable for us to properly meet our responsibility and shape the legislation in reviewing its implementation.

On the other side of that coin, of course, is that again the realities of our political system that the prospects and the problems of having those committees captured by special interest groups because of a long association with the particular legislative subject matter and particular constituencies of the members who find themselves on a particular committee results in a pattern of legislation which is not in conformity with the public interest or the national interest.

Therefore, the question is what mechanism could be adopted in the assignment to committees or the limitations placed on the period of service. For example, on a committee to, on the one hand, balance in a more healthy way the expertise factor against the public interest.

One proposal, Mr. Ford, that has been advanced has been the suggestion that we should have some sort of limitation on the period of service on a particular committee and, in effect, force rotation, the argument being that certain arbitrary cutoff periods would afford the member the expertise available and if people really wanted to rub their noses hard into a public policy matter, they could get into it.

I am always amazed at how quickly our Secretary of Defense can do quick studies on that mass of information with real progress. It seems to me you don't have to be 20 years in a particular environment to learn anything. I think inevitably by osmosis you must learn. However, there could be some different thoughts to putting some kind of limitation on committee service, a forced rotation, which would accomplish two things. One, it seems to me, would be the greater exposure of the House membership to a broader understanding of the various public policy problems the Nation faces and, second, to make it that much more difficult for a particular special interest to gain a dominant influence and position on consideration of legislation in that area.

Mr. FORD. Mr. Culver, I would make two observations. No. 1, if a committee becomes too oriented in one area, you can call it a special interest so that it overemphasizes legislation favorable to that interest. The safeguard to the public is the right and the authority of the House as a whole to overturn that committee's recommendations.

This isn't totally in point but we—and I am not being critical of any one committee—but we have had in the last 2 or 3 years several instances involving several committees where the committee recommendation was overturned by the will of the House as a whole.

I think that capability is a safeguard for the public in general. I would raise questions about kicking a member off a committee just because he had been on it so long. Let me tell you why. For 12 years, I was on the Defense Subcommittee on Appropriations. We used to meet—I think they still do—4 hours a day, 4 or 5 days a week, 4 or 5 months a year and they should. After all, they considered the Defense Department budget recommendations.

There was very little turnover in that subcommittee. I think there still is very little turnover. The net result was that the Members on that subcommittee on both sides of the aisle were really more expert in the history of and the operation of the Department of Defense than most of the witnesses.

The uniformed personnel who used to come and testify and still do are rotated. That is part of their career training. Many of the civilians come before the committee year after year. But when a uniformed witness would come before the subcommittee as a new head of a department or program, the members of the committee sitting on the other side of the table in reality knew more about his budget and his program than he did.

One of my dear friends and one of the most able members of that subcommittee is our colleague Dan Flood. Dan always used to say when a new witness would come before the subcommittee, "Admiral, Skipper," he used to call them. "We have witnesses like you who come and go like Greyhound buses." That was true.

The members of that subcommittee were experts and, if you made a clean sweep of that subcommittee on both sides of the aisle, I think the capability of the Congress or the House at least to make a thorough investigation and analysis and recommendation would be undercut. I can only quote my own experience but I think it would be equally true in most other committees.

Mr. Culver. Mr. Ford, I think that is certainly a most persuasive argument in opposition to such a suggestion, but do you really feel that history would really support such an analysis of the whole of the House Subcommittee on Military Appropriations? Have we enjoyed this kind of intensively critical analysis depending on recommendations and having the effect that it can really point to independent propositions that are determined as far as the defense needs of America or have we not found ourselves for the most part until most recent history in a posture that has been more congenial?

Mr. Ford. I would respectfully disagree. Let me give you illustrations. In the 12 years that I was on that subcommittee running from 1951 to 1964, I had it figured up because it became an issue in my campaign as I recollect, that subcommittee made recommendations accumulatively of cutting the defense budget by about $30 billion. In other words, we didn't buy what the executive branch, the Pentagon, recommended. We made far more reductions than we did add-ons, so we didn't just rubber stamp what they proposed. This was true during that span of time—and I think it is probably true today.

On the other hand, during that period of the 1950's, the Congress through that subcommittee expedited the construction of the Polaris submarine program when the Eisenhower administration was going too slowly. That committee and others in the Congress took the initiative and expanded it so we fulfilled our 41-boat program more quickly, and, I think, it was a right decision.

What I am saying is that subcommittee has not been a rubber stamp. It wasn't then, and I don't think it is today.

Mr. Culver. One of the most deficient areas, which most people acknowledge, for the Congress to address itself to, and one that we are going to develop in order to be a creative legislative group, is the problem of support services, a modern division of the technology and the strengthening of our information-gathering capability and utilization in a more efficient way. One of the things that has always puzzled me is how we in Congress have consistently complained about the power of the Executive being overwhelmed by the superiority of the executive capability.

Let me cite you an example of the 4,000 computers in the executive —and we have three or four. That is illustrative of that imbalance. Then, at the same time, it seems to me particularly in the defense field we have never been the least bit hesitant to make money available to the Pentagon, for example, to contract out for additional information to, say, Rand Corp. on the utilization of, and to utilize countless university faculties, and so forth. I was interested in what thoughts you have about Congress itself giving more consideration, by appropriate thinking, to a more efficient way in which we can draw the very real expertise in all these areas that exist in various quarters throughout the United States on a more efficient information gathering basis for studies.

Mr. Ford. I think we took a step in the right direction last year when we established the Office of Technology Assessment as a joint Senate-House operation. As I envisage that organization's responsibility, it is to hire technical people who will be able to evaluate in a broad scientific nonpartisan way the recommendations of the Executive and the problems that arise because of our society moving more and more into a technical area. I believe that OTA can be very helpful. I am optimistic that it will perform the function that I think you seek and I agree with. . . .

party leaders and standing committees in the House of Representatives

reading 18

by Randall B. Ripley

From Randall B. Ripley, "Party Leaders and Standing Committees in the House of Representatives," a working paper prepared for the Select Committee on Committees, House of Representatives, 93rd Cong., 1st sess. (1973), published in documents entitled *Committee Organization in the House,* vol. 2, part 3, pp. 552–558.

Both party leaders in the House of Representatives and the committees of the House are deeply involved in seeking certain kinds of legislative products. The way the House is structured and the procedures by which it conducts its business dictate that the party leaders and the members of the committees (particularly the more senior members of the committees) will have to interact on a variety of matters if the House is to perform smoothly and well.

As party leaders in the House seek specific legislative ends they must rely on the standing committees of the House for a number of things: the detailed substance of bills, the timetable within which bills are ready for floor consideration, the transmission of leaders' legislative preferences to the members of the committee during committee deliberations, and aid in the transmission of those preferences to all party members during floor consideration. Committee leaders must rely on the party leaders for scheduling business for the floor and helping work for its passage or defeat, for communicating important information about members' preferences to the committee, and for helping distribute committee opinions to non-committee members. . . .

THE NATURE OF LEADER-COMMITTEE INTERACTIONS

There are three particularly important points of interaction between committee leaders and party leaders. First, a major point of actual and/or potential interaction involves assignments to committees. Who sits on a committee may, in many instances, determine what emerges from that committee. As with most facets of House life, change has occurred: the relative influence of party leaders has varied considerably through time. At present the leaders of both parties seem disposed to limit their interference to special occasions. The custom of seniority limits leaders' potential impact on committee assignments to sitting members who desire to change assignments or to new members. And in the case of freshmen members and new assignments the leaders of both parties are generally disposed to exercise only minimal influence unless vital issues are at stake.

This decision by the leaders is not necessarily counterproductive to their interests. The two Committees on Committees use many criteria in making initial assignments of new Representatives and in honoring or refusing requests of sitting members to change assignments. One of these criteria, especially for the most important committees, is loyalty or potential loyalty to generally held party views.

In recent years the leaders, especially in the Democratic Party, have focused their personal attention on a few key committees. A classic instance of leadership impact was the rapid change in ideological complexion of the Democratic contingent on the Committee on Education and Labor engineered by Speaker Sam Rayburn in the 1950's. A similar change has also been wrought in the Democratic side of the Rules Committee both by careful leadership monitoring of new appointments and by the expansion of the Committee's size in 1961 (made permanent in 1963).

In many ways the most important assignments are, of course, committee chairmen and ranking minority members. After seniority hardened as the sole way for members to advance toward these posts roughly after World War I, party leaders have had virtually no leverage in making these choices. They have instead been automatic and dependent only on longevity and electoral fortunes.

In changes made in 1971 and 1973, however, the party leaders have moved into a position to develop some potential for heading movements to prevent individuals from becoming chairmen or ranking minority members if they can persuade a majority of the party that such individuals are undesirable in those positions. In 1971 the Republican Conference agreed to allow the Conference (all Republicans in the House) to vote by secret ballot and one at a time on the individuals nominated by the Committee on Committees to be ranking minority members. If the Republicans should again become the majority party in the House the same procedure would presumably apply to chairmanships. No successful challenges to seniority appointments have been made under the new procedure.

In 1971 the Democratic Caucus (all Democrats in the House) made a similar change. Committee on Committee recommendations come to the caucus one committee at a time and, if ten members request it, nominations can be debated and voted on—not just for chairmanships but for any position on any committee. If a nomination is rejected then the Committee on Committees will submit another nomination. In 1971 an unsuccessful challenge was mounted against reappointment of the Chairman of the Committee on the District of Columbia.

structure of government

In 1973 the Democrats extended their procedure by making it necessary for chairmen to obtain a majority vote in the Caucus. Twenty percent of the members can demand a secret ballot. In 1973 all 21 chairmen (all of whom had advanced to that position by virtue of seniority) were voted on by secret ballot and all won by very large margins.

In short, despite the lack of real change in personnel thus far, both parties in the House have the machinery for rejecting an unacceptable product of the seniority system in the top spot in any standing committee. The Republican Conference members and Democratic Caucus members could, of course, ignore the preferences of the formal party leaders either to retain or reject a chairman or ranking minority member. But it seems likely that members who have come to those positions through seniority will not be deposed if they have the support of the party leaders. And, if the party leaders should ever agree on the necessity of rejecting a nomination for a top position based on seniority they would probably stand a reasonably good chance of carrying either the Caucus or the Conference with them.

A second major point of interaction between party leaders and the committee system involves the scheduling of floor activity that, of necessity, has implications for the scheduling of committee business. If the party leaders of the majority party have an overall program in mind (and this is particularly likely to be the case if the White House is also controlled by their party) they are going to have some need to spread the program out over a Congress. They cannot afford to have all of the important legislation come to the floor of the House in the last two months of a session or, worse yet, the last two months of a Congress. Thus the leaders are going to be consulting with chairmen about major items on the agenda both to get some reading on when reports might be expected and to make some requests either to speed up or, less frequently, slow down, committee consideration and action.

Similarly, committee chairmen have their own agenda to consider. Therefore, they will make timing requests of the leaders for floor consideration on specific dates.

A third point of interaction between party leaders and committees involves the substance of legislative proposals. Party leaders may well be too busy with scheduling matters for the floor and working for their passage (or defeat) to have preferences on the substantive details of legislation. They do, however, have general preferences and, particularly if they are working supportively with representatives of the White House or individual executive departments or agencies, they may have detailed requests on some matters.

In general, leaders in the last few decades have kept their intervention in the substantive work of standing committees to a minimum. They have been much more likely to allow the committee to produce its substantive product by whatever natural processes exist in the committee and then work with the senior members of the committee for the passage (or defeat or amendment) of the committee's handiwork.

A rule adopted in 1973 by the Democratic Caucus increases the likelihood of more substantive input by the leaders into the work of committees. This rule allows 50 or more members of the party to bring to the Caucus any amendment proposed to a committee-reported bill if the Rules Committee is requesting a closed rule. If the proposed amendment is supported by a majority of the Caucus then the Rules Committee Democrats will be instructed to write the rule for floor consideration so that that specific amendment could be considered on the floor. In effect, this will prevent closed rules on bills if a majority present at a Democratic Caucus opposes such a rule. The leeway for leadership intervention is again present here if the Speaker and/or Majority Leader and/or Majority Whip should decide to side with the members who want to force floor consideration of a specific amendment not favored by the committee (including at least some of the Democrats on the committee).

Factors Governing the Nature of Leader-Committee Interactions

There are at least four principal factors that influence the nature of the relationships between any specific party leaders and any specific committee delegation. These factors include the personalities of the individual actors, the policy stances or ideologies of the actors, the relationship between the partisan nature of the committee and the willingness of the committee to accede to partisan requests made by committee leaders, and finally, the majority or minority party status of the leaders and committees.

First, the personalities of the individuals involved in the relationships are important. Some leaders and senior committee personnel just happen to like each other and get along very well; others are at swords points on a very personal basis. In any organization such harmonies and disharmonies are inevitable. They are not predictable, but they are important.

Second, the basic policy stances or ideologies of the party leaders and the committee leaders help set the framework for more or less cooperation between the two sets of individuals. These policy stances are, of course, going to vary through time, with individuals, and between committees. . . .

Third, the relative degree of partisanship acceptable within various committees is related to the willingness of the committee members to entertain specific partisan requests that may be made by the party leaders. Committees vary a great deal in their partisanship. Some, like Education and Labor, are unabashedly partisan. Others, like Ways and Means, exhibit "restrained partisanship," that is, partisan issues are dealt with and final decisions may have a partisan ring but the detailed work of fashioning legislation is handled largely on a nonpartisan basis. Still others, like Appropriations, are virtually nonpartisan even in terms of final outcomes. The more highly partisan committees are more open to the influence of leaders on substantive matters than the less partisan committees.

Fourth, majority or minority status may make a difference. Majority status, particularly when coupled with control of the White House, means that both the party leaders and the committee leaders have a great deal at stake in what the committees produce because what comes out of the committees is likely to pass on the floor. Minority parties are much less

structure of government

likely to prevail on the floor, particularly if the Presidency is also controlled by the majority party. Therefore, there is less pressure on the leaders of the minority party to seek to influence their standing committee delegations. They are more likely simply to follow the lead of those delegations on substance and perhaps on other matters as well. The leaders of the majority party, however, are under pressure to seek specific outcomes either because they know they are responsible in some general sense for what the House produces legislatively or because the White House is stressing to them the necessity for actions of a particular kind.

PATTERNS OF LEADER-COMMITTEE INTERACTION

There are five basic patterns of intervention between party leaders and standing committees in the House. These patterns can be characterized by the degree of intervention by party leaders in various aspects of committee functioning, ranging along a spectrum of leader activism at one end to committee autonomy at the other end. Table 1 summarizes the five patterns of interaction.

There are some conditions that enhance the emergence of patterns of behavior near the leader activism end of the interaction spectrum. Specifically, the following conditions are associated with the leader activism pattern:

1. When the personalities involved (of the party leaders and committee leaders of the same party) are congenial and the party leaders are the more aggressive individuals.

2. When there are relatively few serious policy or ideological disagreements between the party leaders and committee leaders.

TABLE 1
PATTERNS OF PARTY LEADER—STANDING COMMITTEE
INTERACTION IN THE HOUSE OF REPRESENTATIVES

| Type of Pattern | Degree of Party Leaders' Intervention In— | | |
	Committee Assignments	Committee Scheduling	Substantive Questions Before the Committee
Leader activism	High	High	High
Mixed mode: Personnel and scheduling focus	High	High	Low
Mixed mode: Personnel focus	High	Low	Low
Mixed mode: Scheduling focus	Low	High	Low
Committee autonomy	Low	Low	Low

3. When committee traditions permit (or even demand) a relatively large degree of partisanship.

4. When the majority party is involved—particularly a new majority that has just come to power in the House and is full of programmatic zeal.

Other specific conditions can be identified as facilitating the emergence of patterns of behavior near the committee autonomy end of the spectrum:

1. When there are personal strains between the party leaders and committee leaders and/or when the committee leaders possess the more forceful and aggressive personalities.

2. When a large number of fundamental policy and ideological disagreements divide the party leaders and the committee leaders.

3. When the committees put a high value on nonpartisanship in committee deliberations.

4. When the minority party is involved—particularly a long-standing minority that is accustomed to having only a small percentage of its initiatives pass the House, at least in recognizable form for which the minority is given credit.

All of these patterns are drawn from the real world in the sense that they can be illustrated by experience in the House in the 20th century. Different patterns obviously have prevailed over time. Within a single Congress different patterns may apply to the relations between the leaders and different individual committees. Differences between the two parties are also likely to occur. In general, however, the trend of the last 50 years or so has been toward committee autonomy and against leader activism, but there is nothing inevitable about the continuation of that trend. . . .

Congress
as policy-maker

reading
19

by Ronald C. Moe
and Steven C. Teel

Reprinted with permission from the *Political Science Quarterly* 85 (September, 1970), pp. 443–49 and 467–70.

THE LITERATURE of discontent with legislatures in general and Congress in particular has reached immense proportions in recent years. While few will argue that the power of the twentieth-century American Congress has declined in an absolute sense, most would agree that the position of Congress relative to that of the president has declined. Congressional critics maintain that this shift in the balance of power is most apparent in the declining role of Congress as an initiator of legislation and as a force for innovation. This decline, generally regarded to have begun around the turn of the century and to have been subsequently accelerated by the New Deal, the Second World War, and, more recently, the technological revolution, they attribute to the fragmented institutional power of Congress. Critics and defenders alike tend to agree Congress is congenitally incapable of formulating and pushing through a coherent legislative program except under the most unusual circumstances. The Congress now awaits the president's program, for it is he who establishes much of the legislative agenda and sets priorities. The result is both the weakening of Congress vis-à-vis the president and, often, the frustrating of the majority will. . . .

I

Legislation is traditionally a collective endeavor involving a variety of governmental and non-governmental participants. An exact determination of the relative contributions of Congress, the president, the bureaucracy, and interest groups in a given piece of legislation is impossible. Notwithstanding the obstacles that confront any attempt to assign credit for legislation to the several major sets of actors in the political system, the effort is worth making because of the current challenge to our polity.

The evidence indicates that Congress is underrated as an innovator in our political system. Historically, Congress has exhibited more initiative and leadership in policy-making than has the president. In an extensive study of ninety major laws in ten categories spanning a fifty-year period ending in 1940, Lawrence Chamberlain found that the president could be given credit for approximately 20 per cent, the Congress for about 40 per cent. Thirty per cent were the product of both the president and Congress, and less than 10 per cent of external pressure groups. Furthermore, one of the points brought out most clearly by his study was "the depth of the legislative roots of most important statutes." Of the 90 laws, 77 stemmed from bills introduced without the sponsorship of the administration. Chamberlain concludes that while legislation represents a joint effort, Congress has tended to be more aggressive and innovative than the executive branch: "These figures do not support the thesis that Congress is unimportant in the formulation of major legislation. Rather, they indicate not that the President is less important than generally supposed but that Congress is more important."

Looking at the question of which branch is more likely to provide recognition to new policy problems, Chamberlain is once again convinced that Congress has been dominant either by spurring the president to action or by taking independent action. Chamberlain believes that of even greater importance has been the role of Congress as "a center for the origination and maturing of innovative legislation":

> Even the most severe critic of Congress would not deny that it has been sensitive to the ever-increasing areas demanding recognition by the Federal Government. Most of the great mass of regulatory legislation of the past decade, popularly dubbed New Deal legislation, had a well-defined prenatal history extending back several years before it was espoused by the Roosevelt Administration.

There have been no subsequent studies of a comparable nature to determine whether Chamberlain's generalizations remain valid for the post-1940 period. It is widely accepted among contemporary academicians, as we have indicated, that Congress is now relatively weaker in relation to the president than previously and that what innovative influence it might once have enjoyed has been largely dissipated. We would like to ask, therefore, whether in the years since Chamberlain's work appeared, Congress has maintained its influence over the substance of the legislation it handles, or whether the "legislative roots of most important statutes" have, indeed, been entirely displaced by the resources of executive innovation. To answer this question we plan to replicate, to some degree, Chamberlain's approach using as our data the major legislative acts since 1940.

II

The methodology employed by Chamberlain was designed to determine the relative contribution of the president, Congress, and interest groups to the initiation and passage of legislation. The ninety laws he studied were divided among ten categories: business, tariff, labor, national defense, agriculture, federal credit, banking and currency, immigration, conservation, and railroads. Although these categories did not embrace all federal legislation and the choice of specific acts within these fields to some degree reflected a subjective judgment, Chamberlain argued that his mix represented a cross-section of each particular field. Chamberlain classified each law "according to the instrumentality which was chiefly responsible for its substance and passage," but it appears that he weighted influence over passage more than influence over substance. In tabulating the results of his classification, Chamberlain credited the president with preponderant influence over laws which grew out of one or more bills that "had been introduced without administration support and had received substantial consideration in Congress before the administration took a definite position." By discounting this "preliminary activity" and giving disproportionate weight to presidential influence over the passage of given statutes, Chamberlain's tabulation obscured a major area of congressional innovation in legislative policy-making. Perhaps for this reason Chamberlain's conclusions have been so frequently misinterpreted by contemporary scholars. . . .

Credit for an idea is frequently difficult to assign. Because the annual presentation of the president's program is conspicuously treated in the news, it is easily assumed that the major proposals originate in the White House or some executive agency. Although it is true that the president establishes much of the agenda for Congress, his subordinates study the issues and ideas that are under discussion in Congress. In other words, the ideas germinating in Congress are like a shopping list to presidential assistants from which they select those ideas most appropriate for presidential co-optation. Also, it is difficult to determine the exact point at which modification of executive proposals becomes genuine legislative initiative. For these reasons, in attempting to attribute influence, we will give greater prominence to congressional "preliminary activity" and congressional modification of executive proposals than did Chamberlain.

A substantial number of legislative case studies have appeared since the publication of Chamberlain's book. The conclusions of the authors of these case histories will be used, as nearly as these conclusions can be determined, to test whether Chamberlain's results hold true for the period 1940 to 1967. The laws studied over this twenty-seven years span are divided into twelve categories: economic, tariff, labor, transportation, urban problems, technology, agriculture, conservation, immigration, civil rights, national defense, and foreign policy (exclusive of tariff, defense, and immigration).

The selection of legislative categories and of the representative laws within those categories necessarily is, in part, a subjective process. In addition, the selection of individual laws to be evaluated is limited by the material available in scholarly case studies. Nevertheless, the question of whether the Congress is capable of performing a legislative function today and in the future is important enough that the absence of precise measurement techniques ought not discourage investigation. . . .

The limitations of legislative case studies and of the more comprehensive field studies are numerous and obvious; they tend to stress new questions over new answers, the unique over the routine, and bloodshed over peace. Critics of the case study method complain of the absence of integrative theory which would permit data to be analyzed cumulatively. Despite these shortcomings, the existing literature is sufficiently complete to allow us to draw some conclusions about the state of Congress as a policy-maker and the relative strength of Congress and the president in policy formulation.

Our conclusion challenges the conventional wisdom that the president has come to enjoy an increasingly preponderant role in national policy-making. The evidence does not lend support to Huntington and his thesis that Congress ought to recognize its declining state and forego what remains of its legislative function. Quite the contrary, the evidence suggests that Congress continues to be an active innovator and very much in the legislative business. Thus the findings presented here tend to confirm the findings Chamberlain made a quarter of a century ago.

In a period when legislatures throughout the world have experienced a decline in power relative to the executive, why has the American Congress retained its vitality? The answer appears to lie in the decentralized structure of both chambers. Much of the literature on Congress maintains that it is weakened by the dispersion of power inherent in its committee system and by weak chamber and party discipline over members. It is our view, however, that it is precisely this dispersed character of power in Congress which gives it the strength to meet the presidential and bureaucratic challenges. Power in Congress is dispersed because power in the executive is dispersed. Because executive decision-making is essentially incremental and piecemeal, congressional behavior, to be effective, must also be incremental and piecemeal.

It appears that not a little of the criticism of legislative institutions and their alleged inability to introduce innovative policy is based on an inaccurate conception of the policy-making process and a too limited definition of *innovation*. Charles Lindblom suggests that two major approaches exist for making public policy. The approach finding most acceptance in the literature is what he labels the "root method," which starts with fundamentals, "building on the past only as experience is embodied in a theory, and always prepared to start completely from the ground up." This method assumes intellectual capacities and sources of information, Lindblom argues, that are simply beyond the capabilities of man. It is a method which can be described, but not practiced. In contrast Lindblom outlines a "branch method," which is "continually building out from the current situation, step-by-step and by small degrees." This method of "successive limited comparisons" is more modest, but more realistic and thus "superior to any other decision-making method available for complex problems in many circumstances, certainly superior to a futile attempt at superhuman comprehensiveness."

Congress provides innovation in policy through "successive limited comparisons." As an institution Congress shies away from an architectonic role and prefers its public policy interventions to be corrective and supplemental. Its decentralized committee system permits it to be simultaneously involved in many policy fields and to develop the expertise necessary to compete with the bureaucracy. Congress tends to think and act inductively rather than deductively. The concern for details and oversight often obscures the true intent of the body. Like the lawyer, with which Congress abounds, it builds its case from specifics and only concludes with the general proposal. Does change qualify for the appellation "innovation" only when it is comprehensive in nature? We think not.

Congress is often criticized for being too closely tied to local, parochial interests. To critics, the "public interest" does not consist of the sum of the particular interests; a good congressman is one who thinks in national terms and is not unduly concerned with the local interests of his constituency. What appears to some as a congressional deficiency, however, appears to others as a virtue. Because the congressman is close to his constituents and their problems, he is able to keep "distant" government responsive to their needs. It is Congress which provides interest groups, great and small, articulate and inarticulate with access to government. Innovation, then, while occasionally of the dramatic and comprehensive variety, as illustrated in most case studies, is more often achieved in modest, yet important, changes in public policy. These changes act as safety valves for the discontented: [As Ralph Huitt has observed]

> Congress has the strength of the free enterprise system; it multiplies the decision-makers, the points of access to influence and power, and the creative moving agents. It is hard to believe that a small group of leaders could do better. What would be gained in orderliness might well be lost in vitality and sensitiveness to pressures for change. Moreover, Congress resembles the social system it serves; it reflects the diversity of the country. There is much to be said for a system in which almost every cause can strike a blow, however feeble, in its own behalf.

As American society becomes ever more urban, industrialized, and bureaucratic, the need to challenge these impersonal forces increases. Congress, whatever else it may be, is a highly human institution with a demonstrated capacity, when stimulated, to challenge these forces. Congress is not an anachronism. To say that Congress remains a vigorous institution is not to downgrade the role of the president or the bureaucracy. It does suggest, however, that the concept of separated institutions sharing powers remains a vital concept as we enter the last decades of the twentieth century. It also suggests that Congress can have an important part in our struggle to make technological progress serve the interests of our democratic institutions and values.

reading
20

legislative
oversight
of bureaucracy

by Morris S. Ogul

From Morris S. Ogul, "Legislative Oversight of Bureaucracy," a working
paper prepared for the Select Committee on Committees, House of Representatives, 93rd Cong., 1st sess. (1973), published in documents entitled *Committee Organization in the House,* vol. 2, part 3, pp. 701–708.

Legislative oversight of bureaucracy involves some of the most complex forms of behavior that the Congress undertakes. Not surprisingly
then, legislative oversight is less understood than almost any other aspect
of congressional behavior. Both congressmen in interviews and scholars
in their writings concede this lack of sustained insight. In this vortex of
incomplete knowledge (recognizing that the best experts on congressional
behavior are often congressmen) an outsider may make a contribution by
looking at familiar questions from a more detached viewpoint than that
of the immersed participant.

What follows is based on perspectives derived from a variety of
sources, from general reading and observation of the Congress and especially from intensive research in 1965 and in 1966 into the behavior of
several committees and subcommittees. Then, and since, the writer has
interviewed in depth some 40 House members, an equal number of staff
persons, and more than a score of lobbyists and officials in the executive
branch concerned with oversight.

Statements embodying general laws about oversight are scarce. It is
possible, however, to provide some useful insights into the conduct of
oversight. The materials that follow may qualify under this latter heading.
Oversight is defined as the behavior of legislators, individually or collectively, formally or informally, which results in an impact on bureaucratic
behavior in relation to the structure and process of policy implementation.

LEGAL EXPECTATIONS AND ACTUAL BEHAVIOR

There is a large gap between the oversight the law calls for and the
oversight actually performed. The clearest single statement about the over-

sight that the law requires the Congress to perform comes from that often quoted and seldom heeded statement in the Legislative Reorganization Act of 1946 assigning each standing committee the responsibility to "exercise continuous watchfulness of the execution by the administrative agencies concerned of any laws, the subject matter of which is within the jurisdiction of such committee."

Members of the Congress agree that this provision provides a full and direct legal obligation to act. In addition, all those interviewed saw that obligation as an appropriate one for the Congress. In brief, there is consensus in the Congress that extensive and systematic oversight *ought* to be conducted.

One reason for the gap between expectations and behavior lies in the nature of the expectation. The plain but seldom acknowledged fact is that this task, at least as defined above, is simply impossible to perform. No amount of congressional dedication and energy, no conceivable increase in the size of committee staffs, and even no extraordinary boost in committee budgets will enable the Congress to carry out its oversight obligations in a comprehensive and systematic manner. The job is too large for any combination of members and staff to completely master. Congressmen who feel obligated to obey the letter of the law are doomed to feelings of inadequacy and frustration and are laid open to charges of neglect. Fortunately, at least for their own morale, the members of the Congress tend to focus on the immediate more than on the impossible.

The statements above are not intended to suggest that the Congress ignores the oversight function but rather that it performs it selectively. In fact, the Congress oversees formally and informally in many ways on a daily basis. The most visible and perhaps the most effective way is through the appropriations process; the most unnoticed is latently as it considers authorizations, performs casework, and goes about business not directly labeled as oversight.

The remaining part of the gap between expectations and behavior narrows as one considers why congressmen act as they do. Two topics will be given central attention: the multiple priorities of the members of the Congress, and the impact of their policy preferences on their behavior. A discussion of these topics will reveal that there are sound reasons for this gap to exist and that most members do not really mind too much that the gap is as large as it is. Hence, their lack of willingness to do much about it.

MULTIPLE PRIORITIES

Although they seldom seem to articulate it, most members do seem to realize that the performance of oversight is best discussed not in the vacuum of legal expectations but in the more proximate context of multiple priorities and policy preferences. Each member is faced with a variety of obligations that are generally agreed to be legitimate, important, and demanding in time and energy. In principle, he should be working hard at all of them. In fact, since he does not weigh them equally, he is unlikely to give them equal attention.

When any action is perceived to contribute directly and substantially to political survival as well as to other legitimate functions, it is likely to move toward the top of any member's priority list. Extra incentives to oversee come from problems of direct concern to one's constituents or from issues that promise political visibility or organizational support. Conversely, problems not seen as closely related to political survival are more difficult to crowd onto the member's schedule. In the choice phrase of one member: "Our schedules are full, but flexible."

Not all congressional activity is linked directly to political survival. A congressman seems to gain interest in pushing oversight efforts onto his active calendar under the following conditions: new executive requests are forthcoming calling for massive new expenditures or substantial new authorizations in controversial policy areas; a crisis has occurred that has not been met effectively by executive departments; the opposition political party is in control of the executive branch; he has not been treated well either in the realm of personal attention or in the servicing of his requests; he has modest confidence in the administrative capacity of departmental or agency leaders. If key members have confidence in the way that executive department leaders are running their programs, pressure for oversight eases. . . .

In making his choices about what to do, each congressman applies his own standards of relevance; all will be doing those things that they consider most important to them at that time. Problems seen as less pressing may be recognized but may remain untouched. In these calculations, oversight frequently falls into the semineglected category. Choice, not accident, governs this decision.

If one judges from the behavior of congressmen rather than from their words alone, the conclusion seems clear that in oversight as in other congressional activities, selection and choice among worthy tasks is always necessary. Absolute mandates, even if accepted as desirable, will be obeyed only in relative terms. The price of effective action in one area may be the neglect of another.

Members of the Congress, like most other people, manage to compartmentalize their various beliefs and behaviors. Even in the face of continuing imperfect performance, congressmen retain their belief in the desirability of doing a good job at oversight. Yet, concurrently, many members seem comfortable while not doing much to narrow the gap between expectations about oversight and the actual performance of it. One might reasonably conclude then that the main spurs to the conduct of oversight do not come from any abstract belief about its necessity or desirability, but from other sources.

Congressmen through their actions implicitly rank their priorities. A glance at the rules that many seem to use provides some help in trying to understand oversight.

All members have many tasks that they feel should be pursued. The finite limits set by time and energy require that some of these expectations will be met more fully than others. If there is widespread agreement about the contents of a list of high priority tasks, there is less consensus on the relative ranking of them. Only a few things are known about why members choose to give primary attention to some activities and less to others. Even if we can presume that the omnipresent desire to survive politically serves as a major inspiration, still, member selection of other priorities remains a murky area of political analysis.

Because these factors change, the interests of each congressman in oversight will wax and wane despite his continuing adherence to the notion that oversight is an important function for the Congress to be performing.

Examining the policy preferences of members of the Congress moves us toward a more adequate explanation of the gap between expectations and behavior. From interviews and observation, I conclude that congressmen are seldom anxious to monitor those executive activities of which they approve. Oversight efforts to support administrative programs are the exception. A member essentially indifferent to a program is not likely to press for oversight efforts. One of the most important pressures to oversee flows from disagreements on policies, especially those that are of intense concern to the member. The words of members express the abstract desire to oversee; it is when that desire combines with policy disagreement that oversight is more likely to ensue.

A classic example is the experience of the House Judiciary Committee in 1965 and 1966 with civil rights issues relating to race relations. This Committee was an able group vitally interested in civil rights policy-making and administration. Emanuel Celler ran the committee as a strong chairman. Superficially, the Committee was conducting almost no oversight activity on questions of civil rights. What was strange was that the civil rights concerns of the Committee were known to be strong and deep. Several not so obvious factors helped to explain the situation. First, the Committee Chairman felt that he was having an impact on the activities of the Justice Department through informal consultation. Second, the chairman agreed in essence with what the Justice Department was doing and thus had no desire to interfere. Third, in the judgment of Chairman Celler, the net effect of any formal investigations would be harmful to the cause of civil rights since anti-rights forces might find the forum useful to articulate and publicize their views. In this case, the absence of formal oversight could be explained by a simple formula: when policy interests and the obligation to oversee clash, policy preferences will normally prevail as a guide to conduct.

The discussion thus far of member priorities, choices, and policy preferences concerns each member. The fact is that in oversight efforts, as in other activities, all congressmen are not equal. So even an intense desire to oversee, clearly a rarity in the Congress, depends for its fruition on factors other than the individual member's wants. The ability to oversee depends on where one is situated in the legislative process. Individual members, on their own, conduct very little oversight. For reasons of authority, money, and staff, oversight efforts are centered in the standing committees and subcommittees. Where one is placed in the committee system becomes a vital element in translating desires into effective action. A brief look at committees and their oversight activity is thus warranted.

COMMITTEES AND OVERSIGHT

One key to understanding oversight can be discovered by examining those places in the Congress where the division of labor and specialization can most easily be found, the committees and subcommittees. Members individually rarely can expect to conduct much legislative oversight. A comment later in the paper will indicate how even individual members can partially overcome this limitation. The heart of legislative oversight lies in the committees and subcommittees. How and why these units function as they do will tell us a great deal about how legislative oversight is performed. How the committees function is related to their structures for decision-making.

Perhaps the most effective means to enhance a committee's oversight performance is through the presence of an alert, shrewd, active chairman who wants to conduct oversight broad in scope and profound in depth. Most reforms pale in significance before this seemingly simple solution. No one, of course, really knows how to pretest prospective chairmen for these talents and interests. Nor is it clear that the members would want to pick their chairman on the basis of these criteria even if they could. The best practical bet seems to be to assume that a list of committee chairmen and subcommittee chairmen will include a few who are intensely interested in oversight and highly talented in pursuing it and a larger number who are less keen and less talented.

Assuming some such mix of committee chairmen, is there any way to enhance the oversight efforts of those committees headed by chairmen whose appetites and talents for oversight are unimpressive? At least one suggestion merits discussion. The odds for active oversight are better, in the absence of an eager chairman, if there are some semi-autonomous subcommittees with established jurisdictions, budgets, and staffs. The objective is to create additional fields in which ambition may flower. Visibility and ambition are as effective stimulants for subcommittee chairmen as for any other members. An active subcommittee within a quiescent full committee is not an unknown phenomenon in the Congress.

Innovation always has its price. The flexibility of the full committee chairman, his personal power, and perhaps even committee efficiency could possibly suffer. Whether enhancing the prospects for oversight may be worth these costs has to be decided by the congressmen themselves.

What promotes the personal power of the chairman is not necessarily good for committee oversight efforts. Fixed subcommittee jurisdictions may indeed remove some flexibility from the full committee chairman, but the price may be right: promoting the competence prerequisite to oversight activity. Numbered subcommittees without fixed jurisdictions may impede the development of expertise. Besides, from an odds maker's perspective, the presence of several subcommittee chairmen, with defined jurisdictions, separate staffs, and separate budgets, increases the field from which an interest in oversight may emerge. This analysis does not ignore the problems that may arise in some decentralized communities, but merely adds another weight to the scales.

Committee leaders may not dominate all committee behavior, but they do control much of it. What they are willing to do is central. Of course, committee members may press committee leaders to act. One type of situation minimizes the likelihood of member pressure for leadership action: where the members of a committee are there involuntarily. Members view some committee assignments as highly desirable; other assignments are viewed as burdens to be endured. Members appointed to unsought committees frequently transfer to more satisfactory assignments as soon as they can muster sufficient seniority. Given the normal problems in allotting their time and energy, we can expect that few members who see their assignments as undesirable are likely to exert maximum effort on such committees. Some oversight behavior, or the lack of it, is explainable in part by the priority that members assign to their work on a particular committee. In low status committees, those few members who choose to remain probably do so for reasons unrelated to any desire to actively pursue oversight.

SOME GRIST FOR CONTEMPLATION AND DISCUSSION

Four Myths About Oversight

Perhaps the first necessity in thinking more generally about oversight is to suggest that some widely held and deeply cherished ideas are myths. The first of these is that the Congress lacks sufficient authority to oversee properly. In fact, one can argue that the Congress has all of the authority that it needs to oversee much more extensively and effectively.

A second myth holds that the Congress lacks the budget to oversee effectively. With few exceptions, committees have the money that they need even if they wish to sharply augment their oversight efforts. One can uncover, of course, some relatively deprived committees or subcommittees, but these are the exceptions.

A third cherished belief states that the answer to how to improve oversight efforts is more staff. This answer might hold in a few cases, but not generally. Committee staff persons are hired to satisfy a variety of needs. If committee chairmen choose to take on staff exclusively for subject-matter competence, research skills, and investigative talents, they can quickly improve the prospects for oversight. But even then, staff behavior is largely a function of member preferences. A chairman passive about oversight is unlikely to have staff persons, however talented, who view oversight as a high priority. With a few conspicuous exceptions, staff behavior is more a function of member preferences than a determinant of them.

The Legislative Reorganization Act of 1970 spelled out some relationships between the Congress, its committees, and the GAO. The actual impact of the GAO on legislative oversight would be an intriguing study in itself. Such an analysis might well suggest useful paths in a rethinking of how the oversight function is performed.

Legal authority, staff, and money are all important prerequisites to congressional action, but none of these are grossly lacking now. Genuflections before the trilogy of authority, money, and staff do not reach the basic problems.

In my judgment, a fourth myth about oversight is that members of the Congress and their staffs lack the experience, training, intelligence, or creativity to conduct more and better oversight. To put it more bluntly, some critics charge that the members and their staff simply lack the competence, defined broadly in the terms just mentioned, to do the necessary work. One can unearth situations where members lack the competence needed for specific tasks, but one finds little evidence to support the proposition that these deficiencies are universal or, when found, that normally they are beyond remedy. As has been demonstrated in actual performance, useful oversight is practicable in the Congress. Deficiencies in competence in specific circumstances can frequently be remedied if the committees or subcommittees desire to do so.

It is true that even talented generalists (viz., the members of the Congress) can be intimidated by mountains of data, by exotic or technical vocabularies, or by arcane analyses. It is also true that some technical experts at times seem to relish prolix analyses presented in nearly incomprehensive language. The expert may indeed understand that obfuscation is his first line of defense. But legislators and their staffs are predestined neither to succumb nor to be deceived. Effective legislative oversight does not require that all members and all staff persons be competent in all aspects of public policy. If that were necessary the task indeed would be hopeless. The dual practices of division of labor and specialization provide the classical solution to this problem.

SOME SUMMARY PROPOSITIONS

1. Oversight is neither comprehensive nor systematic because that goal is beyond achievement.

2. Oversight is performed intermittently because the factors most relevant to stimulating it are not constantly present. Thus the quality and quantity of oversight vary between the two branches of the Congress, among the committees and subcommittees within each house, and in the same committees and subcommittees from session to session and from issue to issue.

3. It is not too difficult to produce a syndrome of factors which tend to maximize the possibilities for effective oversight. The elements might be: there is a legal basis for committee activity and there is an adequate budget for it; adequate staff resources, defined in terms of numbers, skills, and attitudes are present; the subject matter is not unusually complex or technical; the issue involved has high political visibility; the committee with relevant jurisdiction is decentralized in structure unless the chairman is a strong advocate of oversight in the given area; key committee members are unhappy with their treatment by executive personnel; key committee

members lack confidence in top executive personnel; committee senior members harbor personal antipathy toward executive officials; the executive proposes vast changes in existing programs; committee control rests in the political party opposite to that of the President.

The ease of creating such a list obscures the more difficult problem of assigning weights to each element and to predicting the possible consequences of its presence or absence. Perhaps that is because the primary elements of explanation may well vary from case to case. There seems to be no single pattern which explains legislative oversight in all circumstances. There are only common factors which combine in different ways under specified sets of circumstances. Moreover, even casual inspection of congressional behavior suggests that all the conditions which are part of this syndrome are rarely present simultaneously.

4. Oversight is not a high priority much of the time for most members.

5. Congressional staff behavior is primarily determined by member priorities and policy preferences. The best way to alter staff behavior is to focus on its major determinant.

6. A sense of realism demands recognition of the fact that most members are relatively satisfied with the conduct of legislative oversight of the bureaucracy. They feel little stimulus to alter existing patterns. . . .

III

courts and justice

There are at least three widespread misperceptions of the role that courts play in the governing apparatus of the United States. The first of these is that the Supreme Court of the United States is by far the most important court (and in some ways the only important court). Related to this is the view that it is the Supreme Court's function to state legal principles in a number of well-defined issue areas that individuals and other government agencies (lesser courts, bureaucracies, and legislatures, for example) comply with immediately and without deviation.

The second misperception is that courts function in a world that is very different from the ordinary world of politics. The processes used by courts are thought to be apolitical and judges are thought to be immune from "normal" political pressures.

The third misperception is that courts are aloof from society in a number of ways and easily achieve their presumed goal of dispensing even-handed and equal justice to all citizens. Related to this misperception is the view that justice is something different from public policy of the "normal" sort.

The three misperceptions are all related to each other in that courts and judges, especially Supreme Court justices, are thought to be apolitical, isolated, and working in a world of legal language and precedents that has importance primarily only to the few individuals actually participating as parties in lawsuits.

This note can only suggest the general outlines of why these views are, indeed, misperceptions rather than accurate perceptions. And the readings we have chosen can illustrate contrary views in only some of the areas in which an antidote would be useful.

The view of the Supreme Court as both dominant and legalistic is wrong on several counts. First, there are a very large number of important courts in the United States—including a geographically dispersed federal structure of courts of appeals and district courts and some special courts (for example, the Tax Court and the Court of Military Appeals) and a vast array of state and local courts. The Supreme Court is important, especially on a fairly narrow range of constitutional and legal questions, but most decisions ("justice," if you will) are dispensed through other courts. Second, the domain of judicial activity is constantly shifting. The tone for contraction or expansion is set by the Supreme Court—and this may be one of its most important functions in society. It has shrunk at some points in our history; it has grown in other times. For the last three decades the judicial power has been steadily growing, although there has also been considerable debate over the wisdom of that growth. Third, once the Supreme Court has spoken there still is no particular assurance that compliance will follow even on the part of lower courts let alone on the part of bureaucracies throughout the federal structure. Empirical research has demonstrated a great deal of slippage in many areas. Courts can make pronouncements, but they are notoriously dependent on a whole variety of other officials to enforce those pronouncements. And the task is complicated because most of the time there is latitude left in interpreting the meaning of the pronouncements even if the will to implement them is present.

The Richardson and Vines article (reading 21) deals with policy-making in federal district courts, where much of federal judicial "justice" is accorded litigants. The Glazer article (reading 22) argues that the great expansion of judicial power in recent years has not been without drawbacks.

The view that courts are not involved with politics is also demonstrably wrong. When courts and their activities are studied in detail, a number of familiar political processes begin to come to light. Bargaining and compromise are present. Pressures from a number of organized groups emerge in connection with the making of judicial appointments and in connection with the making of decisions in politically sensitive areas. Given the non-elected status of all federal judges and many state and local judges, these pressures take different forms than they do in the case of elected officials, but generically they are not much different. In many ways courts have constituents about which they must worry. The individuals in the constituencies are not voters but may be other judges, other judicial officials, individual lawyers, organized groups of lawyers, and law clerks. Some of the most important "lobbying" in connection with judicial decision-making occurs within this relatively small, but nevertheless diverse, group of professionals. Interpersonal influence is particularly important in cases of multi-judge courts such as the Supreme Court.

The third misperception—that courts stand aloof from society and dispense equal justice for all—is also inaccurate in several particulars. As indicated, judicial appointments are deeply immersed in politics—and those nominated, after all, come from some portion of society and have personal ties of many sorts as well as organizational and institutional ties. Courts are also intimately related to society in that their decisions do have both potential and actual impact on the ways in which society conducts some of its affairs and on a wide variety of public policies. Despite the slippage between court decisions and compliance alluded to above there is still considerable compliance, and sometimes this is in areas that can have far-reaching ramifications. The representational nature of Congress and virtually all state legislatures has changed dramatically in the last 15 years, for example, because of a series of Supreme Court decisions and a number of lower court decisions. The Glazer article (reading 22) illustrates the policy impact of the courts in a number of areas. We have also included two articles (reading 23 by Engstrom and reading 24 by Slotnick) on policy-making by the judiciary in two specific fields: gerrymandering and obscenity.

decision making in the district courts

by Richard J. Richardson
and Kenneth N. Vines

From Richard J. Richardson and Kenneth N. Vines, *The Politics of Federal Courts* (Boston: Little, Brown and Company, 1970), pp. 80–81, 92–93, 96–98, 100–105, 108–110.

As THE FIRST and only courts that most litigants in the federal system see, the district courts occupy a fundamental position in the federal judiciary. These courts not only receive the great mass of federal cases, but they also settle in final form the great majority of cases decided in the federal courts. This latter point may be illustrated by reference to the year 1960 in which 93.8 per cent of all cases filed in the federal courts were settled in final form at the district level. But important as district courts are in settling cases, they also handle quite a few cases that are later appealed. A large part of the Supreme Court's work and most of the litigation of the appeals courts are cases that have initially been decided by district courts. Because of this, district court cases constitute the decisional building blocks on which much of the work of the appellate courts depends. From several points of view, therefore, the judicial behavior in the district courts and the character of decision making there are of great importance in determining the politics of the federal judiciary. . . .

A SAMPLE OF DISTRICT DECISIONS

For our exploration of decision making in the district courts we went directly to the cases and drew a sample of them for analysis. Our sample included all civil liberties and labor cases from the 33 district courts of the Third, Fifth, and Eighth Circuits decided during the years 1956 to 1961. These cases were selected because they involved policy questions of an unusually important, sensitive, and interesting nature. We chose the district courts of the Third, Fifth, and Eighth Circuits because they constituted a wide geographic distribution. The Fifth contains courts of the

Deep South, the Third a combination of Middle Atlantic and New England industrial states, and the Eighth a combination of Middle Western states and Arkansas.

The character of judicial institutions thus represented is varied, including contrasting social and economic characteristics which are captured within the district boundaries. The range of districts that we have included varies from the southern Mississippi district, with practically no urban and industrial development and a high Negro population, to the western district of Pennsylvania, which is highly urbanized and industrialized and has an average Negro population. In partisan characteristics, the districts range from the Democratic area of western Pennsylvania to the traditionally Republican area of Nebraska, and from the conservative districts of Mississippi to the competitive, partisan districts of New Jersey. . . .

THE DISTRICT AS A DECISION MAKING VARIABLE

The constituencies of district court activity are clearly not simply passive containers of judicial activity. They constitute the environment within which decisions take place, and they mold . . . both the character of the judges that are selected and the nature of district court institutions. . . .

To test the effects of environmental differences, we isolated certain of our cases and observed their relation to an important social variable in the districts. Our group of cases included all race relations cases involving Negroes decided in the Southern district courts. We compared the results of the decisions with the size of the Negro population in the district. Since race relations cases deal with the most sensitive issue in Southern politics, we might expect decisions in the district courts to be related to Negro-white population balance. Other Southern behaviors are strongly related to this factor.

The overall correlation between the direction of decisions and the percentage of Negroes in the district is $r = .42$. (See Figure 1.) The modest but definite direction of correlation indicates that court policies are related to variations in racial population in the same manner as observed in other areas of Southern politics. A close relationship is most visible in districts with extreme population imbalance, either with or without Negroes. The districts of southern Georgia, northern Mississippi, and southern Mississippi all have large Negro populations and low scores in deciding cases for Negroes, whereas the districts of western Virginia, eastern Tennessee, and middle Tennessee have small Negro populations and high scores. In most other districts the relationship is not as pronounced, and in several, notably the northern district of Texas and the eastern district of Louisiana, the relationship is reversed. For example, the northern Texas district has few Negroes but a low civil rights score, and the eastern Louisiana district has a comparatively large Negro population but decided a large proportion of cases favorably to Negroes.

Our evidence indicates that the correlation between race relations policy and Negro-white population balance is weaker in the Southern judiciary than in many other political institutions. Political science litera-

Figure 1. Relationship of Percentage of Cases in District Decided in Favor of Negroes in Race Relations Cases to Percentage of Negro Population in That District

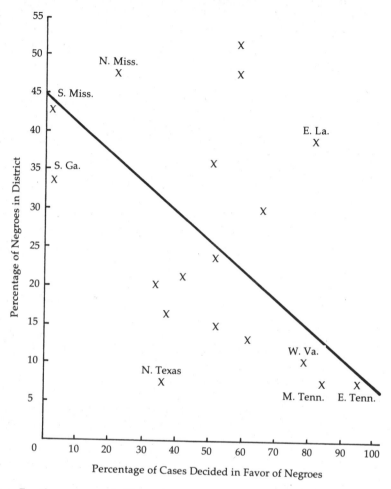

Percentage of Cases Decided in Favor of Negroes

For the purpose of this analysis, we have broadened our coverage to include cases decided from 1957 to 1962 in eleven Southern districts with more than five cases.

Source: *Race Relations Law Reporter.*

ture indicates that the relation is stronger in the actions of Southern officials in registering Negroes to vote and in the behavior of Southern legislators and governors.

In accounting for these differences we note that Southern district judges, unlike most other Southern political officials, are appointed for life, are not removable for political reasons, and are not responsible to Southern

structure of government

public opinion in any formal ways. Although recruitment policies suggest that Southern district judges possess values similar in many respects to those of other Southerners, the life tenures and quasi-insulated positions of the federal judiciary prevent reinforcement of such values through activities like popular elections and public campaigning. In addition, district judges are subjected to pressures from national appellate courts to have their decisions conform to national policies. For these reasons it would seem that Southern judges are less affected by political pressures than are many other political officials in the South.

The district judge is required by statute to live in his district, and he participates as a person in the life of the district community. Thus, although federal judges are insulated from formal links with popular opinion, they are aware of opinions expressed in a community context, and such expression is a variety of popular pressure. . . .

PATTERNS OF DECISION MAKING

In selecting labor and civil liberties cases, we have concentrated on important policy areas in which we would expect differences in political behavior among district judges to be quite visible. Examination of race relations cases in the districts has revealed behavioral differences among judges. Now we examine the entire group of cases.

Our sample of cases in the district courts identified 815 cases that were decided by individual judges; the remaining 76 were decided by three-judge courts and will be discussed later. We have observed the unequal distribution of cases among the circuits, but also interesting is the variation in the amount of decision making among the judges themselves. . . .

The distribution of cases indicates that policy is decided in two crucial areas—civil rights and labor relations—by a minority of district judges. Only to a limited extent does the nature of the district determine decision making distribution, for although certain districts provide more opportunity for district judges to decide significant cases, wide differences exist among judges within districts. In the eastern district of Louisiana, for example, Judge Wright decided five times as many cases as Judge Christenberry, and in the eastern district of Pennsylvania, Judge Gourley handled twice as many cases as did his colleague Judge Clary.

Ostensibly, the courts are passive instruments of policy because they may hear only those cases brought to them, and because judges have little direct control over the flow of cases. It is quite probable, however, that judges discourage or invite litigation by their expressed attitudes and by their past behavior. . . .

In the past, it has been possible for judges to specialize in certain types of cases and to hear these cases because of the manner in which cases were assigned to judges in the court. Schedules describing the times and places judges were sitting made it possible to predict roughly which judges would hear cases scheduled at given times. Through a combination of activities of plaintiffs and the judges themselves, it was thus possible for judges to differentiate the kinds of cases heard. . . .

TABLE 1

NUMBER OF DISTRICT JUDGES DECIDING CASES FOR LABOR AND CIVIL LIBERTIES BY CIRCUIT AND LEVEL OF SUPPORT

| | Number of Judges | | | | | |
| | Third Circuit | | Fifth Circuit | | Eighth Circuit | |
Percentage of Cases	Civil Liberties	Labor	Civil Liberties	Labor	Civil Liberties	Labor
Below 10	7	0	3	0	0	0
10–33.3	3	3	0	0	2	2
33.4–50	0	7	2	2	1	1
51–66.7	0	5	2	2	2	0
Above 66.7	0	5	2	2	0	1

Table 1 compares the decisions of district judges who decided more than five cases in each category according to political direction. A pro-civil liberties decision represented a vote in favor of the liberty claimed, and a pro-labor decision represented one made in favor of the group interests of labor.

Thirty-six judges in the three circuits decided over five cases in one of the areas, and twenty of the judges decided over five in both the labor and civil liberties categories. A dominant pattern in the distribution is the great range of decision scores. Only in civil liberties cases in the Third Circuit was there anything approaching a consensus on the issues that appeared in district litigation. Indeed, it is evident that considerable conflict and political difference exist among district court judges in handling important issues.

The lack of agreement in the districts may result from the solitary role of the district judge who is not exposed to the compromises and other political processes of a collegiate court. A district judge may not take into account the extent to which his decision squares with those of other district courts. On the other hand, appellate bodies may deliberately try to play down disagreements and reach united decisions that can be presented as an impressive consensus to bolster the prestige of a given decision.

The distribution of scores indicates that the behavioral pattern in the district judiciary reflects conflict and a variety of opinion. . . .

Other studies have indicated that different behaviors among judges are related to party affiliation. Our investigation of this relationship was conducted by determining the party identification of judges and then comparing the decisional scores of Republicans and Democrats in each of the subject areas of our investigation. Party membership was related to disposition of cases according to Table 2.

In Table 2, party is shown to be slightly related to disposition of cases for both labor and civil liberties. The more favorable labor scores of the

structure of government

TABLE 2

RELATIONSHIP OF JUDGES' PARTY AND DIRECTION OF DECISIONS
(N = 33)

Labor (349 cases)	Democrats more favorable than Republicans by 8.6 per cent
Civil Liberties (195 cases)	Republicans more favorable than Democrats by 13.3 per cent

Democratic judges parallel the Democrats' tendency in national politics to favor labor interests. The difference is not, however, as great as has been found in studies of national party leaders or national legislators. . . .

The somewhat more favorable decisions of Republican judges on civil rights reflect ambiguity within each party on the subject, particularly among the Democrats. In the South, Eisenhower appointees . . . evinced a more favorable attitude toward civil rights than many Southern Democrats on the bench, and some Democrats in the North . . . had more favorable civil liberties records than Republicans. In addition, studies of party and ideology elsewhere have shown that differences between Republicans and Democrats on civil liberties issues are somewhat blurred. . . .

IMPACT OF THE LEGAL SUBCULTURE

Decision making in the district courts is shaped, as we have seen, by strong local democratic features. So strong and visible has been the influence of local values in the districts that litigants have requested judges to be disqualified in local cases, and a leading law journal has published an article on the problems raised by such judicial behavior and on ways by which district judges might be disciplined.

The eighty-eight district courts are united, however, by certain legal considerations that give uniformity to their decisions and institutional behavior, at the same time that the centrifugal forces of localism are at work. An important experience that pulls judges together is their socialization in legal education. Since most judges have read the same or similar hornbooks, taken similar courses of instruction, and have exposed to many common values in law school, legal education brings some common perspective to decision making. In bar organizations and in further readings in the law, the common elements of legal culture are further disseminated to judges.

The judicial process also provides procedures by which differences among the district courts are refined and common values inculcated into judicial decision making. Since any district decision can be heard in the courts of appeals and may be heard by the Supreme Court, both the regional appellate courts and the Supreme Court can supply uniform standards through review of district court decisions and by remand and vacate order. But it is a mistake to believe that orders and decisions in appellate review are rigidly followed by the local district courts. Indeed, an important political feature of the judicial process is the promptness and the extent to which lower courts observe the directives in appellate decisions. The idea that either the Supreme Court or the appeals courts adequately supervises the district courts is not empirically supportable but, in general, higher court review of district decisions is a cohesive force.

Another important factor unifying the district courts has been their adherence to common legal concepts and rules of procedure. At the beginning of the American court system, the judiciary act passed in 1789 allowed a great deal of local autonomy in legal procedures, providing that actions in district courts were the same in each state "as are now used or allowed in the supreme courts of the same." The general rule of conformity to state practices had many exceptions, and federal procedure dominated in such important matters as the administration of the trial, appellate procedure, and questions of jurisdiction. Conflicting decisions on whether state or federal procedures were more important in the district courts resulted, but the individual judge was ordinarily able to emphasize the procedures of his choice.

It was not until 1938 that Congress, under the urging of legal groups, passed a uniform Code of Civil Procedure, which embodied rules and procedures governing conduct throughout the federal court system. This was followed in 1946 by the passage of a Federal Rules of Criminal Procedure, which provided uniform practices for noncivil cases. The codes were a significant step in providing legal integration of the federal court system, and their success in providing procedural uniformity has been called "quite phenomenal" by one authority. The acceptance of the codes also enhanced the power of legal groups to make the rules under which the courts operate. Although the basic legislation was enacted by the Congress, the rules were originally drafted by a committee consisting of the leading lawyers and law professors in the country and were then submitted to the Supreme Court for revision. When the Congress passed no adverse legislation after submission, the rules as drafted became law. The adoption of the codes was an impressive demonstration of the power of legal groups to enact important modifications of federal judicial institutions.

Judicial conferences and councils, instigated by Chief Justice Taft and urged by legal groups, have provided a further means of unifying the district courts. . . .

reading
22

towards
an imperial
judiciary?

by Nathan Glazer

Reprinted with permission of Nathan Glazer from *The Public Interest*, No.
41, Fall, 1975. Copyright © by National Affairs Inc.

A NON-LAWYER who considers the remarkable role of courts in the
interpretation of the Constitution and the laws in the United States finds
himself in a never-never land—one in which questions he never dreamed
of raising are discussed at incredible length, while questions that would
appear to be the first to come to mind are hardly ever raised. This is
particularly the case when the concern of the non-professional observer
is with social policy rather than with constitutional law as such.

Thus, fine distinctions in the use of evidence in criminal cases are
debated at length, and used as a basic test in judging whether a court or
individual justices are liberal or conservative; whereas one sees little discussion of why judges may hold up hundreds of millions of dollars in
federal payments to states and cities to force them to make numerous civil
service appointments, or why judges may require a state or city to provide
extensive and specifically defined social services. The original *Brown* decision on school desegregation was properly debated at length by our leading
constitutional authorities. But what are arguably the most disruptive decisions ever made by the courts—the requirement that children be bused
to distant schools—have excited much less professional interest than
popular interest.

One reason for this disparity is that judges and lawyers are trained
to see continuity in the development of constitutional law. However far-
reaching the actions the courts take, the lawyers who propose such actions
and the judges who rule on them are committed by the logic of legal
reasoning to insist that they are only unveiling a rule that existed all along
in the recesses of the Constitution or the bowels of legislation: Nothing
new has been added, they say, even though great consequences follow
from their decisions.

Political scientists who study the courts are somewhat freer to see truly original developments in the constitutional law, but they generally do not go beyond interpreting these developments as part of a cycle. If the court changes, to them it changes within a well-understood pattern, in which periods of activism symmetrically contrast with periods of quietism: At some point the Supreme Court, exercising its power to interpret the Constitution and the laws and to overrule the interpretations of legislatures and executives, goes too far—thus, we have the *Dred Scott* decision, or the decisions overruling the actions of the New Deal in the mid-1930's. An explosion then results: as a result of the *Dred Scott* decision, a war; as a result of the anti-New Deal decisions, the court-packing plan. To the political scientist, the court follows not only its own logic but the logic of public opinion. Since it is without the independent power to enforce its decrees, the Court then withdraws. Its withdrawal is assisted ultimately by the appointment power of the President, who is in closer touch with public opinion. A period of quietism thus succeeds a period of activism. . . .

There is, however, another perspective on judicial interpretation, one which is generally identified with outraged legislators, Presidents, governors, and people: The Court has gone too far, they say, and the return of the quietistic phase of the cycle will not satisfy us, for the Court is engaged in a damaging and unconstitutional revolution that even the cyclical return of a period of quietism cannot curb. The lawyers who must operate within the assumption of continuity are inclined to dismiss such outrage, and the legal commentators who look at the long stretch of history are sure that quietism will replace activism—as it has before—and that the courts will retire from the front pages of the newspapers. Yet in 1975, all the evidence suggests that this third perspective is really the correct one: The courts truly have changed their role in American life. American courts, the most powerful in the world—they were that already when Tocqueville wrote and when Bryce wrote—are now far more powerful than ever before; public opinion—which Tocqueville, Bryce, and other analysts thought would control the courts as well as so much else in American life—is weaker. The legislatures and the executive now moderate their outbursts, for apparently outbursts will do no good. And courts, through interpretation of the Constitution and the laws, now reach into the lives of the people, against the will of the people, deeper than they ever have in American history.

FROM WARREN TO BURGER

These are sweeping assertions, yet the course of the law since 1969 supports them. For in 1969 something was supposed to happen, and didn't. In his first term, President Nixon, who opposed the Warren Court's activism, succeeded in making four appointments, and the period of activism that had begun with the *Brown* decision of 1954 was supposed to come to an end, as the Warren Court was replaced by the Burger Court. Instead, there have been more far-reaching decisions—if estimated by the impact on people and their everyday lives—since 1969 than in 1954–1968, even with four Nixon-appointed Justices. In 1971 the *Swann* decision for the first time legitimated massive busing of children to overcome segregation in a large city; in 1974 the *Keyes* decision for the first time legitimated such massive busing in a Northern city, and in addition legitimated standards of proof for *de jure* segregation that were so loose that it guaranteed that *de jure* segregation could be found everywhere (which meant that the Court's narrow 5–4 decision in *Milliken*—which overturned lower court requirements for the merger of Detroit and its suburbs in order to create, through busing, schools with smaller proportions of black children—could very likely be circumvented by demonstrating that the suburbs, too, were engaged in *de jure* segregation). In 1971 the Court legitimated federal government guidelines for the use of tests in employment that required strict standards of "job-relatedness" if, on the basis of such tests, differing proportions of certain ethnic and racial groups were given employment. This decision has, in effect, declared illegal most efforts by employers, public and private, to hire more qualified employees. Since apparently all tests select differing proportions of one group or another, and few tests can be shown to be job-related by the strict standards of the guidelines, most employee hiring on the basis of tests now can be labeled discriminatory and employers may be required, either by lower court orders or by Department of Justice consent decrees, to hire by racial and ethnic quotas—a practice which is specifically forbidden by the Civil Rights Act of 1964 and (one would think) unconstitutional because of its denial of the "equal protection of the laws." In 1973, the Burger Court ruled in *Roe* and *Doe* that just about all state laws on abortion were unconstitutional and decreed that state laws must treat each third of the pregnancy period according to different standards. In 1975 it spread the awesome limitations of "due process" to the public schools, which now could not restrict the constitutional rights of students by suspending or expelling them without at least something resembling a criminal trial. In 1975 it agreed, in the first of a series of important cases on the rights of mental patients, that harmless persons could not be detained involuntarily in mental hospitals.

The list could be extended. It is true that the Court stayed its hand in other cases that could have had enormous consequences: In particular, it refused to accept the argument that states must ensure that financial support of schools be unaffected by differences in community wealth, and it did not allow a challenge by inner-city residents to suburban zoning ordinances. But in both areas state courts are active, and it is hard to see what is to prevent them from decreeing for their states (as the courts of New Jersey already have) the revolution in equalization of school financing and zoning that the Supreme Court has refused to decree for the nation.

What was most striking is that all of these cases—and many others extending the reach of government, whether it wished it or not, into the lives of people, and of the courts over the actions of legislatures and communities—were made despite the rapid appointment of four Justices by President Nixon. The Nixon Justices either supported the majority in 9-0 decisions (e.g., *Swann*), or split (thus only one of the four dissented from the majority in *Doe* and *Roe*), and only rarely (in *Gross*, on due process for students) voted as a bloc against the majority of five who had served on the Warren Court.

Supreme Court analysts and reporters very often tell a different story from this, because in judging the Court, they tend to focus on the endless details of what is or is not allowed in criminal law—the use of confessions, searches, and the like. Emphasizing the criminal law, they apparently see a retreat where another observer might see a modicum of common sense. But I believe all agree that the Burger Court has been surprisingly like the Warren Court; and this raises the question of why the expected turn has not yet taken place—seven years after Nixon was elected, and after four of his appointees were on the court.

THE END OF A CONSERVATIVE JUDICIARY?

Three characteristics of the Burger Court, and of the Warren Court, have excited less interest than they might have, and would suggest that we must at least consider the possibility that there has been a permanent change in the character of the courts and their role in the commonwealth, rather than simply a somewhat extended activist cycle.

First, the activist cycles of the past have always been characterized by conservative Courts, acting to restrict liberal Congresses, Presidents, or state governments—the Marshall Court, the Taney Court, and the Taft-Hughes Courts. This made sense: The Court, after all, was designed by the Founders to be a conservative institution, a check on popularly elected legislatures and an elected (even if not at the beginning *popularly* elected) President. . . .

But something extraordinary has happened when a liberal Court confronts a conservative executive and legislature, as the Warren Court did after the election of President Eisenhower: The *natural* expectations, the order of history, have been reversed. It is even more extraordinary when, after 15 years of appointments to the Supreme Court and the subordinate courts by conservative Presidents (against seven years by liberal Presidents), this strange posture still persists.

A second extraordinary feature of the post-1954 activism is a corollary in part of the first: In the past the role of activist courts was to *restrict* the executive and legislature in what they could do. The distinctive characteristic of more recent activist courts has been to *extend* the role of what the government could do, even when the government did not want to do it. The *Swann* and *Keyes* decisions meant that government *must* move children around to distant schools against the will of their parents. The *Griggs* decision meant that government *must* monitor the race and ethnicity of job applicants and test-takers. The cases concerning the rights of mental patients and prisoners, which are for the most part still in the lower courts, say that government *must* provide treatment and rehabilitation whether it knows how or not. Federal Judge Weinstein's ruling in a New York school desegregation case seems to say that government *must* racially balance communities. And so on.

An interesting example of this unwilled extension of governmental action is that of the Environmental Protection Agency (EPA). It did not wish to issue rules preserving pure air in areas without pollution or imposing drastic transportation controls. To the EPA, this did not seem to be what Congress intended; but under court order, it was required to do both. Similarly, the Department of Health, Education, and Welfare (HEW) apparently did not want to move against the Negro colleges of the South, now no longer segregated under law but still with predominantly black enrollments, nor was this in the interests of those colleges, or their students, or indeed anyone else—but Federal judges required HEW to do so.

In these, as in other cases, government is required to do what the Congress did not order it to do and may well oppose, what the executive does not feel it wise to do, and most important what it does not know how to do. How *does* one create the permanently racially balanced community that Judge Weinstein wants so that the schools may be permanently racially balanced? How does one create that good community in Boston public housing that Judge Garrity wants so that vandalism repair costs may be brought down to what the authority can afford? How does one rehabilitate prisoners? Or treat mental patients? Like Canute, the Judges decree the sea must not advance, and weary administrators—hectored by enthusiastic, if ignorant, lawyers for public advocacy centers—must go through the motions to show the courts they are trying.

RECONSIDERING THE CYCLICAL THEORY

A third feature of the new activism which is also extraordinary: The Court's actions now seem to arouse fewer angry reactions from the people and the legislatures. The power of the Court has been exercised so often and so successfully over the last 20 years, and the ability to restrict or control it by either new legislation, constitutional amendment, or new appointments has met with such uniform failure, that the Court, and the subordinate courts, are now seen as forces of nature, difficult to predict and impossible to control. Thus, one may contrast the outburst over the school prayer decisions of 1962–3 with the relative quietude of response to the abortion decisions of 1973. Or, contrast the effort to adopt a constitutional amendment to control the sweep of reapportionment decisions in 1964–66 with the general view in Congress today that any effort to control the Court on busing by means of a constitutional amendment has no chance of succeeding.

This is, of course, not necessarily witness to the strength of the Court as such: What it reflects, in addition, is the agreement of large sectors of opinion—even if it is still minority opinion—with the Court's actions. But this opinion in favor of the Court is shaped by the reserves of strength the Court possesses: the positive opinion of the Court in the dominant mass media—the national television news shows, the national news magazines, and the most influential newspapers; and the bias in its favor among the informed electorate generally, and among significant groups of opinion-leaders. The Court is further the beneficiary of two accidents of political history (or at least they may be accidents): Because he was running against Barry Goldwater, Lyndon Johnson had an overwhelming victory in 1964, and helped bring into office so many liberal Congressmen that the powerful effort to limit the Court on reapportionment was blunted. And because of the Watergate scandal, so many liberal Congressmen were returned to Congress in 1974 that the natural life of the activist cycle in the Court's history was extended at least two years, and perhaps longer. Thus this Congress will not start any amendment process to limit the Court on busing. (It is understood that liberal Congressmen today, as against our previous history, support the power of the Court. If new appointments bring about the expected conservative switch, that position may change.)

The key point, however, is that the major limitation on the Court's power—public opinion, expressing itself through the Presidency and the Congress—has not come into effect to limit this Court. Outrage at its actions was stronger 12 or 13 years ago than it is today, though the intrusive reach of the Court's actions into the daily life of citizens has become much stronger. . . .

What I am suggesting is that we must reconsider the theory that activist cycles are succeeded by quiescent ones. This belief was based on the view that public opinion in the end controls the Court, which has the power of neither purse nor sword, and that the Court is thus still pretty much where the Founders and Chief Justice Marshall established it, as one of the three coequal branches of government, with great moral authority but little else. In contrast, it appears that the controls on Court power have become obsolescent and that the role of the Court—and courts generally—has changed significantly, such that the most powerful Court and Judiciary in the world have become even more powerful, raising questions of some gravity for the Commonwealth. Of course, any long-range view shortly may be made irrelevant by current events. . . .

However, there are three factors that argue that the activist phase of the present Court will not easily be reversed, and two of them are quite new.

THE NEW CONSTITUTIONAL LOGIC

The first factor is well-known and broadly discussed in the constitutional law literature: The Court must work out the logic of positions once taken, and it cannot easily withdraw from the implications of these positions. Thus, if "standing" to sue has been radically expanded so that many interests and individuals who in the past had no access to constitutional adjudication of their claims now have such access, a systemic change has occurred, and it is not possible to revert to an earlier, more restrictive view of "standing.". . .

WHEN GOVERNMENT EXPANDS

. . . [A] second factor that sustains the permanent activism of the court is the enormous increase in the reach of government itself. When government expands, it could seem reasonable that the Court must extend its reach also. It must consider issues of equity and due process and equal protection in all the varied areas of education, health care, housing, and access to government services of all types. It must consider the varied impact of new subsidies, and controls and restrictions based on safety or environmental considerations. It is true that as government expands it sets up quasi-judicial bodies to adjudicate difficult decisions, but there is one major route of appeal in our system from these multifarious quasi-judicial bodies, and that is to the federal courts, and only one final appeal, to the Supreme Court. The expanded reach of government also means that new bases for decision-making by courts must be taken into account, that the "facts" on the basis of which lower courts rule become more and more complex. . . .

The expanded reach of government not only explains a more activist Court; in the minds of many analysts, it also justifies it. Perhaps it does. But one reason it does is that courts are dissatisfied with how legislatures and executives run their respective spheres, and while they do not egregiously reach out to express their dissatisfaction—courts, after all, must wait for cases to come to them—when the cases do come to them, they stretch their hands out very far indeed to make corrections. Consider issues raised in some recent cases: inadequate medical treatment for prisoners; welfare to applicants delayed beyond some reasonable time; public housing poorly maintained and in poor repair; mental patients not receiving treatment. The courts and their defenders say that if the legislature and executive are incapable of action in these and similar cases, then the courts must act. . . .

THE NEW LITIGATION

Finally, there is a third factor which suggests that a highly activist and intrusive judiciary is now a permanent part of the American Commonwealth: The courts will not be allowed to withdraw from the broadened positions they have seized, or have been forced to move into, because of the creation of new and powerful interests, chief among them the public advocacy law centers. It can hardly be an accident that the failure of the expected conservative cycle to succeed the activist cycle of 1954–68 occurred at the same time that many new centers were established for the promotion of social change through litigation. At the beginning of the 1960's there apparently existed only one such center—the NAACP Legal Defense Fund. Under the Economic Opportunity Act, many poverty law centers were created. Many other centers, receiving government or foundation aid, were established in almost every field of social policy—welfare, education, housing, health, environment—and for almost every group of potential clients—Mexican-Americans, Puerto Ricans, Indians, prisoners, mental health patients, etc. Law for the promotion of social change became enormously popular with law students, and many sought posts in the new centers.

Of course, this revolutionary change in the landscape of the practice of law itself reflected broader changes: a rising critical attitude toward government, a widespread belief among many sectors of the population in the unfairness and unjustness of government, the widespread legitimation among the youth and minorities of an adversary posture and denunciatory rhetoric—which all complemented nicely the standard practices of litigation. Law—for the purpose of the correction of presumed evils, for changing government practices, for overruling legislatures, executives, and administrators, for the purpose indeed of replacing democratic procedures with the authoritarian decisions of judges—became enormously popular. The number of law students rose rapidly, in response to new opportunities for litigation, and also serving as insurance of expanded litigation, owing to the increasing number of lawyers. . . .

reading 23

judicial activism and the problem of gerrymandering

by Richard L. Engstrom

This article was written expressly for the present volume. Professor Engstrom is a member of the Political Science Department at the University of New Orleans.

ON THE EVE of his retirement from the United States Supreme Court the late Earl Warren was requested by an interviewer to reflect upon the achievements of that Court during his service as Chief Justice (1953–1969). Those achievements were often both dramatic and controversial, for the period was one of the most active and aggressive times in the history of the Court. Among them were the demand to dismantle racially segregated public school systems, an expanded recognition of the rights possessed by those accused of criminal activities, the prohibition of prayers in public schools, and a broadening of the constitutionally protected forms of expression. Yet Earl Warren selected as the most significant the Court's decision to investigate and exercise some control over electoral districting arrangements utilized in the selection of the peoples' representatives to legislative bodies. The Court recognized that the purpose of such arrangements was to provide the people with "fair and effective representation" within our system of representative democracy, but in the absence of judicial supervision over this aspect of the electoral process the goal was not being realized.

The basic reason the goal was not being realized was the widespread presence of a condition known as *malapportionment*, large differences in the numbers of people residing within representational districts. These malapportioned electoral arrangements were blatantly unfair. Some people, usually residents of urban areas, were being underrepresented, while others, usually rural dwellers, were being overrepresented. For example, districts for selecting members of the United States House of Representatives from the State of Georgia varied from 272,154 people to 823,680 people. A majority of the members of the lower house of the Kansas state legislature represented only 18.5 percent of the state's population, while a majority of the state senators represented only 26.8 percent. The 68,000 residents of the City of Midland, Texas, selected only one member of their county governing board, while the three other members of the board were each selected from districts of fewer than 1,000 people. Malapportionment was a common condition throughout the United States, and it was the correction of these inequities that Earl Warren thought to be most significant, for such inequities did not provide everyone "an opportunity to participate in his government on equal terms with everyone else" and did not allow everyone to "share in electing representatives who will be truly representative of the entire community."

Malapportionment resulted in the denial of fair and effective representation to many people. But the situation was perpetuated by those immediately responsible for creating and maintaining the arrangements, the representatives themselves. Redrawing the lines of the districts was a politically risky business. To reapportion fairly would reduce the number of rural representatives, could drastically alter the strength of the political parties within a legislature, and, most importantly, was a serious threat to the representatives' own electoral security. It was politically more comfortable to leave the lines alone, or to change them in only the most minimal ways. The recognition that districting was an inherently political process had previously caused the Court to avoid any involvement in this part of the electoral process. But in 1962 the attitude of the Court changed, and a decision was made to involve the federal judiciary in the quest for fair and effective representation.

Soon adopted as the principal medium for the realization of that goal was the "one man, one vote" standard, more recently identified as the "one person, one vote" standard in deference to the women's rights movement. That standard requires every district from which a representative is to be elected to contain approximately the same number of people. Each individual voter is to compete with approximately the same number of other voters in selecting his or her representative. The adoption of that standard has had an impressive impact on the electoral system, for gross malapportionment has been successfully eliminated in this country (except in the United States Senate, where every state is guaranteed two seats by the Constitution). But unfortunately the elimination of malapportionment does not itself mean the realization of fair and effective representation, for districts containing essentially equal numbers of people can be constructed that are still unfair to and ineffective for political, ethnic, and/or racial minorities. In short, the one person, one vote standard successfully prevents malapportionment, but it does not prevent another major obstacle to fair representation, the practice of *gerrymandering*.

Gerrymandering is the practice of creating districting arrangements that prevent or seriously reduce the ability of a recognizable group of voters to translate their voting strength into the selection of representatives favored by that group. It can be directed against a political party or against minority groups such as blacks, Chicanos, or American Indians. A gerrymander operates so as to "waste" a substantial proportion of the group's votes by *dispersing* those votes throughout a number of districts and/or by *concentrating* those votes within one or a few districts. For example, voters in a black residential area can be placed into several districts in which they constitute minorities of maybe 25 to 30 percent, seriously reducing the likelihood of a black person being elected. Alternatively, black voters can be placed into one or a few districts in which they constitute large majorities of maybe 90 to 95 percent, thereby casting many more votes than needed to select a candidate favorable to blacks. In both cases many black votes would be "wasted."

The practice of creating districting arrangements that waste the votes of an identifiable group became known as gerrymandering back in 1812 when Democrats in the Massachusetts legislature attempted to dilute the effectiveness of Federalist voters. As part of that state-wide effort, the Democrats created an elongated senatorial district within Essex County. An artist, Elkanah Tinsdale, added a beak, wings, and claws to the district so that it looked like a monster which was then named a "gerrymander" after the state's governor, Elbridge Gerry. Since then, the practice has been commonly referred to by that name.

Descriptions of weird-shaped districts continue to be a favorite game of commentators. Among the most imaginative recent descriptions have been "The Camel Biting the Tail of the Buffalo Which is Stepping on the Tail of the Dachshund," "The Upside Down Crocodile," and "Jigs and Jags like a Salamander Scurrying Over Hot Rocks." But it is important to be aware of the fact that gerrymandering is not accomplished only through the construction of contorted, weird-shaped districts. Districts that are relatively symmetrical and compact, based on straight lines, may be gerrymanders as well. The shape of the districts is less important than the effect. This is especially true today because computers can be utilized to design districting plans. A computer can be programmed to produce a tremendous variety of compact districts that are essentially equal in population, but which have drastically different electoral consequences. A wide variety of politically relevant information can be incorporated into the computer-districting process in addition to simple population figures. The potential for gerrymandering through a computer is therefore enormous, as the following report on an actual computer-aided districting effort illustrates.

> Political information contained in the final data base included 1968–70 figures for closing and purged registration totals, votes cast in all statewide races, votes cast in all state senate, state assembly, and congressional races, and votes cast in selected local elections. In addition, voting figures for all 1970 propositions, selected 1968 propositions, and selected local bond elections were also included. Demographic information contained in the final data base included 1960 and 1970 census figures for total population counts, total number of blacks, total number of Spanish surnames, and education and income characteristics.

The Supreme Court has recognized that compliance with the one person, one vote standard does not guarantee that districting arrangements will be fair. The Court stated in 1973 that "Fair and effective representation may be destroyed by gross population variations among districts, but it is apparent that such representation does not depend solely on mathematical equality among district populations." But unfortunately this realization has not resulted in the development of effective legal standards through which gerrymandering can be combated. The primary reason appears to be a lack of objective criteria through which gerrymandering can be positively identified. This problem has been pinpointed by Congressman Abner Mikva of Illinois, who has stated, "[Gerrymandering] is somewhat like pornography. You know it when you see it, but it's awfully hard to define." To say that gerrymandering is hard to define really means that it is hard to measure. Malapportionment was easily attacked, once there was a judicial attitude favorable to attacking it, because it was easily measured. Every district's population could be compared to an "ideal" district population—the figure arrived at by dividing the number of people to be apportioned by the number of districts to be constructed. Consequently, judges simply had to decide how much deviation from the one person, one vote ideal they would tolerate (something on which all judges have not agreed). There does not exist, however, an "ideal" set of gerrymandering-free districts. Any set of districts—when combined with our system of winner-take-all elections—will inevitably result in some wasted votes simply due to the residential concentration or dispersion of a group's voting strength. This has led one well-known scholar to assert that "All districting is gerrymandering." This lack of an ideal, gerrymander-free standard places judges in a difficult position. They cannot positively determine how much vote dilution is a function of the residential distribution of a group's voters and how much is a direct consequence of where the district lines have been placed. This confusion causes the judiciary to be very cautious, meaning only the most blatant examples of gerrymandering are likely to be struck down.

The problem was clearly evident the first time the Supreme Court directly confronted the issue. Four congressional districts in the Manhattan area of New York City were challenged for being a gerrymander. In one of these districts, designed by the New York legislature after the 1960 census, black and Puerto Rican residents constituted 86.3 percent of the district population. The other three districts were only 28.5 percent, 27.5 percent, and 5.1 percent black and Puerto Rican. In effect, the legislature had drawn a congressional district boundary around a minority residential concentration. Plaintiffs alleged that this was an unfair concentration of the minority voting strength, which could have more influence over congressional elections if spread in a more equitable fashion throughout the districts. The Court responded, however, that ". . . the concentration of [black] and Puerto Rican voters in one area in the county made it difficult, even assuming it to be permissible, to fix districts so as to have anything like an equal division of these voters among the districts," and denied relief to the plaintiffs because they had not proven that the legislators *intentionally* segregated the vast majority of these voters into only one district. This demand that the motives of those who designed the districts be demonstrated has been criticized as placing upon plaintiffs alleging gerrymandering a burden of proof that is both irrelevant and unrealistic. It is considered irrelevant because unintentional gerrymandering may be just as unfair as intentional. And even if a gerrymander is the product of discriminatory motives, proving intentions independently from an inference drawn from the effects of a districting scheme is an extremely difficult thing to do.

The problem was again evident the only other time the Court directly confronted the issue. A redistricting plan for the Connecticut House of Representatives following the 1970 census was challenged for being "a gigantic political gerrymander" by plaintiffs associated with the Democratic Party. The plan had been enacted by a divided bipartisan apportionment board after the legislature had failed to adopt one. The Republican appointee to the board designed the districts, which were objected to by the Democratic appointee. They were adopted, however, when the third member, who had been selected by the other two, approved of the districts. The Republican member stated that the districts were constructed with the intention of having the proportion of Democratic and Republican representatives elected be approximately the same as the proportion of votes cast for Democratic and Republican legislative candidates throughout the state. The plaintiffs argued that this proportional representation principle was adopted to allow the Republicans to make up for wasted votes resulting from a heavy concentration of Republicans in one part of the state, Fairfield County. In their view, the principle "operated like a referred pain" in that "the excess plurality of a party in one area of the state becomes a justification for maneuvering to elect that party's candidates in another area of the state." The Court again decided against the plaintiffs, however, ruling that the proportional representation goal did not reflect an intention to discriminate, even though the 1972 election held under that plan allowed the Republicans to win 61.59 percent of the seats with only 52.88 percent of the state-wide vote.

The lack of any hard and fast measures through which gerrymandering can be positively identified places judges in a difficult position, but it does not require a helpless judicial posture toward all but the most blatant instances of gerrymandering. When the Court took an aggressive stand against malapportionment it placed the burden of justifying deviations from the one person, one vote principle on those who designed the districts. Many commentators have argued that gerrymandering will remain as a significant hurdle in the pathway to fair and effective representation until the judiciary shifts the burden of proof in these controversies as well. It is argued that plaintiffs alleging gerrymandering should not be required to *prove* those allegations, but rather demonstrate that a *presumption* of gerrymandering is reasonable. If this "reasonable presumption" standard can be met, then the burden of explaining and justifying a set of districts should be placed upon those who designed them. The adoption of such a standard would undoubtedly result in courts ruling against more than just the most blatant forms of gerrymandering.

Congress adopted such a standard to protect blacks in the southern states from gerrymandering when it enacted the 1965 Voting Rights Act. Part of that Act requires that redistricting plans in the South receive federal approval, from either the United States Attorney General or the United States District Court for the District of Columbia, before they can be implemented. To gain this approval, the southern authorities must show that the plans have no racially discriminatory purpose or effect. Following the 1970 census, numerous redistricting efforts in the southern states were rejected because this demand was not satisfied. (In 1976 the Supreme Court seriously altered this demand, however, by ruling that the Act was intended to prevent the implementation of plans that would have a retrogressive impact on the voting effectiveness of blacks, i.e. plans that would be more discriminatory than those they would replace).

This experience under the Voting Rights Act illustrates that gerrymandering could be more generally combated if the courts would adopt a reasonable presumption standard. When an issue is a confusing one, as gerrymandering is, the assignment of the burden of proof is likely to be a very crucial determinant of who wins. But the adoption of such a standard must await another change in the attitude of the Supreme Court. Malapportionment was eliminated as an obstacle to fair and effective representation only after the Court changed its attitude on that issue. Gerrymandering will remain as a further obstacle to the realization of that goal until the Court once again decides that it must exercise a more thorough supervision over the construction of representational districting arrangements.

reading 24

the courts and obscenity

by Elliot E. Slotnick

This article was written expressly for the present volume. Professor Slotnick is a member of the Political Science Department at the University of New Orleans.

ON JUNE 21st, 1973, in the case of *Miller* v. *California,* Chief Justice Burger announced for the Supreme Court's majority that a new policy initiative was being taken in the realm of obscenity law. Frustrated by the Court's seeming inability to pursue a consistent and coherent policy towards obscenity, the Chief Justice asserted that the time was now ripe for a "re-examination" of judicial standards in an effort to "formulate standards more concrete than those in the past." Unfortunately, however, subsequent cases (dealing with, for example, the movie *Carnal Knowledge* and the play *Hair*) have demonstrated that any hopes for policy conclusiveness placed in the *Miller* ruling were unfounded.

The Burger Court was not the first American tribunal to attempt to attack the issue of obscenity and, in fact, Chief Justice Burger's predecessor, Earl Warren, found the issue to be the most perplexing one he ever had to adjudicate. The difficulties faced by the Court in pursuing its policy role in the area of obscenity as opposed to other issue areas, however, are primarily a difference of degree and not of kind. In many respects, the Court's obscenity decisions and their societal impacts can serve as a microcosm of both judicial policy-making and the growth of the law. In essence, both the nature of judicial policy-making and the specific attributes of the *Miller* ruling destined the Chief Justice's decision to be yet another proximate and unsuccessful attempt at definitively determining American public policy towards obscene matter. In view of recent case developments it is impossible to escape the conclusion that the Court has yet to come to grips with a problem largely of its own making.

The judiciary has not always played a primary part in the formulation of obscenity policy and, until after World War II, state legislatures had virtually exclusive control of that policy domain. The states decided what kinds of material could be classified obscene and were, therefore, prohibitable, and the matter generally ended there. The issue did not enter the judicial arena until the constitutional question of the relationship between allegedly obscene material and First Amendment free speech rights was raised by litigants. The judiciary moved to center stage in this policy area with its landmark decision in the 1957 case of *Roth* v. *United States,* which served to open up a pandora's box of adjudication continuing to this day.

Roth had been convicted of sending obscene material through the mails in violation of a federal postal regulation. His defense before the Court was based not upon the question of whether or not the materials at issue were "obscene," but, rather, it was focused on the larger question of whether obscenity was "speech" entitled to First Amendment protection. Justice Brennan answered Roth's query for the Court in the negative: All expression having even the slightest social value was protected by the First Amendment, but obscenity was not since it was "utterly without redeeming social importance." In his opinion, Justice Brennan denotes the obscene as "patently offensive . . . material which deals with sex in a manner appealing to the prurient interest." More specifically the Court would cast its judgment in cases dealing with alleged obscenity by deciding, "whether to the average person, applying contemporary community standards, the dominant theme of the material taken as a whole appeals to prurient interest."

In fashioning the "prurient interest" approach in *Roth,* the Court was implicitly establishing itself as the adjudicator of obscenity and, consequently, as the prime policy-maker in this area. But just what was the policy established in *Roth?* On this question, there was much uncertainty. "Prurience" was an infrequently used term which the dictionary defines as having "lustful, lascivious, lewd . . . longings." As the Court's critics were quick to point out, there was logically no way to apply the *Roth* standard according to the views of the average person since average people would not have lustful, lascivious, and lewd prurient longings. In effect, anyone who *could* gauge "prurience" was abnormal and not average, and "average" people would have no prurient interest. In this "Catch 22" situation, it was virtually impossible for the lower courts that would have to implement *Roth* and for the members of the public who would have to live with it to get a handle on the Court's policy. For while obscenity was taken out of the realm of First Amendment concerns, and was, therefore, subject to government regulation, Justice Brennan's pronouncements appeared to narrowly circumscribe the kind of material which could be classified as "obscene."

The confusion emanating from the Court's *Roth* guidelines became painfully evident in less than a year after the decision. Apparently lower federal courts had misunderstood what the Supreme Court had said, as three *unanimous* obscenity convictions obtained after *Roth* were overturned when they reached the high tribunal. Yet, in these reversals, as in many more which were to follow, the Supreme Court did little to articulate more effectively their obscenity policy. Thus, in case after case, lower court decisions were either upheld or overturned with terse per curiam opinions (unsigned, undeveloped judgments penned "by the Court"), summary judgments without written opinions, or through pronouncements simply citing *Roth* as authority. In those instances when members of the Court did speak, they often appeared to make matters even worse. Thus, for example, Justice Stewart offered his guidelines for determining obscenity in a case dealing with the movie, *The Lovers:*

> I shall not attempt further to define the kind of material I understand to be embraced within that shorthand description, and perhaps I could never succeed in intelligibly doing so. But I do know it when I see it, and the motion picture involved in this case is not that.

What Stewart "knew" when he "saw it" was, apparently, less obvious to his colleagues on the bench, lower court judges, and the public at large. Thus, between 1957 and 1968 the Supreme Court dealt with the problem of obscenity in 13 major cases containing 55 separate written opinions. The fact that lower courts continued to misread (or disobey) the thrust of the Supreme Court decisions was also quite evident. In 1967, for example, the Supreme Court overturned 13 state and federal obscenity convictions without even entertaining argument on the merits. It struck some analysts, including Justice Harlan, that the Supreme Court was demanding that the states and the federal government draw their obscenity statutes more precisely than the Court itself had drawn its own guidelines. As Harlan noted in dissent in a 1968 case which struck down a Dallas obscenity ordinance because of the wide discretion granted in this "unconstitutionally vague" law, "the truth is . . . that the Court has demanded greater precision of language from the City of Dallas than the Court itself can give." The dissenting Justice's comments are all the more revealing when it is added that the Dallas statute in question was modelled after the Court's *Roth* decision guidelines!

Implicitly, what the Court's majority appeared to be doing in the line of cases following *Roth* was to establish a "hard core pornography" approach to obscenity. Apparently, it was hard core pornography which members of the Court recognized when they "saw it" but were unable to precisely define. To the Court's majority, the *Roth* standard was meant to be a liberal test which worked to grant constitutional protection to materials which had been censored under state and federal obscenity statutes for many years prior to *Roth*. The Court's decision making, while generally liberal, was unprincipled, and the seemingly random course of case development contributed to two somewhat contradictory societal consequences. Firstly, the Court's narrow view of what constituted the obscene gave relatively free reign to the purveyors of pornography. Thus, throughout the 1960's the country witnessed an unprecedented boom in "X" rated movie theatres, "adults only" bookstores, etc. Apparently, commercial entrepreneurs were willing to take their chances on a run-in with the law which would probably end in ultimate acquittal. Secondly and conversely, serious artists in diverse media who were not, perhaps, as tied in to and economically dependent on the mass pornography market stifled their own creative expression because of the "chilling effect" of possible obscenity arrests and potential conviction.

In the years following *Roth* it also became clear that *Roth*, with nothing more, was simply inadequate to handle the myriad manifestations of the obscenity dilemma. Judicial policy making differs from policy making in other governmental branches in that courts must attack problems in a piecemeal fashion. The Court cannot attack a problem simply because it is there but, rather, must wait for the issue to be framed in a case properly brought before it. What this meant in the obscenity realm was that over time the issues changed substantially. For the most part, the Court used this opportunity to muddy further the judicial waters as new decisions were grafted to the old, even when they were seemingly contradictory. In the process, the policy established by the *Roth* guidelines became even more incomprehensible.

Thus, in the case of *Ginzburg* v. *United States* (1966) the Court moved towards a "variable" approach to obscenity under which Ralph Ginzburg was sent to jail for mailing materials which were not deemed in and of themselves to be obscene. As the Court put it, "The deliberate representation of petitioner's publications as erotically arousing . . . stimulated the reader to accept them as prurient. He looks for titillation, not for saving intellectual content." Ginzburg was convicted, in effect, of "pandering" to prurient interest. As evidence of his intention the Court noted that he had unsuccessfully attempted to get mailing privileges for his wares (and a postmark) from Intercourse and Blue Ball, Pennsylvania, before settling for the larger postal facilities of Middlesex, New Jersey. The Court's use of a variable obscenity approach where material is judged not in a vacuum but in the context of its distribution led First Amendment absolutists Black and Douglas to their usual obscenity dissent, to be joined by the more conservative Justices Harlan and Stewart. As Black pointed out, Ginzburg was being sent to jail for selling something and doing something which neither he nor anyone else could have known in advance was illegal.

Two years later, the implications of the variable obscenity approach were drawn out in the case of *Ginsberg* v. *New York.* The case dealt with a New York statute which permitted material which was not obscene for adults to be considered obscene for minors. Mr. Ginsberg was convicted for selling such an obscene magazine to a teenager in violation of the statute. Placing the case's development in perspective, dissenting Justice Fortas noted, "A sixteen year old boy was enlisted by his mother to go to the luncheonette and buy some girlie magazine so that Ginsberg could be punished."

One final issue addressed by the Court in the late 60's was that of private possession of obscene matter versus its public distribution. In 1969 the Court held that *Roth* was never meant to be applied to perusal of obscene material in the privacy of one's home. Yet in an apparent about-face the Court announced in a 1971 decision that the 1969 case did *not* mean that an individual was constitutionally protected in the securing of obscene matter even if intended solely for private use. Thus, the Court succeeded in placing itself in the position of implicitly requiring that privately used obscene matter had to be produced in the confines of one's home or, alternatively, the material had to be spontaneously generated or immaculately conceived.

It became increasingly apparent to the public at large and to the executive and legislative branches of government that the Court was wrestling with the obscenity issue and losing badly. The populace blamed the Court for what was perceived to be widespread permissiveness and degradation in American society. People demanded action of their government and, not wishing to handle the ball personally, President Johnson responded by appointing a blue ribbon Obscenity Commission headed by Dean William Lockhart of the University of Minnesota Law School. The Lockhart Commission was charged with the task of creating legislative guidelines for dealing with and defining obscenity. Since the Courts had obviously failed in fashioning a workable and coherent policy, perhaps the independent commission could set the problem straight and provide direction for the returning of policy initiative in this area to the legislature.

After studying the problem for two years the Lockhart Commission issued its report in 1970. They began by accurately assessing what the ultimate negative societal consequences of the *Roth* decision and its progeny had been.

> This subjectivity and vagueness produces enormous uncertainty about what is "obscene" among law enforcement officials, courts, juries, and the general public. It is impossible for a publisher, distributor, retailer, or exhibitor to know in advance whether he will be charged with a criminal offense for distributing a particular work, since his understanding of the . . . tests and their application to his work may differ from that of the police, prosecutor, court, or jury. This uncertainty and consequent fear of prosecution may strongly influence persons not to distribute new works which are entitled to constitutional protection and thus have a damaging effect upon free speech.

Thus, the Commission concluded that present obscenity policy was ineffective based on standards and criteria which were illusory. At this juncture, however, the report took a surprising turn. Eschewing their mandate the Commission announced that they would *not* attempt to formulate a workable definition of obscenity and that such an effort would be futile. Instead they proposed that nothing should be deemed "obscene" per se. Rather, limitations should be imposed on the kinds of audiences sexually oriented materials could be sold to and the manner in which the material could be distributed. At bottom, the Commission concluded that the only legitimate state interest involved in inhibiting sexually oriented expression was the protection of juveniles, sexual deviants, etc. from the potential harmful effects of the sexually oriented materials. By imposing "traffic" controls but not absolute prohibitions on the distribution of sexually oriented materials, the Commission reasoned that the State interest involved could be reconciled with First Amendment rights of expression.

Stunned by the Commission's Report, many officials in the government as well as members of the public at large felt that they had been double crossed. The great controversy fanned by the Commission's report led to its rejection in the Senate by a vote of 60–5. Only five Senators— (Clifford Case (Rep.-N.J.), Jacob Javits (Rep.-N.Y.) George McGovern (Dem.-S.D.), Walter Mondale (Dem.-Minn.), and Stephen Young (Dem.-Ohio)—were willing to accept the risk of being publicly identified with the scandalous document and of being perceived as friends of pornography. Apparently 35 Senators decided that discretion was the better part of valor and did not participate in the roll call vote. Reaction to the report from the Nixon White House was just as negative and just as swift. At the urging of a vast majority of the Republican Congressional membership, the President totally repudiated the recommendations of the Commission established by his predecessor, terming the report "morally bankrupt." Going even further, the President urged every state in the union to enact anti-obscenity legislation, promising to give such measures his full support.

It was in the wake of the abdication of the Obscenity Commission and in the midst of ongoing judicial confusion that the newly reconstituted Nixon–Burger Court decided to attack the controversial issue anew. Through the primary vehicle of *Miller* v. *California* the Court's majority established new standards for gauging obscenity, including the following criteria.

1. Would the average person applying contemporary community standards find that the work, taken as a whole, appeals to the prurient interest?

2. Does the work depict sexual conduct specifically defined by applicable state law in a patently offensive way?

3. Does the work, taken as a whole, lack serious literary, artistic, political, or scientific value?

When an affirmative answer is given to all three of the above queries, a work may be circumscribed as obscene. Several crucial policy differences between the Court's rulings in *Roth* and *Miller* were immediately evident to constitutional analysts. While under *Roth* the "community standards" to be applied were those of some mythical "national" community, in *Miller* the national standards emphasis was clearly rejected. As Burger put it, "Our nation is simply too big and too diverse for this Court to reasonably expect that such standards could be articulated for all 50 states in a single formulation . . . To require a state to structure obscenity proceedings around evidence of a national 'community standard' would be an exercise in futility . . . It is neither realistic nor constitutionally sound to read the First Amendment as requiring that the people of Maine or Mississippi accept public depiction of conduct found tolerable in Las Vegas or New

York City . . . People in different states vary in their tastes and attitudes and this diversity is not to be strangled by the absolutism of imposed uniformity." Apparently the Court was acquiescing in and supportive of the President's position that initiative in defining obscenity and regulating it should be placed in the states.

Thus, while the Chief Justice was attempting to establish new obscenity standards, the *Miller* decision placed the court in the curious and paradoxical position of saying that the new standards would be relative ones. Further, the thrust of the Court's new obscenity policy is underlined by the third criterion listed above. While under *Roth* a work was protected unless it was *utterly without* redeeming social value, under *Miller* to be automatically protected a work had to have *serious* value. Thus, the policy established by the Court in *Miller* appeared to be aimed at allowing the prohibition of a greater amount of material under the rubric of obscenity than was possible under the *Roth* standard. In basing its test on local communities the Court also appeared to be relinquishing some of its control of the obscenity issue back to the state legislatures and state tribunals.

In a companion case decided along with *Miller,* Justice Brennan articulated in dissent his dissatisfaction with the new obscenity ruling. Brennan's dissent was not surprising since he had written the initial *Roth* opinion, a significantly less harsh approach to obscenity than *Miller.* What was surprising, however, was Brennan's total rejection of *any* definitional approach to obscenity including his own earlier *Roth* guidelines. Commenting on the Chief Justice's revision of *Roth*, Brennan remarked, "I am convinced that the approach initiated 15 years ago . . . and culminating in the Court's decision today, cannot bring stability to this area of the law. . . . In my view the restatement leaves unresolved the very difficulties that compel our rejection of the underlying *Roth* approach, while at the same time contributing substantial difficulties of its own." Thus, Brennan argued, the Court would be continuing to solve cases among individual parties while failing to offer workable guidelines for legislation, adjudication by other courts, and primary public conduct. Insufficient notice would continue being given by the judiciary to persons potentially violating the law while judicial decision making at all levels would likely remain irregular and unpredictable. The new ruling would also serve to further the "chilling effect" of prior cases on legitimate speech while adding a fresh ingredient into the ongoing internal court problems the entire obscenity issue had generated. In short, Brennan concluded, the time had come for the Court to leave behind the elusive attempt to define obscenity. Rather, like the Lockhart Commission before him, Brennan favored the turning of attention to the issue of the valid and legitimate state interest involved in the regulation of distribution of sexually oriented materials to specific impressionable identifiable subgroups in the population.

In large measure, Justice Brennan's prophecies about the weaknesses of the *Miller* formulation have proven true. Certainly, if the Chief Justice felt that *Miller* would rid the Supreme Court of hearing further cases on the obscenity issue he has been proven wrong. Justice Harlan once lamented that the Court was tied in to the "absurd business of perusing and viewing the miserable stuff that pours into the Court." Further, as Justice Brennan noted, "While the material may have varying degrees of social importance, it is hardly a source of edification to the members of this Court who are compelled to view it before passing on its obscenity." One thing that had become clear by the time of the *Carnal Knowledge* case one year after *Miller* in 1974 was the fact that the Supreme Court *still* would be the ultimate judge of obscenity and that their decision would remain focused on the "absurd business" of their personal perusal of the material in question.

Carnal Knowledge was just one example of many movies, plays, books, etc., which disparate local communities had found obscene in view of their understanding of *Miller*. In overturning the obscenity conviction won in an Albany, Georgia case for the showing of the Academy Award nominated film, Justice Rehnquist noted for a unanimous Court that, "It would be a serious misreading of *Miller* to conclude that juries have unbridled discretion in determining what is 'patently offensive'." In a statement substantially blurring the policy change from *Roth* to *Miller* Justice Rehnquist concluded, "*Our own view of the film satisfies us* (emphasis added) that 'Carnal Knowledge' could not be found under the *Miller* standards to depict sexual conduct in a patently offensive way." The reality that the Court had not progressed far in over 15 years was evident in Rehnquist's discussion of the guarded camera shots employed in the film as a primary basis and justification for his decision. As Justice Brennan remarked in his concurrence, "Today's decision confirms my observation . . . that the Court's new formulation does not extricate us from the mire of case by case determinations of obscenity. . . Thus, it is clear that as long as the *Miller* test remains in effect one cannot say with certainty that material is obscene until at least five members of this Court, applying inevitably obscure standards, have pronounced it so."

Looking back over nearly two decades of obscenity litigation inevitably brings into focus many unique aspects and consequences of judicial policy-making. Clearly the Court never worked on a clean slate once the *Roth* ruling was announced but, rather, grafted new decisions onto the old ones. Thus the Court's doctrine changed slowly, if at all, while the specific issues to which the doctrine was being applied were changing a great deal. Since new judicial standards never superseded the old (and Chief Justice Burger still insists that *Miller* is a logical outgrowth of *Roth*, Justice Brennan's protestations to the contrary notwithstanding), the result has often been the attempted co-existence between internally inconsistent and mutually exclusive rulings. Under these circumstances, the lack of clear, consistent and enforceable guidelines left lower courts with a great deal of decisional discretion and failed to offer the public at large any predictability through which they might have been better able to plan their own actions.

Changes in the Court's obscenity doctrine can be traced to many factors. Perhaps, above all else, personnel changes occurred on the High Court, and the liberal First Amendment stances of Chief Justice Warren and Justices Black, Goldberg, and Fortas were replaced by the more conservative and restrictive obscenity postures of Chief Justice Burger and Justices Blackmun, Rehnquist, and Powell. Personnel changes aside, however, changes in judicial doctrine can be traced to changes in the positions of long sitting Justices as well, reacting to what they now perceive were the weaknesses of their original formulations. Witness Justice Brennan's total repudiation of the approach that he himself had initiated in *Roth.* Finally, judicial decision making does not go on in a vacuum, and it is clear that members of the Supreme Court were well aware of the criticism that their obscenity rulings had evoked from all levels of American society including the Presidency, Congress, lower courts, the Lockhart Commission, all the way down to the man on the street who perceived his neighborhood being ruined by the influx of X-rated movies.

In the final analysis, to say that the *Court's* obscenity policy changed through the years does not necessarily say that American public policy towards obscenity changed concurrently. Ultimately it is not solely judicial doctrine that is important for understanding judicial policy making, but, rather, the behavioral consequences of that doctrine upon those charged with obeying the Supreme Court mandates. As Alexander Hamilton aptly noted, the judiciary lacks both the power of the purse and the power of the sword. For judicial policy to be translated into public policy necessitates cooperation and support from coordinate branches of government and from the lower courts to insure compliance with the Court's decisions. Clearly, such requisites for successful judicial policy-making have not been met in the obscenity realm. Executive and Congressional unhappiness with the Court's decision making led to the creation of the Lockhart Commission and the encouragement of restrictive state obscenity policies. Lower courts, both federal and state, continually had their restrictive obscenity decisions overturned on appeal to the Supreme Court. It is difficult to judge to what extent lower court behavior represented outright defiance of the Supreme Court policy or, alternatively, an inability to assess just what that policy was. There does appear to be some validity in both explanations. In any event, inconsistency in judicial decision making at all levels has been an integral part of the crazy quilt patchwork that is American obscenity policy.

In situations such as this where the Supreme Court policy is unclear at best and is meeting substantial resistance as well, the ultimate "policy makers" may be the individuals themselves whose activities touch on the issue. Thus, with regard to the distribution of obscene books one researcher, James Levine, noted, "The lines of communications connecting appellate courts, trial courts, political elites and booksellers may be so tenuous and haphazard that policy messages emanating . . . either become garbled or peter out entirely before reaching the local bookstall. Even if judicial dictates are successfully transmitted, they may be disregarded by local judges, police, prosecutors, and merchants." Thus, empirical research demonstrated that only 5 percent of the booksellers surveyed initiated any changes in their merchandising policies as a direct result of the Supreme Court's *Ginzburg* ruling. This was so despite the fact that 70 percent of the booksellers claimed they usually found out about Court rulings, suggesting that these rulings were either misunderstood and/or ignored. As Levine put it, "The Supreme Court may have donated a wealth of raw materials for the benefit of legal scholars, but its influence on the dissemination of sex literature in the general bookstore has been miniscule." In the same study it was also found that the bookseller's personal attitudes about obscenity were the most accurate predictors of what materials were generally sold in the bookstore.

It is on a cautionary note, then, that we must conclude. It is to the courts we must look to seek the initial source of judicial policy-making, yet our search must not end there. An assessment of judicial policy-making must ultimately focus on the behavior of those people whose activities are directly affected by legal decisions. For the most part, because of the nature of judicial policy-making in the obscenity realm, the Court has failed in its main objectives.

the federal structure
and intergovernmental
relations

Federalism is a system of government in which there is a constitutionally based sharing of powers between a central, national government and regional governments. In the United States, the national government (also called the federal government) is headquartered in Washington, D.C., and the regional governments are the fifty states (and their local governments).

The U.S. Constitution lays out the approximate powers and responsibilities of the national and state governments. The Constitution gives the national government certain enumerated powers; through interpretation by the Supreme Court, the national government also has certain implied powers (arising from the "elastic clause" of the Constitution); because it is a government, it also has certain inherent powers. Under the 10th Amendment, "the powers not delegated to the United States by the Constitution, nor prohibited by it to the States, are reserved to the States respectively, or to the people." And finally there is the concept of concurrent powers (those that are exercised by both national and state governments).

Federalism has been evolving since the Constitution was first framed in 1787, and this evolution has been guided by two things. First, the Supreme Court has been critically important in shaping federalism by its interpretations of the Constitution in cases involving questions of "states rights" and national supremacy. The Court's interpretations have changed over time. A tilt toward national supremacy was initiated by Chief Justice John Marshall with his famous decision in the case of *McCulloch* v. *Maryland* (1819), but later justices favored a states rights position. By the time of the New Deal, the Court was again inclined toward national supremacy (with considerable urging from President Franklin Roosevelt).

The second factor influencing the evolution of federalism has been the steady expansion of the national government's involvement in numerous policy areas over time. This expansion has included involvement in many areas previously exempt from governmental activity, as well as a greater degree of involvement in more traditional areas of governmental action. In part this expansion has come about because state governments could not or would not deal with the problems, and in part because the problems were widely perceived to be national in character and therefore best dealt with by the national government.

Probably the most notable feature of federalism is its dynamic character. It has been continuously changing since the 1780's and will continue to change as Court interpretations change, and as new needs are perceived. But federalism is dynamic in another sense as well, and that is its interactive aspect. Federalism is first and foremost an experiment in intergovernmental relations. From the perspective of the local official, federalism and intergovernmental relations pervade decision making and government operations every day. He must deal with federal grants, program evaluators, and auditors; with state personnel and programs; and with other local government personnel in counties, townships, cities, and school districts. From the national point of view, federalism is also important, as federal grants to states and localities become increasingly larger in an absolute sense and in a percentage sense of share of the total national budget, and as the awareness of the need for concentrated coordination of efforts at all levels of government to solve problems increases. The impetus for intergovernmental interactions involves the basic questions of politics—decisions that affect who is to get what share of something, or who is going to make decisions and have particular powers.

Increasingly since the New Deal Americans have looked to the national government to solve problems and provide resources to solve problems; increasingly Washington has initiated programs aimed at improving the quality of life and at achieving other broad national objectives, such programs to be administered at the local level. But this kind of federalism (policies initiated in Washington and implemented in Peoria, Pocatello, and elsewhere) has not always succeeded. As James Sundquist writes: "The basic dilemma . . . is how to achieve goals and objectives that are established by the national government, through the action of other governments, state and local, that are legally independent and politically may be hostile. Those state and local governments are subject to no federal discipline except through the granting or denial of federal aid. And that is not very useful, because to deny funds is in effect to veto the national objective itself."

In addition to the problem identified by Sundquist, federalism has other policy implications. Initiatives for policy can come from many different sources—local governments, state governments, the federal government. There is no single point of responsibility for initiating a policy recommendation, and this fact helps lead to a fragmented, uncoordinated approach to problems. Fragmentation is enhanced under a federal system because only parts of a problem are likely to get addressed at any given time, rarely the problem as a whole. And policy initiatives, regardless of the sources, may be of a positive, creative nature or of a negative, obstructionist nature, or may be both simultaneously.

The readings in this section illustrate the intergovernmental interactions that characterize federalism in action in two different policy areas. The Derthick selection (reading 25) shows state-national interaction over social services spending. The federal government (in the shape of Congress and the Dept. of HEW) had begun a program of unlimited federal matching funds for unspecified social services spending by the states in a 1962 amendment to the Social Security Act. No one recognized the financial implications of this very broad, vague amendment that contained no specific standards of application—except the states, who simply had to show up and collect their money. The California illustration shows how one state caught on very early to claiming matching funds, while the Illinois case illustrates how one state successfully pressured the federal government into significantly reinterpreting federal regulations to allow states to displace or substitute state expenditures with federal money. The article by Franklin on manpower revenue sharing (reading 26) describes a set of interactions between the national government and local governments under a relatively new mechanism to provide funds for the training and employment of the disadvantaged and the unemployed. As that article illustrates, the quality of local manpower decision making is deeply affected by intrusions from Congress, the federal bureaucracy, and local political groups.

reading

25

uncontrollable spending for social services grants: California and Illinois

by Martha Derthick

From Martha Derthick, *Uncontrollable Spending for Social Services Grants* (Brookings Institution, 1975), chapters 5 and 7. © 1975 by The Brookings Institution, Washington, D.C.

A LOOSE LAW, the changed character of administration, the rising demand for federal benefits, the development of a reform doctrine of greater federal responsiveness to the states—all these were conditions antecedent to the explosion of services spending, conditions that made the explosion highly probable but still do not fully explain it. For the outburst actually to occur, the state governments had to take certain specific steps. They had to make their claims and have them approved by federal administrators. The first and for several years the only state to do this in a big way was California.

From 1967 through 1971, as the following breakdown shows, California received 25 to 36 percent of the federal grants for social services and training:

Fiscal year	Total Grants (thousands of dollars)	Grants to California (thousands of dollars)	Percent of Total Grants to California
1967	241,567	59,907	25
1968	295,094	86,367	30
1969	396,691	143,229	36
1970	689,062	205,068	30
1971	776,221	216,633	28

It began drawing heavily on services funds even before the 1967 amendments, and when the subsequent change in federal policy occurred California detected it promptly. . . .

California relied on no single technique for exploiting services grants. It culled the rules and designed responses to fit. . . .

Activities that were already being performed—such as attendant care for infirm persons or day care for children receiving benefits under Aid to Families with Dependent Children (AFDC)—were now provided in such a way as to maximize federal money. . . .

How much of the federal money went for new services and how much replaced state-local effort would be hard to establish, even program by program. . . .

California officials had a sophisticated grasp of the implications of the open end in social services and of the ways in which private as well as state and local public funds could be used to tap it. A legislative staff report early in 1969 recommended that the state Department of Rehabilitation be redesignated the Department of Social and Rehabilitation Services and given responsibility for all social service functions, an arrangement that would facilitate the fullest use of services grants. . . .

The same report also recommended creating an intergovernmental and interdepartmental services fund, again for the purpose of managing funds to maximize federal matching. The report explained that private agencies would also be able to participate to their advantage. . . .

To maximize federal grants, California took fairly obvious steps—steps that a close reading of the federal rules would have suggested to men who read them with that purpose in view. California is remarkable more for the way in which the state government proceeded than in what it did. The degree of legislative initiative is striking.

By and large grantsmen have operated from offices in the executive branch or private consulting firms under contract to executive agencies. California was different in that initiatives came from legislative staffs that had been built up in the 1960s under the leadership of a powerful and ambitious speaker of the Assembly, Jesse Unruh. . . . With the legislature more than supporting them, indeed showing the way, administrators in the California Department of Social Welfare had a license to organize and enlarge their activities so as to capture services grants.

Federal regional officials were fully informed of California's actions. They met regularly with executives of the state welfare department who were in charge of social services. They cleared the state's proposals with Washington headquarters, and headquarters imposed no restraints. Ordinarily, state officials had a clearer perception than did federal regional officials of what the Social and Rehabilitation Service (SRS) headquarters would approve. "We had a better pipeline than they did," a California official recalled. "It became a joke." Federal regional officials would seek policy interpretation from state officials instead of the other way around. Initiative lay with the state. "It would have been difficult to have a regional staff that could stand up to them," according to a veteran member of the central staff. Certainly no regional staff could stand up to California with-

structure of government

out backing from headquarters, and such backing, which was not always firm even before the reorganization, crumbled altogether when the SRS was created.*

With California drawing so heavily on services funds, it was only a matter of time before other states would learn from the example. Conceivably, however, a conservative administration after 1969 might have forestalled state action by reversing the expansionist course of federal policy. When it did not, the way was open for massive state claims. . . .

The state that touched off the spending explosion of 1972 was Illinois, which advanced a bold interpretation of federal regulations on the purchase of services and precipitated a fresh and permissive statement of federal policy. . . . The Illinois demands engaged the personal attention of the President, involved the governor's office in a confrontation with the Office of Management and Budget, and culminated in a victory for the state on the floor of the Senate.

Illinois was one of many states in which budgets were badly strained by rising welfare costs. . . .

In Illinois, coping with the welfare and fiscal crisis was up to a progressive Republican governor, Richard B. Ogilvie, who had been elected simultaneously with President Nixon in 1968, and to the very able, well-educated young men whom he had attracted to his staff. . . .

In the fall of 1970, as [the Illinois Bureau of the Budget] prepared the budget for fiscal year 1972, they foresaw a sizable deficit, on the order of $140 million, as the result mainly of rising welfare costs. The governor and his staff were determined not to make up this deficit at the expense of the poor by cutting welfare grants. . . . And, unwilling to cut welfare grants, Ogilvie and his staff were downright unable, so they believed, to raise taxes. . . . . He and his staff concluded that they must make up their deficit with federal funds. . . .

At about the time that Illinois budget officials were making their plans for fiscal year 1972—that is, in the fall of 1970—they discovered the possibilities in social services grants, and on December 30, 1970, they submitted several major amendments to the Illinois plan for social services to Donald F. Simpson, the regional commissioner of the Social and Rehabilitation Service (SRS) in Chicago. They then proceeded to base their 1972 budget on the assumption that the Department of Health, Education, and Welfare (HEW) would approve and fund these proposals. . . .

Bold as a budgeting tactic, the Illinois social service proposals were bolder still in what they contained. In fully exploiting the loophole that federal laws, rules, and administrative practice had opened, Illinois went well beyond what California or any other state had done.

Illinois proposed that its Department of Public Aid should make substantial purchases of service from other state agencies, including Mental Health and Corrections. . . .

The specter that had troubled veteran public assistance adminis-

---

* [Editors' note: SRS was created in 1967 as part of a general reorganization of HEW.]

trators—that the states would exploit the open end for the purpose of fiscal relief, simply to transfer ongoing costs to the federal government—was raised by the Illinois plan. . . .

Besides enlarging the scope of purchased services and concentrating on state agencies, Illinois proposed a procedural breakthrough, complementary to its substantive proposals and highly important even if technical. It asked for a waiver of the single-state-agency requirement—several waivers, actually, one for each of the departments from which the Department of Public Aid would make purchases. . . . Here again, as with the purposes of expenditure, Illinois was profoundly challenging traditional public assistance administration. The single-state-agency requirement had been used by the Bureau of Family Services (BFS) to hold state welfare departments directly accountable for the use of federal grants. If the purposes of spending could be broadened and if the single-state-agency requirement could be bypassed, the states could easily turn services grants into a form of shared revenues, transferring federal public assistance funds to other state agencies more or less at will and using appropriations to other state agencies as matching funds in the federal public assistance program. . . .

It became clear to Illinois officials after they made their proposals that HEW would not soon or lightly approve. Illinois had stepped into an area where rules were unclear and stakes were high. Technically, Simpson could have given approval. Under SRS rules, regional commissioners can approve state plan amendments but must refer disapproval to headquarters. Yet Simpson drew back once the plan was submitted, choosing instead to insist that officials in Washington decide. No neophyte, Simpson was a career federal official who had been assistant secretary of HEW for management in the Johnson administration. He fully recognized the national implications of the Illinois proposals. If national policy was in the making, he declared, it was up to officials in Washington to make it. . . .

Simpson's demand for guidance brought no response from the SRS headquarters. . . . Simpson saw the national implications; so did officials at the SRS headquarters. As he shrank from taking responsibility, so, with less justification, did they, and this reluctance deepened after the decision was taken and the magnitude of the costs became apparent. . . .

The decision to approve the Illinois plan, like most important decisions in government, was not taken at one point by one identifiable official. It was the outcome of a complicated stream of events in which HEW's commitments evolved and choices narrowed as time passed. Approval came in three steps. The first was a memorandum issued to SRS regional commissioners on June 17, 1971, which set forth guidance on the purchase of services from public agencies. The policy stated in this memorandum was highly favorable to Illinois. The second came at the end of September 1971, when the SRS formally approved the plan submissions—that is, the responsible federal official, Simpson, signed them. The last came in February 1972, when HEW Secretary Elliot Richardson granted Illinois four waivers of the single-state-agency requirement.

At each of these three steps, Ogilvie's staff put as much pressure on the federal administration as they could. Assuming that Simpson had already done all he could for them, they concentrated on officials in Washington. Illinois had an office in Washington, which the Ogilvie administration had upgraded. . . . It received reinforcements from Springfield. Budget officials traveled to Washington repeatedly to press their case, and the governor himself was active. He too came to Washington, and got on the telephone to urge the Nixon administration to help. In repeated meetings with federal officials, Illinois officials advanced political, fiscal, and legal arguments, mixing these according to the audience. . . . During the first and crucial round of lobbying in the spring of 1971, Illinois met resistance from the Office of Management and Budget (OMB) and from career officials and program specialists in HEW. The Illinois officials' success came with appointive, policy-level officials in HEW—Tom Joe and John Twiname. . . .

In the end it was Tom Joe who took matters in hand. With the assistance of Joel Cohen, HEW's assistant general counsel for the SRS, he drafted the memorandum of June 17, 1971, that gave regional offices guidance on the purchase of services from public agencies. Though cast in general terms, this memorandum was a response to the Illinois case. . . .

The June 17 memorandum repudiated the old BFS * policy that purchase should not be used to pay for activities that are normally the responsibility of other state agencies. . . .

A policy that federal public assistance funds should not pay for activities that are normally the responsibility of other state agencies had finally been turned upside down. They *should* be so used, when public services are being offered to poor people. . . .

The authors of the June 17 memorandum did not regard it as a wholesale concession. . . . In the context of the Illinois demands, the memorandum seemed a compromise and an instance of drawing lines where none had been drawn before. Besides drawing the line at certain types of expenditures desired by the state (Illinois, after all, was much interested in matching institutional expenses, and in negotiations it had begun to advance claims for education), the memorandum reasserted the single-state-agency principle. . . . it explicitly declined to discuss the use of state funds, other than public assistance appropriations, as the state matching share of services costs. . . . Finally, the memorandum provided that federal funds should not be used "merely to replace State and local funds.". . .

In all, this memorandum was an extraordinary public document. In content, it was high policy. Basic principles of public assistance administration and possibly hundreds of millions of dollars in federal funds were at stake. In form, however, it was treated as less than policy. This was a memorandum of "clarification," not a regulation; thus Twiname's office did not put it through the elaborate process of review and clearance that is used for regulations. It was not cleared with the HEW comptroller or

* [Editors' note: The Bureau of Family Services (BFS) was a predecessor agency of the Social and Rehabilitation Service created in 1967 within HEW.]

with the secretary. It was not addressed to state governments but to federal regional officials "as a basis for negotiations with State agencies and evaluation of State plans." And it was signed by a man who had ceased to hold office.*

Naturally, SRS regional officials were puzzled by this document and asked guidance on what to do with it. The reply from headquarters in July surpassed the original in equivocation. A memorandum from Commissioner Bax explained . . . that headquarters did not "intend to publish the statement or issue it formally to State agencies at this time . . . it is a flexible document, subject to such change as may prove to be necessary." Bax then proceeded to add: "I urge you to share the content of this statement with the States. However, if you distribute copies of the actual statement, they should be clearly marked DRAFT." Draft or not, the regional offices were instructed to use the memorandum as "guidance material" in assisting the states in program development. . . .

Equivocal as it was—or as its sponsors wished it to be—the memorandum made crucial concessions to Illinois. Though they professed disappointment at the time, Illinois officials were "very gratified," as one later acknowledged. After June 17, it would have been difficult for HEW to reject the Illinois plan proposals. Yet approvals did not immediately follow. Ostensibly a clarification, the memorandum still left much to interpretation, especially as to whether federal funds would supplant state funds. Negotiations went on.

As the end of September approached, Illinois pressed for a decision. The SRS could not delay forever, and September 30 was a deadline in the eyes of state officials who believed that Illinois would lose the right to certain retroactive federal reimbursement if approval were not received before the start of the second quarter of fiscal year 1972 on October 1, 1971. As that date approached, Illinois secured a meeting in Washington with Twiname.

At this session, which took place on September 27, there was one last round of negotiation. Illinois officials put forth their proposals. Simpson raised questions, which Illinois answered. . . . Twiname did not have much to say. As usual, it was Joel Cohen who put the hard questions. To the surprise and disappointment of the Illinois delegation, Joe was also challenging and critical. Immediately afterward, Simpson, with Twiname's approval, had signed [the plan], and . . . SRS had approved interagency agreements covering the purchase of service by the Illinois Department of Public Aid from the departments of Mental Health and Corrections. . . .

Yet this was not the final decision. The climactic confrontation between Illinois and the Nixon administration was still to come. Ordinarily, plan approvals would have disposed of the case, but this was not an ordinary case. HEW still had to grant single-state-agency waivers. . . . But there was no halt in the rise of welfare costs. In the fall of 1971 Ogilvie's

---

* [Editors' note: The memo was signed by Community Services Administration Commissioner Simonds. CSA was created in 1969 and subsumed under SRS.]

structure of government

budget office was estimating the state's welfare deficit for fiscal year 1972 at $107 million. . . .

In Springfield, the governor moved to cut welfare costs in a highly selective way. . . .

In Washington, the state prepared to take legislative action. The Illinois office in Washington had conceived the idea of emergency federal legislation to relieve the states of increases in welfare costs for a year beginning on June 30, 1971. That is, the states would be "held harmless" against the rise in welfare costs. This relief would be offered only to states that had not tightened eligibility standards or lowered standards of cash payment in the categorical programs, which of course included Illinois. . . .

Success, . . . was not far off for Illinois. Fortuitously, the attempt to cut welfare at home made it possible to achieve victory in Washington, for it drew the state's senior senator, liberal Republican Charles H. Percy, into the contest on Ogilvie's side. . . . After consulting with Ogilvie's Washington office, Percy responded by promising active support for hold-harmless legislation for the states. He thereupon set out to gather support for the proposal from governors and other senators. He announced that he would introduce the bill if it had administration support. . . .

On November 15, Senator Percy introduced the hold-harmless proposal as an amendment to the President's tax reduction bill, part of a package of economic legislation to which the administration attached highest priority. . . . Opposed to the Percy amendment as such, the administration also wanted to prevent extraneous amendments to the tax bill, especially if they related to social security or welfare, subjects that would have opened up an interminable debate. Accordingly, no sooner had the Percy amendment been introduced than the administration offered to pay to remove it. . . .

Illinois was told that if Percy would withdraw his amendment, the administration would make several concessions, among them that HEW would complete action on the state's social services proposals. Other items included backing for some of the cost-cutting measures that the governor had announced. . . .

On November 17, the Illinois group met with O'Neill.* Sensing a strong bargaining position, for the administration thought the Percy amendment had a good chance to pass, Illinois was lengthening its list of demands, which now ran to fifteen or sixteen items. . . . Not much was said of social services, which were mutually understood to be part of the package. In particular, it is not clear that there was a shared understanding of what the Illinois social services proposals would cost. In the spring, Illinois officials had $75 million in mind. In November they seem to have been anticipating a greater yield but not to have revealed the precise magnitude of their aspirations to O'Neill. The open-endedness of the law and the uncertainty of federal laws and regulations left that figure in doubt. . . .

* [Editors' note: O'Neill was the Assistant Director at OMB.]

Presidential support proved helpful to Illinois in the last stages of its negotiations with HEW. . . . For a while the question of whether Illinois should be granted waivers of the single-state-agency requirement moved through bureaucratic channels. . . .

On February 1, 1972, Governor Ogilvie and Tom Corcoran called on Secretary Richardson to argue for the waivers and to urge that they be granted retroactively from the date on which plan amendments had become effective (October 1970). Richardson agreed. Behind the scenes, Illinois officials were claiming that the waivers were integral to the state's social services proposals, which Ehrlichman and O'Neill had agreed in November to approve, and they were insisting that O'Neill deliver on the commitment made then. An honorable man, he did. . . .

Once again, federal policy was being shaped to meet the needs of the governor of Illinois. . . .

As planned, Illinois made up its budget deficit with federal funds. . . .

Governor Ogilvie lost the 1972 election. Reflecting soon thereafter on his four years in office, he identified the welfare crisis of 1971 as "the climactic issue," which he had dealt with by cutting general assistance costs and getting "large federal commitments on several fronts." His budget staff, too, took satisfaction in the outcome. . . .

federalism in action: manpower revenue sharing

reading 26

by Grace A. Franklin

This article was written expressly for the present volume.

THE COMPREHENSIVE EMPLOYMENT AND TRAINING ACT (CETA) is a form of special revenue sharing passed by Congress and signed by President Nixon in December of 1973. It consolidates and decategorizes a number of federal manpower programs previously funded through categorical grants and it decentralizes program administration to state and local elected officials (known under the Act as "prime sponsors"). CETA is important not just because of its scope (almost $5 billion were spent and almost 2½ million people were served in fiscal year 1976), but also because of the rearrangement in federal and local government relationships that it has stimulated by changing the way money is distributed for manpower programs.

The CETA legislation is divided into parts called Titles, three of which are of primary importance. Title I authorizes prime sponsors to provide training and work experience programs to persons who are economically disadvantaged, unemployed, or underemployed. Title II authorizes prime sponsors to employ unemployed persons (those who have been out of work at least 30 days) in public service jobs. Public service employment is employment of a person in the local community in a job designed to provide some useful public service, with the salary being provided by CETA funds. Title VI was added to the basic legislation in December of 1974 as economic conditions, especially unemployment, worsened in the country. It is also a public service employment program, but it is aimed at recently unemployed workers.

Under CETA, prime sponsors (state, city, and county elected officials from areas with populations greater than 100,000) are given responsibility for planning and administering a comprehensive manpower system for their jurisdictions. Within guidelines established by the federal government, they decide what programs will be operated, which service providers will operate them, what the budgets for the programs will be, and who will be served by the programs. The money for the prime sponsors' programs is appropriated annually and is distributed to prime sponsors according to different formulas for Titles I, II, and VI. Because the resources available are insufficient to serve all who need manpower services, the importance of prime sponsors' decision-making latitude is emphasized—they not only decide who will get served, they also decide who won't get served. The CETA legislation also mandates that each prime sponsor have a citizen advisory council whose members are representative of local community and manpower interests. These councils are to assist the prime sponsors in developing their plans for manpower services.

WHY CETA EMERGED

Prior to CETA's passage in 1973, manpower training and employment programs were funded through a variety of federal categorical grants authorized under the Manpower Development and Training Act of 1962, the Economic Opportunity Act of 1964, the Emergency Employment Act of 1971, and their amendments. There was a proliferation of categorical programs in the 1960's, each with separate guidelines and target groups, and gradually an awareness developed that the categorical grant approach to solving national problems had drawbacks. For example, in the manpower program area, there was a lack of coordination among the many categorical programs operating in a given locality. Elected officials and program operators often did not know programs were operating, and they had no authority to coordinate those programs. Participants often got shuffled from one program to another; there was no central agency to tell a potential enrollee whether or not he or she was eligible for any of the programs in the community or what those programs were. In addition to lack of coordination, there was a feeling that programs designed in Washington were too standardized and could not bend sufficiently to meet needs and conditions in Oshkosh, Oceanside, and other localities. There was little coordination among manpower programs at the federal level, either, so similar programs were enacted, with separate appropriations accounts and guidelines, even though they may have been duplicative. And rival federal agencies guarded their turf jealously.

HOW CETA EMERGED

The problems cited above led to a movement to reform manpower programs. In 1969, as part of his "new federalism," President Nixon proposed a consolidation of manpower programs, stressing decategorization of administration to local levels, and local decision-making flexibility. The enactment of CETA followed a long and stormy legislative process, a presidential veto, and many failed compromises and coalitions. As is often true when major changes in policy are proposed, there was much resistance to altering the status quo, and several divisive issues impeded easy compromise solutions.

The principal actors or factions in the evolution of CETA included President Nixon and conservative congressional Republicans (who favored decategorization and decentralization and who opposed public service employment), liberal congressional Democrats (who were more supportive of the categorical programs and favored public service employment), the service providers (who felt threatened by consolidation and decategorization), the rival federal agencies and their lobbies (HEW, the Department of Labor, and the Office of Economic Opportunity, which were competing for administrative jurisdiction over manpower programs), and representatives of the lobbies for state and local governments that stood to gain under CETA (U.S. Conference of Mayors, National League of Cities, National Governors Conference, National Association of Counties).

These groups disagreed and argued about three major questions. First, would there be any guarantees under the new system for the old service providers, and what form would these assurances take? Second, to what level would funds and decision-making authority be decentralized? The states, cities, and counties all had vigorous proponents and opponents, and none trusted the others very much. Third, and most divisive of all, was the issue of whether the consolidation of manpower programs should include a public service employment component, and if so, what kind and how large.

Despite the lack of agreement on these and on lesser issues, CETA did emerge, and like much legislation, it was a bundle of compromises and ambiguously worded language. The inclusion of ambiguity in the legislation is probably not accidental—it allows both sides to feel as if their position has been vindicated. But such an approach to law-making creates problems later on for administrators trying to interpret and apply the law.

INTERGOVERNMENTAL RELATIONS UNDER CETA: THE FEDERAL PERSPECTIVE

The principal feature of intergovernmental relations involving manpower programs prior to CETA was the lack of involvement by local governmental officials. The federal government was supreme, authorizing and funding categorical programs, overseeing their implementation, writing and monitoring contracts with service providers. In general, local government units were bypassed by the federal government, which dealt directly with service providers. To the extent that local government units did interact with the federal government it was in the role of service provider of a particular program, and the interactions were over details of contracts. Local government units were simply one of many equals, all subordinate to federal officials.

The principal change in intergovernmental relations under CETA (see Figure 1) has been in the impact that federal decisions had on local manpower programs. Prior to CETA a decision to fund a categorical program was made at the federal level in the regional office of the Department of Labor (DOL) or the Office of Economic Opportunity (OEO). A categorical grant was approved and a program came into being at the local level—in other words, a federal budgetary decision became a local program fact. Under CETA the federal role has shifted from a program decision focus to a focus on administration and monitoring. There are now three areas

Figure 1. Changes in Intergovernmental Relationships Before and After CETA

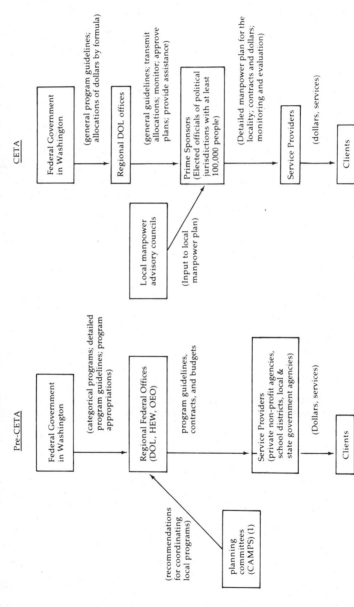

Pre-CETA

Federal Government in Washington	
↓ (categorical programs; detailed program guidelines; program appropriations)	
Regional Federal Offices (DOL, HEW, OEO)	
↓ program guidelines, contracts, and budgets	
Service Providers (private non-profit agencies, school districts, local & state government agencies)	
↓ (Dollars, services)	
Clients	

(recommendations for coordinating local programs)

planning committees (CAMPS) (1)

CETA

Federal Government in Washington
↓ (general program guidelines; allocations of dollars by formula)
Regional DOL offices
↓ (general guidelines; transmit allocations; monitor; approve plans; provide assistance)
Prime Sponsors (Elected officials of political jurisdictions with at least 100,000 people)
↓ (Detailed manpower plan for the locality; contracts and dollars; monitoring and evaluation)
Service Providers
↓ (dollars, services)
Clients

Local manpower advisory councils
(Input to local manpower plan)

* The Cooperative Area Manpower Planning System committees, begun in 1967 to coordinate the efforts of many federal agencies involved in manpower, were comprised of agency delegates and some representatives of governors' and mayors' offices. There were more than 400 local area committees.

structure of government

of federal activity—plan approval, monitoring prime sponsor program activity, and providing technical assistance to prime sponsor staff. All of these activities are conducted in order to assure compliance with broad CETA goals, and all of them take place principally in the person of the federal representative, an employee of the regional office of the Department of Labor (RDOL) assigned as the liaison between a prime sponsorship and RDOL (hereafter referred to as fed rep).

The legislation and regulations are flexible enough to allow either an aggressive or a passive federal stance in administering CETA. For example, in approving a prime sponsor's plan, a federal representative and his superiors must judge whether a prime sponsor has made "maximum efforts" to achieve the goals of his previous year's plan. No criteria for "maximum efforts" are laid down in the law, so interpretation and application vary according to personal outlook and necessity. The flexibility and ambiguity inherent in reliance on personal interpretation are not clarified by the policy directives issued to RDOL from the office of the Assistant Secretary of Labor for Employment and Training, and from relevant actors in Congress, and by RDOL directives issued to its own staff and to the prime sponsor staff. The directives of one source are not always consistent with those of another source, nor are they consistent with themselves over time.

The Place Of The Federal Representative

It falls on the fed rep to relay and interpret to the prime sponsor staff all of the directives and guidelines being issued and reissued. The fed rep is the formal link between the prime sponsors and DOL. The fed rep becomes the Department of Labor to the staff in the prime sponsorship. He communicates the news of budget allocations, plan approval, definitions, and new directives, and he helps the staff with data requests and training to upgrade their skills and administrative ability. Depending on what aspect of his role he chooses to emphasize, the fed rep may be viewed as a good guy or a heavy by the prime sponsor staff.

Most fed reps were program specialists before CETA, working as grant officers assigned to a categorical program (like the public employment program or Neighborhood Youth Corps). With CETA, they were transformed into generalists, responsible for all programs being operated in a single prime sponsorship. But they received limited training for their new assignment and had to learn on the job. Although their jobs take them into the heart of local politics, they have no training in this area, and a rapid turnover of fed reps' geographic assignments in the first 18 months of CETA (some prime sponsors had as many as five reps in that time) severely hampered their ability to become familiar with the local political situation.

The fed rep has an uneasy dual role to play under CETA, and different reps have emphasized different aspects of their assignment. On the one hand, they are friends and counselors of the prime sponsor staff, giving advice and assistance, helping design solutions to meet local manpower problems, in general acting as sympathetic resource persons. On the other hand, they must be critics of the system they have helped design and enforcers of the CETA regulations. They must conduct independent assessments, prescribe corrective actions, and monitor the implementation of corrective actions.

The fed rep faces a number of pressures that emphasize the attractiveness of nonaggressive role interpretation, and of the "friendly counselor" over the independent critic aspect. First is the fact that because CETA is new, roles are being defined for the first time, at both federal and local levels. There were no established CETA routines for the fed rep and the prime sponsor staff to utilize. Second is the tendency to smuggle in familiar routines, even if they are not really appropriate, simply because they are familiar. Thus some fed reps have been handicapped by their pre-CETA experiences of grant approval, which tended to make them think in terms of paper processing and report submittal (while others have been handicapped by another pre-CETA mentality that stresses the superiority and authority of the federal government over subgrantees). They have not been told by DOL nor do they know themselves how to evaluate the substantive aspects of prime sponsor's programs, so the paper focus retains its grip.

Third, the reward structure within RDOL has an effect on the fed rep's outlook, because if his prime sponsorship looks good in its plans and performance, then the fed rep, too, looks good. Thus the tendency again to stress timely report submittal, not to look too hard at substantive concerns, and occasionally to reinterpret reality in order to produce a more favorable report.

Fourth, the prime sponsor staffs have not uniformly welcomed the federal presence. Many believed that the rhetoric of revenue sharing characterizing the debates leading to CETA would be and should be followed, and they are resistant to any federal role except distributor of funds.

All of these factors contribute to the likelihood that the fed rep will interpret his role to be less rather than more aggressive, which in turn leads to an increased chance that the rep will be "co-opted" by the prime sponsor staff and will become simply a nonindependent spokesman for the prime sponsorship.

Plan Approval

The prime sponsor must submit a comprehensive manpower plan for each CETA title annually. Each annual plan, plus any significant modifications to it, must conform to federal requirements regarding format, narrative content, timetables, and procedures to be followed. Failure to conform results in delays in funds reaching the prime sponsor, and potentially could result in DOL refusing to fund a grant. (Although DOL has delayed funding, and has refused to approve modifications of a prime sponsor plan when it judged that the reprogramming of funds was improper, it has never permanently withheld money from a prime sponsor.) Causes for disapproving a plan include discrimination; failure to serve the economically disadvantaged, the unemployed, and the underemployed in an equitable manner; unreasonable administrative cost; failure to honor maintenance of effort (this refers to a prohibition against *substituting* CETA funds in the prime sponsor budget, rather than using CETA money to *supplement* the prime sponsor's budget). Plans cannot be disapproved because of the way the prime sponsor allocates funds among program activities, such as classroom training, work experience, or supportive services.

The prime sponsor plans must state (among other things) what groups in the population are to be served, what programs will be offered, who the deliverers of the programs will be, what the rationale for program and service deliverer selection are, and the results and benefits expected from the programs. Before submitting a plan to RDOL, the prime sponsor must solicit input from his advisory council, from the general public, and from a variety of governmental agencies.

Once submitted, the fed rep assesses the plan against a standard checklist. Missing or incomplete data must be provided by the prime sponsor staff. When the plan is judged to be acceptable, it is signed by the fed rep's superiors, and the prime sponsor receives the CETA funds.

The interaction between the fed rep and the prime sponsor during the planning process is almost always a friendly one. Usually the fed rep has many opportunities to make informal comments and suggestions about the plan during his field visits and when viewing drafts. Changes to the formal submitted plan can be negotiated between the fed rep and the prime sponsor staff on an informal basis, with the rep recommending changes and the staff supplying information. An effort is made by both parties to avoid formal rejection and any appeals process. Formal approval comes when the fed rep's superiors review and sign off on the plan—only rarely does a plan get sent back at this stage, but even then, an effort is made to exhaust negotiation and compromise informally before going to formal administrative or judicial hearings.

Monitoring

The legislation and regulations give DOL ample authority to monitor prime sponsors' program operations. The federal monitoring presence takes several forms. One is simply through the frequent visits of the fed rep to the prime sponsorship. Many prime sponsors regard any visit as federal monitoring, whether or not the fed rep has that as his purpose. Another form of monitoring occurs through the submission of periodically required reports that prime sponsors are required to submit to DOL. In addition to regular reporting, DOL conducts formal audits of all prime sponsor's fiscal operations on a periodic basis.

Major "field assessment" of the prime sponsors' Title I programs is conducted annually by the fed reps and other RDOL personnel in the fourth quarter of the fiscal year. The field assessment allows a comprehensive review of the prime sponsors' manpower operations during the year to detect any problems not observed in the regular reports to RDOL, and to make input into the next year's plan. The results of the assessment are the major tool DOL has in deciding whether to refund a prime sponsor. Despite its importance as a decision-making tool, the assessment has serious shortcomings. The first assessment conducted in fiscal year 1975 relied heavily on rate of expenditures, rather than on more substantive evaluation of the manpower programs. Second, the standard assessment instrument was not applied in a uniform fashion. Different fed reps had different perceptions of the same problems, and a problem common to two prime sponsorships would not necessarily be recorded as a problem in both assessment reports. Third, despite many serious problems in the prime sponsorships during the first year of CETA, DOL was willing to be lenient in "grading" the prime sponsors.

Technical Assistance

Technical assistance is a shorthand name for the resources available to the prime sponsor staff from the DOL staff, usually at the RDOL level. Technical assistance takes several forms, all aimed at sharing the presumed expertise of RDOL personnel in program planning, operations, and evaluations with the presumably less experienced staff at the prime sponsor level.

In the six months between the passage of CETA and its official implementation, a number of Technical Assistance Guides (TAGs) were written at the national office of DOL and distributed to regional offices and to prime sponsors. These handbooks covered a variety of aspects of planning and operating a CETA program, with special attention to administrative matters.

Another form of technical assistance occurs when the prime sponsor staff seeks clarification of definitions in the law or regulations, or seeks a ruling on the permissibility of some local procedure under CETA. Sometimes these questions can be resolved by the fed rep, sometimes they go higher up in the RDOL hierarchy, and occasionally a prime sponsor raises a question that becomes an issue with national implications and is resolved in the national office. Especially in the first year of CETA's implementation, there was a serious problem with inconsistent definitions and interpretations being given to prime sponsors. Prime sponsors in the same state could be operating under very different guidelines, depending on the interpretations of their fed reps.

Formal unsolicited communications from DOL to the prime sponsor staff comprise another class of technical assistance, and cover matters such as reporting requirements, planning procedures, plan timetables, participant eligibility, and expediture rates. Communications from DOL to prime sponsors were especially prone to being revised or reversed in the first year of CETA. The changes were very confusing to prime sponsors, who sometimes simply ignored the changing directives because they had no confidence in their content.

DOL staff may also provide personal technical assistance in a group setting such as a training seminar either at the request of the prime sponsor staff or at the initiative of the fed rep, who has detected a weakness in staff operations in some area that a training session could help improve.

Most technical assistance efforts in the first year of CETA were aimed at prime sponsor staff, usually to help them develop reporting systems to meet federal requirements, but during the second year, DOL was taking more interest in upgrading the expertise of the manpower advisory councils, particularly in those areas where the councils seemed to be under-utilized.

In providing technical assistance to prime sponsor staff, RDOL staff, particularly fed reps, have the potential to be viewed and used as an important asset, but in general, utilization of RDOL resources has been limited for a number of reasons. The main problem with the early technical assistance efforts was that the resources that RDOL had to offer were not themselves well developed, they were not well organized and promoted to best advantage, nor were they manned by the most able personnel. As mentioned earlier, fed reps haven't received any particular training before going out to their geographic assignments. They read the same TAGs, law, and regulations as the prime sponsor staff, and learned on the job. Often they could have benefitted from some technical assistance sessions themselves. This inexperience helps to explain the conflicting advice that prime sponsors received from different fed reps. The large percentages of marginal performers and significant underperformers following the FY 75 field assessment suggest that RDOL was less than successful in providing preventive technical assistance to prime sponsors, and in monitoring prime sponsoring during the year.

Enforcing Broad CETA Goals

Much of the legislative debate preceding CETA, as well as the CETA legislation and regulations themselves, contains language about a variety of broad goals to be realized as a result of manpower reform: decentralization, decategorization, citizen input, maintenance of effort, comprehensiveness, and serving the economically disadvantaged, the unemployed, and the underemployed. None of these goals is defined precisely, with the result that they may be given different interpretations at different times, or they may be ignored.

From the national level, there have been no mandates during the first two CETA years making these goals concrete for the purpose of helping to focus RDOL monitoring on the technical assistance activities and prime sponsor implementation activities. Partly this lack of leadership has been due to DOL's concern with getting a major piece of new legislation operational.

At the RDOL level, attention to broad CETA goals has also been sporadic. RDOL staff has developed a paperwork focus and a fixation on expenditure rates to the exclusion of a concern for programmatic comprehensiveness, decategorization, or participant service patterns within the prime sponsorships. This focus is the result partly of the absence of directives from the national office regarding broad CETA goals, and partly because the regional offices have also been immersed in the process of getting a new system operational.

To some extent the national economic condition in 1974 and 1975 was also responsible for distracting DOL's attention at both the national and regional level from broad CETA goals. As the unemployment rate worsened, pressure mounted from Congress and the White House for DOL to increase the number of public service employment (PSE) jobs and the rate of expenditures for PSE, and this pressure led to the DOL fixation on Titles II and VI and to the near exclusion of Title I from DOL consciousness.

THE LOCAL PERSPECTIVE

Most local-federal interactions occur between the offices of the prime sponsor staff and RDOL, and are related to the various federal requirements discussed above. There are more than 400 prime sponsors interacting with ten regional offices on a variety of usually routine matters. Generally the local perspective is a mirror image of the federal perspective discussed above. But several features of the local perspective on intergovernmental relations are unique and deserve mention.

Chief elected officials (CEOs) of prime sponsorships are formally actors in the local manpower decision-making arena on a large scale for the first time, but in terms of actual involvement, their participation is low. Some few mayors began to develop manpower interest and staffs under the CAMPS system, but most local officials, especially at the county level, came into CETA with little manpower experience. In general CEOs are more interested in Titles II and VI (the public service employment titles) than in Title I, but their interest and involvement in manpower overall has increased since pre-CETA days. The general stance of the CEO toward CETA is to delegate authority for the program operation to his staff. Some CEOs may set broad policy guidelines for the staff to follow, some may require periodic briefings, others may simply ignore manpower unless some crisis arises.

Thus, most of the day-to-day contact between the prime sponsorship and the federal government involves interaction between RDOL and the prime sponsor's manpower staffs and concerns issues like getting a plan approved, submitting a required monthly or quarterly report, and instituting uniform management systems. These interactions occur between the prime staff and the fed rep, and while most are handled in a routine manner, the interactions have not been free of problems. For example, many prime sponsor staffs feel that the numerous federally imposed requirements have diminished local flexibility in planning and operating programs. They tend to regard the requirements, especially those related to the planning process, more as a hoop to be gotten through than a help to local forecasting. Another sore spot in local-federal interactions concerns the uncertainty of funding from one year to the next because of delays in the congressional appropriations process (over which DOL has no control). In the absence of a firm figure for actual appropriations, DOL makes "planning allocations" to prime sponsors, and when final appropriations become available, readjustments to the planning figure are made. Thus prime sponsors must plan for a range of possible allocations, rarely knowing until the last minute how much their actual allocation will be.

Prime sponsor staff also complain about the quality of technical assistance they receive from their regional offices—most frequently cited problems involve the accuracy, timeliness, and type of assistance rendered.

In general, prime sponsor staff feel that much DOL involvement introduces unnecessary standardization and decreased local options.

Generally, the CEO's and staff that had manpower experience prior to CETA are not particularly awed by the DOL presence nor intimidated by DOL requirements; less experienced prime sponsors are more easily impressed. The primary characteristic of most local-federal interactions is one of independent power centers coming together and bargaining to resolve differences. The interactions are definitely not characterized by the pre-CETA hierarchical relationship between the feds and the locals. Prime sponsors are willing to question and to challenge DOL requirements and interpretations, and they will bring outside pressures (from their congressional delegations, or from any national DOL or White House ties they may have) to reinforce their positions. More than one CEO has indicated a reluctance to submit passively to the instructions of mere federal bureaucrats.

Most prime sponsors have found ways to work with federal requirements and fed reps in order to maximize local benefits. There are several techniques used. One is a genuinely productive relationship where the fed rep and the regional office are actively used by the prime sponsor staff as resources to improve the local staff and program capability. Another technique is to co-opt the fed rep so that the rep becomes a mouthpiece, consciously or not, for the prime sponsorship, rather than an independent critic. Another is the selective use of "scapegoating," where the prime sponsor staff in making decisions will shift the responsibility for those decisions onto the shoulders of the feds. DOL thus bears the brunt of many unpopular local decisions.

THE PROGRAMMATIC IMPACT OF INTERGOVERNMENTAL RELATIONS IN CETA

An early and persistent fear of opponents of decentralization in government programs was that elected officials would use those programs politically, and that persons most in need of services would be least likely to receive them if elected officials were in charge. The reasoning goes that the neediest segments are traditionally the least influential politically at the local community level (although they may have important national lobbies), and elected officials would not unnaturally be inclined to serve those groups in their areas that were more politically influential and active.

Evaluation studies of the transition to CETA and its early years provide some data that may be used to examine this fear (although it is too early to draw definite conclusions). For example, in terms of change in service delivery agents, nearly half of all local prime sponsors have assumed responsibility for delivery of some services to participants. On the other hand, most pre-CETA service providers have continued to receive funding under CETA. The pre-CETA delivery agents most often cut were community action agencies, agencies that traditionally served the most disadvantaged. In terms of changes in the characteristics of CETA participants, the changes that have occurred since 1974 are not dramatically large, but they are consistently in the direction of favoring the less disadvantaged participant, especially in Titles II and VI. There are many reasons for these shifts besides a conscious decision by local officials to serve more or less of certain target groups. The sick national economy in 1974 and 1975, a changing pool of eligible participants, and a national emphasis on the recently unemployed worker are all at work.

But regardless of why the shift is occurring, it seems clear that if the national government is going to retain more than a rhetorical commitment to providing employment opportunities to segments of society that traditionally lack employable skills, then it will have to exercise a conscious and continuous effort to assure that that goal is being achieved at the local level. The impact of federal-local interactions in the first two years of CETA has been a focus on administration and paper details and an avoidance of evaluating broader questions of who is receiving services and who should be receiving them. Federal attention to this broad CETA goal, and others like it, must advance beyond rhetoric if the goal is to be achieved and not simply be displaced by day-to-day detail.

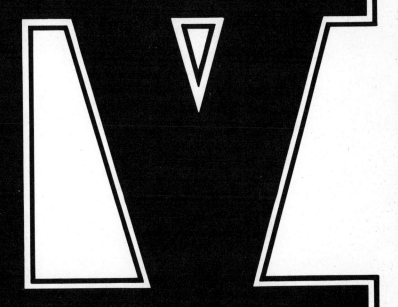

IV

governmental
responses to
public needs

domestic policy

The national government in the United States is involved in a broad range of activities, both foreign and domestic. There are very few areas of life that are not at least touched by some activity of the federal government.

In the present section our focus is on the policy activities of the government that are intended to impact primarily on the domestic life of the nation. (The distinction between domestic and foreign policy is, of course, not perfect. Many domestic policies have international spillover and vice versa. Not only are nations interdependent in the modern world but the policies of any given nation also all tend to be interrelated with each other.)

Naturally, in the course of a few selections we cannot hope to show the government in action and the consequences of that action across the whole range of policy areas in which the national government is active. However, we have chosen readings that offer illustrations in clusters of related fields in summary fashion rather than only a few issues in more detail.

In broad terms government activity in the domestic sphere can be thought of as having three major perceived impacts. The labels were first suggested by Theodore Lowi in 1964 and are adopted here as providing insights into what the government does. First, government policy can be thought of as *distributive*. Such policies are perceived to be aimed at inducing various activities in the private sphere that at least theoretically would not be undertaken otherwise and are thought to be desirable from a society-wide point of view. Thus, for example, in the mid-19th century the first transcontinental railroads were induced to undertake construction in part by grants of land from the federal government. Distributive policies, then, involve *subsidy* for specified private activities of one sort or another. Once some portion of the private sector begins to receive a subsidy that portion is likely to begin to look on it as a matter of right and an interlocking network of supporters both in and out of government forms to support the continuation and probably the expansion of the subsidy. This is the "subgovernment," discussed in the general introduction to this volume, operating in its classic role.

Second, some government policies principally involve *regulation* of private activities. Such policies set the conditions under which various private activities can be undertaken (for example, banks and other credit-granting institutions are required to make certain disclosures about true interest rates; railroads and truck lines are permitted to charge only certain rates for carrying specified commodities between various cities). They may also give the exclusive franchise to use some public good or engage in some activity to one group of petitioners while denying other petitioners the same right (for example, licenses to operate television and radio stations are given to some individuals and corporations and denied to others).

Third, some government policies are perceived to involve *redistributive* ends. These policies shuffle the wealth of society in a seemingly identifiable way from one broad group of individuals (such as a social class or a racial group) to another broad group of individuals. For example, the personal income tax is perceived to impact more heavily on the more well off in society and less heavily on the less well off. Thus, in part depending on the spending pattern with the revenues thus collected, this policy seems to redistribute in a more egalitarian way. At the same time, however, the impact of the Social Security tax and benefit package tends to redistribute in the opposite direction.

In the readings that follow the selection from the staff study for the Joint Economic Committee (reading 27) deals with distributive policies in the agricultural area. The article by Wilson deals with regulation. The articles by Rivlin (reading 29) and Orfield (reading 30) both deal with redistribution.

The readings also illustrate some other general points about domestic policy in the United States.

First, there seems to be a dynamic in the national policy-making system that pushes toward the reduction of controversy in advance of decision making. This means that there is a natural tendency for all policies to become distributive because the least controversy is involved there. Usually the beneficiaries (the subsidized) do not object to subsidies for other groups and activities as long as their own subsidy is at least stable or perhaps growing and seemingly not threatened by anything else the government does. Thus distributive policies tend to perpetuate themselves and both regulatory and redistributive policies are often redefined over time in distributive terms. Also, some regulatory policies become, in practice, exercises in presumed self-regulation (which, in fact, becomes another form of subsidy). The Wilson article details this process.

Second, in the distributive area there is a phenomenal range of activities, agencies, and programs involved. The reading from the Joint Economic Committee staff study addresses only one field out of many and is intended to give the reader a sense of the diversity of subsidizing activities in just one field.

Third, the distributive area is often the target of different kinds of policies simultaneously, and those policies may be pushing in contradictory directions. A classic example of such contradiction is evident by the fact that the federal government simultaneously supports regulatory policy aimed at reducing smoking and at the same time supports distributive policy encouraging the production of tobacco and stable high prices for that commodity.

Fourth, the federal system is also a complicating factor in the design and implementation of public policy in the United States. The Orfield article, for example, describes how the federal government helped create the very conditions of housing and educational segregation that plague virtually all of the major metropolitan areas of the country, conditions with which the cities must now cope.

Fifth, individual policies do not have their desired impacts (or even undesired impacts) in isolation. Rivlin makes the very sensible suggestion in her article that it is appropriate, for example, to think of clusters of policies as "strategies" for dealing with broad problems.

Sixth, unintended consequences of programs often emerge along with, perhaps, some of the publicly proclaimed intended consequences. The Orfield article is good in identifying some of the unintended consequences of federal housing policy and programs over a period of years.

federal agricultural subsidy programs

by Staff of the
Joint Economic Committee,
U.S. Congress

reading 27

From *The Economics of Federal Subsidy Programs,* a staff study for the Joint Economic Committee, 92nd Cong., 1st sess. (1972).

Agricultural, or farm subsidies are here distinguished from food subsidies. Farm subsidies are designed to increase farmers' incomes, chiefly by increasing the price, including subsidy, that they receive for their crops. They operate in the area of economic activity of agricultural production. Food subsidies are intended to benefit primarily the consumers of foodstuffs, chiefly through a lowering of food market prices.

The farm subsidy is accounted for in part by a market failure originating in the high degree of unpredictability of agricultural output from a given input of labor, fertilizer, and the like, for any one year. Weather conditions and the reaction of other farmers to past swings in the market are the chief causes of this unpredictability. Farming is thus a risky business, if risk is taken in the sense of a high degree of dispersion of probability-weighted outcomes around some average outcome. This difficulty is exacerbated by the unwillingness of the market to absorb a large increase in output without a drastic fall in price—the demand for farm products usually expands less than in proportion to a change in price. Hence, the farmer may actually get less total receipts from a large crop—if all other farmers are having much the same experience—than from a small crop. In the past, such a fall in household income for a farmer has driven him to try to increase his output the following year; and, if all farmers react in much this way, a further decline in gross and net receipts may occur.

This situation of excess output has been aggravated by the rapid growth of agricultural productivity. The use of new techniques and the substitution of machinery and fertilizer for land and labor have drastically reduced the manpower requirement for agricultural production in the United States. For the U.S. farm economy as a whole, man-hour requirements per unit of output fell by 1.8 percent per year from 1910–14 to 1940–44, and have since then declined at a 5.9-percent annual rate.

The result has been that agricultural output has increased faster than demand, and without any market controls, low farm prices and incomes recur. The increased work and misery that farm families undergo before incomes rise again, or before farmers are willing to leave the farm for other jobs, has been deemed too high a price to pay to obtain a free market in farm products. Farm subsidies have therefore been introduced.

Farm subsidies are commonly direct cash payments designed to persuade producers to reduce the acreage that may be used in the production of a certain commodity. The acreage restrictions reduce farm output and thereby raise market prices to the desired price support level. Wheat and grains are among the most important commodities receiving this kind of farm subsidy.

The Government also makes direct payments to farmers to both encourage certain conservation practices and to withdraw cropland from production. While these subsidies are accounted for under "Natural Resources," . . . they would have to be included in any full accounting of the cost of agricultural subsidies. This includes such activities as Rural Environmental Assistance, Great Plains Conservation, Cropland Adjustment, Conservation Reserve, and Emergency Conservation Measures.

Another way the Government keeps farm prices up is by taking some of the commodity off the market through purchases, and then disposing of it abroad or in other ways that do not directly affect the domestic price. Typically, these programs also restrict crop acreage. The net amount of money laid out in thus supporting the market price is included here as a farm subsidy, even though no direct cash payment is made. The money payment may be in the first instance a loan to the farmer, with his crop held as collateral. But if, as in the United States, it is a no-recourse loan where the Government can look only to the collateral, not to the farmer personally for getting its money back, the loan is obviously a subsidy to the extent that the loan value is above the market value. In that case, the farmer makes no effort to pay off the loan, regarding it simply as a purchase by the Government of his crop.

Finally, farm subsidies may take the form of special tax reductions and credit assistance. It is not clear how the tax subsidy listed below, "Expensing and Capital Gains for Farming," relates to agricultural production. The credit subsidies appear to be aimed at improving the general operation and maintenance of farms rather than affecting the production of any particular commodity.

To the extent possible, the gross budgetary costs of the above agricultural system have been identified for fiscal year 1970 in Table 1. These costs of approximately $5.2 billion are paid by taxpayers. But consumers also pay a part of the cost of price support programs through the higher agricultural prices brought about by subsidies that restrict agricultural output. These higher prices are themselves a type of subsidy paid directly by consumers to farmers. The income transfer cost of these subsidies has recently been estimated by Charles Schultze to be approximately $4.5

TABLE 1

**GROSS BUDGETARY COSTS OF FEDERAL AGRICULTURAL
SUBSIDIES, FISCAL YEAR 1970**

[in millions of dollars]

Program	1970 actual
Direct cash payments:	
Direct payments for commodity purchases	398
Feed grain production stabilization	1,644
Sugar production stabilization	93
Wheat production stabilization	863
Wool and mohair payments	53
Cotton production stabilization	328
Conservation related programs	—
Dairy and beekeeper indemnity payments	—
Tax subsidies:	
Expensing and capital gains for farming	880
Credit subsidies:	
Emergency credit	6
Farm operating loans	8
Soil and water loans	17
Price-support loans	87
Storage facility and equipment loans	2
Farm ownership loans	68
Rural electrification loans	179
Rural telephone loans	67
Crop insurance	9
Order of magnitude total	5,202

billion annually. Thus, the total transfer cost of farm subsidies—the money transferred from taxpayers and consumers to farmers—is in the range of $10 billion annually. . . .

DIRECT PAYMENTS FOR COMMODITY PURCHASES

Administering agency . . . . Agricultural Stabilization and Conservation Service, Department of Agriculture.

Objectives . . . . To improve and stabilize farm income, to assist in bringing about a better balance between supply and demand of the commodities, and to assist farmers in their orderly marketing of their crops. This is accomplished through Government purchase of eligible commodities in this case, although this may also be done through nonrecourse loans.

Financial form. . . . . Direct cash payments (purchase subsidy).

Direct Recipient	Any person who, as owner, landlord, tenant, or sharecropper who is entitled to share in crops on a farm, that has history of producing is eligible. Eligible commodities are feed grains and feed grain products, wheat and wheat products, rice, rye, blended food products, dry edible beans, castor beans and oil, flaxseed, soybeans and soybean products, honey, upland cotton, extra-long staple cotton, cotton products, dairy products, peanuts, tung nuts and oil, vegetable oil products, linseed oil, rosin and turpentine, tobacco, tallow or grease, and seeds and plants.

FEED GRAIN PRODUCTION STABILIZATION

Administering agency	Agricultural Stabilization and Conservation Service, Department of Agriculture.
Objectives	To adjust the production of surplus crops to keep crops in balance with demand, to reduce public cost, and to make price-support programs more effective. The payments are used for production costs and to help farmers maintain their income. Producers of feed grains who participate can earn payments by setting aside an acreage from crop production equal to a specified percentage of the base and maintaining the farm's conserving base.
Financial form...........	Direct cash payments.
Direct recipient..........	Any person who as owner, landlord, tenant or sharecropper on a farm that has history of producing the commodities is eligible. Eligible commodities are wheat, corn, barley, grain sorghum, and oats.

SUGAR PRODUCTION STABILIZATION

Administering agency	Agricultural Stabilization and Conservation Service, Department of Agriculture.
Objectives	To protect the welfare of the U.S. sugar industry, to provide U.S. consumers with ample sugar supplies at reasonable prices, and to promote and strengthen the export trade of the United States.
Financial form...........	Direct cash payments.
Direct recipient..........	Sugar beet and sugarcane producers in the continental United States, Hawaii, and

Puerto Rico are eligible for payments. To be eligible, producers must (a) not harvest an acreage in excess of the proportionate share (acreage allotment) established for their farms; (b) pay all farmworkers at rates not less than those established by the Secretary of Agriculture; and (c) if they are also processors of sugar beets or sugarcane, pay fair prices for cane or beets purchased from other growers. If they employ children under 14 years or permit those 14 years and 15 years to work in excess of 8 hours per day, a $10 deduction is made from their payment for each day the child is employed.

WHEAT PRODUCTION STABILIZATION

Administering agency . . . . Agricultural Stabilization and Conservation Service, Department of Agriculture.

Objectives . . . . To adjust the production of surplus crops to keep crops in balance with demand, to reduce public cost, and to make price-support programs more effective. The payments are used for production costs and to help farmers maintain their income. Producers of wheat who participate can earn domestic marketing certificates by setting aside an acreage from crop production equal to a specific percentage of the allotment and maintaining the farm's conserving base.

Financial form. . . . . Direct cash payments.

Direct recipient . . . . Any person who as owner, landlord, tenant or sharecropper on a farm that has history of producing the commodities, is eligible.

WOOL AND MOHAIR PAYMENTS

Administering agency . . . . Agricultural Stabilization and Conservation Service, Department of Agriculture.

Objectives . . . . The wool program is designed, through the use of annual incentive payments, to supplement the income of growers from sheep production and thereby to encourage increased domestic production of wool at prices fair to both producers and consumers in a way that has the least adverse effects on foreign trade. It also seeks to encourage producers to improve the quality and marketing of their wool and mohair.

Financial form........... Direct cash payments.

Direct recipient......... Any person who owns sheep or lambs for 30 days or more and sells shorn wool or unshorn lambs during the marketing year. Any person who owns angora goats for 30 days or more and sells mohair produced therefrom.

COTTON PRODUCTION STABILIZATION

Administering agency .... Agricultural Stabilization and Conservation Service, Department of Agriculture.

Objectives .... To adjust the production of surplus crops to keep crops in balance with demand, to reduce public cost, and to make price support programs more effective. The payments are used for production costs and to help farmers maintain their income.

Financial form........... Direct cash payments.

Direct recipient......... Any person who as owner, landlord, tenant, or sharecropper on a farm that has history of producing the commodity is eligible.

DAIRY AND BEEKEEPERS INDEMNITY PAYMENTS

Administering agency .... Agricultural Stabilization and Conservation Service, Department of Agriculture.

Objectives .... For necessary expenses involved in making payments to dairy farmers and manufacturers of dairy products who have been directed to remove their milk or milk products from commercial markets because it contained residues of chemicals registered and approved for use by the Federal Government, and to beekeepers who through no fault of their own have suffered losses as a result of the use of economic poisons which had been registered and approved for use by the Federal Government.

Financial form........... Direct cash payment.

Direct recipient......... Dairy farmers, dairy manufacturers, and beekeepers.

FARMING: EXPENSING AND CAPITAL GAINS TREATMENT

Financial form........... Tax subsidies.

Description .... Farmers, including corporations, may deduct certain costs as current expenses even though these costs represent inventories on hand at the end of the year or capital improvements. For example, the cost of producing crops or raising livestock may be deducted as an expense even if not sold by the end of the tax year. Certain capital improvements are also deductible during the year incurred rather than capitalized and depreciated. This treatment also extends to the sale of orchards, vineyards and comparable agricultural activities.

Although the special farm accounting rules were adopted to relieve farmers of bookkeeping burdens, these rules were used by some high-income taxpayers who were not primarily engaged in farming to obtain a tax, but not an economic, loss which was then deducted from the high-bracket, nonfarm income. In addition, when these high-income taxpayers sold their farm investment, they often received capital gains treatment on the sale. The combination of the current deduction against ordinary income for farm expenses of a capital nature and the capital gains treatment available on the sale of farm assets produced significant tax advantages and tax savings for these high-income taxpayers.

After the Tax Reform Act of 1969, capital gains from the sale of farm assets may be taxed as ordinary income to the extent farm losses (over $25,000) previously reduced nonfarm income exceeding $50,000. This provision is much more complicated than it appears here.

EMERGENCY CREDIT

Administering agency .... Farmers Home Administration, Department of Agriculture.

Objectives .... To assist farmers and ranchers in continuing their normal farming and ranching operations where they are unable to obtain credit from normal sources because of losses caused by natural disasters. This includes acquiring, enlarging, improving farms, farm buildings, water development and conservation, operating loans, and replacing equipment and livestock damaged or destroyed by natural disaster.

Financial form . . . .   Credit subsidy (direct loans).

Direct recipient . . . .   Farmers or ranchers who have suffered severe property damage or crop losses due to natural disasters. These will usually lie in areas designated by the Secretary of Agriculture; however, the Secretary may make loans without regard to the designation of emergency areas to persons or corporations who have suffered severe production losses not general to the area.

FARM OPERATING LOANS

Administering agency . . . .   Farmers Home Administration, Department of Agriculture.

Objectives . . . .   To enable operators of not larger than family farms make efficient use of their land, labor and other resources by extending credit and supervisory assistance. Loan funds may be used to: (1) purchase livestock, poultry, fur bearing and other farm animals, fish, and bees; (2) purchase farm, forestry, recreation, or nonfarm enterprise equipment; (3) provide operating expenses for farm, forestry, recreation, or nonfarm enterprise; (4) meet family subsistence needs and purchase essential home equipment; (5) make minor real estate improvements; (6) refinance secured and unsecured debts; (7) pay property tax; (8) pay insurance premiums on real estate and personal property; (9) other miscellaneous purposes.

Financial form . . . .   Credit subsidy (direct loans).

Direct recipient . . . .   Operators of not larger than family farms. Family farms are those on which a working operator and his family furnish the major portion of the labor. This decision is made on an individual basis by USDA.

SOIL AND WATER LOANS

Administering agency . . . .   Farmers Home Administration, Department of Agriculture.

Objectives . . . .   Through loans and supervisory assistance to facilitate the improvement, protection, and proper use of farmland by providing adequate financing for soil conservation, water development, forestation, drainage of farmland, the establishment and improvement of permanent pasture and related measures.

Financial forms.......... Credit subsidy (direct loans).

Direct recipient.......... Farm owners and farm tenants.

PRICE SUPPORT LOANS

Administering agency .... Agricultural Stabilization and Conservation Service, Department of Agriculture.

Objectives .... To stabilize, support, and protect farm income and prices.

Financial form........... Credit subsidy (direct loans). Price support loans to producers are "nonrecourse." Producers are not obligated to make good any decline in the market price of the commodity they have put up as collateral. If market prices rise above support, producers can pay off their loan and market their commodity. If market prices fail to rise above support prices, producers can pay off the loan through forfeiture of collateral. If the commodity is stored on the farm the farmer is responsible for maintaining the condition of the commodity.

Direct recipient.......... Any U.S. producer of eligible commodities. Eligible commodities are feed grains and feed grain products, wheat and wheat products, rice, rye, blended food products, dry edible beans, castor beans and oil, flaxseed, soybeans and soybean products, honey, upland cotton, extra-long staple cotton, cotton products, dairy products, peanuts, tung nuts and oil, vegetable oil products, linseed oil, rosin and turpentine, tobacco, tallow or grease, and seeds and plants.

STORAGE FACILITY AND EQUIPMENT LOANS

Administering agency .... Agricultural Stabilization and Conservation Service, Department of Agriculture.

Objectives .... To complement the price support commodity loan program by providing adequate financing for storage facilities and drying equipment, thereby affording farmers the opportunity for orderly marketing of their crops.

Financial form	Credit subsidy (direct loans).
Direct recipient	Any person who, as owner, landlord, tenant or sharecropper produces one or more of the following commodities: barley, corn, grain sorghum, oats, rye, wheat, soybeans, sunflower seed, rice, dry edible beans, flaxseed and peanuts.

FARM OWNERSHIP LOANS

Administering agency	Farmers Home Administration, Department of Agriculture.
Objectives	Through the extension of credit and supervisory assistance, assist eligible farmers and ranchers to become owner-operators of not larger than family farms; to make efficient use of the resources; to carry on sound and successful operations on the farm, and afford the family an opportunity to have a reasonable standard of living. This includes (1) enlarge, improve, and buy family farms; (2) refinance debts so as to place the farming operation on a sound basis; (3) improve, establish, or buy a farm-forest enterprise; (4) finance non-farm enterprises including recreation on all or part of the farm; (5) buy and develop land to be used for forestry purposes.
Financial form	Credit subsidy (guaranteed and insured loans).
Direct recipient	Eligible farmers.

RURAL ELECTRIFICATION LOANS

Administering agency	Rural Electrification Administration, Department of Agriculture.
Objectives	To finance dependable, modern, central station electric service in rural areas. A small number of loans are also made for wiring of premises, plumbing, and electrical equipment and appliances. These loans are made to REA borrowers for relending to individual consumers on their lines.
Financial form	Credit subsidy (direct loans).
Direct recipient	Rural electric cooperatives, public utility districts, power companies, municipalities, and other qualified power suppliers.

RURAL TELEPHONE LOANS

Administering agency .... Rural Electrification Administration, Department of Agriculture.

Objectives .... To finance the improvement, expansion, construction, acquisition and operation of telephone lines, facilities, or systems to furnish and improve telephone service in rural areas.

Financial form........... Credit subsidy (direct loans).

Direct recipient.......... Telephone companies or cooperatives, nonprofit, limited dividend, or mutual associations, who in turn pass on services to persons in rural areas defined as any area of the United States not included within the boundaries of any city, village, or borough having a population in excess of 1,500 inhabitants, and such term shall be deemed to include both the farm and nonfarm population thereof.

CROP INSURANCE

Administering agency .... Federal Crop Insurance Corporation, Department of Agriculture.

Objectives .... To improve the economic stability of agriculture through a sound system of crop insurance by providing all-risk insurance for individual farmers to assure a basic income against droughts, freezes, insects, and other natural causes of disastrous crop losses.

Financial form........... Credit subsidy (insurance).

Direct recipient.......... Any owner or operator of farmland, who has an insurable interest in a crop in a county where insurance is offered on that crop, is eligible unless the land is not classified for insurance purposes.

reading
28

the dead hand
of regulation

by James Q. Wilson

AFTER DECADES of public and journalistic neglect, the government
agencies that set prices, control entry, and regulate conduct in many of
our most important industries have suddenly found themselves in the
limelight. Owing to the efforts of Ralph Nader and other advocates of
"consumerism," a considerable segment of attentive opinion has become
convinced that the prosaic, often arcane decisions of these little understood
commissions are not always in the public interest. Such a view is correct,
and for dramatizing the fact we owe Nader and the others a debt of
gratitude.

But dramatic confrontations between "raiders" and "bureaucrats,"
however useful in creating an issue, are not so useful in understanding the
issue. Persons easily convinced that the government is not acting rightly
tend to assume that it is because the government is not righteous; if
industries are being regulated wrongly, then (in this view) it must be
because bad people are doing the regulating. It would be unfortunate if
the resolution of the regulatory issue were framed in terms of the moralis-
tic premises that first gave rise to it.

It would be all the more unfortunate considering that a number of
scholars, chiefly economists, have developed over the last ten years a
substantial set of analytical tools and empirical findings which, taken
together, constitute an impressive contribution to our knowledge of what
happens when the government tries to intervene in the economy. Yet
compared to the enormous influence of those economists who have developed ways of managing our tax, fiscal, and monetary policies, the influence
exercised by the regulatory economists has been negligible. About the only
serious effort to move in the direction suggested by their analyses was
President Kennedy's 1962 transportation message calling for the abandon-

ment of minimum-rate regulation in the shipment of bulk commodities on trucks, trains, and barges. The plan was buried in Congress, opposed by the truckers, the barge operators, and the rate setters (in this case, the Interstate Commerce Commission).

If the economists' success in getting their aggregate strategies accepted reaffirmed what the invisible hand of the market could do under proper guidance, their failure in getting government to accept their critique of non-aggregate strategies testified to the enduring strength of the dead hand of regulation. . . .

The problems of regulatory agencies go beyond price setting . . . and involve issues ranging from allocation (e.g., deciding who will get a television broadcast license) through the approval of business practices (e.g., deciding which firms may merge and which may not) to the control of what may or may not be broadcast (e.g., deciding whether radio stations will be allowed to editorialize or whether television stations show too much violence or too many commercials). In evaluating these and other kinds of government regulations, there are two standards one may employ—efficiency and equity. By "efficiency" I mean that a given regulatory policy achieves a desirable objective at minimal cost; by "equity" I mean that the regulatory policy, whether efficient or not, treats those subject to it fairly—that is, treats like cases alike on the basis of rules known in advance and applicable to all.

Until the end of the 1950's, the many criticisms of regulatory commissions were generally based on rather narrow or truncated versions of these two criteria. Those concerned with efficiency tended to emphasize the problem of who would determine what the desirable social objective should be and thus to whom regulatory agencies would be accountable. . . .

Critics concerned with equity, who on the whole were less favorably disposed to the idea of administrative regulation at all, concentrated their fire on the administrative procedures of the commissions, and sought by various legal and judicial remedies to insure that parties appearing before the commissions would receive ample notice, a fair hearing, an opportunity for review, and the other elements of due process as then conceived. . . .

THE EFFECTS OF REGULATION

The economists have cut through much (though as we shall see, not all) of the fuzzy rhetoric and empty reforms addressed to these issues and have asked instead the simple question, "What effect does a regulatory policy have and, given certain goals, how can that effect be improved?" The first thing to decide was whether regulatory policies, especially in the rate-fixing area, *had any effect at all.* Everyone, of course, assumed that they had. Why else would businessmen complain so much about these rates and an aroused public demand even lower ones? . . .

EFFICIENCY

The inefficient use of economic resources in fields such as transportation does not result from the fact that stupid or corrupt men regulate these industries, but from the fact that well-meaning and reasonably intelligent men do. . . .

Nor are the economic inefficiencies limited to the transportation field. By a combination of policies administered by various agencies, we insure that the nation produces too much crude oil and too little natural gas. Restrictions ("quotas") on the importation of foreign oil guarantee that the price of oil in the United States will be higher than it need be (i.e., than the world price) and that there will be more drilling in scarce domestic oil reserves than is justified. At the same time, the Federal Power Commission until recently has set the field price of natural gas below the rate necessary to clear the market, and thus below the rate many think is necessary to encourage vigorous exploration for new sources of supply. This means that while present-day consumers of gas may have been benefited because prices have been kept low, future consumers may well have been harmed because of the shortages they will encounter (and to some extent, already are encountering).

WHO HAS CAPTURED WHOM

Scholars as diverse as the radical historian Gabriel Kolko and the conservative economist George Stigler offer a simple explanation for the behavior of these and other regulatory agencies: They have been captured by, or were created to serve the interests of, the industries they are supposed to regulate. To Kolko, business regulation, like all other "reform" efforts in American government, has had the intended effect of making secure the control over wealth exercised by the dominant economic class. To Stigler, any industry with sufficient political influence will use the coercive power of the state to limit entry into the industry and thus to restrict competition; failing that, it will take the second-best strategy of obtaining cash subsidies from the government to help defray the cost of competition. ("Second best," because a cash subsidy, without entry control, would have to be shared with all new entrants into the industry, and the bigger the subsidy the more numerous the entrants.)

There are examples of regulation that seem to have no other explanations than those. The benefits given to the petroleum industry by import quotas and tax-depletion allowances represent an enormous subsidy (perhaps as much as $5 billion a year). The CAB has not allowed the formation of a new trunk airline since it was created in 1938. At one time the butter producers virtually suppressed the use of margarine by obtaining laws that forbade coloring margarine to look like butter. Plenty of other instances could no doubt be added.

But just as striking are the cases contrary to the theory of industry capture. The Federal Power Commission can hardly be called the tool of the natural gas producer interests; until recently it has set wellhead prices below what the producers would like and indeed what the public interest probably requires. If the ICC was once dominated by the railroads, it is not today: So generous has that agency been to the chief rivals of the railroads, the truckers and barge lines, that today the rail industry favors deregulation altogether. Television broadcasters (such as WHDH in Boston) that have lost their license to a rival claimant because of the action of the Federal Communications Commission, or newspaper owners who face the possibility of having to divest themselves of television station ownership, or television networks that have had the amount of programming they could supply in prime viewing time reduced by a half-hour each day are not likely to think of themselves as playing the role of captor with respect to the FCC.

Indeed, there may well be as many industries that have been "captured" by their regulatory agency as agencies captured by the industry. But the term "capture" reflects a simplistic view of the politics of regulation. Though there have been very few good studies of agency politics, what probably happens is this: An agency is established, sometimes with industry support and sometimes over industry objections, and then gradually creates a regulatory climate that acquires a life of its own. Certain firms will be helped by some of the specific regulatory decisions making up this climate, others will be hurt. But the industry as a whole will adjust to the climate and decide that the costs of shifting from the known hazards of regulation to the unknown ones of competition are too great; it thus will come to defend the system. The agencies themselves will become preoccupied with the details of regulation and the minutiae of cases in whatever form they first inherit them, trying by the slow manipulation of details to achieve various particular effects that happen to commend themselves from time to time to various agency members. . . .

Louis Jaffe has probably stated the political situation more accurately—the agencies are not so much industry-oriented or consumer-oriented as *regulation-oriented*. They are in the regulation business, and regulate they will, with or without a rationale. If the agencies have been "captured" by anybody, it is probably by their staffs who have mastered the arcane details of rate setting and license granting. . . .

In any event, most regulatory agencies have been doing pretty much what Congress has asked of them. Congress never intended that competition should govern in transportation, and the ICC has seen to it that it hasn't. The ICC was supposed to "co-ordinate" our transportation system, and though one may question (and I certainly question) whether co-ordination can be achieved by detailed regulation, the fact is that the ICC, supposedly "owned" by the railroads, has in the name of co-ordination been quite generous to the trucking and barge industries—so much so that now the railroads are in favor of deregulation. Indeed, if any agency has been "captured" by its clients, it has been, under certain presidents, the National Labor Relations Board; but again, this is exactly what Congress intended in the Wagner Act. (Curiously, academic criticism of business domination of regulatory agencies rarely extends to organized labor influence in the NLRB.) The Securities and Exchange Commission has had a running feud with much of Wall Street, just as Congress hoped it would. Indeed, if any single political force benefits from economic regulation, it is Congress—or more accurately, those key Congressional committee and subcommittee chairmen with a substantive interest in, or appropriations responsibilities over, the regulatory agencies. The FCC has been reluctant to make any change in its controls over cable communication without checking with key Senators, and the NLRB regularly hears from members of the House Education and Labor Committee about matters pending before it.

But even Congressional intervention, like industry control, is not in itself a problem; everything depends on the ends toward which such intervention or control is directed. The problem of efficiency, in short, is not wholly a problem of clientelism, political meddling, or agency incompetence; in substantial part it is a problem of the nature of the tasks which we have given the agencies. These tasks probably could not be performed well even in theory, and amid the practical realities of confused ends and ambiguous standards they are, through the fault of no one in particular, performed abominably.

EQUITY

The economic analyses thus far described have rather little to say explicitly about the problem of equity, though their criticism of piecemeal rate making has clear implications about the fairness with which (for example) shippers of similar products over similar distances are treated. The general question of equity is not raised by economists, and those who do raise it—chiefly business firms that feel unjustly treated—are often ignored on grounds, quite plausible in many cases, that they are engaged in special pleading.

But the issue remains, even if it is difficult to get people to take it seriously. . . .

[I]t seems clear . . . that a person or corporation subject to regulation cannot in many cases know in advance where he stands, nor expect to be treated tomorrow by the same rule that governed his actions today. The theory of regulation advanced in the earlier part of this paper—that it tends to be an ad hoc, particularistic process, affected, but not determined, by a policy habit or inclination—suggests not only that agencies will not operate on the basis of general rules, but that they will go to some pains to avoid developing such rules.

There are two reasons for this. One is that the greater the codification of substantive policy, the less the power the agency can wield over any client in the particular case. As Michel Crozier has argued with respect to bureaucracy generally, power depends in part on uncertainty—I have power over you to the extent you cannot be sure in advance what my reactions to your behavior will be. If the agency could only apply known rules to corporate behavior, it would still constrain that behavior, but far less than if it improvised its action in each case. In a baseball game the umpire has power because he can call me out after three strikes; but his power over me would be much greater if every time I came to the plate he told me that how many strikes I would be allowed depended on how well I swung the bat, or maybe on how clean my uniform was.

The second reason for avoiding codification is related to the first: The agency and its staff wish to be able to achieve particular goals in particular cases. Though the goals may be ambiguous and the cases all different, the general desire to realize a particular state of affairs is more important to the agency than the desire simply to insure that the rules are followed. To continue the analogy, it is as if the baseball umpire desired not just to see that the game was played fairly, but also that a certain number of runs were scored (so the fans would be happy), a certain number of pitches thrown (so the pitcher would get a good workout), and a certain price charged by the owners (so they would be either happy or unhappy, depending on his intentions). . . .

THE UNLIKELIHOOD OF CHANGE

Neither industry nor the agencies have much need to fear major reforms, or at least reforms that reduce the item-by-item discretionary regulation that now exists. Quite the contrary. The reform impulse, except among economists who specialize in the problems of better use of regulated resources, is now of an entirely different sort—increased regulation, increased discretion, more numerous challenges to existing corporate practices. Commissioner Nicholas Johnson of the FCC has even published a book, *How To Talk Back To Your Television Set,* that is a manual of ways to challenge broadcasters; if its lessons were followed by a large number of citizen groups, the already considerable tendencies of broadcasters to provide programs that offend absolutely no one would be given a powerful impetus. What the pursuit of audience ratings has started, the law suits and renewal hearings would consummate. (In fairness it should be noted that Commissioner Johnson has also been an advocate of cable television and the greater diversity it promises.)

With respect to rate-fixing agencies, a move toward greater reliance on market forces in industries where competition is adequate is also unlikely. Not only would the agencies oppose it, but some groups will lose in the short run from any deregulated rate: Consumers might have to pay more for natural gas, oil companies might earn less from crude oil, and some shippers would pay more in rail and truck rates. Everyone who stands to pay more will naturally oppose deregulation, and those who will pay less (consumers, future generations, some firms) are typically not organized to seek such benefits—if, indeed, they are even aware of them.

But most importantly, the most articulate segment of public opinion has recently become aroused by the issue of "consumerism," and this almost surely will lead to demands for increasing the power and aggressiveness of the regulatory agencies. There is, of course, no necessary contradiction between a desire to protect the consumer and the desire to use scarce resources more efficiently; the efforts of the Federal Trade Commission or the Food and Drug Administration to insure that false and misleading claims are not made for products and that harmful substances are not sold to unwitting buyers are in principle unobjectionable. Indeed, one of the ironies of economic regulation is that it has generally existed with respect to those tasks it can do only poorly (such as setting rates and prices and controlling market entry) and has not existed, or has been indifferently managed, with respect to those tasks it could do well (such as controlling the effects of business activity on third parties or on the environment).

Reducing the emission of noxious fumes or preventing the sale of a harmful drug is conceptually and perhaps administratively easier than deciding what allocation of television licenses will be in "the public interest" or what price levels are "reasonable"; yet until recently Congress has encouraged the agencies to do the latter but not the former. In so far as the contemporary concern for ecology and public health redresses this balance, it is all to the good.

But it is unlikely that the desire to improve and perfect human affairs will stop there. An effort will be made to "protect" the consumer by setting the price he can pay or forbidding him to buy certain products of whose dangers he is fully aware. Moreover, enhancing the powers or stimulating the activity of regulatory agencies for whatever reasons will lead the agencies themselves to enlarge their mandate and extend their influence. Consumer advocates, including as they do many of those most skeptical on other grounds of the manageability of large government organizations, should be the last to suppose that bigger consumer-protection agencies will work as intended; but of course, they are among the first to suppose it.

reading

29

social policy: alternate strategies for the federal government

by Alice M. Rivlin

From a revised version of the Woytinsky Award Lecture given on October 12, 1972. Originally published as Woytinsky Lecture No. 3, Department of Economics and Institute of Public Policy Studies, University of Michigan.

. . . I WANT TO direct your attention to a global, perhaps mind-boggling question: What alternative means does the federal government have of carrying out social policy? In particular, what strategies are available for allocating budgetary resources to the solution of social problems?

By the ominous military term "strategy" I mean a conception of the federal government's role, of the type of activity the central government should undertake. A strategy may involve hundreds of complex laws and amendments enacted over several years or even decades, but once it has been accepted it provides some general rules about the nature of federal activity to guide the maneuvers of legislative and budgetary tacticians.

Social insurance is an example of such a strategy. In the mid-1930's the public and the Congress decided that one kind of activity appropriate to the federal government was the creation of a national contributory "insurance" system that would protect people against various kinds of income losses beyond their control—losses due to old age, unemployment, death of the breadwinner, and similar disasters. The original law gave only limited protection to a minority of the population, but acceptance of the strategy provided an agenda for forty years of legislation and continues to be a major influence on the size and allocation of the federal budget.

"Federal grants for human services" is a second example of a strategy, albeit a less clearly articulated one than social insurance. Social reformers over a long period argued that an appropriate role of the federal government in alleviating social problems was to give grants to state and local governments and certain other institutions to support specific kinds of human services (education, health care, manpower training, and the like). This strategy made slow headway from the 1930's through the 1950's but had a major impact on legislative and budgetary decisions in the 1960's.

A large proportion of federal spending for social programs reflects one or the other of these two strategies. For the last 40 years they have provided the liberal-moderate majority with a framework for decisions. A liberal-moderate congressman or senator did not have to understand every detail of every bill. Within limits, he could invoke the two general strategies. If the measure in question was an extension of social insurance or provided more federal grants for education, health, or other human services, he was disposed to favor it. This did not mean that every proposal passed—far from it. There were bitter arguments at every stage. But the principles provided a framework within which to argue about specific questions such as "how much?" and "how fast?"

I would like to discuss these two existing strategies and where they have brought us and then turn to the following four options for the future:

The first of these is an individual cash income strategy which would involve concentrating federal efforts over the next few years on reducing disparities in individual disposable incomes, presumably by reforming the federal tax structure to increase taxes paid by high income people and reduce those paid by the poor and by increasing cash transfers to low income people.

The second is an individual service-financing strategy under which the federal government would concentrate on equalizing ability to pay for certain services produced in the private market, but considered "essential" to well-being. Health insurance, housing allowances, child care allowances, aid to students in post-secondary education, and perhaps even "vouchers" for elementary and secondary education could be elements of such a strategy.

The third is a revenue-sharing strategy which would involve concentrating federal resources on increasing and equalizing the budgetary capacity of state and local governments either to provide general governmental services or to support broad functions such as education for health services.

The fourth, and by far the most difficult, strategy might be called an institution-changing strategy, under which the federal government would attempt to change how states, localities, universities, enterprises, markets, and other institutions operate and what they do, by providing incentives for more effective operation, stimulating the introduction of new kinds of services, discovering and publicizing new techniques or training people in new skills. . . .

WHY TALK ABOUT STRATEGIES?

It is unusual to organize a discussion of social policy around strategies. Policy analysts—and other people—usually organize their thoughts around objectives, such as eliminating poverty or improving health, or sub-objectives such as curing cancer or reducing unemployment. They talk about the priority to be accorded a particular objective (although there is rarely much of substance to be said on the subject) and about the merits and demerits of particular ways of approaching it. These analyses are highly useful, but I suspect that the most vociferous political debates of the next few years will center not on competing objectives but on competing strategies, alternate views of the appropriate role of the federal government that cut across objectives and functional areas such as health or housing. Policy analysts may find themselves more relevant if they focus their thoughts—at least part of the time—around the advantages and disadvantages of these major strategies and their implications for movement toward social goals. . . .

SOCIAL INSURANCE AS A STRATEGY

In retrospect—looking back from the vantage point of four decades at the state of the nation in the depths of the Great Depression—it is not at all obvious why setting up a long-range program of social insurance against income loss appeared to contemporaries an appropriate response to the conditions of the day. The economy had ground to a screeching halt; millions were out of work; businesses were failing; banks were closing. Why should the nation have chosen this particular moment in its history to set up a permanent social insurance system, financed by a new and regressive tax, which would not even start paying benefits for several years? Indeed, many people argued at the time that recovery should precede such long-range reforms.

It is also no longer obvious why the aged were deemed so deserving of income protection. One might have argued—and some did—that the needs of children deserved high priority. Nor is it clear now why a contributory system seemed so attractive to the decision-makers of the 1930's. One might have argued—and some did—for paying pensions to the aged out of general revenues rather than out of a payroll tax.

But although the decisions made on social insurance were by no means the only defensible ones, several things coalesced to bring them about. The magnitude of the economic disruption convinced people that something was radically wrong with the American economic system, that individuals were too vulnerable to disasters outside their control, and that some permanent system was needed to protect them against income losses that were not their fault. President Roosevelt and others around him had a longstanding commitment to the social insurance idea. Moreover, faith in the fiscal reliability of governments was at a low ebb. The idea of collecting contributions in a trust fund attracted people as a means of increasing the probability that the government's commitment to pay out benefits in the future would actually be honored. The worker's contribution appeared to establish his right to a benefit in time of need.

Whatever the reasons, the fact is that Congress passed the Social Security Act in 1935. Its proponents realized at the time that it was just a first step. . . .

[T]he strategy of social insurance won acceptance and for the next

35 years a dedicated group of people worked to improve the system by increasing benefits, extending coverage, and adding to the list of disasters that people were to be insured against. In 1939, the Social Security Act was amended to provide benefits for dependents and survivors. After time out for World War II liberalizing the social insurance system became a regular ritual in the Congress in election years:

1950—coverage broadened by adding the self-employed, benefit levels raised

1952—benefits increased

1954—coverage extended to farm workers and domestics, benefits increased

1956—benefits added for disabled workers aged 50 to 64 and for disabled children of retired or deceased workers; coverage extended, retirement age lowered for widows, wives, and working women

1958—benefits added for dependents of disabled beneficiaries

1960—disability benefits extended to people of all ages and their dependents

1961—early retirement provisions extended to males and survivors benefits liberalized.

Then came the fight over medical benefits which ended in 1965 when Congress added Medicare for the aged. More recent Congresses have increased benefits for widows, extended Medicare to the disabled and continued to raise benefits. An across-the-board benefit increase of 20 per cent preceded the 1972 election.

The combined result of demographic changes and amendments to the social security, unemployment compensation, and railroad retirement programs is that we now have a comprehensive social insurance system whose outlays come to well over $60 billion a year or close to a quarter of the federal budget.

The amazing thing is that—except for Medicare, which was a substantial departure from the original concept of protection against income loss—the extensions and liberalizations of the social insurance system generated little controversy. . . .

FEDERAL GRANTS FOR HUMAN SERVICES

The second strategy—federal grants for human services—is a more complex one and cannot be identified with any single piece of legislation, as the social insurance strategy can be identified with the Social Security Act of 1935. The strategy made slow headway over several decades, then suddenly commanded wide support and enthusiasms in the mid-1960's when it became the vehicle for a renewed attack on poverty. . . .

The breakthrough came in the mid-1960's when the nation rediscovered poverty and Congress passed a spate of new federal programs to fund various kinds of human services mostly for the poor, including the Elementary and Secondary Education Act, the Higher Education Act, Head Start, neighborhood health centers and other community action programs, model cities, and other efforts under the rubric of "The Great Society." Most of these programs provided federal funds for human services to be delivered at the local level; but they reflected a more complex and ambitious strategy than had been evidenced in the simpler proposals for, say, federal aid to education. The federal funds were to be targeted on the poor. Moreover, the Great Society programs were intended to change the way in which services were delivered, to provide new kinds of services, and to increase the participation of the poor in the decision-making process. . . .

In retrospect, the human services strategy was not an obviously appropriate response to the rediscovery of poverty—any more than social insurance was an obviously appropriate response to the Great Depression. If a nation was so concerned about the poor why did it not choose to raise their incomes directly? Clearly it would have been more efficient, at least in the short run, to give poor people money through cash transfer programs than to embark on a long range chancy effort to raise future incomes by offering services to the poor and to their children. Some people argued for the more efficient cash transfer approach, but they lost. The services strategy appealed to people because it stressed self-reliance and providing an opportunity for the poor to earn their own way. It also picked up the political support of those who had fought so long and hard for federal aid to education and federal support for other human services.

Whatever the reasons, the "Great Society" approach was accepted by the liberal-moderate majority with what now seem naive hopes for quick and dramatic results. They hoped both that relatively small amounts of federal money (plus federal guidelines specifying what was to be done with the money) would radically alter how state and local governments and other institutions functioned and that relatively small doses of human services would drastically and visibly alter the lives of the poor.

Ironically, the new human service programs might have been judged a great success if their enactment had not quite accidentally coincided with another development: a new demand for "accountability," for demonstrable "outputs" and measurable results of government spending. The new emphasis started with the reasonable sounding notion, very appealing to scholars, that it ought to be possible to identify the benefits of government programs and that spending decisions should involve judgments about whether anticipated results are worth the cost. The basic idea spawned the planning programming budgeting system, led to the earmarking of substantial federal funds for "evaluation" (and the growth of a whole new industry to spend that money) and enticed a great many academic researchers away from their relatively comfortable, theoretical pursuits to the harder task of measuring the costs and benefits of public programs.

Beyond the campuses and the think-tanks, the main effect of the new emphasis was that a whole new set of questions were asked by Congress and the public about what government programs actually do. . . .

Strangely, the new questions were directed almost exclusively at new programs, not at established ways of spending the federal budget. Established programs, such as impacted area school aid, vocational education, farm subsidies, and hospital building programs, continued to be funded without anyone asking for measurable results.

The new questions are basically good ones, but the efforts to answer them have revealed how ill-equipped educators, health professionals, city officials, and others are to produce evidence of measurable output. In the past they have not put much effort into identifying exactly what they are producing and how to measure it, and they find the new questions threatening and perplexing. . . .

THE NEED FOR NEW STRATEGIES

What has come out of the 1960's experience at the federal level is a new realism, indeed, several different kinds of realism:

—about the difficulties of bringing about social change
—about the limited knowledge that exists at any level about how to run effective service programs

—about the limits of federal ability to manage service programs

—about the limits of federal resources and the necessity of choice.

All of this new realism underlines the necessity of rethinking federal strategies in the social policy area. . . .

Beside social insurance, these seem to me to be at least four sets of strategies that might guide the allocation of increments in federal resources in pursuit of social objectives in the next few years. Each has a plausible rationale and each involves problems on which policy analysts need to do more work. Clearly no one strategy is likely to be followed to the total exclusion of the others, but a clearer understanding of the implications of each will help guide decisions on the relative emphasis to be placed on each.

Strategy I: Reducing Disparities in Individual Cash Income

One could make a strong case for concentrating increments in federal resources over the next few years on reducing disparities in individual money incomes, especially on raising incomes at the low end of the scale. One could argue that the persistence of huge differences between the affluent and the poor, especially the fact that many people are still forced to live on incomes well below what most of the population regards as a decent minimum, is both inherently inequitable and a cause of many other serious social problems, such as high crime rates and decaying neighborhoods.

Enthusiasm for the cash income strategy involves giving priority to the objective of reducing inequality and poverty over other possible objectives of the federal government. It implies a respect for the individual's ability to make choices about how to spend his income and a rejection of the idea that the government ought to make choices for people, especially poor people, by providing them with food stamps, housing, or medical care rather than money. It implies skepticism about the feasibility of reducing poverty by offering services, such as education or manpower training, and a preference for the more direct methods of narrowing income disparities through manipulating tax and cash transfer programs.

On the tax side, the cash income strategy presumably involves reform of the federal income tax to increase effective income tax rates paid by upper income people and other tax reforms, including reduced reliance on the payroll tax to finance social insurance, to lower the tax burden on the poor. On the expenditure side, the cash income strategy implies increases in transfers to low income people, but here several distinct substrategies are possible. Two of them might be designated the "neat" version and the "fill-in-the-cracks" version. Both would be less costly if the economy were operating at full employment.

The essence of the "neat" version of the cash income strategy is replacement of most of the existing patchwork of income transfer programs (and perhaps some service programs as well) with a single comprehensive program, such as a negative income tax. The new program would guarantee everyone a basic minimum income with amounts depending upon family size, but would encourage people to work by allowing them to retain a substantial fraction of their earnings. . . .

The difficulties of designing and arousing support for the "neat" version might lead one to opt for a less drastic version of the strategy which would focus on improving existing income transfer programs and developing new ones only to fill-in-the-cracks where current programs leave groups without income protection. This strategy might involve: (1) putting a federal floor under the incomes of the aged, the blind, and the disabled poor whose social security is not adequate—a step largely accomplished by amendments to the Social Security Act passed in 1972; (2) retaining veterans benefits to protect poor people who happen to have served in the armed forces; (3) increasing unemployment benefits and making them more uniform; (4) moving to a national benefit schedule for families with dependent children by raising benefits in states where they are low.

This set of reforms would still leave a substantial number of people in poverty, mostly the "working poor" who are in the labor force but are not able to earn enough to keep their families out of poverty. To assist this group one might propose wage supplements or incentives to private business to encourage more employment of low skill workers or a public employment program or some combination of the three.

A government program that guarantees jobs at adequate wages to those able to work may be more attractive to the voters than a cash "handout." For able-bodied adults not covered by other income maintenance programs, the government could act as "employer of last resort," standing ready to provide a public job at a specified wage to anyone who cannot find other employment. . . .

Strategy II: Financing Individual Services

Another major strategy would be for the federal government to concentrate additional resources on helping individuals and families to pay for certain services that are widely regarded as essential to a decent life and to opportunities for advancement, but which are, or could be produced in the private sector. Medical care, child care, housing, and various forms of education and training are the most usual candidates for inclusion in this strategy.

Instead of giving people cash transfers to be spent at the discretion of the recipient, under this strategy the government would in effect give people vouchers good only for the purchase of particular services. The rationale for earmarking the funds might be (1) that the need for the particular service occurs in large lumps and would cause hardship even to people with adequate incomes; (2) that people, especially poor people, cannot be expected to devote as much of their income to the particular service as is deemed to be in their own or the national interest; (3) or that it was easier to gain political support for financing a particular service than for a cash transfer program. The additional political support might come from the producers of the service (e.g., the housing lobby) or from middle-income groups which expected to benefit from a program designed to finance special kinds of services (e.g., a college scholarship program), but not from a general income transfer program focused on the poor.

Choice of this strategy implies considerable faith in the efficiency and effectiveness of the private market. One could, of course, argue for providing health care or housing as a public service, but the strategy of financing individual services assumes that private production (perhaps with some regulation) is preferable as long as the government provides people with access to the private market. . . .

Strategy III: Revenue Sharing

Another possible strategy is for the federal government to put major emphasis on increasing and equalizing the ability of state and local governments to perform their general functions or to carry out some broad responsibility such as education. Specific decisions about how the money would be spent would be kept at the state and local level with the federal government playing the role of resource equalizer.

One rationale for the revenue sharing strategy is that it is inequitable for public services available to an individual to be determined by the tax base in the jurisdiction in which he happens to live. Indeed, the courts are beginning to suggest that state education financing systems may be unconstitutional if they make the amount spent on a child's education depend heavily on the local tax base in the jurisdiction where he lives. Movements toward equalizing expenditures on public services within the state will tend to strain state resources since there may be strong pressure to bring the lowest expenditure jurisdictions up rather than cutting the highest down. Great inequality in resources available for tax purposes also exists among states. Moreover, state and local governments depend upon taxes that are less progressive and less responsive to economic growth than the federal income tax. Hence, it is argued that the federal government should put substantial resources into general revenue sharing and perhaps also into block grants to equalize expenditures on education and other broad functions of government.

This strategy too has its problems. The basic difficulty arises out of the conflict between the goal of maximizing local autonomy and the goal of preserving accountability to the federal taxpayer. Local governments may, indeed, not act in the national interest, maybe even waste money—or worse. Efforts to control local uses of federal funds, however, violate the spirit of the revenue sharing strategy which is that local citizens are the best judges of what they need from local government. Federal controls clearly may lead to rigidity and stifle the initiative. But lack of controls implies lack of accountability to those paying the federal tax bill.

Strategy IV: Institution Changing

These three strategies are all plausible and if undertaken in a major way separately, or in combination, could drastically alter the distribution of income and access to services both public and private. But all three are hands-off strategies that rely on private markets and political processes at the state and local level to produce services and use federal power simply to equalize resources among governments and individuals. These strategies do not change what institutions—markets, persons, governments, school systems—actually do and how they do it. But we all know that private markets often work badly. It is not at all clear that we can rely on private markets to produce attractive low cost housing or to break down residential segregation by race. Nor is it clear that private markets can be relied on to provide effective medical care to everyone who needs it, even if the financing problem is solved. It will not do much good to give ghetto residents or the rural poor health insurance if no health facility exists in these areas and doctors will not practice in them.

Moreover, the problem is not just with private institutions. Governments are not always responsive to their citizens, especially the poor and minorities, and may have little incentive to seek new methods or provide more effective service.

All of this argues for a fourth strategy: A major federal effort to induce various kinds of institutions to operate more efficiently and in the public interest as perceived at the national level. But this is the hardest strategy of all and one about which policy analysts have, at present, the least to say. The tools of such a strategy must be varied but they clearly include research and development, especially social experimentation to test out new methods of delivering services, dissemination of the results of such experiments, and training people in new methods and techniques. The tools may also involve federal efforts to specify who must be involved in decision processes at local levels—specifying that recipients of the services must be represented.

In addition, the strategy clearly involves bribes, more politely known as incentives. The federal government can try to induce state and local governments to provide new kinds of services by giving grants earmarked for those particular services and can even specify who is to benefit and how the services are to be produced. Tax and other kinds of incentives can also be used to encourage or discourage various kinds of private activity. For example, industrial pollution could be discouraged by taxes on effluents or hiring of disadvantaged workers could be encouraged by special tax breaks for businesses that do it.

The myriad of problems of this strategy are of two sorts. Some involve the basic problem of deciding what sort of changes are desirable and what kinds of incentives, penalties, or other devices are likely to bring them about. Policy analysts have a lot of homework to do on this front —developing performance measures, designing testing and evaluating incentives to institutional change.

The second set of problems is how to get rid of the programs designed to bring about institutional change when they are no longer needed, or have turned out to be counter-productive. The federal landscape is littered with narrow categorical grants whose original purpose was desirable institutional change but which have outlived their usefulness, and special tax provisions originally designed for a worthy purpose which have become loop holes for the protection of the affluent. . . .

federal policy, local power, and metropolitan segregation

reading

30

by Gary Orfield

Reprinted with permission from the *Political Science Quarterly* 89 (Winter 1974–75), pp. 777–78 and 784–91.

THROUGH MUCH of American history, the most elemental flaw of the American federal system was its inability to protect basic rights of black Americans in the southern and border state regions. It is ironic that only a decade after the decisive exercise of national power to force change in the South, American federalism should once again be entangled in a set of seemingly intractable issues of race. No sooner did public action clear away the most blatant denials of the right to vote, to use public accommodations, and to attend desegregated schools, than fundamental issues were raised about the implications of pervasive and rapidly spreading segregation in the center of the great metropolitan areas of the North and West.

Even the rhetoric is similar. Once again the defenders of the existing arrangements appeal to the tradition of local control and once again the state governments join the battle against national regulation in Congress and in the courts. Once again the civil rights organizations turn to the federal courts and appeal to executive agencies, searching for the power to force the changes in the structure of local government, which they see as the only alternative to a future of metropolitan apartheid.

The United States today faces racial segregation in its urban complexes on a scale that would have been virtually unimaginable a generation ago. Great cities, long considered typical American cities, have become the sites both of ghettos of unprecedented vastness and of spreading economic malaise. Two decades after the 1954 Supreme Court decision, school segregation continues to worsen in many of these cities. After a decade and a half of state and local fair-housing laws and six years after enactment of a sweeping federal law, statistics show only a slight and uncertain change in the pattern of overwhelming residential segregation. A decade after the enactment of federal legislation against job discrimination the very rapid movement of jobs to the suburbs and beyond is geographically screening out many minority workers in the concentrated urban centers.

Metropolitan segregation increasingly is giving racial and class definitions to units of local government, particularly in the older urbanized areas. The highly fragmented structure of political power tends to exacerbate the problems and severely limit the resources of the central city and inner suburban communities with minority concentrations. Racial polarization often serves to obscure common area interests and to produce an increasing coalescence of suburban political power, power used to forestall change and to redistribute resources to the suburbs. Increasingly, disputes over race may become disputes between jurisdictions, a pattern very evident in the unsuccessful efforts of the city school authorities in Richmond, Virginia, and Detroit as well as several other cities to invoke the power of the federal courts to prevent virtually complete segregation of the central city school systems by imposing desegregation plans incorporating most of the metropolitan areas. . . .

GOVERNMENT RESPONSIBILITY FOR SEGREGATION

Although governmental action by no means bears the full responsibility for metropolitan segregation, the power of the federal, state, and local governments was invoked on behalf of segregation throughout the basic period of the development of the ghetto system and the construction of the early post-World War II suburbs. Although the Supreme Court ruled in 1917 that the ordinances of a number of cities openly zoning neighborhoods on racial lines are unconstitutional, state and local governments soon found highly effective alternative ways to support private discrimination organized by the real estate industry. Some southern cities even continued to enforce their unconstitutional ordinances.

The basic device was the restrictive covenant, an agreement among initial property owners, written into the deed of the property. The covenants which forbade sale of the property to blacks and other locally unpopular minorities gained great power because they could be enforced through litigation in the state courts. The covenants often were reinforced by school zoning decisions intended to keep schools segregated. Widespread violence and intimidation which commonly appeared when blacks attempted to obtain housing outside the ghetto were abetted by the general policy of refusing local police protection to black families attempting to occupy their residences outside black communities. These public policies played a basic role in creating the ghetto system when substantial black migration from the South began between 1910 and 1920. . . .

When the collapse of the private housing market brought the government massively into the housing business in the New Deal period, the new federal agencies adopted and reinforced the racial practices of the real estate and mortgage lending industries. As banks collapsed and people rushed to withdraw money from still-solvent institutions, funds for mortgage finance evaporated and banks were forced to call many of the short-term renewable mortgages then widely used. Mounting unemployment brought a widespread defaulting on mortgage payments. Foreclosures reached record levels and there was no money for new construction.

The federal government intervened decisively to revive the industry through two extremely successful insurance programs. Federal insurance for bank deposits and federal regulation of insured banks eliminated the risk of loss for depositors. Federal Housing Administration (FHA) mortgage insurance eliminated the lending institution's risk in providing mortgage financing for properties meeting FHA standards. The assets of savings and loan associations, a dominant source of mortgage money, multiplied more than 200 times in the sixteen years after the federal deposit insurance system began. By 1960, they had invested $67 billion, mostly in home mortgages.

FHA mortgage insurance revolutionized home financing by guaranteeing payment on mortgages which met the agency's standards of housing quality and appraised market value. With risk eliminated, lenders were willing to accept lower interest rates and much longer periods of repayment. These changes substantially cut the size of monthly payments, helping millions of Americans become home owners. Since approval for FHA financing greatly expanded the potential market for a new development, builders complied with the agency's intricate quality standards. At the same time, FHA became the leading force in rationalizing national home appraisal practices. Within a year of its creation, FHA was insuring 40 percent of new home mortgages. Home building had doubled and mortgage costs were at an all-time low.

As the government emerged as the decisive force in the massive but highly fragmented housing and home finance industries, it adopted a segregationist policy and refused to insure projects that did not comply. The common wisdom of the white realtors and appraisers was that integration inevitably damaged property values. Although there was no evidence for this assumption, it became official policy for FHA appraisals. The FHA shaped the housing market through policies spelled out in successive revisions of its *Underwriting Manual.* The manual was one of those decisive but little-known bureaucratic documents which help form American civilization. It compelled FHA officials to prevent fiscal risk by requiring effective guarantees against "inharmonious racial groups." Appraisers were told to look for physical barriers between racial groups or restrictive covenants. "Incompatible racial elements" was officially listed as a valid reason for rejecting a mortgage.

While the FHA provided extremely important services for young white families, blacks were viewed only as a liability on an appraisal balance sheet. Other FHA policies deepened the discriminatory impact. Since it was easier to accurately appraise the value and life expectancy of housing in new developments of similar units, the FHA refused insurance for mortgage commitments in large areas of central cities which it judged to be deteriorating and to have uncertain future value, thus channeling funds and buyers outward and denying federal assistance for the only housing on the black housing market.

The New Deal period also saw the first small and tentative efforts to construct public housing for a fraction of the millions of families still priced out of the private housing market. The Public Works Administration eventually built fifty-one projects, readily accepting the policy of segregation. Congress reinforced the localism of the early experiments in 1937 when it set up a public housing agency largely limited to financing projects in which local authorities made most of the decisions. Federal officials were considered bold to even enforce a separate-but-equal policy requiring that black projects get a proportionate share of the units built.

When Congress finally committed the country to a permanent housing program in 1949, it set off major political battles over the location of the new public housing it authorized. Blacks needed housing most urgently and their need was to be intensified by the large-scale destruction of ghetto housing authorized by the slum clearance sections of the 1949 law. Rapid construction of housing would logically have employed vacant sites available at reasonable costs in the outlying areas of cities. These areas, however, were white. The issue came to a head in a period of tense race relations and widespread racial turmoil intensified by rapid black urbanization during World War II, a time of acute general urban housing shortages. As in World War I, the wartime boom brought whites and blacks pouring into cities during a period when there was virtually no new housing construction. Bombings and violence against black "invasions" of white areas were commonplace. In Birmingham, Alabama, the city fathers actually set up a fifty-foot "no man's land" between white and black neighborhoods on the town's west side.

Federal officials adopted a policy of "local option" on segregation in the new projects. The policy produced pervasive segregation of residents in buildings constructed on segregated sites. Instead of increasing the black housing supply, frequently the net effect of the new urban programs was to diminish it, since more black housing units were eliminated for "slum clearance" than were constructed under the public housing programs. The record was particularly dismal within the urban renewal program. By 1967, about 400,000 units of housing had been destroyed in urban renewal areas, displacing a great many poor black families. Less than 3 percent of these units had been replaced by new public housing within the renewal areas.

When black public housing was constructed the projects usually offered a concentrated and intensified version of ghetto life. In order to maintain segregation the local public housing authorities usually purchased and cleared expensive, intensely used ghetto land. Since the site cost was so high, the planners could stay within federal per-unit cost ceilings only by constructing high-rise buildings. Many housing experts knew from the start that high-rise buildings with hundreds of apartments built on ghetto sites were unsuitable for families with small children. As the policy of constructing "vertical ghettos" unfolded, thousands of black families desperate for decent housing found themselves trying to survive in the midst of social chaos and even physical terror. The environment, of course, was one of almost absolute racial separation.

Although the public program left some dismal monuments on the urban landscape, it was a relatively small effort. The urban renewal experience was more devastating. Financially strapped central cities often forgot the social goals of the program in a futile rush to escape the vicious cycle of urban deterioration and escalating costs. To get the projects moving, local officials often certified that replacement housing was available for poor blacks when there was none. Federal officials who knew they were lying accepted their assurances and provided funds.

The definition of successful renewal became efficient removal of blacks from an area and their speedy replacement by higher-income whites or businesses. Local offices chased after the chimera of a restored tax base while pushing black families from terrible housing conditions in old deteriorated areas to terrible housing units, which cost more, in nearby deteriorated areas. . . .

Federal housing and renewal policies respected the fragmentation of local power in metropolitan areas. Very few suburban communities built public housing and some even used the urban renewal program to wipe out small pockets of long-time poor black residents. Most of all, however, the FHA and Veterans Administration (VA) mortgage insurance programs shaped and reinforced the racial and economic segregation of suburbia. FHA appraisers required assurances that insured properties "shall continue to be occupied by the same social and racial group." The agency even drafted a model restrictive covenant and urged its adoption. Private developers who wanted to sell without discrimination met unending bureaucratic delays.

The FHA policy was so deeply rooted that it continued in effect for a time even after the Supreme Court's 1948 ruling against restrictive covenants. Even when the formal policy changed, the operating assumptions within the program were largely untouched. After the Court struck down judicial enforcement of the covenants, the FHA at first maintained that administrative agencies still had the right to insist on segregation. After the FHA announced in 1950 that it would insure no more homes with new covenants, realtors soon learned that the agency had no objection to "gentlemen's agreements." FHA did not probe beneath the surface of new covenants requiring approval of sales by a group of neighbors, screening by the board of a community club, options to repurchase property, and other devices. The Veterans Administration had a similar record, with nonwhites holding only 2 percent of its guaranteed mortgages in 1950. The extremely favorable VA program allowed families to become home owners with virtually no downpayment, but black veterans generally were denied the opportunity to obtain inexpensive new housing and thus begin building an equity. . . .

The first significant action against discrimination in federal housing programs did not come until 1962, when President Kennedy signed an executive order on the subject. The order, however, was narrowly drafted to cover only a limited segment of the housing industry and to exclude the regulation of federally supervised mortgage lending institutions. Only a tiny staff was provided to oversee the policy's implementation and sanctions were almost never invoked. In 1967, a study by a fair-housing group testing the extent of actual access of potential black buyers to FHA insured housing concluded that virtually nothing had changed. When the FHA finally conducted its own national survey of the race of those benefiting from its programs, it made similar findings. The agency's deputy commissioner, Philip Maloney, reported in late 1967 that in "a number of large urban centers . . . virtually no minority family housing has been provided through FHA."

During the half-century when the ghetto system was consolidated and the basic structure of suburbia set, the federal government was a powerful force for segregation. As the dominant economic force in the housing and home finance industries after the early 1930s, the government underwrote the industries and reshaped the way they operated. Governmental standards not only influenced that part of the market directly participating in federal programs, but also profoundly affected the way the rest of the business worked. In a highly fragmented industry dependent on federal support with many thousands of builders, realtors, lenders, salesmen, and rental agents, federal standards had a powerful national impact. The record of this half-century can only be read as a powerful and persistent use of public power to segregate American cities.

GOVERNMENTAL ACTION AND SCHOOL SEGREGATION

The record of official action on behalf of school segregation in urban communities is less clear and less dramatic because federal agencies played only a very minor role in educational policy during this period. The actions which shaped the racial patterns of the schools were overwhelmingly local ones. Until the recent past there was relatively little serious investigation of the racial history of city school decisions. Now, as increasing numbers of cases are filed in which civil rights lawyers allege intentional official action to intensify educational segregation, the necessary research is being conducted in city after city. With striking uniformity, the research is producing evidence sufficient to persuade federal courts that local school boards in the North and West are guilty of a history of *de jure* segregation. In the first years of serious urban litigation, this conclusion has been reached by state and federal courts in cases in Detroit, Los Angeles, parts of New York City, Denver, San Francisco, Las Vegas, Boston, Indianapolis, and a number of other cities. The records of these cases are replete with evidence of racial gerrymandering of attendance lines, overcrowding of minority students while there is empty space in white schools, selection of school sites intended to intensify segregation, student assignment policies which allowed white students to transfer out of integrated schools, and a variety of other local actions.

Given the intense level of housing segregation, even a neutrally administered neighborhood assignment policy would obviously often lead to a high level of segregation. The fact is, however, that school authority has commonly been used not to alleviate the consequences of housing segregation, but to intensify them, making maintenance of integrated neighborhoods extremely difficult and denying an integrated education to children who lived in reasonably close geographic proximity. . . .

IVB

foreign and
defense policy

Foreign and defense policy is like domestic policy in that it can be thought of in broad categories in which different things are at stake. Thus the patterns of bargaining and compromise production and the content of the bargains and compromises struck will also vary. Again we think that three categories, although far from perfect in terms of mutual exclusivity and other "rigorous" criteria for judging categories, can be used to account for most specific cases of foreign and defense policy.

The first category can again be labeled *distributive*. Basically policies in this area have to do with the distribution of personnel and materiel after basic strategic guidelines have been adopted that will presumably be used to guide specific decisions. But, even assuming that the guidelines are present and are clear and are the subject of behavior aimed at adherence, there is still lots of latitude left in such policies for variation between individual decisions. Thus the bargaining process much resembles the bargaining in the domestic field when governmental subsidy is being parceled out.

The two major types of specific decisions that are distributive both involve defense policy. One involves the entire defense contracting procedure—from initial requests for proposals, through bidding for the contract, letting the contracts and subcontracts, testing the product, and the making of payments for the product at various stages of the process. Presumably strategic guidelines set the overall mix of forces deemed necessary to protect the United States. But once those decisions have been made, then a great deal of federal largesse is at stake in the decisions about what weapons to procure from what contractors and subcontractors under what contractual arrangements. The second distributive policy involves decisions on the placement, expansion, contraction, and closing of military bases in the United States. A great deal of payroll money is involved in such decisions for local communities and, in a variety of ways, they compete for that money.

The second category of defense and foreign policy involves the *strategic* decisions themselves (or what is usually thought of as "policy" as opposed to the details of implementing it—although that distinction is rarely very clear). For example, broad decisions on foreign aid and trade (should the Soviet Union be extended certain kinds of economic advantages or should those advantages be tied to a change in their policy making emigration to Israel very difficult for Soviet Jews? Should Turkey be denied aid until progress is made on a peaceful settlement of the Cyprus problem?) are strategic. The extent of United States involvement overseas either in general (with, for example, the disposition of American troops and bases abroad) or with regard to specific cases (for example, Vietnam at any point in the 1950's, 1960's, or early 1970's; or Angola in late 1975 and early 1976) is another strategic issue. The stance toward the world in general and specific countries in particular in terms of the movement of people (immigration policy) affords another example.

Third, some policies are best designated as *crisis* policies. That is, some happenings in the world are perceived by high officials (and perhaps by the general public as well) to be important threats to the national well-being of the United States that must be answered in a short period of time. Some of these threats appear in the guise of incidents that seem small in retrospect but may have larger implications at the time that a decision is thought to be necessary in short order. In the last several decades a number of instances come to mind: the landing of American Marines in Lebanon in 1958; the decision of the United States to land Marines in the Dominican Republic in 1965; the decision not to contest the North Korean seizure of the U.S. naval ship *Pueblo* in 1968; the decision to recover the U.S. merchant ship *Mayaguez* by force from the Cambodians in 1975.

Other crisis situations have large-scale and/or long-term implications at the time they arise. President John Kennedy clearly risked nuclear war with the Soviet Union in the confrontation over the placing of Soviet missiles in Cuba in 1962. President Eisenhower decided to avoid the risk of becoming embroiled in a land war in Asia by refusing to go to the aid of the French in Vietnam during the last throes of their rule there in 1954. President Eisenhower again decided to avoid the risk of confrontation with the Soviet Union by not supporting the British and French in their seizure of the Suez Canal in 1956.

Foreign and defense policies are, in some ways, less familiar to the average American than many domestic policies. But, when understood as additional instances of the functioning of institutions and individuals subject to a variety of pressures and producing a variety of outcomes they do not seem as arcane or esoteric. Rather they can be understood and analyzed in much the same vein as domestic policies.

The readings that follow provide examples of the three major kinds of policy. The article by Ognibene (reading 31) explores some aspects of the defense contracting business as an example of distributive policy.

The article by Abrams and Abrams (reading 32) explores the workings of current U.S. immigration policy as an instance of strategic foreign policy. The article is particularly useful in underscoring the problems that arise when decisions are made in the absence of good data or planning. Major slippage between what is desired and what can be achieved is almost unavoidable in such situations.

Finally, part of a memoir by the late Robert Kennedy (reading 33) focuses on the lessons he sees being learned about crisis decision making as a result of the Cuban missile crisis of 1962.

reading 31

getting and spending

by Peter J. Ognibene

IN WASHINGTON every spring the Congress celebrates the new season with an uproar of hearings, investigations, requests, appeals, and theatrical demands. The ceremony in both Houses takes the form of a morality play in which the actors cast themselves in the role of the returning hero. With rhetorical denunciation (of the President, the special interests, the Pentagon, etc.) they seek to renew the blossoming of conscience in the American wilderness.

The evil figure of the defense establishment has become a stock character in the play, and tradition requires that it be reviled with ritual abominations. Each year the Congress must bring forth an unwilling conspirator, most often a large corporation, on whom it can drape the vestments of infamy. The role in recent years has been played (not without talent) by General Dynamics, by ITT, and by the Lockheed Aircraft Corporation. This year it has been assigned to Litton Industries.

The shipyard division of this conglomerate, ranked thirty-fifth in the Fortune 500 on $2.5 billion in sales, has fallen behind schedule on its contracts with the U.S. Navy, and its delinquency promises to cost the taxpayers no less than $500 million in unforeseen overruns. The conglomerate also happens to have been put together by Roy Ash, the man Richard Nixon chose to appoint director of the Office of Management and Budget.

The irony is too obvious to ignore. Accordingly, throughout the winter and early spring, the Senate has been demanding the right to pass judgment on Ash's appointment; at the same time, as if to sustain its prerogative, it has been inquiring into the affairs of Litton Ship Systems. The preliminary evidence appears to encourage the expectations of inefficiency, incompetence, and possible fraud.

As the bad news gradually becomes public, the Congress gives voice to dramatic anger, and the newspaper editorialists write their customary sermons. The general outcry depends upon the assumption that large government contractors do business in the familiar ways of American free enterprise (i.e., he who fails the trial of the marketplace goes broke). That assumption is necessary to the morality play, but it has little to do with the prevailing economics.

The lessons of the past ten years suggest that the government intends to support the defense establishment at no matter what cost. The government conceives of that establishment as a precious mechanism (or, in the usual phrase "a national asset"), and it will spend whatever money is required to maintain production, to keep the people employed, and to continue the orderly accumulation of credit. All other considerations give way to this national imperative. Anybody still possessed of illusions on the subject had only to listen to John Connally testifying before Congress on the occasion of the Lockheed bankruptcy. At the time Connally was the Secretary of the Treasury, and he spoke with extraordinary candor: ". . . What do we care whether they perform? We are guaranteeing them basically a $250 million loan. What for? Basically, so they can hopefully minimize their losses, so they can provide employment for 31,000 people throughout the country at a time when we desperately need that kind of employment. That is basically the rationale and justification."

The large defense contractor thus operates within a system that absolves him of risk. When the money and politics reach sufficient magnitudes, the supposedly iron laws of free enterprise melt like so much wax. The government guarantees, however, do not extend to profits. The corporations remain in existence, but the stockholders almost invariably lose money.

Consider one other quotation, again from a man who should know whereof he speaks. Also in 1971, also testifying on the matter of the Lockheed loan, Admiral Hyman Rickover offered the following opinion: ". . . Large defense contractors can let costs come out where they will, and count on getting relief from the Department of Defense through changes and claims, relaxations of procurement regulations and laws, government loans, follow-on source contracts, or other escape mechanisms. Wasteful subcontracting practices, inadequate cost controls, shop loafing, and production errors mean little to these contractors, since they will make their money whether their product is good or bad; whether the price is fair or higher than it should be; whether delivery is on time or late."

If Rickover and Connally can be accepted as honest witnesses, then, at the upper limits of the political and financial spectrum, the conventional forms of business are transformed into an elaborate charade. The government and its contractors perform the ritual arguments about prices, claims, and competitive bids, but their arguments have no more substance than the speculations in a gossip column. The ritual supports a system of waste and incompetence, but it also supports a great many voters, who, in turn, support the politicians who complete the ritual by pretending to condemn it. Without somebody masquerading as villain, who can play the part of hero?

Not all the members of Congress agree to the hypocrisy of the charade, and a few of them do what they can to dismantle it. But for the most part Congress approves a system of defense spending that makes nonsense of the virtues supposedly inherent in the character of American enterprise. The theoretical or schoolbook virtues become liabilities in a system governed by ritual rather than by the exigency of the marketplace.

The two Litton contracts presently in question provide an exemplary demonstration of the new capitalism. The first of the contracts is for amphibious assault ships (the LHA) and the second is for large destroyers (the DD-963). The government has appropriated $3 billion for the two series of ships, all of which are to be built in the Litton yard in Mississippi on the Pascagoula River. The first of the ships, i.e., the first LHA, is already two years behind schedule.

Both contracts have come under extensive scrutiny during the past year (in the House Armed Services Committee and in the Joint Economic Committee of the Senate), and the following principles have been derived from a study of the relevant testimony.

I. THE CONTRACTOR NEED NOT DELIVER WHAT HE HAS CONTRACTED FOR

The original contract the Navy signed in May 1969 was for nine LHAs at a total cost of $1.4 billion, but in February 1971 the Navy informed Litton that the program would be reduced to five ships. The official reason was overall fleet reductions, but others suspect that the Navy realized the LHAs would be late and might consequently delay the DD-963s that were to be built in the same shipyard. Under the terms of the 1969 contract, the four-ship cutback in the LHA program put Litton in line to receive cancellation costs of $110 million. The Navy publicly estimates the five LHAs will cost $970 million, but the Senate's foremost opponent of military waste, William Proxmire of Wisconsin, claims the Navy's unpublished figures show "it will cost $1.4 billion to complete" the five LHAs. In other words, the Navy would be getting five ships for the price of nine—a cost overrun of some $400–500 million.

At the end of March last year, Litton submitted a fifteen-volume, 6,000-page "reset proposal" for the LHA program that included a $270 million claim against the Navy. (Having initially tapped the treasury by winning the contract, the successful "competitor" then begins to seek ways to make up for his low bid. Although the particular maneuver chosen—in this case a "reset proposal"—may be Byzantine in its complexity, the purpose is simple: to raise the price of the ships.) The details of the reset proposal were not made public because the Navy considers the information to be "corporation confidential." Asked the basis for Litton's claim of $270 million, the Navy wrote: "The contractor's alleged basis of the claim is Navy interference in Design Development and over management, late GFE and GFI [government-furnished equipment and information]." (A "claim" is another of those rituals for increasing the price of your product: blame the Navy for your own mismanagement, threaten the government with a large claim, and settle out of court for all you can get.)

Two months later the Navy gave its official response to the Litton reset proposal or, as it unaccountably came to be called, "reproposal." In a letter dated June 23, 1972, Admiral R. C. Gooding, the Acting Commander of the Naval Ship Systems Command, opened fire on the Litton proposal with blunt language: "In our opinion this 'Program Reproposal' as submitted is almost completely unresponsive to the obligations undertaken by Litton in the 23 April 1971 Memorandum of Agreement with the Navy and thus has breached the terms of that instrument. . . ."

Admiral Gooding then listed the conditions under which the Navy would be willing to "negotiate a new delivery schedule" for the LHAs. He ended the letter with this warning: "If you do not agree with the course of action proposed herein, the Navy may have no alternative but to pursue its remedies under the 'Default' clause."

Recognizing the ritualistic character of the warning, Litton remained unimpressed, and it responded with its own press release after the Navy's letter was made public by Senator Proxmire. One sentence in that one-page release stands out: "Litton does not expect to subsidize the construction of LHAs nor be required to finance the Navy during the construction period." It was, in effect, an ultimatum, and on August 31, the date on which Litton was to begin receiving payments only on the basis of physical progress on the LHAs, the Navy gave Litton a six-month extension and continued reimbursing the company for its incurred costs.

II. THE WEAPON NEED NOT BE NEEDED

The LHA was designed to transport and land a battalion of marines (1,900 troops), twenty-five to thirty helicopters, and four large landing craft. About the size of an aircraft carrier of the *Essex* class, the LHA is supposed to do the work now done by four separate amphibious ships: it would no doubt have been ideal for Gen. Douglas MacArthur's Inchon landing in Korea. The DD-963s have been designed as antisubmarine warfare (ASW) vessels with the principal mission of supporting the force of aircraft carriers. Not all naval analysts think they will be very good ones. . . .

There is no unanimity . . . in knowledgeable circles that the Navy needs a new destroyer or, if it does, that the DD-963 would be the right one. Nonetheless, Litton has a thirty-ship contract for the DD-963. The Navy had originally wanted fifty.

III. THE CONTRACTOR CAN AFFORD TO BE WRONG

After two rounds of bidding, the competition for the destroyer contract narrowed to Litton Industries and Bath Iron Works of Maine. On February 2, 1970, the third round of secret bids was submitted, and the two shipbuilders were close: Litton's ceiling price was $80.8 million per ship and Bath's was $81.1 million. According to a GAO analysis of the bidding released in August 1970: "The [Navy's] Source Selection Advisory Council ultimately concluded that the proposal of either contractor would provide destroyers suitable for the future needs of the Navy." So, on March 20, 1970, the Navy asked Litton and Bath for their "best and final offers," but unlike the earlier rounds for which the contractors were given about a month to prepare their bids, the Navy gave them just six days.

No technical changes were made in the ship's design by either contractor, but both dropped their prices. Bath dropped its ceiling price per ship a modest $1.4 million to $79.7 million. Litton's drop was more dramatic: a $9.5 million decrease to a ceiling price per ship of $71.3 million. Litton underbid Bath by almost a quarter of a billion dollars even though it had not changed its design.

The key to Litton's drastic cut in price centered on the company's estimate of what effect inflation would have on the prices it had to pay for labor and material. Litton was optimistic and estimated it would recover $144 million *more* from the Navy than it would actually pay out because of inflation. Bath's estimate was pessimistic: it expected to recover $146 million *less* from the Navy than it would actually pay out because of inflation. In short, because Litton's crystal ball predicted a rosy future whereas Bath's figures took inflation into account, Litton got the contract. This $290 million disparity apparently did not trouble the Navy even though it was, in the words of the GAO report, "the largest single point of difference between them in the final bid."

The Navy now puts the price (to Litton plus government equipment) of one DD-963 at $90.5 million, but if one includes an electronic warfare system cost overrun discovered by Rep. Les Aspin of Wisconsin, the cost is closer to $95 million. How much higher might it go? At the moment no one is saying, but there are signs that the DD-963 could match the LHA's lamentable performance.

IV. THE CONTRACTOR MUST PROMISE MIRACLES

Litton won the contract to build the LHAs in competition with General Dynamics and Newport News Shipbuilding and Dry Dock. Departing from precedent, the Navy issued performance (rather than design) specifications for the LHA and invited shipbuilders to submit their own designs, the winner of the competition to build the entire class of ships. The Navy's choice of Litton, a relatively inexperienced shipbuilder, was controversial because (among other reasons) Litton had yet to build the automated shipyard on the west bank of the Pascagoula River in Mississippi, where the ships were to be built on an assembly line.

When the LHA contract went to Litton, some thought it signaled a great leap forward for the American shipbuilding industry. Long envious of the innovations of Japanese, European, and Russian shipbuilders, the Navy was excited by Litton's aerospace concepts of modular construction applied to shipbuilding. Admiral Isaac C. Kidd, the present Chief of the Naval Material Command, which is responsible for ship construction, now believes that the Litton shipbuilders "promised more than they have been able to produce. We've got to remember," he told the House Armed Services Committee, "that we made a decision on the basis of a shipyard that was nonexistent at the time, and a technique for production that was still sort of a gleam in somebody's eye."

The DD-963 contract was distinguished by two "firsts." It was the first time the Navy had turned over the responsibility for designing a major combat vessel to a shipbuilder, and it was the first time since World War II that so many Navy ships had been awarded to a single contractor. These two breaks with established practice were controversial, and now, three years later, they appear to have been serious mistakes. . . .

V. THE CONTRACTOR CAN MAKE ABSURD MISTAKES

Litton prides itself on decentralized management, and the company's Beverly Hills headquarters claims to give its managers in the field a free hand as long as their performance reports are within acceptable limits. At Litton, however, "decentralization" can mean that headquarters simply does not know what its various divisions are doing. A labor union official from Pascagoula, Dean L. Girardot, told Proxmire's Joint Economic Committee in December about what happened to the second commercial container ship being built at the west bank yard. A Litton official at Pascagoula decided to build the ship in one piece rather than in modules and was well along in his work when headquarters found out about it. Beverly Hills ordered Pascagoula to "cut the ship in two," said Girardot.

"Then they had to put it back together again?" asked an incredulous Proxmire.

"Yes," said Girardot, "but it was module construction at that point." . . .

In its successful bid for the LHA contract, Litton estimated that 36.8 million labor-hours would be required to develop and build nine LHAs: about 4.1 million hours per ship. In its reset proposal, Litton raised its estimate to 55.8 million labor-hours for five LHAs: about 11.2 million hours per ship. In other words, Litton's labor estimate for each ship nearly tripled. Of the 55.8 million hours, 42 million were for actual production of the ships. When the hearings were held a year ago, less than 2 percent of the 42 million production-line labor-hours had been expended. By year's end, however, the company had collected about $400 million of the $970 million contract.

Admiral Gooding told the House Armed Services Committee in April 1972 that Litton's west bank shipyard was "several hundred men short" and that the prospects for improvement were bleak. "The projection is [that] even with their current hiring rate, they will be 2,000 men short by the end of the calendar year," he said. Asked about Litton's labor turnover rate, Gooding said it was inordinately high, "about 50 percent."

"In other words," Chairman F. Edward Hébert asked, "if the program is continued and the contract [i.e., the reset proposal] is awarded, they don't have the manpower to carry it out if they don't show an improvement?"

"That is correct, sir," Gooding replied.

VI. THE CONTRACTOR MUST UNDERSTAND THE ART OF BOOKKEEPING

Litton is fighting the Navy not only on the LHA and DD-963 but for "claims" it says the Navy should pay for work performed on other Navy ships in the east bank shipyard at Pascagoula. Litton, indeed, has already begun counting a portion of these claims as money in the bank. Although the company's sales for both 1971 and 1972 were $2.5 billion, after-tax profits dropped from $50 million in 1971 to just $1 million last year. Litton would have been in red ink but for the legerdemain of its accountants, who counted $41 million in *claims* against the Navy, which Litton may never be paid, as *assets*. It was all perfectly legal and in accordance with the magical mathematics in the handbook of "generally accepted accounting principles." Had these claims not been included as assets, the company would have shown a net *loss* of some $23 million (by my rough calculations).

Litton's imaginative bookkeeping was exposed by Senator Proxmire in August 1972 when he found that $32 million in claims were being carried by Litton as assets and that this had not been reported to Litton's stockholders. After Proxmire made Litton's "profit formula" public, the company owned up to it in its 1972 annual report and revealed that its "assets" had increased from $32 million to $41 million by another stroke of the pen in the last quarter. Litton's stock now sells for about a tenth of its 1967 high of 120.

VII. A CONTRACTOR IS IN THE BUSINESS OF POLITICS

Although Litton's profits and the price of its stock have been on the downside in recent years, Litton has been cornering an increasing share of the Pentagon's business. Ranked fourteenth in 1968, in the space of two years Litton moved up to ninth largest defense contractor (based on the dollar amount of defense contracts held). That this rise occurred after the election of Richard Nixon to the Presidency may have been a coincidence.

The authoritative *Congressional Quarterly* reported that "officials of companies ranking among the top 25 defense, space and nuclear contractors in fiscal 1968 contributed at least $1,235,402 to political campaigns during the 1968 Presidential election year." Of what was reported, the largest amount given to either political party came from the officers and board members of Litton Industries: $151,000, all of it to the Republican party.

Campaign contributions are one way to influence elected officials, but a more effective way is to have one of your own in the inner councils of state. Roy L. Ash was a cofounder of Litton in 1953 and its president from 1961 until he resigned in December 1972 to become President Nixon's director of the Office of Management and Budget. Ash, who admits giving "five figures" to each of Mr. Nixon's successful Presidential campaigns, did not meet the President until after the 1968 election. Apparently impressed, Mr. Nixon appointed Ash in April 1969 to head the President's Advisory Council on Executive Organization: one of the council's recommendations led to the creation of OMB.

In the past, OMB and its predecessor, the Bureau of the Budget, have been two of the more effective internal checks on the power of the Pentagon. As a matter of course, OMB reviews the performance of defense contractors, and of necessity it will have to evaluate Litton's performance on the $3 billion in Navy shipbuilding contracts it holds and the validity of the half-billion dollars in claims against the service. When Ash was designated for the OMB post, he said he would divest himself of his 233,000 shares of Litton stock, and when asked if he would be in line to receive any "deferred compensation" from the company, he said he had "no pension plan or anything else." With his financial connections to Litton thus severed, Ash averred there would be no "potential conflict of interest" if he were called upon to pass judgment on the company he founded.

Will Ash hold defense contractors to their contractual obligations or will he advocate a continuance of the present corporate welfare system to maintain their prosperity?

A Navy memorandum raises doubt that Ash will be able to see matters from other than the defense contractor's point of view. The memo recorded a meeting on June 6, 1972, which was one of a series between Ash and Admiral Kidd. The meeting, convened at Ash's request, was to discuss the LHA contract. The memo notes that the meeting opened with Ash indicating that "based on consultations with his lawyers" Litton and the Navy had to choose one of eight alternatives on the LHA. These ranged from outright termination of the contract to continuing "cost reimbursement payment basis beyond the 40-month current contract limit," which was when payments based only upon physical progress were to begin. Ash also indicated that "if Litton were required to convert to a physical progress payment basis in September 1972" the company "would be unable to perform due to the impact on an already tenuous cash flow position." (As earlier noted, the Navy continued reimbursing Litton for its incurred costs.)

The memo ends noting that Ash "indicated that it appears that some in the Navy have a built-in sense of self-righteousness concerning Litton's performance, and that the Navy would have to relax this view if Litton is expected to proceed with the [LHA] contract." Ash indicated he would go "to the White House to explain the problem" if the Navy's action did not satisfy him.

Ash is now one of the most powerful men *in* the Nixon White House. He presides over a $250 billion budget, and, equally important, he makes policy decisions and recommendations to the President concerning the management of the Executive Branch. How the Pentagon purchases weapons, its procurement regulations, and what legislation the Administration will promulgate are matters he can control directly or indirectly. If he reaches the conclusion—as others have—that the United States has too many defense contractors for its needs, perhaps he will recommend that this excess capacity be eliminated through free market mechanisms: a course that would probably result in the demise of one or more contractors. If, on the other hand, he continues to think like a Litton executive, we will probably see even greater subsidies for the already heavily subsidized shipbuilding and aerospace industries. The budget for fiscal year 1974 allocates $81 billion to the defense establishment, the largest such appropriation since World War II.

Litton's mismanagement of the LHA and DD-963 contracts may or may not prove to be the worst example of bungled Pentagon procurement, but it will certainly not be the last as long as defense contractors are allowed to inhabit a world where there is no penalty for failure. If the five LHAs are ever built, the cost overrun will be on the order of a half-billion dollars. If comparable errors were made in the labor and cost estimates for the DD-963, those thirty ships could cost $1 billion to $2 billion more than anticipated. Although Congress has appropriated some $1.6 billion of the $2.7 billion required for the thirty-ship contract, it is still too early to know if there will be delays or cost overruns that would make the final price much higher. When will we know?

I asked that question of Congressman Aspin who, with Senator Proxmire, has been one of the individuals most responsible for exposing Litton's mismanagement of the LHA and DD-963. Aspin's answer was not comforting: "Everything indicates that Litton is going to overrun the DD-963 maybe even worse than it has the LHA, but we can't prove it. By the time we can, it will be too late."

immigration policy— who gets in and why?

by Elliott Abrams
and Franklin S. Abrams

Reprinted with permission of Elliott Abrams and Franklin S. Abrams
from *The Public Interest,* No. 38, Winter 1975. Copyright © 1975 by National Affairs, Inc.

In 1965, a major reform which had been urged by liberals for decades
made radical changes in American immigration policy. The passage of the
Immigration and Nationality Act of 1965 was hailed as a great advance
in American social policy, for it abolished the discriminatory "national
origins quota system" which had so heavily favored Northern and Western Europeans. The 1965 reform was proclaimed as both the most humanitarian and the most sensible immigration policy in the nation's history,
for it asked of the alien not what was his place of birth, but what family
ties he had to America or what skills he possessed. The reuniting of
families and the admission of needed workers were the keystones of the
new policy.

After the passage of the bill, the attention devoted to the immigration
issue declined immediately, and the matter was removed from the agenda
of pressing reforms. It may therefore come as a surprise to many that while
the new law has indeed, in many ways, proved more sensible and more
humane than its predecessor, and has eliminated discriminatory quotas,
it has also produced a number of entirely unanticipated results, some of
them directly contrary to the intent of its authors.

It was probably not foreseen, for example, that the population gain
from immigration would come to equal a figure one-third as high as natural
population growth (excess of births over deaths). It was probably not
expected that immigration from Asia would rise nearly 500 per cent. Nor
was it foreseen that so many Asian professionals would enter the country
that, today, there are more Filipino doctors in America than there are black
doctors. Since the 1965 Act assumes there will be great difficulty choosing

between Eastern Hemisphere applicants, while all Western Hemisphere applicants will be accommodated, it was clearly not anticipated that the reverse would turn out to be true: Today the supply of visas meets the total demand from Europe, Asia, and Africa, while the demand far exceeds the supply for North and South America. Intent on reuniting families, the supporters of the bill would undoubtedly have been surprised to learn that the current 30-month backlog in Western Hemisphere visas means a husband and wife may be separated for that long a period. Least of all would supporters of the bill have expected their handiwork to have given impetus to an unprecedented wave of illegal immigration.

Now, 10 years later, the effects of the 1965 reforms are becoming clear, although significant areas of debate remain. . . .

CHOOSING THE IMMIGRANTS

Though the numerical totals in the 1965 Act are arbitrary, the need to set some limit is, for the United States today, incontrovertible. America's wealth, political freedom, and economic opportunities would probably attract more immigrants than even the most hospitable native is likely to welcome. The next question which faced the reformers in 1965 was, accordingly, how to choose among the would-be immigrants.

From the time immigration was greatly limited, in 1921, until 1965, the "national origins quota system" was in effect. Based on a melange of bigotry and pseudoscientific racial theories, the policy had been to admit Northern and Western Europeans and to exclude all but a few immigrants from any other region outside our own Hemisphere. . . . This policy was effectively implemented by laws which determined each country's quota by reference to the composition of the U.S. population. Under the 1952 statute, the quota was 65,631 for England, 5,635 for Italy, 308 for Greece, and 100 each for most Asian countries.

While the 1921, 1924, and 1952 quota laws had most successfully implemented the policies which produced them, support for those policies eroded steadily after the Second World War. The desire for increased population and for admission of workers with needed skills, compassion for the plight of European refugees, and diminishing support for the view that our "basic strain" had to be protected combined to produce a tangle of public laws, new regulations, and private bills designed to create paths through and around the national origins quota laws. Although the national origins system was theoretically the heart of American immigration policy until 1965, by the 1950's two thirds of all immigrants were being admitted under exceptions to it. The quota law had become an anachronism, so effective in implementing the beliefs and policies of another era that reactionaries rallied round it with the same passion liberals devoted to attacking it. In the end, it took the irresistible pressure of the 1964–65 Great Society tide to bring about a change.

The broad outlines of the new policy were a matter of general agreement. "Reunification of families is to be the foremost consideration," the Senate report stated, meaning that close relatives of American citizens and aliens admitted for permanent residence would be given priority. In addition, needed workers were to be admitted: "aliens who are members of the professions, arts, or sciences, and . . . skilled or unskilled laborers who are needed in the United States." Finally, provision was to be made, continuing the American tradition, for the admission of "certain refugees."

Once it was decided to give priority to relatives and to workers needed by our economy, the first question that arose was how much priority to give to each. The 1965 law gives special treatment to the very closest relatives of American citizens: Parents of citizens over 21, and spouses and unmarried minor children of citizens, are admitted without numerical limitation. This priority is difficult to criticize, but beyond it the choices are less clear.

A DUAL SYSTEM

For the Western Hemisphere, it was thought that such choices could be avoided. Historically, there has been no limitation placed on Western Hemisphere immigration, and the national origins quota had not been applied. Continuation of this treatment was included in the early proposals for reform in 1965 and the Administration backed this position as being part of our "Good Neighbor" policy. The assumption was, simply, that no numerical limitation was necessary. Attorney General Katzenbach told the House subcommittee hearings that "if you look at the present immigration figures from Western Hemisphere countries there is not much pressure to come to the United States from these countries. There are in a relative sense not many people who want to come." Therefore, he concluded that "there simply is not a real immigration problem with respect to the Western Hemisphere countries. It is not a practical problem."

How the Attorney General reached his conclusion is unknown. Statistics were available showing that immigration from the Western Hemisphere had averaged about 160,000 annually in the years 1961–65, and the high birth rates and comparatively low economic opportunities prevailing in much of the Hemisphere are not state secrets. Despite Katzenbach's assurances, the Congressmen and Senators were sufficiently worried to tack on the numerical ceiling of 120,000, effective after a three-year transition period, before passing the bill.

Since the original reform proposals had been drawn up with no numerical limit for Western Hemisphere immigration, and since in any case the supply of visas was expected to exceed the demand, no attempt was made in the 1965 Act to give relatives preference over workers, or to distinguish between closer and more distant relatives or between workers of varying levels of skills. Applicants are simply granted visas on a first-come, first-served basis. However, in order "to protect the American economy from job competition and from adverse working standards as a consequence of immigrant workers entering the labor market," a "labor certification" program was established. Under it, a Western Hemisphere applicant who will be employed in the United States can obtain a visa only after the Labor Department certifies that there are not enough U.S. workers "able, qualified, willing, and available" to perform the job he is seeking, and further that the alien's terms of employment will not adversely affect prevailing wages and working conditions. But in accord with the goal of reuniting families, the labor certification is not required of parents, children under 21, or spouses of citizens or permanent resident aliens.

Unlike the Western Hemisphere, the Eastern Hemisphere had since 1921 been subject to numerical limitations, and in most countries demand had regularly exceeded supply. Therefore, the problem of selection had to be faced, and Congress has made its choices clear.

Within the limit of 170,000, immigrants are selected not on a first-come, first-served basis but through a system of seven preference categories, each of which is limited to a certain proportion of the visas available. . . .

PREFERENCES AND PRIORITIES

This preference system is not at all illogical, but many of the choices it makes may be questioned. . . .

Many of the potential problems in the preference system established for the Eastern Hemisphere have been minimized by the moderate number of applicants. Since the overall supply of visas usually meets demand, at present almost all qualified applicants are being admitted—unless, of course, they are excludable for reasons such as disease, subversive activities, or (like John Lennon) a criminal record. Meanwhile, in the Western Hemisphere, where demand for visas far exceeds the supply, there is no procedure available for choosing between applicants. This combination of excess demand and lack of selection procedure has produced chaos.

THE WESTERN HEMISPHERE: DISORDER AND DELAY

If only 120,000 people each year applied for visas from Western Hemisphere countries, the system established by the 1965 Act would work. The alien would apply for a visa, and after some paperwork (obtaining a labor certification or an exemption therefrom based on family relationship), he would be admitted a few months later. In fact, however, the delay in getting a visa is now nearly two and a half years, meaning that 300,000 more people have applied for visas than the State Department, doling them out at the mandatory rate of 120,000 Western Hemisphere visas per year, has been able to process.

While the cause of the delay is obvious—more applicants than visas—the great leap in the number of applications is not really understood. Demand for visas is simply much higher than virtually anyone had predicted. . . .

DELAY MEANS DISTORTION

The resulting two and a half year delay in the reuniting of a Western Hemisphere family is clearly contrary to the key goal of the 1965 Act. Similarly, a two and a half year delay in permitting the entry of needed workers destroys the responsiveness of the Act to the conditions of our economy.

Some less apparent effects of the law are equally significant. First, no distinctions whatsoever are drawn among applicants, an acceptable policy when all are admitted, but a foolish one when all are not. Thus, close relatives receive no preference over workers, and highly skilled or professional workers are admitted no sooner than the unskilled—doctors get no preference over maids so long as there is some degree of shortage of both. One fine example of inequity in the system, certainly unintended by Congress, results from the section of the law providing, for the Western Hemisphere, that parents of U.S. citizens are exempt from the labor certification requirement. Thus, a woman without any skills, whether married or not, may establish her right to a visa if she gives birth while in the United States. She is then the parent of an "American citizen," exempt from the labor certification requirement and thus entitled to a visa. Such "baby cases" have now come to take up a noteworthy proportion of the 120,000 visas available in the Western Hemisphere.

Second, a two and a half year wait between job offer and ultimate admission is most likely to deter those who are doing best at home due to their ability and training. Thus, we may well be discouraging some of the prospective immigrants whose talents are greatest and whom we would most like to admit.

Third, the backlog gives rise to a substantial amount of illegal immigration. . . .

THE DEMOGRAPHIC PROFILE

While introducing delay and disorder in the handling of Western Hemisphere immigration, the 1965 reforms have had only slight impact on the patterns of either national origin or occupational skill of the immigrants. In 1973, about 173,000 immigrants arrived from this Hemisphere. By far the largest number—70,000—came from Mexico, and Cubans constituted another 24,000. The following lists show the top 10 countries, and the number of immigrants from each, for 1965 and 1973:

TABLE 1
WESTERN HEMISPHERE IMMIGRATION: 1965, 1973

1965		1973	
Canada	38,327	Mexico	70,141
Mexico	37,969	Cuba	24,147
Cuba	19,760	Dominican Republic	13,921
Colombia	10,885	Jamaica	9,963
Dominican Republic	9,504	Canada	8,951
Argentina	6,124	Trinidad & Tobago	7,035
Ecuador	4,392	Colombia	5,230
Haiti	3,609	Haiti	4,786
Costa Rica	2,911	Ecuador	4,139
Brazil	2,869	Guyana	2,969

As can be seen, one effect of the new law was to cut immigration from Canada; in 1965, it sent us more immigrants than any other Western

Hemisphere nation, but it now ranks only fifth. The next two nations on the 1965 list were Mexico and Cuba, which have, in 1973, simply moved up one notch each. The Dominican Republic, Colombia, Ecuador, and Haiti were also among the top 10 in 1965, and remain so today.

In regard to the occupational mix, statistics show very few changes of great magnitude, especially when compared to those brought about in the Eastern Hemisphere by the preference system. The only noticeable changes appear to be a drop in professionals and a rise in laborers and service workers—that is, a downgrading of the skills of arriving aliens. The lack of a preference system and the two and a half year backlog are almost certainly the culprits here.

In short, the "reforms" introduced in 1965 have managed, in the Western Hemisphere, to defeat many of the basic purposes of the 1965 Act, to increase illegal immigration, to downgrade slightly the average skill of arriving immigrants, and to create a two and a half year backlog of would-be immigrants. What makes this picture more ludicrous than grim is that the new system for the Eastern Hemisphere is working so well.

THE EASTERN HEMISPHERE: A RADICAL CHANGE

Under the old McCarran-Walter Act, immigration from Northern and Western Europe was greatly favored. Quotas were 65,631 for the United Kingdom, 24,814 for Germany, 17,756 for Ireland; the somewhat less favored Italy got 5,645 visas, and Poland 6,488; Greece received only 308 each year, while most Asian nations received only 100. With the introduction of the new preference system, the countries sending the most immigrants changed entirely, as the following lists show:

TABLE 2
EASTERN HEMISPHERE IMMIGRATION: 1965, 1973

1965		1973	
United Kingdom	27,538	Philippines	30,700
Germany	24,045	Korea	22,930
Italy	10,821	Italy	22,151
Poland	8,465	China	17,297
Ireland	5,463	India	13,124
China	4,057	Greece	10,751
France	4,039	Portugal	10,751
Japan	3,180	United Kingdom	10,638
Philippines	3,130	Yugoslavia	7,582
Netherlands	3,085	Germany	6,600

It should be added that immigration from Italy and Greece (where the backlog of fifth-preference brothers and sisters which existed in 1965 has been exhausted) appears to be dropping. Immigration from Northern and Western Europe is also dropping, due in some cases to favorable economic conditions in the home country and in other cases to the introduction of the labor certification requirement. Germany is an example of the former situation, and Ireland, with its largely unskilled labor force, of the latter. The great reduction in immigration from Ireland has been a source of concern to many Irish-Americans, and special legislation has been offered to raise the Irish total (down to 2,000 in 1973). But the proponents of the legislation have never been able to square special treatment for Ireland with the overall principle that national origins are no longer to be a factor in our immigration laws, and the special legislation has never come close to passing.

In 1965, only one of every 14 immigrants was Asian; in 1973, the figure had risen to almost one in three. The top two countries are now the Philippines and Korea, where immigration is hitting up against the 20,000 per-country maximum, plus the immediate relatives exempt from numerical limitation. The reason is, of course, that the national origins quota system has been replaced by the preference system, bringing to the United States individuals who, due to family ties or to special skills, are believed to be the most worthy of the limited number of visas available.

As striking as the shifts in the national origins of Eastern Hemisphere immigrants are the changes in the patterns of their occupational skills. Briefly put, Eastern Hemisphere immigrants, and especially Asians, are much more likely to be highly trained or professional workers than are immigrants from any other area. In 1973, 54 per cent of Asian immigrants workers were in the professional or technical fields; 83 per cent of Indian immigrant workers and 67 per cent of Filipinos were in this category. (It may be added that 52 per cent of the 6,700 immigrants from Africa were also in this category.)

No figures are kept by the U.S. government on the religion of immigrants, but the changing pattern of national origins clearly will result in increasing diversity in American religious life. Although most Filipino immigrants are Roman Catholics, immigrants from the rest of Asia are a mix of Buddhists, Hindus, Sikhs, and other religions hitherto largely unfamiliar to Americans. Increased immigration from Egypt, Pakistan, Turkey, Iran and other Moslem countries is producing a considerable rise in the number of American Moslems, although the absolute figures are still comparatively small. The bulk of Christian immigrants are Catholics from the Western Hemisphere, the Philippines, and Europe, but many belong to other churches. The Greek Orthodox Church has grown with immigration from Greece, Turkey, and Yugoslavia; Armenian Christians from Turkey and Assyrian Christians from Iran, unhappy with what they see as discrimination at home, are enlarging the size of these groups in the United States. At any rate, the proportion of white Protestants among the immigrants is very small.

The political effects of these changes in the ethnic composition of the American population are unknown. It has been suggested, notably by Daniel Patrick Moynihan, that the effect of large new nationality groups on American foreign policy will be significant. This argument cannot yet be evaluated, since the number of immigrants from any one nationality group admitted under the new law is not yet large enough to be a politically significant force, especially in view of the fact that many have not yet become citizens. In any event, the decision in 1965 to eliminate considerations of national origins from our immigration laws necessarily carries with it the acceptance of any such political effects as entirely legitimate: Our commitment to political and personal liberty extends to immigrants as well as to citizens. . . .

THE AMERICAN DILEMMA

Many of the problems resulting from the new immigration law are soluble, and the next session of Congress is likely to see remedial legislation passed. But new legislation cannot, of course, resolve the irreconcilable conflicts built into our immigration policy. As has been noted, if we emphasize the economic role of immigration and admit more and more skilled workers, we sacrifice the goal of reuniting families; if we stress (as is now the case) the admission of relatives, we lose control of the effect of immigration on our labor markets. If we admit highly skilled immigrants, we may be hurting their home countries and our own less privileged citizens; if we fail to admit the highly skilled applicants, we deprive our country of their badly needed talents. Remedial legislation can, however, deal with problems which, if not unpredictable, were at least unpredicted—above all, the dilatory and haphazard treatment of Western Hemisphere immigrants caused by the great rise in demand and the lack of a preference system for this area.

It is important, however, to distinguish criticism of some aspects of our present statutes and administrative procedures from criticism of our basic immigration policy. The fact is that the Immigration Act of 1965 brought into being both the most humanitarian and the most sensible immigration policy in our nation's history. Despite the many criticisms that may be directed at our immigration laws, the United States remains, of all the world's countries, by far the most hospitable to immigrants. Not only do we admit more immigrants than any other country, we treat all applicants without regard to religion, race, color, or national origin. No serious proposal has been made to reduce non-white immigration—a step already taken by Canada. Further, we allow immigrants to become full-fledged citizens after only five years. Moreover, the evidence indicates that chauvinistic prejudices against newcomers are rare, and opportunities for economic and social integration are widespread.

None of this is news to the millions of aliens now planning on, or dreaming of, making their futures in the United States. Though Americans may be used to hearing our society described as racist, oppressive, or sick, this country remains a symbol of political freedom, social mobility, and economic opportunity to millions around the world. The difficulties we face in implementing our immigration policy are not the result of gross incompetence or meanness of spirit (though both can be found in Congress and in some of the pressure groups seeking to influence the writing of immigration laws). On the contrary, we face difficult choices because our country remains immensely attractive to enormous numbers of aliens, and because we are willing to admit a substantial number of these. It is in this context that the successes and failures of the 1965 reforms must be evaluated.

thirteen days: the Cuban missile crisis of 1962

reading

33

by Robert F. Kennedy

ON TUESDAY MORNING, October 16, 1962, shortly after 9:00 o'clock,
President Kennedy called and asked me to come to the White House. He
said only that we were facing great trouble. Shortly afterward, in his office,
he told me that a U-2 had just finished a photographic mission and that
the Intelligence Community had become convinced that Russia was placing missiles and atomic weapons in Cuba.

That was the beginning of the Cuban missile crisis—a confrontation
between the two giant atomic nations, the U.S. and the U.S.S.R., which
brought the world to the abyss of nuclear destruction and the end of
mankind. From that moment in President Kennedy's office until Sunday
morning, October 28, that was my life—and for Americans and Russians,
for the whole world, it was their life as well. . . .

I often thought afterward of some of the things we learned from this
confrontation. The time that was available to the President and his advisers
to work secretly, quietly, privately, developing a course of action and
recommendations for the President, was essential. If our deliberations had
been publicized, if we had had to make a decision in twenty-four hours,
I believe the course that we ultimately would have taken would have been
quite different and filled with far greater risks. The fact that we were able
to talk, debate, argue, disagree, and then debate some more was essential
in choosing our ultimate course. Such time is not always present, although,
perhaps surprisingly, on most occasions of great crisis it is; but when it
is, it should be utilized.

But more than time is necessary. I believe our deliberations proved conclusively how important it is that the President have the recommendations and opinions of more than one individual, of more than one department, and of more than one point of view. Opinion, even fact itself, can best be judged by conflict, by debate. There is an important element missing when there is unanimity of viewpoint. Yet that not only can happen; it frequently does when the recommendations are being given to the President of the United States. His office creates such respect and awe that it has almost a cowering effect on men. Frequently I saw advisers adapt their opinions to what they believed President Kennedy and, later, President Johnson wished to hear.

I once attended a preliminary meeting with a Cabinet officer, where we agreed on a recommendation to be made to the President. It came as a slight surprise to me when, a few minutes later, in the meeting with the President himself, the Cabinet officer vigorously and fervently expressed the opposite point of view, which, from the discussion, he quite accurately learned would be more sympathetically received by the President.

We had virtual unanimity at the time of the Bay of Pigs. At least, if any officials in the highest ranks of government were opposed, they did not speak out. Thereafter, I suggested there be a devil's advocate to give an opposite opinion if none was pressed. At the time of the Cuban missile crisis, this was obviously not needed.

It is also important that different departments of government be represented. Thirty years ago, the world was a far, far different place. The Secretary of State and his department could handle all international problems. Perhaps they were not always handled correctly, but at least this handling by one department was manageable. Our commitments were few—we were not as widely involved as we are today—but we were nevertheless a very powerful nation. We could and did, in places we felt our national interests were involved (such as Latin America), impose our will by force if we believed it necessary. The Secretary of State dealt with all the responsibilities without great difficulty, giving foreign-policy advice to the President, administering the department, directing our relationships with that handful of countries which were considered significant, and protecting the financial interests of our citizens around the world.

But that position has very little relationship with that of the Secretary of State today. The title is the same; it still deals with foreign affairs; but there the similarity virtually disappears. Today, the Secretary of State's position is at least five jobs, five different areas of responsibility, all of which could properly require his full time.

The Secretary of State must deal with more than one hundred twenty countries, attend to the affairs of the United Nations, and travel to numerous countries. He must receive ambassadors, attend dinners, and handle other protocol and social affairs (and lest anyone believe this to be unimportant, we might remember that Secretary Rusk missed President Kennedy's extremely important meeting with Prime Minister Macmillan in Nassau because of a diplomatic dinner he felt he should attend). The Secretary of State must deal with a dozen crises of various significance that arise every week all over the globe, in the Congo, Nigeria, Indonesia, Aden, or elsewhere. He must deal with the one or two major crises that seem to be always with us, such as Berlin in 1961, Cuba in 1962, and now Vietnam. Finally, he must administer one of the largest and most complicated of all departments.

Beyond the time and energy that are required in administering the office, there is another major difference in foreign affairs. Thirty years ago, only the State Department was involved in international matters. But that is no longer true. A number of other agencies and departments have primary responsibilities and power in the foreign-relations field, including the Pentagon, the CIA, the Agency for International Development, and, to a lesser degree, the USIA and other independent or semi-independent departments.

In some countries of the world, the most powerful single voice is that of the AID administrator, with the Ambassador—even though he is representing the State Department and is ostensibly the chief spokesman for the United States and its President—having relatively little power. In some countries that I visited, the dominant U.S. figure was the representative of the CIA; in several of the Latin American countries, it was the head of our military mission. In all these countries, an important role was played by the USIA and, to a lesser degree, the Peace Corps, the Export-Import Bank, the American business community in general, and, in certain countries, particular businessmen.

Individual representatives of at least the Pentagon, the CIA, and AID must be heard and listened to by the President of the United States in addition to the State Department. They have information, intelligence, opinions, and judgments which may be invaluable and which may be quite different from those of the State Department.

It is also true that because of the heavy responsibility of the Secretary of State, he cannot possibly keep himself advised on the details of every crisis with which his department has to deal. There is also the risk that as information is sifted through a number of different hands up to him or to the President, vital facts may be eliminated or distorted through an error of judgment. Thus it is essential for a President to have personal access to those within the department who have expertise and knowledge. He can in this way have available unfiltered information to as great a degree as is practical and possible.

During the Cuban missile crisis, the President not only received information from all the significant departments, but went to considerable lengths to ensure that he was not insulated from individuals or points of view because of rank or position. He wanted the advice of his Cabinet officers, but he also wanted the opinion of those who were connected with the situation itself. He wanted to hear from Secretary Rusk, but he also wished to hear from Tommy Thompson, former (and now again) Ambassador to the Soviet Union, whose advice on the Russians and predictions as to what they would do were uncannily accurate and whose advice and recommendations were surpassed by none; from Ed Martin, Assistant Secretary for Latin America, who organized our effort to secure the backing of the Latin American countries; also from George Ball, the Under Secretary of State, whose advice and judgment were invaluable. He wanted to hear from Secretary McNamara, but he wanted to hear also from Under Secretary Gilpatric, whose ability, knowledge, and judgment he sought in every serious crisis.

On other occasions, I had frequently observed efforts being made to exclude certain individuals from participating in a meeting with the President because they held a different point of view. Often the President would become aware of this fact and enlarge the meetings to include other opinions. At the missile-crisis conferences he made certain there were experts and representatives of different points of view. President Kennedy wanted people who raised questions, who criticized, on whose judgment he could rely, who presented an intelligent point of view, regardless of their rank or viewpoint.

He wanted to hear presented and challenged all the possible consequences of a particular course of action. The first step might appear sensible, but what would be the reaction of our adversaries and would we actually stand to gain? I remember an earlier meeting on Laos, in 1961, when the military unanimously recommended sending in substantial numbers of U.S. troops to stabilize the country. They were to be brought in through two airports with limited capability. Someone questioned what we would do if only a limited number landed and then the Communist Pathet Lao knocked out the airports and proceeded to attack our troops, limited in number and not completely equipped. The representatives of the military said we would then have to destroy Hanoi and possibly use nuclear weapons. President Kennedy did not send in the troops and concentrated on diplomatic steps to protect our interests.

It was to obtain an unfettered and objective analysis that he frequently, and in critical times, invited Secretary of the Treasury Douglas Dillon, for whose wisdom he had such respect; Kenny O'Donnell, his appointment secretary; Ted Sorensen; and, at times, former Secretary of State Dean Acheson, former Secretary of Defense Robert Lovett, former High Commissioner of Germany John McCloy, and others. They asked the difficult questions; they made others defend their position; they presented a different point of view; and they were skeptical.

I think this was more necessary in the military field than any other. President Kennedy was impressed with the effort and dedicated manner in which the military responded—the Navy deploying its vessels into the Caribbean; the Air Force going on continuous alert; the Army and the Marines moving their soldiers and equipment into the southeastern part of the U.S.; and all of them alert and ready for combat.

But he was distressed that the representatives with whom he met, with the notable exception of General Taylor, seemed to give so little consideration to the implications of steps they suggested. They seemed always to assume that if the Russians and the Cubans would not respond or, if they did, that a war was in our national interest. One of the Joint Chiefs of Staff once said to me he believed in a preventive attack against the Soviet Union. On that fateful Sunday morning when the Russians answered they were withdrawing their missiles, it was suggested by one high military adviser that we attack Monday in any case. Another felt that we had in some way been betrayed.

President Kennedy was disturbed by this inability to look beyond the limited military field. When we talked about this later, he said we had to remember that they were trained to fight and to wage war—that was their life. Perhaps we would feel even more concerned if they were always opposed to using arms or military means—for if they would not be willing, who would be? But this experience pointed out for us all the importance of civilian direction and control and the importance of raising probing questions to military recommendations.

It was for these reasons, and many more, that President Kennedy regarded Secretary McNamara as the most valuable public servant in his Administration and in the government.

From all this probing and examination—of the military, State Department, and their recommendations—President Kennedy hoped that he would at least be prepared for the foreseeable contingencies and know that—although no course of action is ever completely satisfactory—he had made his decision based on the best possible information. His conduct of the missile crisis showed how important this kind of skeptical probing and questioning could be.

It also showed how important it was to be respected around the world, how vital it was to have allies and friends. Now, five years later, I discern a feeling of isolationism in Congress and through the country, a feeling that we are too involved with other nations, a resentment of the fact that we do not have greater support in Vietnam, an impression that our AID program is useless and our alliances dangerous. I think it would be well to think back to those days in October 1962.

We have not always had the support of Latin American countries in everything we have done. Frequently, our patience has been sorely tried by the opposition of some of the larger South American countries to measures we felt to be in our common interest and worthy of their support. During the Cuban missile crisis, however, when it was an issue of the greatest importance, when the United States was being sorely tried, those countries came unanimously to our support, and that support was essential.

It was the vote of the Organization of American States that gave a legal basis for the quarantine. Their willingness to follow the leadership of the United States was a heavy and unexpected blow to Khrushchev. It had a major psychological and practical effect on the Russians and changed our position from that of an outlaw acting in violation of international law into a country acting in accordance with twenty allies legally protecting their position.

Similarly, the support of our NATO allies—the rapid public acceptance of our position by Adenauer, de Gaulle, and Macmillan—was of great importance. They accepted our recitation of the facts without question and publicly supported our position without reservation. Had our relationship of trust and mutual respect not been present, had our NATO allies been skeptical about what we were doing and its implications for them, and had

Khrushchev thus been able to split off the NATO countries or even one of our chief allies, our position would have been seriously undermined.

Even in Africa, support from a number of countries that had been considered antagonistic toward the United States was of great significance. With a naval quarantine around Cuba, our military reported, Soviet planes could still fly atomic warheads into Cuba. To do so they had to refuel in West Africa, and the critical countries with sufficiently large airports and the necessary refueling facilities were Guinea and Senegal. President Kennedy sent our two Ambassadors to see the Presidents of those two countries.

Sekou Touré of Guinea had been the subject of great criticism in the United States because of his friendship with the Communist nations; but he also admired President Kennedy. When our Ambassador visited him, he immediately accepted as true President Kennedy's description of what was happening in Cuba; said Guinea was not going to assist any country in constructing a military base on foreign soil; and announced that Russian planes would not be permitted to refuel in Conakry.

In Dakar, Ambassador Philip M. Kaiser had a close personal relationship with President Leopold Senghor, who a short time before had had a very successful visit to Washington. He, too, quickly perceived the danger and agreed not to permit Russian planes to land or refuel in Dakar.

In short, our friends, our allies, and, as Thomas Jefferson said, a respect for the opinions of mankind, are all vitally important. We cannot be an island even if we wished; nor can we successfully separate ourselves from the rest of the world.

Exasperation over our struggle in Vietnam should not close our eyes to the fact that we could have other missile crises in the future—different kinds, no doubt, and under different circumstances. But if we are to be successful then, if we are going to preserve our own national security, we will need friends, we will need supporters, we will need countries that believe and respect us and will follow our leadership.

The final lesson of the Cuban missile crisis is the importance of placing ourselves in the other country's shoes. During the crisis, President Kennedy spent more time trying to determine the effect of a particular course of action on Khrushchev or the Russians than on any other phase of what he was doing. What guided all his deliberations was an effort not to disgrace Khrushchev, not to humiliate the Soviet Union, not to have them feel they would have to escalate their response because their national security or national interests so committed them.

This was why he was so reluctant to stop and search a Russian ship; this was why he was so opposed to attacking the missile sites. The Russians, he felt, would have to react militarily to such actions on our part.

Thus the initial decision to impose a quarantine rather than to attack; our decision to permit the *Bucharest* to pass; our decision to board a non-Russian vessel first; all these and many more were taken with a view to putting pressure on the Soviet Union but not causing a public humiliation.

Miscalculation and misunderstanding and escalation on one side bring a counterresponse. No action is taken against a powerful adversary in a vacuum. A government or people will fail to understand this only at their great peril. For that is how wars begin—wars that no one wants, no one intends, and no one wins.

Each decision that President Kennedy made kept this in mind. Always he asked himself: Can we be sure that Khrushchev understands what we feel to be our vital national interest? Has the Soviet Union had sufficient time to react soberly to a particular step we have taken? All action was judged against that standard—stopping a particular ship, sending low-flying planes, making a public statement.

President Kennedy understood that the Soviet Union did not want war, and they understood that we wished to avoid armed conflict. Thus, if hostilities were to come, it would be either because our national interests collided—which, because of their limited interests and our purposely limited objectives, seemed unlikely—or because of our failure or their failure to understand the other's objectives.

President Kennedy dedicated himself to making it clear to Khrushchev by word and deed—for both are important—that the U.S. had limited objectives and that we had no interest in accomplishing those objectives by adversely affecting the national security of the Soviet Union or by humiliating her.

Later, he was to say in his speech at American University in June of 1963: "Above all, while defending our own vital interests, nuclear powers must avert those confrontations which bring an adversary to the choice of either a humiliating defeat or a nuclear war."

During our crisis talks, he kept stressing the fact that we would indeed have war if we placed the Soviet Union in a position she believed would adversely affect her national security or such public humiliation that she lost the respect of her own people and countries around the globe. The missiles in Cuba, we felt, vitally concerned our national security, but not that of the Soviet Union.

This fact was ultimately recognized by Khrushchev, and this recognition, I believe, brought about his change in what, up to that time, had been a very adamant position. The President believed from the start that the Soviet Chairman was a rational, intelligent man who, if given sufficient time and shown our determination, would alter his position. But there was always the chance of error, of mistake, miscalculation, or misunderstanding, and President Kennedy was committed to doing everything possible to lessen that chance on our side.

The possibility of the destruction of mankind was always in his mind. Someone once said that World War Three would be fought with atomic weapons and the next war with sticks and stones.

As mentioned before, Barbara Tuchman's *The Guns of August* had made a great impression on the President. "I am not going to follow a course which will allow anyone to write a comparable book about this time, *The Missiles of October*," he said to me that Saturday night, October 26. "If anybody is around to write after this, they are going to understand that we made every effort to find peace and every effort to give our adversary room to move. I am not going to push the Russians an inch beyond what is necessary."

After it was finished, he made no statement attempting to take credit for himself or for the Administration for what had occurred. He instructed all members of the Ex Comm and government that no interview should be given, no statement made, which would claim any kind of victory. He respected Khrushchev for properly determining what was in his own country's interest and what was in the interest of mankind. If it was a triumph, it was a triumph for the next generation and not for any particular government or people.

At the outbreak of the First World War the ex-Chancellor of Germany, Prince von Bülow, said to his successor, "How did it all happen?" "Ah, if only we knew," was the reply.

index

Bureau of Reclamation, 134
Bureaucracy, 151-90; and budget, 174-82; attitudes toward democratic ideology, 163-73; control of, 153-54; relations with Congress, 195-200, 207-11, 212-19; relations with President, 126-27, 128-39; size, 151
Burger, Warren, 232, 233, 234, 245, 250, 253
Burns, Arthur, 130

Cabinet, 121, 126, 141
Califano, Joseph, 136, 137
Case, Clifford, 250
Celler, Emanuel, 215
Central Intelligence Agency, 343
Civil Aeronautics Board, 300
Civil Rights Act of 1964, 233
Clark, Kenneth, 100
Clifford, Clark, 112
Code of Civil Procedures of 1938, 230
Commerce, Department of, 131, 138
Commissions, regulatory; see Regulatory commissions
Committees of Congress; see also individual committee names: and oversight, 216-17; assignments, 201-03; relations with party leaders, 201-06
Comprehensive Employment and Training Act of 1973, 267-78
Confidence, 32-34
Congress, 4, 192-219; and budgeting, 174-82; and courts, 230; and defense procurement, 325-32; and immigration policy, 333-40; and policy-making, 207-11; committees, 193, 195-206, 216-17; see also individual committee names; party leaders, 201-06; relations with bureaucracy, 195-200, 207-11, 212-19; relations with President, 140-49, 207-11; relations with regulatory commissions, 302
Congress of Racial Equality, 97
Congressional Budget Office, 181
Congressional liaison office (White House), 125-26, 140-49
Connally, John, 325
Coolidge, Calvin, 129
Council of Economic Advisors, 123, 124, 130
Court of Military Appeals, 221
Courts, 221-54; see also names of

specific courts; and Congress, 230; and judicial activism, 231-38, 239-44; and politics, 221, 222; and public opinion, 236; and society, 221, 222-23; overview, 4-5, 8
Crisis policy, 323, 341-48
Cuban Missile Crisis, 341-48
Cynicism; see Confidence

Defense, Department of, 137, 142, 145, 146, 167, 198, 324-32
Defense procurement, 324-32
Democratic ideology, 163-73
Democratic Party, 67-84; see also Political parties
Dillon, Douglas, 344
Distributive policy, 284, 322; see also Subsidy
District of Columbia Committee, 202
District courts, 224-30; impact of judges' party affiliation, 228-29
Dodd, Thomas, 88
Domestic Council, 123, 124, 137, 138, 139
Douglas, Paul, 158-59
Douglas, William O., 248

Economic Opportunity Act of 1964, 237, 268
Education and Labor Committee, 202, 204, 302
Ehrlichman, John, 124, 137, 138, 266
Eisenhower, Dwight D., 75, 108, 113, 114, 122, 125, 127, 130, 142, 149, 199, 229, 234, 323
Elections, 45-53, 67-84
Elementary and Secondary Education Act of 1965, 309
Ellsberg, Daniel, 113
Emergency Employment Act of 1971, 268
Employment Act of 1946, 175
Environmental Protection Agency, 234-35
Executive branch: overview, 4
Executive-legislative relations, 8, 109-10, 128-39, 140-49
Executive Office of the President, 109, 120-27, 128-39, 181
Export-Import Bank, 343

Farmers Home Administration, 293-95, 296

McCarran-Walter Act (immigration), 338
McCloy, John, 344
McGee, Gale, 90
McGovern, George, 75, 250
McNamara, Robert S., 344, 345

Malapportionment, 239; see also Gerrymandering
Manpower Development and Training Act of 1962, 268
Manpower program, 267-78
Marshall, John, 234, 236, 256
Mass media; see Media
Mayo, Robert, 137
Media, 38-39, 43-65; agenda-setting function, 43-44, 45-53
Medicaid, 178
Medicare, 308
Mikva, Abner, 242
Mitchell, Clarence, 100
Mitchell, John, 118, 119, 137
Mondale, Walter, 250
Moynihan, Daniel P., 339
Muskie, Edmund, 88, 90, 181

Nader, Ralph, 298
National Association for the Advancement of Colored People, 97, 237
National Association of Counties, 269
National government: channels of access, 5-6; coercive power, 5-6; complexity, 3-5; overview of characteristics, 3-10; uniquely American characteristics, 6-10
National Governors Conference, 269
National Labor Relations Board, 301, 302
National League of Cities, 269
National policy: domestic, 284-320; foreign and defense, 322-48; general nature, 10-11; impact of Congress, 207-11; impact of political parties, 67-68, 77-84; strategies, 305-14: federal grants, 305-06; individual cash income, 306, 310-11; individual service financing, 306, 312; institution-changing, 306, 313-14; revenue-sharing, 306, 312-13; social insurance, 305, 307-10

National Security Council, 123, 124, 138
Nelson, Gaylord, 90
Nessen, Ron, 125
Nixon, Richard M., 45-52, 88, 89, 91, 92, 108, 109, 111-19, 121, 122, 123, 124, 125, 127, 136, 138, 161, 162, 179, 180, 232, 233, 250, 261, 264, 267, 268, 324, 330, 331

Obscenity, 245-54
Obscenity Commission, 249-50, 251, 253
O'Donnell, Kenneth, 344
Office of Economic Opportunity, 98, 167, 269
Office of Management and Budget, 109, 123, 124, 125, 128-39, 174, 179, 180, 181, 188, 189, 261, 263, 324, 330-31
Office of Technology Assessment, 200
Ogilvie, Richard B., 261, 262, 263, 265, 266
Oversight, congressional, 212-19; and committees, 216-17

Patman, Wright, 88, 90
Peace Corps, 343
Percy, Charles, 265
Planning programming budgeting, 180-81
Pluralism, 87, 100-02
Poage, W. R., 90
Policy advocacy, 123
Policy implementation, 123-24
Policy initiation, 123
Policy types: domestic, 284-86; foreign and domestic, 322-23
Political parties, 23-24, 67-84, 146-48; in courts, 228-29; in Congress, 193, 201-06; platforms, 81-83; popular support, 67-68, 69-76
Powell, Lewis, 253
President, 8, 108-49; and budgeting, 174-82; and legislative clearance, 128-39; and legislative liaison, 140-49; institutionalization, 120-27; relations with Congress, 140-49, 207-11
Proxmire, William, 88, 90, 158, 326, 327, 329, 330, 332
Public opinion, 18-41; and courts, 236; defined, 18; linkages to gov-

page 352

ernment, 19-20, 21-30; sources of opinion, 18-19

Public service employment, 275-76, 278

Public Works Administration, 318

Public Works Committees, 156-62

Purcell, Graham, 90

Rational budgeting, 179-80

Rayburn, Sam, 202

Redistributive policy, 285

Reedy, George, 127

Regulation, 9, 183-90, 284-85, 298-304

Regulatory commissions, 183-90, 298-304; *see also names of individual commissions;* and Bureau of the Budget, 188, 189; and Congress, 184, 185, 186, 187, 188, 189, 302; and President, 185, 187; and Supreme Court, 185; life cycle, 183-90; gestation, 183-84; maturity, 187-89; old age, 189-90; youth, 184-87

Regulatory policy; *see* Regulation

Rehnquist, William, 252, 253

Representation, 21-30, 100-02; and interest groups, 37-38, 87, 98-99; and political parties, 23-24

Republican Party, 67-84; *see also* Political Parties

Revenue; *see* Taxes

Revenue-sharing, 267-78, 306, 312-13

Richardson, Elliot, 262, 266

Rickover, Hyman, 325

Rogers, William, 114, 119

Roosevelt, Franklin D., 108, 120, 122, 129, 130, 161, 256, 307

Rules Committee, 202

Rumsfeld, Donald, 121

Rural Electrification Administration 296-97

Rusk, Dean, 342, 343

Saylor, John, 161

Schultze, Charles, 288

Securities and Exchange Commission, 301

Segregation, racial, 315-20

Social and Rehabilitation Service, 259-66

Social security, 177, 178, 182, 257, 307-08, 311

Social Services Grants, 259-66

Social welfare policy, 9; *see also*

Redistributive policy

Soil Conservation Service, 161

Sorensen, Theodore, 136, 344

State and local government, 5, 7-8, 31-41

State, Department of, 137, 142, 146, 342-43

Stewart, Potter, 247, 248

Strategic foreign and defense policy, 322-23

Student Non-Violent Co-ordinating Committee, 97

Subgovernments, 11

Subsidy, 9, 284-85, 287-97

Supreme Court of the United States, 221, 224, 229, 230, 232-38, 239, 256, 315, 316

Taft, William H., 230, 234

Taney, Roger, 234

Tax Court, 221

Taxes, 177-78, 182

Transportation, Department of, 133, 136

Treasury, Department of, 131

Truman, Harry S., 122, 130

United States Conference of Mayors, 269

United States Information Agency, 343

United States Navy, 324-32

Unruh, Jesse, 260

Urban League, 97

Vice President, 126

Vietnamese War, 111-19

Voting Rights Act of 1965, 243-44

Wallace, George C., 47-52, 118

Warren, Earl, 232, 234, 239, 240, 245, 252

Ways and Means Committee, 182, 204

Weaver, Robert, 96, 132

Westmoreland, William, 116

Wheeler, Earle G., 116

White House Office, 109, 125, 129, 130, 136, 138, 139, 141-49, 181

Wood, Robert, 132

Young, Stephen, 250

Young, Whitney, 100

THE BOOK MANUFACTURE

National Government and Policy in the United States was composed (Videocomp), printed and bound at Kingsport Press, Kingsport, Tennessee. Internal and cover designs were by John D. Firestone & Associates. The type is Palatino with Futura Medium display.